INSIGHT GUIDES

The world's largest collection of visual travel guides

Baltic States

Edited by Roger Williams
Photography by Lyle Lawson
Editorial Director: Brian Bell

T 20001

APA PUBLICATIONS
Part of the Langenscheidt Publishing Group

INSIGHT GUIDES

BALTIC STATES

© 2000 APA Publications GmbH & Co. Verlag KG
(Singapore Branch), Singapore. *All Rights Reserved*

CONTACTING THE EDITORS: Although every effort is made to provide accurate information in this publication, we live in a fast-changing world and would appreciate it if readers would call our attention to any errors or outdated information that may occur by writing to us at Apa Publications,
P.O. Box 7910, London SE1 1WE, England.
Fax: (44) 20 7403-0290.
e-mail: insight@apaguide.demon.co.uk.

First Edition 1993
Second Edition 1995, updated 2000

Distributed in the United States by
Langenscheidt Publishers Inc.
46–35 54th Road, Maspeth, NY 11378
Fax: (718) 784 -0640

Distributed in the UK & Ireland by
GeoCenter International Ltd
The Viables Centre, Harrow Way
Basingstoke, Hampshire RG22 4BJ
Fax: (44) 1256-817988

Worldwide distribution enquiries:
APA Publications GmbH & Co. Verlag KG
(Singapore branch)
38 Joo Koon Road, Singapore 628990
Tel: 65-8651600. Fax: 65-8616438

Printed in Singapore by
Insight Print Services (Pte) Ltd
38 Joo Koon Road, Singapore 628990
Fax: 65-8616438

www.insightguides.com

This guidebook combines the interests and enthusiasms of two of the world's best-known information providers: Insight Guides, whose titles have set the standard for visual travel guides since 1970, and Discovery Channel, the world's premier source of nonfiction television programming.

Insight Guides' editors provide practical advice and general understanding about a place's history, culture and people. Discovery Channel and its website www.discovery.com help millions of viewers to explore their world from the comfort of their homes and also encourage them to explore it firsthand.

For much of the 20th century Estonia, Latvia and Lithuania were faceless places in grey history books. So when light fell upon them as the former Soviet Union began to break up, Apa Publications was one of the first on the scene to record the countries coming into the light.

The project editor for the book was **Roger Williams**, an experienced journalist who has edited numerous *Insight Guides,* including those to Great Britain, Normandy and Catalonia. Williams was on an extended visit to the three Baltic states for London's *Sunday Times* when this guide was first published.

Williams

Working with Williams was veteran photographer **Lyle Lawson**, who spent a whole summer exploring the three Baltic states and then returned to capture the first snows of winter.

Williams began assembling his writing team by drafting two UK-based experts. The historian **Rowlinson Carter**, fresh from an epic journey through Eastern Europe for *Insight Guides*, provided background perspective. **Lesley Chamberlain**, a former Reuters Moscow correspondent and author of two milestone books, *The Food of Russia* and *The Food of Eastern Europe*, flew out to sample the countries' food and culture accompanied by her daughter, Elizabeth.

Lawson

An Insight regular, **Anne Roston**, who edited the guides to France and Provence, was rediscovered in Helsinki where she had been writing for the London *Times* and the *New York Times,* among other publications.

Carter

Roston

Lucas

Lüfkens

"It was one of the few corners of the world that kept a steady eye on Estonia," she says. "Estonia is much less Nordic than its cousin across the Baltic, but many people understood my pidgin Finnish."

Four contributors were recruited in Tallinn. **Mihkel Tarm** is an American Estonian who runs the monthly *Tallinn City Paper* and works for Associated Press. He arrived after independence, and met and married his Estonian wife, Eve. "I had grown up knowing about Estonia," he says. "It was like coming back to Never Never land." His expertise has been tapped for a look at the future of the countries' economies. The managing editor, responsible for the paper's listings, turned out to be **Andrew Humphreys**, who had contributed to the *Insight Guide* to Cairo. He volunteered to provide the exhaustive Travel Tips for Estonia.

Lisa Trei is an American-Estonian journalist who began working on a book about the Baltics after independence. Her special concern has been pollution and her contribution is a chapter on The Environment.

Estonia has a well regarded and successful weekly paper, the *Baltic Independent*. Part owner and managing editor **Edward Lucas** is a former Eastern Europe correspondent of London's *Independent* newspaper. Although working in Tallinn, he was commuting every week from his home in Vilnius. Having lived and worked the length and breadth of the three states, he welcomed the opportunity to analyse the Baltic character and write about Life Today.

Contributors in Latvia included the Canadian-Latvian **Karlis Freibergs**, editor-in-chief of the other successful and respected English-language weekly, the *Baltic Observer*. He provided invaluable Travel Tips, with the help of colleagues **Alda Staprans**, **Marika Berzina**, and **Marita Ozolina**.

Also in Riga was **Juris Lorencs** of the World Federation of Free Latvians and an expert on religious affairs, who writes on The Church and Religion. Not far away was **Valdis Muktupavels** who is widely recognised as Latvia's leading authority on traditional musical instruments, which he plays and makes. His piece on The Singing Tree is added to the weight of information about folklore provided by **Anatol Lieven**. Lieven was working as Baltics states' correspondent for London's *Times*. On his father's side, he is descended from a Baltic German noble family in what is now Latvia, and his book, *The Baltic Revolution*, is published by Yale University Press. For this guide, he also writes about Ethnic Diversity.

In Lithuania, we found two outstanding experts: **Matthias Lüfkens** and the late **Professor Ceslovas Kudaba**. Lüfkens, a former correspondent for France's *Libération* newpaper and Britain's *Daily Telegraph*, also edits the Baltics' bright and invaluable *In Your Pocket* city guides to Vilnius, Kaunas, Klapeda, Riga, Tallinn and Pärnu. He lives in France, where he now works for *EuroNews* television. Still a frequent visitor to the Baltics, Lüfkens wrote the chapter to the Lithuanian capital and the country's second city, Kaunas. He was also responsible for the update of this guide in 2000. For the rest of the Lithuanian country, we turned for enlightenment to Professor Kudaba, a lecturer in geography at Vilnius University who was also a deputy of the Supreme Council of Lithuania from 1990 to 1992.

Another contributor from Vilnius is **Mykolas Mikalajunas**, former director of the state encyclopedia publishers. He writes about one of the country's heroes, the athlete and transatlantic flyer Steponas Darius.

Mikalajúnas, his wife Jurate and their family provided Lyle Lawson with invaluable help in Lithuania, as did Leons and Ludmilla Alksnis and their daughter Christina in Riga. Maila Saar, Vivien Rennel and Silvi Blaumovitz at the Estonian Association of Travel Agents and Eriks Saks and Gundega Zeltina of the Latvian Association of Travel Agents also went out of their way to help. Susan Maingay and the British Council in Riga were very supportive, and in London Tereza Svilans and Imants Liegis at the Latvian Embassy were good to have around. The book was proofread by **Carol Mansur**.

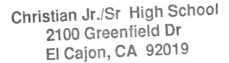

CONTENTS

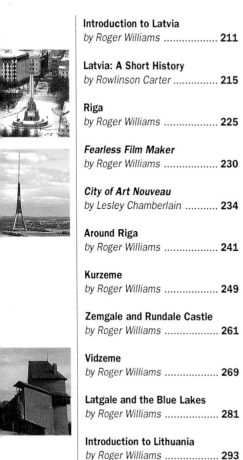

Maps

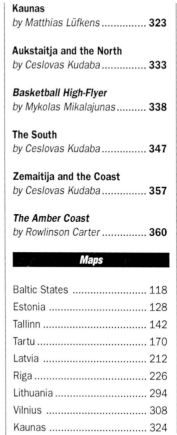

Getting Acquainted

Government 370
Geography & Population 370
Climate & Clothing 371
Language 371
Time Zones 372
Religion 372
Business Hours 373
Electricity 373
Public Holidays 373

Planning the Trip

Visas & Passports 374
Customs & Export 374
Currency & Exchange 374

Getting There

General Information 375
Tour Operators 375
Getting to Estonia 376
Getting to Latvia 377
Getting to Lithuania 378

Practical Tips

Postal Services 380
Telephone & Fax 380
Area Codes 380, 381
The Internet 381
The Media 382
Emergencies 383
Crime 383
Medical Services 383
Emergencies 383
Health 383
Dentists 383, 384
Estonian Tourist Information ... 384
Latvian Tourist Information 385
Lithuanian Tourist Information . 385
Embassies & Consulates 386

Getting Around

Distance Guide 391
Estonia 391
Latvia 392
Lithuania 394

Where to Stay

Estonia 395
Latvia 398
Lithuania 400

Where to Eat

Food in the Baltics 403
Estonia 403
Latvia 405
Tipping 405
Vodka 405
Lithuania 407

Attractions

Estonia 409
Latvia 411
Lithuania 413

Culture

Estonia 417
Estonian Films 418
Latvia 418
Lithuania 418

Shopping

Estonia 419
Latvia 420
Lithuania 421

Sport

Estonia 422
Latvia 422
Lithuania 422

Language

Estonian 423
Latvian 423
Lithuanian 424

Further Reading

General 425
Other Insight Guides 425

Art & Photo Credits 426
Index 427

PEOPLE OF THE BALTICS

The people of the three Baltic nations are as different from each other as the Norwegians are from the Poles, or the Irish from the Dutch, but they share one characteristic: a quite remarkable tendency for self-absorption, accompanied by a constant need to discuss their plight. This is partly a consequence of being small countries but, more importantly, it is the result of a systematic, and partially successful, attempt by their eastern neighbour to exterminate them.

If repression had been any harsher, Estonians, Latvians and Lithuanians would have met the same fate as the Ingrians, Kalmuks, Tatars and other small nations who got in Stalin's way. As it is, the debasement of the language and national culture through Russification and Sovietisation has been as pervasive and damaging in its way as the destruction of the natural environment.

Soviet hangover: People in all three republics are still afflicted by a sometimes surprising inferiority complex. This is partly because these countries are small: Lithuanians, Lativans and Estonians frequently tend to assume that the world is largely ignorant of their countries and ignorant of their needs. More acutely, perhaps, it is a legacy of Soviet rule, under which national identity was placed firmly in second place to the supposedly superior language and culture of Russia. This can make people seem dour. Estonians in particular sometimes find foreigners' cheerfulness shallow and irritating.

Lithuanians have perhaps the most complex Baltic national character. A memory of the Grand Duchy that ran from the Baltic to the Black Sea still has a profound influence. Sometimes the result is attractive: national self-confidence gives Lithuanians a zeal to succeed and regain their rightful place among what they consider to be Europe's "real" countries. The desire not to be outstripped economically by Poland, their historical partner and sometime coloniser, is deep.

Preceding pages: Latvian girl; mother and daughter, Lithuania; harvesting the rye; Vytautas Ciplijauskas, Lithuanian painter of the famous; behind the scenes at a parade in Rezekne; children in the Old Town, Riga. Left, the Latvian look.

"The world may not know much about us, but it should" is a deeply ingrained attitude. The "think big" *Weltanschauung* meshes neatly with a continuing fixation with America, the promised land to which many tens of thousands of Lithuanians have emigrated over the past hundred years. Despite its distance, America remains a dominant cultural influence: televised NBA basketball games attract an avid following, while the American ambassador's comings and goings are front page news. Conversely, Lituanians tend to be remarkably uninterested in their neighbours. Few could name the current prime ministers of major neighbours such as Poland, Sweden or Belarus.

be the warmest, with the austere Nordic character of the former complementing the exuberant chaos of the latter.

Solid stock: Latvians, by contrast, have fewer distinctive national features, but make up for this with a striking and very attractive streak of kindness. The German influence, as in Estonia, results in a solid, reliable work ethic which has largely survived the effects of communism. Slow starters, Latvians initially lagged behind their Baltic neighbours in economic reform. Now they have easily overtaken Lithuania in attracting investment from abroad, and on some scores do even better than Estonia, previously the unquestioned star performer.

The idea, therefore, that economic or political self-interest should lead to a close engagement with countries such as these is regarded with amused indifference in the case of the first two, or, in the case of Poland, with suspicion and defensiveness.

Lithuanians like talking about Baltic cooperation, but are generally much less enthusiastic about following it up in practice. Despite linguistic ties with their Baltic cousins, the Latvians, Lituanians treat their northern neighbours rather as Americans treat Canadians: benignly and with sweeping ignorance. Contacts between Estonians and Lithuanians, when they happen, seem to

Much of Latvia's booming private sector, however, is run by Russians – reflecting the fact that most of the large cities have a majority of Russian speakers. Latvians' roots are in the countryside – something apparent in everything from folk art to the national cuisine. Where they do venture into urban culture, however, they excel. Riga's "Untamed Fashion Show" is one of the avantgarde events of the year in Europe. And the rich architectural heritage (much of it stemming from long-gone Germans and Jews) in cities such as Riga is prized by all.

Latvians' good nature is sometimes said to be their undoing. Whereas the Estonians maintained a stony inner resistance to Russification, this process advanced far further in Latvia: mixed marriages were more frequent, and national consciousness seemed the weakest in the Baltics when the independence struggle began in the late 1980s. Whereas Lithuanians make up 80 percent of the population of their country, Latvians are in a bare majority (around 58 percent at the last count) in theirs – which now adds a bitter edge to the question of naturalising the hundreds of thousands of post-war settlers.

Not to be forgotten among the Latvians are the Livs, a handful of descendants of the original coastal tribe who speak a Finno-Ugric language like the Estonians. Latvians

two nations, are members of the Finno-Ugric ethnic family, whose origins lie deep in the marshes of Siberia. Despite substantial influences from their Swedish, Danish, German and Russian rulers over the past six centuries, Estonians still prize their bloodline – sometimes comically: "War is an Indo-European phenomenon," one visitor was startled to hear. "It's because of your settlement pattern: you live in villages, while we prefer solitary forest clearings."

How the Finno-Ugric Attila the Hun fitted into this world view is not divulged. Equally incongruously, the Finno-Ugric neighbours, the Finns, are regarded rather disparagingly, frequently refered to as "moose" by Estoni-

have a special respect for this almost extinct race and its mystical link with the past.

The difference between Estonians and their Baltic neighbours – and indeed most of Europe – is well illustrated by the language. Whereas Latvian and Lithuanian sound recognisable to the outsider, Estonia, with its unfamiliar vocabulary, chirruping intonation, ultra-complex grammar and distinctive word-order is as impenetrable to the Indo-European outsider as Hungarian or Finnish. This is not surprising: Estonians, like these

Left, Estonian father and daughter. <u>Above</u>, floral tribute, Lithuania; Estonian island fisherman.

ans. Of course, for many Estonians contact with Finns was limited for several decades merely to the boatloads of them who turned up in Tallinn for the weekend intent on drinking themselves half to death – this is a pastime that is not unfamiliar to residents in all three states.

Estonians have had many years to brood on the misfortune that has soured their history. Just as Lithuanians like to tell you that their country is the geographical centre of Europe, that their language is archaic and their folk art extraordinary, and just as Latvians will point out that in the pre-war years of their first independence they were one of Europe's great dairy exporters, so do Estonians relish any chance to explain that they were, before the war, more prosperous than Finland.

Estonia has its face set squarely towards Helsinki and Stockholm. The majority of young, economically active Estonians have visited one or both of these cities. Unlike Lithuanians or Latvians, whose emigrations are dispersed in other hemispheres, one of the most active Estonian diasporas lies just across the Baltic Sea, in Sweden. Estonians are only too aware of the importance of their Scandinavian neighbours: indeed, many Estonians would be glad to shed their "Baltic" tag altogether. With their backs set firmly against Moscow, marriages between Rus-

sians and Estonians, unlike Latvians or Lithuanians, are rare. When the Moscow correspondent of the London *Times* mentioned to a Russian in 1980 how much he liked Estonia, he was told:" Ah, now I can see you are anti-Soviet."

But it is not a rational attitude to geopolitics that distinguishes the Estonian national character, but rather its astonishing degree of reserve, which is in start contrast to the other Baltic states. Staying for more than a few days in Vilnius, a foreigner will find it impossible to avoid being invited into a Lithuanian household, stuffed with food, offered presents, taken on guided tours, in-

troduced to family, friends and pets, and generally made to feel at home. In Latvia the visitor will find hospitality, too, though the atmosphere will be more relaxed and not quite so intense. Invited to a house, you will not escape without sampling some home produce, some of which may be pressed on you to take away.

Friends for life: Estonians, however, have mastered the art of being impeccably polite without being friendly. A visitor waiting for an invitation to an Estonian home risks dying of old age before it is proffered. Friendship, an Estonian may tell you, is for life and it would not be right for a new acquaintance to be invited into their home when they know that sooner or later he or she will go away. Though the idea that real friendship is like a precious cordial which should only be offered to one's nearest and dearest can be offensive and off-putting to foreigners, it must be said that Estonians are not truly selfish or unfriendly. Once the friendship is actually made, it is as solid and lasting as a steel rod.

The standard Estonian excuse for this behaviour is that most people's apartments are so cramped and run-down that they would feel ashamed to invite a foreign guest home. (This may be offered as a genuine excuse elsewhere.) More importantly, a natural tendency to reserve has been heightened – or distorted – by the imposition of an alien occupation. "Ugh! Just like a Russian" may be the response to an attempted hug. Displays of affection, eating garlic and wearing hats when it isn't winter are all regarded by Estonians with utmost disdain because, like hugging, they associate these things only with their least favourite neighbours.

Despite their differences, Estonians, Latvians and Lithuanians are united by a love of nature. Admittedly, they enjoy it in different ways: Lituanians will drive their car to a beauty spot and blast their surroundings with pop music, whereas Latvians will organise marvellous barbecues or swimming parties. Estonians tend to regard such habits with horror, going to great lengths to find a truly solitary spot where they can sit in silence with their loved ones – or, even better, entirely alone.

Left, Riga teenager. **Right**, with the grandchildren on the allotment, just outside Vilnius.

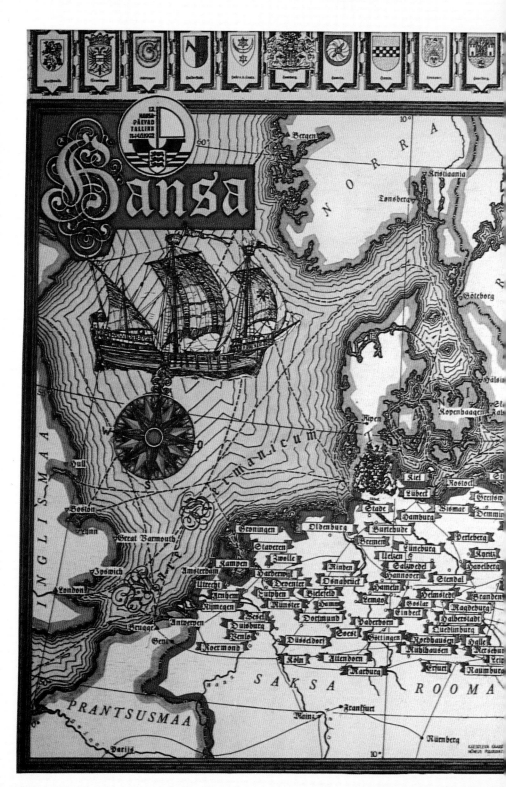

Teostanud
OLEV SOANS
Kaastegevad:
JÜRI KOHA, ENDEL SOANS
Käsitrükk
VOLDEMAR KANN
Tallinn 1991—92

27

6000 BC: Finno-Ugric peoples from southeast Europe reach Estonia.

2500 BC: Indo-European culture arrives and merges with indigenous population in Latvia and Lithuania. Baltic tribes established: Kurs, Semigallians, Letgallians, Sels and Finno-Ugric Livs.

1000–1200 AD: Estonian tribes beat off Russian (Slav) attacks.

9th–10th century: Vikings on the coast utilise trade routes to Byzantium and the Caspian Sea via the River Daugava.

1009: The name Lithuania is written for the first time.

1201: German crusaders establish a bishopric in the Liv settlement at Riga under Albrecht of Bremen. It becomes the basis for the Baltic conquest.

1207: Livonia (Terra Mariana) is recognised as part of the Holy Roman Empire, with Riga as its capital.

1219: Danes take Tallinn.

1230: Mindaugas unites the Grand Duchy of Lithuania. For convenience he adopts Christianity and is crowned King of Lithuania (1252).

1236: A brief victory is achieved for Latvian and Lithuanian forces when they defeat crusaders at Saulė.

1237: The German crusaders' Order of the Knights of the Sword becomes the Livonian Order.

1280: Semigallian tribes fail in their attack on Riga and retreat to Lithuania.

1282: Riga joins Hanseatic League; Tallinn joins three years later.

1316: Under Duke Gediminas, the founder of Vilnius and the Jogaila dynasty, the struggle against Teutonic Knights continues and Lithuanian expansion begins.

1343: Estonian rebellion on St George's night fails to bring lasting independence, but leads to Danes selling duchy of Estonia to the Teutonic Order.

1386: Lithuania and Poland are united in marriage between Duke Jogaila and Queen Jadviga. The two countries remain united until 1795.

1410: Duke Vytautas and Jogaila defeat the Teutonic Order in the Battle of Tannenberg (Grünwald).

1520s: The Reformation establishes Lutheranism in Latvia and Estonia.

1558–83: Livonian Wars between Sweden and Russia result in Livonia being divided up (1562). Northern Estonia comes under Swedish rule; southern Estonia under Polish rule. Duchies under Polish suzerainty established in Kurzeme (Courland) and Pārdaugava in Latvia. The German bishop of Piltene (Latvia) and Oesel (Saaremaa Island) sells land to Denmark.

1579: Vilnius University founded by the Jesuits.

1581–1621: Riga swears loyalty to Stephan Bathory, king of Poland and Lithuania, who introduces Counter-Reformation.

1600–29: Polish-Swedish War leaves Estonia and northern Latvia in Swedish hands; southern Latvia and Lithuania in Poland's.

1632: Tartu University founded.

1642–82: Flowering of Courland under Duke Jēkabs.

1694: St Peter's steeple, Riga, the tallest in the world, is completed.

1700–21: Great Northern War between Charles XII of Sweden and Peter the Great results in Russian victory. Russia occupies Estonia and Latvia. It also produces the first poem to be written in Estonian, by Kasu Hans, about the destruction of Tartu by the Russians (1708).

1712: Martha Skavronska, a peasant from Latvia, marries Peter the Great and 12 years later is crowned Catherine, Empress of Russia.

1768: Rundāle Palace, Latvia, is completed.

1795: Lithuania becomes part of the Russian empire. Lithuania Minor (now Kalliningrad) falls to Germany.

1812: Napoleon marches through, on his way to Moscow, raising hopes of freedom from Russia.

1832: Vilnius University is closed down by Russians following attempts to restore independence.

1860–85: The era of National Awakening. The abolition of serfdom combines with new educational opportunities and leads to a great literary and artistic movement.

1864: A 40-year ban on the printing of books in Lithuanian begins.

1869: The first national singing festival is held in Estonia.

1872: The first strike is organised by women workers in Narva.

1885: An era of intense Russification begins following unsuccessful uprisings against Russia; local languages displaced.

1905: The first socialist revolution demands independence. Manors are burned and hundreds of citizens executed.

1914–18: War waged on three fronts, between Germans and white and red Russians.

Duchy. Poland, also newly independent, seizes Vilnius.

1923: Lithuania reclaims Klaipėda.

1934: Bloodless coup in Estonia. Parliament is dismissed in Latvia.

1939: Hitler-Stalin Pact puts Estonia and Latvia under Soviet sphere of influence and Soviet soldiers arrive. Baltic Germans are ordered back to Germany.

1940–41: Red Army terror. Thousands are deported or shot.

1941–44: German occupation of Baltics.

Bolsheviks seize power in bloodless coup in Estonia, but unable to maintain control. Germany occupies Latvia, Lithuania.

1918: The Republic of Estonia is declared in Tallinn, Latvia in Riga. The German army moves in, and manors and power are given back to German aristocracy. Germany loses the war and the Soviets move in. With some allied help, the Soviets are fought back.

1920: Independence is finally achieved, for the first time in Estonia and Latvia, and for Lithuania the first time since the Grand

Concentration camps set up. Extermination of Jews, especially in Vilnius. Russians and Germans fight over Baltic soil.

1944: The Soviets reoccupy Baltics and turn them into Soviet republics. The Stalinist era begins. Mass reprisals, deportation to Siberia.

1952: The armed resistance to Soviet occupation is finally crushed.

1988: Opposition parties established.

1989: A 430-mile (688-km) human chain, from Tallinn to Vilnius, links up in protest.

1991: Soviet intervention results in 14 killed at TV tower, Vilnius; five die in Riga. Republics finally restored to independence.

1994: Russian troops pull out of Lithuania.

Preceding pages: the Baltic and the Hansa ports.
Above, crusader and bishop, Dundaga Castle.

One of the most perplexing problems facing the Paris peace conference in 1919 was what to do about the Baltic provinces of tsarist Russia which the Bolsheviks, not without a fight, had consented to let go. Lithuania had once ruled the largest empire in Europe. It was somewhat overwhelmed by Poland before both were swallowed, almost but not quite whole, by Russia in the 18th century. Estonia and what was put forward to the peace conference as an independent state which called itself Latvia were, by any his-

sions to autonomy, they became virtual Russian provinces once again.

Among few other peoples did the Soviet mill grind finer than in Estonia, Latvia and Lithuania. They occupied a special place in Soviet strategy, an updated version of Peter the Great's "window to the West", which began with the founding of St Petersburg but envisaged expansion southward to maximise Russia's access to the Baltic, often referred to as the "Northern Mediterranean". Like its southern counterpart, it had a coastline over

torical or political criteria, equally elusive. Nevertheless, three independent states were internationally recognised under these names, although first the Bolsheviks and then Stalin made it plain that it was not a situation that could be tolerated forever. Their independence was sentenced to death by the Nazi-Soviet Pact just before World War II. The pact implied that the Baltic states would be parcelled out between the two, but it was overtaken by events with Hitler's invasion of the Soviet Union. The three states were incorporated into the Soviet Union in 1940 and at the end of the war they were reconquered and though there were some minor conces-

which the adjacent nations were ready to fight for every inch. Russia had initially been held to ransom by German Balts who controlled the Estonian and Latvian ports, and Peter the Great was determined that it would never happen again, a view with which the Soviet regime totally concurred. Lithuania was regarded in exactly the same light, and it was agents of the tsar, long before any thought of Soviet Man, who vowed to obliterate all signs of national Baltic identities.

The Russification of the Baltic provinces in the 19th century was so successful that when the matter of their independence came up at the Paris peace conference one of the questions asked was sublimely naive: "Who are these people and whence did they come?" For three nations buried so deep in the history of others that their identities were long presumed to have been lost, they have surprisingly robust tales to tell.

The countries also have common bonds. With their backs to the Baltics, they have been hemmed in by the great powers of Sweden, Denmark, Germany and Russia, who have interfered in their affairs for 800 years. In fact, the peoples of the three coun-

garian, those words are *jumal*, *poeg* and *päev*. But it was a long time before the languages, with their extended alphabets and complex word endings, were written down.

Baltic peoples also took longer than the rest of Europe to embrace Christianity, preferring their sacred oaks and thunderous gods. Some of the earliest Christian teaching came from Orthodox traders from the east. The trade routes were well established, up the River Daugava and down the Dnieper to the Black Sea. Amber was the singular com-

tries come from two distinct groups, neither Slavic like the Russians nor Teutonic like the Germans. In the north were the Finno-Ugric tribes of Estonia and the Livs of Latvia, of whom only a handful remain. Latvia was otherwise peopled by Letts who, like Lithuanians, were Indo-European Balts whose language has some similarities with Sanskrit. For instance, the words for "god", "day" and "son" in Lithuanian are *dievas*, *diena* and *sunus* and *devas*, *dina* and *sunu* in Sanskrit. In Estonian, which has similarities with Hun-

Left, German crusader. **Above**, Catherine, the Baltic peasant empress, and Peter the Great.

modity the Balts possessed, and others wanted it. This gem, made of fossilised pine resin, made its way to ancient Egypt and Greece.

First conquerors: Among those taking this trade route were the Vikings, and it was their leader, Vladimir I, who first united the Slavic Russians and made a capital on the Dnieper at Kiev. When the Scandinavians settled down on the Baltic coast, they did so in Estonia: *Taani Linn* (Tallinn) is Estonian for Danish town. By then the real conquering force of the Baltics was beginning to dig in. The German crusaders appeared in 1201 in Riga where they installed a bishopric for Albrecht of Bremen. From there, they set down roots of a ruling class in all three countries that lasted into the 20th century.

This elite arrived in religious orders, which fought among themselves as much as they fought against those who opposed them. There were the ministerials of the archbishop, the burghers of the city and the Knights of the Sword, who became Knights of the Livonian Order. The country of Livonia which they created put the different peoples of Latvia and Estonia under the same authority and established a healthy and lucrative environment for the merchants of the Hanseatic League, the German trading confederation which followed in their wake. Their architecture, of half-timbered *Fachwerk*, and store-

had similar problems with the Teutonic Knights. This union also gave Poland access to the sea, which was crucial to the success of its empire-building ambitions. At its height the Duchy was one of Europe's largest countries, stretching from the Baltic to the Black Sea. Gediminas's grandson married the Polish queen and the houses were united for the next 400 years.

Jesuit builders: Poland brought a strong Catholic influence to Lithuania, and the Jesuits arrived to build their schools and fancy baroque churches, while the Reformation whipped through the Germanic northern Baltic lands in a trice, converting everyone overnight. In the brief period when half of

houses with gables stepped as high as those beside Amsterdam's canals, spread from Klaipéda and Kaunas to Riga to Tallinn.

Lithuania, however, was not so easily brought to heel, and it frequently joined forces with the Kuronian and Semigallian Letts in clashes with the German knights. By the middle of the 13th century the Lithuanian tribes had been unified under Mindaugas who briefly adopted Christianity so the Pope, in 1252, could crown him king. When the German knights opposed him, he reverted to his pagan beliefs, and stood his ground against the knights. In 1325 the Lithuanian ruler Gediminas allied himself to the Poles who

Latvia became a Polish principality, everyone converted back to Catholicism. The Balts had little say in this matter as in everything else. Compulsory church attendance made them indifferent as to how the service was conducted.

The local inhabitants were denied virtually every privilege and for centuries were not permitted to build houses of stone nor live within the city walls. Membership of the greater guilds was forbidden; even semi-skilled workers, such as millers and weavers, were brought in from abroad. The ruling society was impenetrable. In Estonia and Latvia the German descendants of the knights ruled; in Lithuania there was a rigid aristocracy of Poles. This survived even the break up of Livonia by the Swedes during the mid-16th century.

The Swedish period is sometimes looked on as an enlightened one, in spite of wars against Poland, then Russia. But there was more talk than action. In Tallinn in 1601 Charles IX demanded peasant children be sent to school and learn a trade. "We further want them to be allowed, without hinderance, to have themselves put to use as they like, because to keep children as slaves is not done in Christendom and has been discontinued there for many years." Despite noble intentions, however, his words fell on deaf ears.

fugitives branded and even mutilated. Little became of her demands for change. In 1771 public auctions of serfs became illegal, but there are records of auctions for years afterwards, while in Lithuania a noble who killed a serf could face a fine. The barons remained powerful, making laws and practising their *droit de seigneur*. Serfdom was not finally abolished until the middle of the 19th century.

In the 18th century the idea of nationhood had begun to be fomented by teachers such as J.G. Herder, but it wasn't until the 19th century and the Romantic movements, with towering poets and intellects such as Lithuania's Adam Mickiewicz, that the idea really started gaining ground. There was much lost

Further upheaval followed in the 18th century. When Charles XI threatened to take away more than 80 percent of the domains occupied by the descendants of the Teutonic Knights, these German Balts called him a "peasant king" and turned to their other enemy for help. Russia was soon in charge and thereafter took control of Lithuania as well. In 1764 Catherine the Great visited Estonia and Latvia and found serfs still being sold or exchanged for horses or dogs, and

time to catch up on. The more enlightened German landlords did their best to make amends, starting schools and themselves learning the local languages perhaps for the first time.

Tartu University, near the Latvian border, was the intellectual force behind the National Awakening in both Estonia and Latvia. However, Lithuania suffered a setback with the closing of its university in 1832, followed by a ban on printing Lithuanian books, punishment for uprisings against the tsar. Paradoxically, throughout the Baltics there was as much Russification towards the end of the century as there was national fervour.

Left, a 19th-century Estonian fishing village. **Above**, anti-Soviet demonstrators in 1990; and the aftermath as Stalin is finally toppled.

Discontent with the unenlightened tsars broke out into the Russian Revolution of 1905. It was a horrifically violent time that affected all the Baltic states, where many were delighted to torch the grand manors and other buildings of the ruling class. The destruction sparked was the start of a savage century. The two world wars were particularly fiercely fought and heaped destruction on the Baltic states.

Wars' wasteland: The retreating Red Army scorched its way homeward at the end of World War I, leaving the land in ruins. After World War II, only a few dozen people crawled from the rubble of major ports such as Klaipėda, Ventspils and Narva. Vilnius, the Jerusalem of Lithuania, witnessed the wholesale extermination of the Jewish population. The scars of both wars are still deep in the landscape, which is dotted with cemetaries and memorials.

The final injustice was the permanent imposition of Soviet rule and Stalinist terror. Anyone a visitor meets today in the Baltics is likely to have a relation who was sent to Siberia or shot.

The period between the two world wars saw the extraordinary flowering of three quite separate cultures, each coming into their own as nation states. From 1918 to 1939 the land belonged to the people of the Baltics for the first time for more than seven centuries. The German Balts were sent home, first through land reforms, and in the end by Hitler who, under his pact with Stalin, ordered them out. There was great hardships to overcome, but the economies, based on agriculture, grew to match those in the West. Political life was not all roses, but at least it was their own.

This golden age of political autonomy was an era that the people of the Baltic states looked back to for 50 years thereafter. This was a time to which they wanted to return. Only in the late 1980s did the citizens of Estonia, Latvia and Lithuania turn away from the past and start to build a new future for themselves. The struggle for independence during this period cost many lives, but secured for the three countries the freedom of self-determination and a future over which they were to have control.

<u>Right</u>, Soviet tank outside the broadcasting centre in Vilnius, January 1991, when 14 were killed.

LIFE TODAY

Ask a Balt what real differences independence has made to their own lives and the answer is no longer necessarily a gloomy sigh followed by a catalogue of complaints, as was frequently the case immediately following independence. The initial effects of independence were impressive but almost entirely superficial. Once-banned flags flew over government buildings in which a sluggish and hostile Soviet bureaucracy still reigned. Passports were issued, but private citizens still needed Soviet-style exit visas to leave the country. Fear of repression by the state gave way to worries about crime. Living standards plummeted, and although western goods began appearing in the shops, many ordinary people had not lived so poorly for decades. Some major cities spent most of the winter without hot water or heating, while politics seemed to be locked into a series of futile squabbles.

The old certainties have now gone, and some of them are missed. Drunks are no longer whisked away for compulsory drying out, nor is homelessness disguised by Soviet vagrancy laws. No longer picked up by the Soviet system, the truly feckless, and the very unlucky, have become poor, sometimes pitiably so.

The *nouveaux pauvres* contrast with the other spectacular economic phenomenon of post-communism, the *nouveaux riches* – there are pockets of real prosperity in the Baltics. Life for many more ordinary citizens has changed too. During the Soviet occupation, only the most enthusiastic collaborators of the *nomenklatura* (officially listed influentials) could hope to live in a solid, spacious house, drive a western car or take holidays in the "real (non-communist) abroad". Today such "luxuries" are in reach of tens of thousands of people and the numbers are growing every day.

All three countries have their own currencies, which are smartly printed and rock solid. Inflation is down to annual single figures, and those who try pay with American dollars put the price up, not down.

Preceding pages: housing block, Latvia. **Left**, students on Graduation Day in Riga.

Privatisation too has begun dividing up the state's monopoly of wealth and power, putting real property into the hands of ordinary citizens for the first time in more than two generations. Within three years of independence, most housing in Lithuania, for example, was sold off to the tenants, creating a nation of owner-occupiers.

So much has changed that it is sometimes tempting to forget how bleak conditions once were: areas from health care and public hygiene to education, morality and family structure had been broken and contaminated by an incompetent system of government.

Although Estonians, Latvians and Lithuanians may not seem at first sight to differ

the communists – as elsewhere – then constructed a system which methodically perverted the moral and intellectual basis of everyday life. For all but the very young and the very old, it was under this system that they spent their formative years.

Once the overriding task of overthrowing Soviet rule was out of the way, the leaders of the independence struggle proved unimpressive at the day-to-day running of their countries, and politics and politicians fell into a low esteem from which they have not yet recovered. Parties are plentiful in number, puny in membership, short of ideas and fractious in behaviour. The political reporting by the media remains largely shallow and sen-

greatly from their neighbours elsewhere in post-communist Europe, their history is radically different. Poland, Hungary and Czechoslovakia suffered repression, but not the almost genocidal hostility that the Kremlin displayed to the Baltic states.

For many locals, the problem is so basic as to be biological. "All the good ones died in the forest or left," is a local woman's typical complaint. In 1944, most of the brightest Estonians, Latvians and Lithuanians (of both sexes) fled westwards. Of those who stayed behind, many more died in Siberia, or in the hopeless, bloody resistance struggle of 1944–53. With the intelligentsia all but eliminated,

sationalist, while the state-dominated national television channels have yet to shed the docile (and tedious) journalistic culture of the Soviet era. Corruption among office-holders of all kinds remains notorious.

Yet the beginnings of change are at hand. Voters are showing considerable enthusiasm in voting out politicians who are seen as excessively corrupt, squabbling or incompetent. After the disastrous era of right-wing rule in Lithuania, voters plumped heavily for ex-communists who, if not exactly over-engineered intellectually, were at least pragmatic enough to worry about losing office, which they eventually did in 1996, ushering back in a conservative government. In Estonia, there are even more promising signs of a new generation in public life, and an encouraging willingness to forget party differences when dealing with the most fearsome problems, such as organised crime.

It is this – establishing the rule of law – that is probably the greatest remaining challenge facing politicians, and indeed the Baltic states in general. Protection rackets, in particular, are endemic, with shopkeepers, market gardeners and restaurateurs among the most prominent victims. Better armed, better off and better motivated than the police, the gangsters see little standing in their way. The homes of the humble are little safer than the

high, but they are way below Western figures and hardly a threat for the average tourist.

The pressure of dealing with practical problems is steadily ridding politics, and life in general, of one of the most unappealing habits of the post-independence era: the habit of blaming everything on the past fifty years of repression. A fair excuse for incompetence in 1989, it sounds increasingly lame ten years after independence. For many ordinary people, the realisation that they are not only practically responsible for their own lives, but also have considerable power to determine the outcome, is the most substantial achievement of independence. Added to this is the realisation that while the rest of the

limousines of the wealthy. The assassination of Lithuania's top investigative journalist, Vitys Lingys of the *Respublika* daily newspaper, was a brutal reminder of the mafia's reach and audacity.

Yet even here, there are signs that the tide is turning. Private security companies are beginning to offer a clean, if expensive, alternative to paying protection, while the need to collect taxes is forcing politicians to rein in the wilder excesses of the private sector. Rates of robbery and murder remain

Left, professional musicians busking in Riga.
Above, Latvian art class.

world may have been fascinated by the Baltic independence struggle of 1988–91, interest has now declined. Despite expectations foreign investors did not flock to the Baltics in the post-Soviet era.

The effects of this steady change in the psychological climate are pervasive and positive. For example, to begin with, a shop or restaurant was the height of creativity and enterprise. Now, the same establishment needs sharp prices, customer-friendly opening hours and polite staff. Foreign visitors are less likely to be lectured on what they should know, and more likely to be quizzed about what their hosts could be doing better.

The changing mentality, and the remarkable growth of the private sector in the past few years, have gone furthest in Estonia. Buoyed by a booming trade in metals and cars, the northernmost Baltic economy is now set for Europe's highest rate of economic growth. Latvia too seems to have turned the corner, and there are even signs that the largest, but most sluggish performer, Lithuania, may be reaching the end of its long slump.

There is, however, a long way still to go for all three countries. Civil society – the thickly woven net of voluntary organisations, clubs, charities, pressure groups and self-help associations that makes up the roots of a civilised

management of the Soviet era is improving. Roads, which were never very good, have now been resurfaced and are clearly marked and well sign-posted, although you may come across vicious pot-holes on secondary roads. The telephone system has gone from Stone Age to state of the art in less than a decade. All three countries should soon be digitalised, allowing direct-dial international calls from almost any phone, while mobile phones and the internet are all the rage. Of all the infrastructure, public transport is unpleasantly crowded; trains in particular are slow and often squalid but always on time.

Most city dwellers live not in the charming historic centres but in grim Soviet-era high-

democracy – is still fragile. There is a vast amount to learn, on everything from managing public finance works to how to run a proper office. Human relations are still pervaded by the secretive, mistrustful habits of the Soviet era. "How can I get my staff to talk to each other?" exclaims one foreign businessman despairingly – his employees, almost compulsively, hoard information that logic and business sense suggests they should share. Basic concepts of punctuality, politeness and service have taken only shallow and partial root.

The physical environment, which for years remained degraded by the neglect and mis-

rise blocks, plagued by expensive and unreliable heating systems. Overcrowding is endemic with parents and sometimes two children squeezed into a single-room apartment. Young couples, even with children, often have to live with their parents. The electrical systems in many apartments are unable to support more than a few kilowatts, making even the use of electric fires hazardous.

The health system is a particular source of worry and uncertainty. Medical salaries are low; supplies are erratic. Public health inspection is patchy, meaning that diseases such as TB and diphtheria, as well as food poisoning are all on the increase. Although visitors are most likely to be struck down with little more than an upset stomach, for someone living entirely on a local diet, the results in life-expectancy and infant mortality figures are clear to see. For men life expectancy is 65 years, for women 76, that is around 8 years fewer than in neighbouring Finland. Infant mortality in Latvia is about 15 deaths per 1,000 live births. In Sweden this figure stands at 4 deaths per 1,000 births.

All this may be bad enough for adults, but for children times are particularly grim. Childcare in the Baltics has become expensive, and Soviet habits die hard. Taking a pushchair onto public transport, for example, is unusual and generally an unpleasant

sight that was practically unknown in these countries a few years ago, are now an increasingly common sight here.

In general, women seem to be faring much better than men. This is perhaps because they did not suffer the frequently spirit-crushing experience of military service in the occupation army. Women in the Baltics often seem more enterprising, resilient and capable of adapting to rapid change than their husbands and brothers. The skills that a modern economy increasingly demands such as the ability to deal politely and easily with total strangers seems on the whole to come more easily to women than men (waiters, for example, frequently seem painfully ill-at-ease

experience, making it difficult for anyone with such dependents to travel far afield; discipline seems harsh to European eyes, while potty training starts, by Western standards, ruthlessly early. The tireless promotion of Western toys such as Barbie dolls and similar costly childhood crazes creates an extra strain on the household budget. Some parents respond to the trouble and expense of child-rearing by taking to drink: child beggars and street children, a

Far left, modern banking, Tallinn. **Left**, high-tech communications, Estonia. **Above**, Virve and Vidrik Kivi, B&B proprietors, Viljandi, Estonia.

and pompous, whereas waitresses increasingly show a relaxed, friendly manner that is indistinguishable from the behaviour of their counterparts elsewhere in the world).

There is still a considerable number of social, financial and political problems to resolve in the Baltics. Many people remain frightened of Russia, organised crime is still a major concern and there is widespread poverty, ill-health and insecurity across all three countries. However, the foundations have been laid for the life that more pampered Europeans regard as "normal" – if not for this generation of Balts, then, with luck, for the next.

At least since the 13th century, when the German and Scandinavian crusaders arrived to impose Christianity at the point of the sword, the territory of the present Baltic states has been one of mixed settlement. Over the intervening period, apart from the various native peoples who later came together to make up the Estonians, Latvians and Lithuanians, the area has also been settled by large numbers of Germans, Poles, Jews and Russians. There are also West European merchant communities in the ports of Riga, Tallinn and Narva. Today, the question of relations between the Balts and the large Russian population in the region is one of the key problems hanging over the future of the Baltic states.

Centre of Jewry: Jewish settlement began in the 14th century, when Jews were invited into Lithuania by the Grand Duke Vytautas. Precisely because the rulers of Lithuania, and later of Poland-Lithuania, were relatively tolerant towards the Jews, Lithuania became a great centre of world Jewry, and the "Litvaks" one of its most important branches. "Lithuania", as understood by the Jews, embraced the whole area of the former Grand Duchy, including Belarus and parts of the Ukraine. By the 18th century, its capital, Vilnius (in Yiddish, Vilna or Vilne) was known as "the Jerusalem of Lithuania", because of its large number of synagogues and its many *yeshivas*, or Hebrew schools.

Later that century, Vilnius became a centre of Jewish Orthodox resistance to the Hasidic religious movement then sweeping eastern Europe. Gaon Street in the centre of the city's old town is named after the Gaon or "Genius" of Vilna, the rabbi who led the Orthodox, and whose prayer house stood on that street until it was demolished by the Nazis along with most of the ghetto. Nearby was the Great Synagogue (now a playground), which had the dimensions of a cathedral.

Before the holocaust, Jews made up eight percent of the population of what is now Lithuania, and a much larger proportion of Kaunas (Kovno) and Vilnius. Many Lithuanian Jews had also moved to Latvia, and there was a small population of 5,000 or so in Estonia. The Nazis were to wipe out those populations almost completely, and today the few thousand that remain are being steadily diminished by emigration. The Lithuanian-Jewish writer Grigory Kanovitch has warned that if things go on as they are, "there will soon be more Jewish organisations here than there are Jews".

Jewish emigration from the Baltics was much encouraged by the memory of the holocaust, in which Baltic partisans and volunteers played a major part; indeed, the initial massacres in Lithuania were conducted entirely by Lithuanians without direct German involvement. This has cast a very severe shadow over subsequent relations and, a year after independence, the allegation that the Lithuanian government was giving a blanket rehabilitation to former war criminals led to much sweeping criticism in the Western press.

Baltic participation in the holocaust was due partly to anti-Semitism (though there

Preceding pages: Vilnius's synagogue. **Left,** the heart of the 1930s Polish ruler Marshal Piłsudski is buried in Vilnius. **Above,** priest at Kurämäe Orthodox nunnery, Estonia.

was no history of attack as there is in other parts of Europe), but more to the belief that Jews had played a major part in supporting the Soviet regime that was imposed on the Balts in 1940. This was indeed true, but what the Balts who make this charge forget is that the Jewish communists also turned on their Jewish opponents, and that in fact a higher proportion of Jews than Balts was deported to Siberia in 1940–41.

The lack of a serious dialogue between Lithuanians and Jews, of the sort that has occurred in Poland, means that the great majority of Lithuanians are unaware of this fact. However, all three Baltic governments have condemned the holocaust and Baltic

helped by the Catholic church, the Polish nobility, and the fact that, as in all the Baltics until the 16th century, there was no written form of their language.

It is hard to point to specific Polish monuments in Vilnius (Wilno, in Polish), because the whole of the old city is in effect such a monument, built by Polish architects, studded with Polish inscriptions and similar to many Polish baroque towns. Czesław Milosz, the Nobel prizewinning writer who lived there until 1941, described it as "narrow cobblestone streets and an orgy of the baroque: almost like a Jesuit city somewhere in the middle of Latin America". Vilnius still retains its character as a Catholic frontier outpost.

participation in it, though they have not yet admitted its scope.

Poles' position: The official Polish presence in what is now Lithuania also began in the Middle Ages, with the marriage union of the Lithuanian Grand Duke Jogaila and the Polish princess Jadviga in 1386. However, for a century and more before that the Lithuanian Grand Dukes had ruled over large numbers of Slavic peoples, many of whom were ultimately to see themselves as Poles.

After the union, many Lithuanians, especially from the upper classes, also became Poles – a cause of enduring resentment in Lithuania. The Polonisation of Lithuania was

Until World War II, Lithuanians were a small minority in Vilnius, with Poles the largest community, followed by the Jews. Vilnius was the home city of a number of great Polish cultural figures like Milosz and Adam Mickiewicz. The latter's epic, *Pan Tadeusz*, begins with the famous invocation:

O Lithuania, my fatherland,
Thou art like health; what praise thou
shouldst command
Only that man finds who has lost
thee quite.

The passage also refers to the Gate of Dawn, the chapel in Vilnius dedicated to Our Lady which is still a place of pilgrimage for Poles as well as Lithuanians. Worshippers from the two communities sometimes scuffle there as the Poles coming in for a Polish-language mass bump into Lithuanians coming from a Lithuanian-language service. The heart of Marshal Józef Piłsudski, the ruler of Poland between the wars and himself a Polish-Lithuanian nobleman, is buried in Vilnius's Rasų (Rossa) cemetery beside his mother.

In the 19th century Lithuanian peasants participated in rebellions against Russian imperial rule along with their Polish-speaking landlords. But by World War I Lithuanian nationalists were distinguishing themselves from the Poles, whom they blamed for many of Lithuania's historical problems.

reconquest in 1945, when almost all the Polish intelligentsia and upper classes emigrated to Poland (or were deported to Siberia). It still numbers more than 270,000. Tens of thousands of Poles also live in Latvia, the southern parts of which also used to be part of Poland. However, whereas in Lithuania, fear of Lithuanian nationalism made many Poles support the Soviet communists in the independence struggle in the late 1980s and early 1990s, in Latvia most Poles were pro-independence. The Lithuanian nationalisation and land-ownership laws have caused considerable tension between Poland and Lithuania. For some time this caused difficulties on the Polish-Lithuanian frontier

After Lithuania and Poland achieved independence from Russia in 1918, the two countries clashed over Vilnius, until in 1921 it was seized by a Polish expeditionary force under General Lucijan Żeligowski. Newly independent Lithuania made the recovery of Vilnius the centrepoint of its foreign policy, and finally received the city back from Stalin in 1940, when he had won it from Poland following the Molotov-Ribbentrop Pact.

The Polish minority in Lithuania dropped by more than 50 percent after the Soviet

Left, A last look: Russian soldiers, pulled out in 1994, sightseeing at Trakai, Lithuania. <u>Above</u>, children in Narva, Estonia.

and hindered trade going to and from the Baltic states.

Relations between Lithuania and Poland tend to be warmer than between Lithuanians and local Poles. The authorities in Warsaw have shown little sympathy for the complaints of the ethnic Polish organisations in Lithuania, concentrating instead on building solid diplomatic and economic ties with their new neighbour. After several years haggling over whether Poland needed to "apologise" for seizing Vilnius in 1920, the two countries signed a long-overdue friendship treaty.

By the year 2000 relations between Warsaw and Vilnius had considerably improved with both countries eagerly co-operating to enter the European Union.

The Catholic church, to which many people in Lithuania and Poland belong, may do something in the future to bridge the gap between these two countries. So far, this has not been the case, because of the close identification between the church in Lithuania and Lithuanian nationalism. However, with a Lithuanian émigré and former papal nuncio to Holland as Archbishop of Vilnius, and the Pope a Pole, there are signs that both sides will be able to overcome the prejudices that have been bequeathed by history.

Russians who remain: Lithuania's problem with the Poles appears fairly minor, how-

ever, when compared to those of Estonia and Latvia with the local Russian-speakers, who make up 32 percent and approximately 37 percent of the respective populations. Small communities of Russians had lived in the area since the early Middle Ages, when some Baltic tribes paid tribute to Russian princes. After the conquest by Peter the Great, these were joined by Russian soldiers, merchants and officials. At the end of the 19th century a major influx of Russian workers began. This was interrupted by World War I and the Russian Revolution, which drove considerable numbers of white Russian refugees to the Baltics.

Prior to 1940, Riga was the greatest Russian émigré centre after Paris. When Stalin occupied the Baltic states in June 1940, these émigrés were among the first to suffer from the secret police. Newspapers and cultural centres were closed and churches converted for secular purposes.

The reconquest of the Baltics by the Soviet Union in 1944–45 began a process of Russian immigration which drastically altered the region's demography. Today, Tallinn's population is less than 40 percent Russian, while Riga's is just under 40 percent (in 1939, it was 63 percent Latvian).

The great majority of Russians now living in the Baltic are immigrants from the Soviet period or their descendants. The Latvian and Estonian parliaments have decided that these people are allowed no automatic right to citizenship, and may only obtain it by a process of nationalisation modelled on rigid criteria generally employed by other European countries.

Contrary to some expectations, however, the unsympathetic attitude of the Latvian and Estonian governments to the Russian "settlers" has not led to any noticeable increase in ethnic tension – not least, perhaps, because of the comparative prosperity and stability of the Baltic states, even for those with a distinctly second-class status.

The withdrawal of the Russian troops from the Baltic states in 1994, after a great deal of anxiety and complaint, has also helped to relieve tension. A few thousand Russian civilians had already headed back to the motherland, and some tens of thousands have since plumped for Russian citizenship. The rest wait, somewhat passively, in legal limbo, neither wanting to integrate, nor leave the place they have come to regard as home.

The Estonians and Latvians, although not especially overjoyed at the prospect of continued co-existence with the legacy of the former empire, have largely given up any hopes of any large-scale repatriation. The wealth and influence of the burgeoning Russian business class is providing an important counterweight to political adventurism from any quarter and, barring interference from outside parties, flare-ups on either side seem increasingly unlikely.

Left, Orthodox cemetery, Mustvee, Estonia. **Right**, mosque of the community of Tatars, Lithuania.

COUNTRY LIFE

The return to independence has brought with it the desire to go back to the pre-war idyll of the self-sufficient smallholder. Many of the old Soviet collectives have now been broken up into smallholdings, much as the land was redistributed during the First Independence when the Baltics became famous for their dairy products. However, for nearly half a century under the so-called "progressive" Soviet system, agricultural productivity increased overall by less than 2 percent. By turning the clock back, a great number of people believe the land will flow with milk and honey once more.

Land for all: Even those without access to farmlands, particularly newcomers to the towns or the region, often have allotments, typically plots of around 6,50 sq. ft (600 sq. metres), which were provided for company and factory workers under the Soviet regime. Densely planted with fruit trees, berry bushes, vegetables, herbs and flowers, these allotments sprawl around most of the towns and cities. In spite of completely inadequate plumbing or other such high-tech facilities, increasingly solid weekend shacks have been constructed on such land over the years, and now that planning permission has slipped into the morass of largely unenforceable laws, two-storey brick-built houses are rapidly rising, their new roofs "topped out" with wreaths of oak leaves.

Whether farmhouses or summer houses, there is a great pride in constructing both the buildings and their contents by hand, by creatively using what materials are available. The poor general condition of many buildings in the country – places that have been destroyed by revolution, war and neglect – means that there is much work to be done. Such a large number of buildings had been burned out by the end of World War I that the first of the popular open-air ethnographic museums was established to conserve a few specimens of traditional building craft before they completely disappeared. Some of the old crafts, such as thatching and weaving, were already declining in the bleak

Preceding pages: milkmaid, Lithuania. **Left,** gathering winter fuel in Alūksne, Latvia.

years after World War II. And after the next World War came the Soviet occupation, which sent landowners to Siberia and joined farms together in collectives, leaving even more neglected buildings to fall into decay.

Restoration is already in hand, and new farms and country homes are being built as many people are buying land with nothing on it at all. Among the new smallholders' priorities is a sauna, built away from the main house because of the risk of fires. The hands of a farmer are ingrained with soil, with no hot running water to wash it away. Only the sauna, fired up at least once a week, has a chance of getting rid of the dirt, while a swish of the birch twig stimulates the blood.

acquaintances without a small bunch as a present. Herbs, notably dill (an especially popular addition to Latvian cooking), rue, caraway and sage, are also grown for culinary or medicinal use. Tomatoes and small cucumbers, which can be pickled with cherry and currant leaves, are typically grown in vegetable plots. In Lithuania *rūta*, or rue is widely grown. Not only is this the national flower and a girl's name, but also a symbol of virginity – a wreath of it is traditionally burned on a wedding night.

Chickens, ducks and geese are common farm animals. Cows are kept in unfenced fields: brown cows in Latvia, black-and-white "Dutch" ones in Estonia and Lithuania.

Also indispensable is the cellar where harvest produce can be stored through the long, harsh winter. Sometimes the cellars are entered through doors in small mounds in the gardens, which look like bomb shelters. Even in a city the size of Riga, modern blocks of flats have cellars in which residents keep their country produce fresh. A considerable number of homes also have their own facilities for smoking meat and fish.

Surrounding the farm buildings there are often beds of bright flowers: roses, chrysanthemums, dahlias, fuschias, lilies and sweet peas. Flowers are an everyday part of Baltic life. It is rare for anyone, of either sex, to visit

They are milked where they stand two and sometimes as often as three times a day. Country meals are incomplete without spoonfuls of sweet or sour cream.

There is a theory that farm buildings are spread out and not huddled in villages for defensive purposes, because scattered communities are a more difficult target for a concentrated attack. However, in the south, in Lithuania, smallholders and country people seem to prefer the community of villages; there, the pull of the land, though still strong, does not embrace with such energy the ideal of daily rural toil that is encountered in Latvia and Estonia.

The changing year: Winters in the Baltic states are long and dark. For up to four months of the year the ground may be rock hard, and snow forces cattle and poultry to remain sheltered indoors. Sledges make haulage easier in these harsh conditions, and trees are felled and chopped into neat piles around the house. Holes are made in the lakes' thickly iced surfaces and fish, attracted by the light, can be scooped up by the bucketful. Illegal hunters follow beaver tracks in the snow. Wild animals seeking food may wander into the region from the icier heartlands of the great continent: bears have been sighted in Estonia, while wolves are said to move into Lithuania in hunting packs.

banks. On the Teiči nature reserve near Madona in Latvia, Old Believers, who have no access to newspapers or televisions, are even more isolated than usual, as the waters rise around them. On the delta of the Nemunas in Lithuania, some houses are constructed on stilts, so that they escape the spring floods; in some places, the floors of cattle barns can be raised by means of a winch, in order to escape the rising water levels.

As the earth warms, violets carpet the woodlands, and bird cherry blossom creates a beautiful fresh white blanket on the trees, which lilac soon turns to blue. Sweet water is tapped from beneath the barks of birch trees, and sometimes also maples, and then stored

Elk, deer and wild boar – species that live in nearly every forest – are sought by licensed hunters, as are wild duck, capercaillie, black cock and hares as big as hounds (there are no wild rabbits). The stalkers are professional countrymen: hunting is not a great Baltic pastime. Dogs tethered up on the farms warn of attacks by foxes or hawks or by packs of eastern Usurian wild dogs which have been growing in numbers recently.

When spring melts the snow, swamps rise and rivers are frequently known to burst their

<u>**Left**</u>**, the plough is now back in private hands, Lithuania. <u>Above</u>, slaughtering a pig in Latvia.**

in the cellar to slake thirsts on scalding summer days.

However, it is the arrival of the majestic storks that really signifies the arrival of spring. Each year these long-legged birds faithfully fly back to their nests, which are perched high in treetops, on old chimneys or on cartwheels that farmers have put up on poles – the storks' presence is a guarantee of good fortune. The birds then repair and build up their nests and settle down for the summer, when they high-step through the meadows feasting on frogs. During spring and summer, this area becomes home to the world's largest population of black storks.

In summertime everyone who can leaves the towns and cities to stay in the country with friends and family. Children break up from school at the beginning of June and are often sent to relations in the country for the whole of their three-month holiday; family bonds do not seem as close, on a daily basis, as they are in the West. Their mothers may join them; fathers usually come at weekends.

Sunday evenings see trains full of people returning from the country laden with buckets, baskets and bags. There is also a harvest to be had in the wild, of blueberries, cloudberries, whortleberries and tiny delicious strawberries. In addition, every garden has red and black currants, and glass jars are

filled with jellies and jams. It is typical for visitors to be offered plates of berries with perhaps a few vegetables, such as pods of fresh garden peas. All this farm produce is sold in the colourful markets in the nearest large town, where old ladies sit by their basket of strawberries, herbs and salad to eke out a living.

Vodka economy: Harvest time is hard work and as many people are involved as possible to help allieviate the load. Estonia and Latvia are reasonably mechanised, but horses and carts are still evident in some parts of Lithuania. Agricultural machinery is slowly being upgraded: straw is not automatically baled;

hay is not bagged up for silage. Scythes and pitchforks are as indispensable as they have always been. Under the Soviet system, a tractor driver was liable to be the local alcoholic: he was called on to plough and harvest the small plots people were allowed to keep, in return for which he was often paid in moonshine vodka. Many smallholders still use vodka as a currency. They make it from rye, or from just sugar and water with perhaps a few peas. It can ferment in milk churns which are kept in the sauna.

Barley and rye, which are used in the preparation of beer and sourdough bread, are the main crops. Sugarbeet and maize are also grown. In this new age of nostalgia there is talk of planting the fields with flax again. It used to be a staple, for linen and rope, and in past summers its flowers turned the fields blue. Cannabis is also grown for hemp, and *kaņepu sviests* (cannabis butter) is a Latvian treat spread on rye bread.

Summer weather is unpredictable. It can be as hot as in southern Europe, and occasionally there are even mini tornadoes. Harvests are unreliable and nobody knows what will appear in the shops. This, coupled with a precarious economy, means that people view their smallholdings as an insurance against hunger and deprivation.

The summer comes to an end as the storks start to gather in the fields preparing for their migration south. At the beginning of September, amid parades, children go back to school and the speed limit on the roads is reduced for a few weeks to take account of their holiday-induced doziness. Those with apartments in the city will return to settle in with their produce for the winter.

But there are still a few autumn weekends left in the country, to go picking nuts and, the favourite of all, mushrooms. And there is one last berry to preserve, that of the rowan, after the first frost has made it sweet.

Then the woods and the flat fields fall under the grey skies of winter, and skiers and skaters wait hopefully for snow. It is then that the smallholder will reap the rewards of the summer's harvest. For, whatever happens to the economy, to unemployment, there will always be something in the cellar to keep the wolf from the door.

Left, retrieving water from the well , Estonia.
Right, milking a "Dutch" cow in Lithuania.

Baltic cooking today is basically pretty straightforward country fare. The plain, wholesome, unspicy dishes characteristic of all three of the states – although especially Latvia and Estonia – demand little artistry, but nevertheless can be very good.

If your schedule allows, take an hour or two to peruse the disused Zeppelin hangars, which house Riga's massive – and extremely crowded – market. Scores of indoor stalls tout fresh and fermented dairy products: vast slabs of soft white cheese, harder yellow cheese, bottles of sour cream, yoghurt and cultivated sour milk. In another hall, high-quality fresh pork gleams pink, and many varieties of sausage and ham wait to be sampled. Smoked fish sells at one end of the market, while delicious fresh fruit is on offer at the other.

In summer, baskets are piled high with early apples and pears – small irregular specimens that are not subject to the trading controls that are all too familar in Western Europe; glass tumblers spill over with red and black berries and tiny yellow mirabelle plums. Look out for the different varieties of nuts, the dried fruit, the umbrils of caraway seed drying on the branch, huge bunches of fresh, strong, flat-leaf parsley, pots of honey, barrels of sauerkraut lined up for tasting and trays of fresh, home-made black, brown and white bread. These staple foods, which are brought in by private sellers from the nearby countryside, are the raw materials of traditional Baltic cooking.

These ingredients are usually served at the table with very little seasoning. In the vegetable hall you may smell dill and garlic – but for flavour Latvia mostly relies on fermented milk, smoked fish and cheese, and bacon, with a sprinkling here and there of caraway seed, rather than strong herbs and spices. Fresh milk is the predominant flavour in Estonian food, and onions are considered too strong a taste to feature heavily. Lithuanian cooking, which has been partly influenced by the Orient, is the most pungent of the three.

Preceding pages: meat stall, Riga central market. Left, Sunday lunch in Lithuania. Above, *cepelinai*.

This hint of Oriental spice in Lithuanian cooking is a result of the country's complicated political past. From the 15th century exiled Crimean Tatars and refugees from the Golden Horde flocked to this powerful state to coexist with Russians, Belarussians and Poles under the leadership of the Polish/Lithuanian noble class. The results today are a half-forgotten legacy of exoticism and luxury, recipes which dare to include black pepper and nutmeg and marjoram. Spices were imported from the East;

marjoram was probably brought into the country from Italy, via Catholic Poland.

Since independence in the early 1990s Lithuanians, Latvians and, to a lesser extent, Estonians have rediscovered the richness of their traditional country-style cooking. In each of the three capitals, countless traditional restaurants have opened, typically offering heavy butter-doused Lithuanian *zeppelinai* and other traditional dishes. However, the best local cooking can usually still be sampled in private homes.

Bread baskets: Excellent natural resources, quality farming and careful husbandry contribute to the goodness of Baltic food.

The lush land provides rich harvests of grains and berries, dark forests provides ideal environment for mushroom growth, fish populate the rivers, lakes and sea, and pig and dairy farming are important industries.

Excellent bread, especially rye bread, comes from this northern part of the world, where the hardiest of the cereal crops flourishes even in cold, poor soil. Rye bread, which has a strong rich taste, is enhanced by molasses, made from native-growing sugarbeet, and caraway seed. This bread keeps well and is an ideal accompaniment to the local beer, cheeses and pungent cured meat and fish. One type of pale rye loaf, which has a smooth, shiny, tan-coloured

These breads, which are also very popular in Germany, Poland, Russia, Sweden and Finland, are top class, especially now that private producers are offering previously rare wholegrain varieties. More than one Western traveller has made a meal out of bread alone, to the consternation of the locals who cry: "But where's the sausage to go with it, or the butter?" (In the Baltics they still love their meats and fats.)

Porridge and potatoes: Although porridge used to be a staple food in these parts, porridges made from cooked grain are now rarely seen on menus except on special occasions. The ancient Latvian version, called *putra*, is made of barley (or a mix of barley

crust, is widely known as Riga bread and is best eaten when it is fresh and sweet. (Most bakers hang a two-pronged testing fork beside their self-service shelves.)

Other Baltic speciality breads include the plain dark rye variety that is often served in hotels and which should not be judged by the dryness and sourness it exudes when left indefinitely exposed to the air. (Don't let this put you off.) Among the white breads are the robust and versatile French *baton*, not at all like its Gallic counterpart, and the creamy-coloured sourdough loaves that are usually home-made and well worth seeking out for their extraordinary muscular texture.

and potato) and typically served with a ladle of bacon fat, some smoked meat or fish, or perhaps also with milk products, as a main course. In Estonia mixed grain porridges are sometimes served with milk.

There is also a breakfast speciality that is akin to porridge: *kama*, made of ground toasted grains and raw oats is mixed with yoghurt or milk and eaten with salt or honey.

These gruels make good use of the region's barley, which doesn't have enough leaven in it to be used in the preparation of modern bread. There is another dish that is similar to porridge; this speciality is made of mushy peas and then eaten with bacon fat. Grey field peas eaten with fat bacon is another local favourite in Latvia.

If a Lithuanian were asked to name his or her favourite dish, it would probably be something prepared with potato. The Baltic Germans introduced this exotic tuber to the Baltics at the start of the 18th century, and the whole region fell for its charms, especially the Lithuanians. Today they eat boiled potatoes with everything from yoghurt to bacon fat, and, like the Poles and the Jews, they are fans of grated potato pancakes. The same grated potato is used to make a variety of filled rissoles, such as *cepelinai*, meaning that this potassium-rich foodstuff plays a part in most daily diets. Yeast-leavened wheat

is strongly influenced by the Russian and Polish fondness for Slavic *tortellini* – another Baltic treat.

Fat feasts: One of the hallmarks of Baltic food is the non-prevalence of protein. Meat and fish, at least in Latvia and Estonia, are traditionally eaten in very small quantities, almost as a dressing or garnish to the bread, pasta or porridge at the focus of a meal. Rich, fatty foods, rather lean meats, tend to prove most popular at special feasts.

Although fat features so prominently in the Baltic diet, however, it's interesting to note that traditional food here is rarely fried. Vegetables and carbohydrates are typically boiled first and then covered later with fat –

dough – the food stuff from which genuine pizza bases are made – is another staple carbohydrate here. On street corners in Tallinn you can buy slightly sweet white dough made from this yeast-leavened wheat, which tastes deliciously fresh.

In Latvia the array of savoury baking is highly enviable. Special treats include cheese- and meat-filled yeast-dough buns and yeast-dough horns stuffed to the brim with minced bacon. If pizza makes you think of pasta, look no further than Lithuania, where cooking

Left, cabbage seller in Ventspils; Latvian fish-monger. Above, Lithuanian festive treecake.

whether in the form of bacon, cheese or, quite simply, butter.

Pork is without doubt the most commonly eaten meat, followed in Lithuania by game. (The term pork covers salt pork, sausage and the black pudding – blood sausage – that Estonians traditionally eat every year on Christmas Day.)

In the 15th century Lithuania was highly renowned for its smoked wild boar. Domestic pig farming was later introduced by the Germans with exceptional results. This pork-production industry was so successful that smoked lean pork from the Baltics, all pink, wrinkled, juicy and tender, is believed to have been the stuff of many a privileged Communist Party banquet. Smoked lean pork is certainly more inviting than the whole wedges of salted pork fat, the dietary mainstay of the labouring male peasant in the early 1900s, which are still classed as a delicacy.

On commercial menus you will come across hot, fresh meat dishes more familiar to the visitor than anything mentioned so far. In many restaurants, meat cutlets, fried escalopes, meatballs and boiled and fried sausages are more often than not prepared by foreign chefs.

Fish dishes: If you like fish, you'll find there is much in the way of local delicacies to tempt you here. Local fish preparations, such

difficult to find and is now very expensive. More affordable are the Estonian fresh fish soups, which are made with vegetables and then thickened with flour and milk.

Cold dishes: Until early in the 20th century two-thirds of traditional Baltic dishes were those for its cold table. This is something that seems to come especially into its own at breakfast time, when a mix of cheese and meat, as well as vegetables and cream, is served. At other times of the day, the cold table is often supplemented with soup.

Salads are an important part of the cold table. They are usually accompanied by dressings and eaten with bread. One of the culinary highlights of a visit can be a bowl of

as smoked saltwater salmon, pickled herring, smoked sprats and smoked eel, rank among the best fish dishes in the world. In fact, smoking fish is so much part of the national heritage that the Latvian national poet Imants Ziedonis appeared on television following the independence to remind people of the best home-cure techniques for fish. If you travel around the inland lake districts you are also likely to encounter freshwater fish dishes, notably those using trout and pike.

In Latvia and Lithuania fish is often cooked in bacon fat – a rare case of frying. Russian caviar, which was once the pride of every restaurant menu, is becoming increasingly

tomatoes and cucumbers picked straight from a country garden, tossed with fresh dill and parsley and sour cream. Sometimes strips of meat or cheese are used in the same way as raw vegetables to make composite salads for the cold table but often these are covered in bottled flavourings. Unfortunately, they represent only a poor attempt at a quick urban cuisine adapted from the country.

Soups: Although there are old recipes in Lithuania for varieties of beetroot soup along the lines of the Russian/Ukrainian/Polish beetroot-based *borshch*, and for mushroom soup, this liquid dish is most typically found on the menus of cheaper eateries. Lithuanian beetroot soup has a sweet-and-sour base and is usually flavoured with sorrel, which is a rich source of iron and vitamin C.

Estonian food is generally fairly mild and its soups are no exception. A classic Estonian soup contains milk, dried peas and buckwheat grains and the majority of varieties on this are made with milk and vegetables, or with yoghurt and dill cucumber.

Under German influence, Latvia and Estonia used to make a sweet bread soup, which used up leftover fruit. Since the bread was probably sour and black the soup was closely related to the sour-sweet kīsels made with summer berries. Beer soups belong to this curious category.

Garden produce: The country garden is something that is celebrated in all three states, and it cannot be stressed highly enough how vital a part it plays in Baltic culture. One of the most charming and notable poems in Lithuanian literature – one that is frequently, and many believe quite rightly, compared to Virgil's *Eclogues* – is called *The Seasons*, written by an 18th-century clergyman, Kristijonas Donelaitis.

In the kitchen garden, which became popular in Donelaitis's time, the sweetest tomatoes, ridge cucumbers, courgettes, beets, kohlrabi, potatoes, swede and turnips grow in profusion alongside peas and cabbages and rhubarb. Somewhere near the vegetable

Special occasions: Christmas Day is celebrated with pork dishes in Estonia, goose in Protestant Latvia and Lithuania, and fish and mushrooms in Catholic Lithuania. At midsummer – an important date in the Baltic calendar – the dairy products come into their own. A special dense yellow country cheese, smoked and flavoured with caraway seeds, is traditionally produced for midsummer (Jani – St. John's Day) in Latvia; a similar spicier cheese is eaten in Lithuania. You can sample both varieties in Riga's main market.

Left, homemade beer, Lithuania; wild mushrooms, Estonia. **Above**, picking berries in Latvia.

garden you will also find apples and plum trees and, in an ideal world, a bee-hive. A guest might enjoy an inspiring summer tea made from baked sour windfall apples sweetened with clear plum jam and macaroons. Nothing is wasted.

Cakes: At the opposite end of the spectrum from the healthy ideal of the country garden is the Baltic sweet trolley. Nowadays cakes are generally more popular than desserts in the Baltics. In Lithuania, look out for treecakes and honey cakes. Treecakes are made by adding dough in layers to a rotating wooden pole in front of a hot fire. The result is a cake with many age lines and fungi-like

appendages clinging to its outer bark, where dollops of egg and lemon dough have been added. Despite its peculiar appearance, it is quite delicious.

In cafés, where many varieties of shortbreads, shortcrust and flaky pastries, and eclairs are sold, you can't help noticing that Latvians and Estonians have a German-style penchant for eating large amounts of sweet whipped cream with their cakes.

Drinks: Coffee is one dietary feature that distinguishes Russia from the Baltics: coffee is far more prevalent here. Note that both tea and coffee are served without milk. Soft fizzy drinks are widely available here. Mineral water is normally good quality, although some varieties are pumped full of unpalatable salts and are hence rather unsuccessful at quenching thirst. Note that it is not safe to drink tap water in Riga – always buy bottled water instead.

If you are in the mood for something stronger, you'll find that the majority of bars and cafes serve beer on tap rather than in bottles. The main breweries (Kalnapilis and Utenos in Lithuania, Aldaris in Latvia and Saku in Estonia) have recently been upgraded thanks to foreign investment. The local brews are now available on tap in most restaurants. Varieties range from dark beer to the latest craze of ice beer.

Herbal *eau-de-vie*, Riga Black Balsam (a dark brew, which tastes like a mixture of treacle and Campari), sweet Lithuanian liqueurs, locally produced Russian vodka and sparkling wines complete the standard alcoholic line-up. You may also find expensive wines from France and less costly but decent vintages from Georgia, Hungary and Romania.

Soviet life did nothing for the quality of food and service in restaurants. Today, however, the majority of Baltic restaurants have shed their Soviet past. Baltic food is best enjoyed in private homes or in the form of a picnic, composed of some of the delicacies offered at a typical Baltic cold table – excellent fresh vegetables, cold meats and tasty, albeit mild cheeses. Although the fare served in long-established hotels may seem rather heavy and fatty to the diet-conscious, health-obsessed Westerner, it can certainly work wonders for an empty stomach.

Left, summer café society in Tallinn.

Throughout the Baltics churches and monasteries have re-opened their doors for business. Property has been denationalised, religious schools are starting up, tracts are being published and the media is open to preachers. In the streets there are saffron-robed Krishnas and smart-suited evangelists from Sweden, Germany and the United States. Money from the Vatican, from northern Europe's Lutherans and from America's varied sects is pouring in to refurbish the fabric and educate the eager congregations.

The Baltics, ever at the mercy of changing spheres of influence, have amassed a collection of churches with an extraordinary variety of styles. Their history has also left the countries with some two dozen differing belief codes and has created such a tolerance towards other people and their religions that there are Lutherans who regularly attend Catholic Mass and Catholics who sing in Orthodox choirs. In Tallinn, for example, Methodists and Seventh Day Adventists both share the same church.

Orthodox beginning: With the help of Greek Orthodox Russian merchants, the first teachings of Christ were voiced here in the 11th and 12th centuries but Christianity did not arrive in full force until the early 13th century when the German crusaders subjugated Estonia and Latvia. This belated start meant that the early European ecclesiastic style, Romanesque, was on the decline. Only St George's in Riga and the remains of Ikškile church on an island on the River Daugava give a glimmer of that expiring style. Church architecture in the Baltics begins with Gothic.

In Estonia the earliest stone churches, built of limestone and dating from the end of the 13th century, are on the islands. These were simple Gothic buildings without towers, and were used for protection. On Saaremaa the churches at Kaarma and Valjala have interesting murals and the one at Karja has beautiful sculptures.

Lithuania converted to Christianity nearly two centuries after its Baltic neighbours, in

1387. Although nothing remains of Vilnius's first church, it must have echoed the red-brick building of the castle. When St Anne's and the Bernardine monastery were built in the 15th century, its bricks, like those of the cathedral in Kaunas, would not have looked as out of place as they do today.

The Reformation took hold almost immediately after Martin Luther published his thesis in 1520 and its first centres were Tallinn and Riga, where sacred paintings began to be destroyed. There is a strong

painterly tradition in Baltic churches, on collection chairs, *priedieux*, pews, galleries, altars, triptychs, tablets and doors. Many churches had decorated walls and ceilings, which were painted over during the Reformation, and in subsequent years. These were mostly done by Balts, and only the "easel" paintings were produced by foreigners.

In Tallinn, the late 15th-century Baltic painter Bernt Notke, who produced the High Altar of Aarhus cathedral, Denmark, and Lübeck cathedral's great cross, was responsible for the folding altar at the Holy Ghost Church (1483), which has more paintings than any other in the Baltics. He also pro-

Preceding pages: Assumption Day pilgrims in Aglona. **Left,** Catholic procession, Rēzekne, Latgale. **Above,** Lutheran minister, Alūksne.

duced the macabre *Dance of Death* painting now in the Niguliste church museum. In the middle of the 16th century the newly formed Duchy of Courland sought to secure its power base by ordering the building of 70 new Lutheran churches.

Catholics sought refuge in the Polish territories of southern and eastern Latvia and Lithuania where the Jesuits began to build their sumptuous churches. Many of Vilnius's 40 Catholic churches are in the highly decorative baroque style. The first, begun in 1604, was dedicated to Lithuania's patron saint, Casimir. Among the finest is the Sts Peter and Paul church, supposedly built on the pagan temple to the goddess Milda. Its

church all trustworthy bishops were eliminated and it was impossible to ordain new priests. Today the world's largest Old Believers congregation, numbering some 20,000, is in the gold-domed Grebenschikova temple in the Moscow district of Riga. The church's walls are lined with stunning icons depicting only the saints' faces, and services are led by someone from the congregation, elected teachers (*nastavniki*) of the church.

Class distinctions: Though they tend not to last as long, there are still a number of wooden churches throughout the three countries, mostly in Lithuania. The oldest examples date from the middle of the 18th century. The ethnographic museum near Riga has a typi-

Italian sculptors adorned it with more than 2,000 white stucco figures, many of them quite beautiful. The churches, which typically feature a twin-towered facade, show Hispanic influence. In Latgale both St Peter's in Daugavpils and the huge, isolated church at Aglona, which attracts pilgrims from all over eastern Europe on the Feast of the Assumption are in this style.

Catholics were not the only refugees. A split in the Russian church in the 17th century brought an influx of Old Believers to the Baltics and elsewhere. They belong to the *bezpopovci* (without ministers) faction: during Russia's great repressions against the

cal example. Its figurative carvings and round log walls were all hewn with nothing more refined than an axe. It has a special fancy seat for the local German landlord and the front pews were more elaborately made for German workers. The native peasants were obliged to sit at the back – and were put in the stocks if they failed to attend services.

Because the Lutheran churches in Estonia and Latvia served the interests of the overlords, the Herrnhuters, or United Brethren Church, gained many followers during the 18th and 19th centuries. Services were conducted in farmers' houses or specially built prayer halls, and it became known as "the people's church", with an emphasis on education and religious enlightenment.

The United Brethren's activities diminished during the middle of the 19th century as pressure was put on them by both the Lutheran church and the tsar who won some conversions to Orthodoxy after promising support to farmers against the demands of German land barons. After Poland failed to gain independence in the 1863 uprising, the tsarist government also came down heavily on Old Believers, whom it looked on as renegades, and Catholics, whom it thought were a threat to the empire. A huge building programme brought a crop of onion-domed churches including the Orthodox cathedrals

people changed their convictions quite freely and even became involved in the old pagan religions, a romantic revival which was stoked up in the independence movements. After World War I and the break with Russia the countries formed independent Evangelical Lutheran churches, while all the Catholic churches came under the direct subordination of the Pope.

Jewish populations were well established in the Baltic region, which was one of the world's largest Yiddish language centres. Vilnius, the "Jerusalem" of Lithuania, had 98 synagogues, and there were synagogues in nearly every town in the countryside where a large proportion of the shops and small

of the Holy Theophany of Our Lord in Riga (1844) and the Alexander Nevski in Tallinn (1900). Many can be seen, abandoned, throughout the countryside today. There are still a few practicsing Orthodox Latvian and Estonian churches, though commercial links with Moscow have been severed.

Towards the end of the 19th century the first Baptist churches appeared in Estonia and Latvia, and around the beginning of the 20th century Seventh Day Adventists and other Protestant sects arrived. At that time

Left, Krishnas on the streets of Vilnius. **Above**, Judrenai Catholic church, Lithuania.

businesses were Jewish-run. Almost the entire population was deported or killed during the Nazi occupation: more than 200,000 died in Vilnius. Estonia was the only country Hitler triumphantly declared *Judenfrei* (Jew-free). Though some of the synagogue buildings around the countries remain, it is hard to identify them. One or two synagogues have re-opened in the capitals to serve the several thousand who have not yet left on their hoped-for emigration, and the one in Riga has been beautifully restored.

The church underground: During the Soviet years, all church properties and holdings were nationalised and many churches became concert halls or museums. St Casimir's in Vilnius was turned into a Museum of Atheism, and Riga's Orthodox cathedral became a planetarium and cafe. The state continually interfered with the works of the church and those who attended it: their careers were threatened, and their children were banned from higher education.

Even though Soviet rule was harsh, local authorities in the Baltics were more lenient and liberal compared with the Soviet heartland. There were many more working churches in Riga than in Leningrad, which had nearly three times the population of the former. Because it was easier to register a church and educate children in the Baltics,

many Baptists, Adventists, Pentecostals and other believers emigrated here from Russia, the Ukraine and elsewhere.

The Roman Catholic Seminary in Riga educated all new priests from the entire Soviet Union, except for Lithuania. Other institutions survived, such as the only Orthodox nunnery in the Soviet Union, at Kuremäe in Estonia. The church battled on, and many priests, evangelists and activists were imprisoned for their work. Estonia lost more than two-thirds of its clergy in the first Soviet years. The Catholics, along with the smaller Protestant churches (Baptist, Adventist and Pentecostal), were most successful in organ-

ising their opposition and keeping in touch. A group of Catholic priests regularly published the underground *Chronicles of the Lithuanian Catholic Church*, which informed the world about repression and human rights violations. The people, too, remained resilient. The Hill of Crosses, just north of Šiauliai on the Kaunas-Riga highway was bulldozed by the Soviets three times, but each time the crosses were rebuilt

Changing congregations: Today the Baltics are still centres of religion. The Commonwealth of Independent States has its bishop's chair for the German Evangelical Lutheran church in Riga and Vilnius is re-establishing itself as one of Catholicism's citadels in Europe. People are returning to the church but things have changed. The Lutheran and other Protestant congregations have fallen in the intervening years, and many country churches have only a handful of worshippers. By contrast, the Catholic church, through its diligence, organisation and might, has held its flock. In Latvia, where there are nearly twice as many Lutheran as Catholic churches, the number of baptisms in each is now about the same, around 10,000 a year.

Everywhere there are still signs of the religious mix. In Trakai and Vilnius are two *kenessas*, prayer houses of the Karaites, a surviving Jewish sect of Tatars who arrived in the 14th century at the behest of Grand Duke Vytautas. There are Muslims and Mormons, Uniats and *dievertu*, pagan Latvians whose churches are holy places around sacred oaks.

Not all the ecclesiastic splendours are on the beaten track. The splendid Pažaislis monastery should be sought out near Kaunas. One of Riga's architectural secrets is hidden behind the Academy of Sciences: the 1822 Church of Jesus, the Lutheran bishop's seat, is a wooden octagonal building in the empire style. The largest wooden church in the country, it measures 90 ft (27 metres) wide and has eight Ionic columns supporting elliptical domes.

When you have seen everything in Estonia, get a Russian visa and visit Petchory in the Pskov region. A great fortress wall encircles this 15th-century monastery, an abiding symbol of the churchs' struggles and endurance.

Left, Mother Superior, Kuremäe. **Right**, Lutheran confirmation in Šilutė, Lithuania.

Folklore is at the very heart of Baltic culture. Indeed, until the 19th century, folklore in effect *was* Baltic culture, because German and Polish rule from the Middle Ages onwards had meant that no real indigenous literary culture had been able to evolve. In the 19th and 20th centuries, the Baltic scholars and writers who developed the new Baltic cultural identity primarily used peasant folklore as their starting point.

Fortunately this folklore was of immense richness, especially in the field of music. Songs appear to have played an important part in the worship of the ancient Baltic gods, and ever since have been at the heart of the Balts' sense of themselves. Almost every Baltic village has its own choir, many of them of a professional standard. State and public occasions often begin with folksongs. As a Latvian *daina*, or folksong, has it:

I was born singing, I grew up singing,
I lived my life singing.
My soul went singing
Into the garden of God's sons.

A visit to some sort of folk-performance is recommended for any visitor. Fortunately, apart from the major festivals, performances of one sort or another go on all year round. From the beginning, folklore and the Baltic national movements were mixed up together. The first Estonian and Latvian national song festivals, held in 1869 and 1873 respectively, were also political events of the first importance, symbolising the reawakening and unity of the new nations. The independent republics between 1920 and 1940 turned them into great official symbolic events.

The Singing Revolution: Under Soviet rule, these festivals were among the very few ways in which national feeling could be legally displayed, although several of the more patriotic songs were banned. After Mikhail Gorbachev came to power, these songs were restored, and the various folklore festivals became key symbols of the national independence movements in a process which has been dubbed, especially in Estonia, the

"Singing Revolution". It was at the "Baltica" festival in 1987 that the old national flags of the former republics were publically displayed together for the first time under Soviet rule and without those responsible being promptly arrested.

The national song festivals are astonishing affairs, with the choirs numbered in thousands and the audiences in tens or even hundreds of thousands – a considerable proportion of the population. A charming element of informality is added by the lovely

tradition that, after every song, young girls run on to the stage to present flowers to their favourite conductors.

Folklore was also the key to rediscovering, or reinventing, the beliefs and society of the pagan Balts which existed before the Christian conquest. These seem to have been based on the idea that the world was itself created partly through song and story-telling:

"Once upon a time, the Lord God walked through the world, telling stories and curses, asking riddles..."

Modern-day scholars such as the great French-Lithuanian semiologist, Algirdas Julien Greimas, have used surviving folktales

Preceding pages: a senior citizens' singsong in Lithuania. **Left**, folk-art painting, Lithuania. **Right**, Saaremaa wedding socks.

to try to establish the nature of the ancient gods and their worship. Many gods have been rediscovered: Perkūnas or Pērkons, god of thunder, akin to the Slavic Perun and the Scandinavian Thor; Laima and Māra, goddesses of luck (good and bad, because Laima, like some Indian goddesses, also brings the plague); Aušra (the Dawn), and many lesser gods and goddesses, some of them figures in their own right, others merely subsidiary aspects of the main divinities.

The 14th-century priest Peter of Dusburg wrote that the Balts of his time "worship all of creation... sun, moon, stars, thunder, birds, even four-legged creatures down to the toad. They have their sacred forests, fields and

waters, in which they do not dare to cut wood, or work, or fish."

Until the 18th century, Catholic priests in Lithuania were still cutting down sacred oaks in an effort to stop their worship, and until the 20th century some of the ancient spirits lived on in folk tales about forest spirits such as the leprechaun-like *Kaukai*, the *Aitvarai* (who can lead people to hidden treasure) and the *Barzdukai*, a form of bearded gnome. The *Kaukai* were originally neutral spirits who could be won over with gifts. Later, however, they came to be identified with the Christian devil. The Devils Museum in Kaunas, unique in the world, contains a magnificent collection of portrayals of the Devil by Lithuanian folk-artists. Unfortunately, this is also to some extent a museum of historical anti-semitism, since most of the devils are meant to be Jewish.

Midsummer frolics: By the 18th century, awareness of the old Baltic religions as such had disappeared or become completely mixed up with Christian beliefs. Thus the great pagan festival of Midsummer Night was renamed St John's Eve, but it has retained many of the old pagan legends and customs, especially those connected with fertility. One of these is that on that particular night and only then, a flowering fern appears, and if a boy and a girl find it together, it will fulfil their heart's desire. Of course, ferns don't actually flower, but the tradition is a good excuse for young couples to go off together into the forest at night.

For many centuries, Christian priests and ministers did their best to stamp out much of Baltic folklore, precisely because it embodies so much paganism. The earliest records of Latvian folksongs are provided in evidence for 17th-century witch-trials, and it has been suggested that the "witches" of this period were in fact the linear descendants of the old pagan priests and sorcerers.

In the 1920s and '30s, efforts were made by some people to resurrect the old pagan religions. In Latvia, this took the form of the *dievturība* movement, which continues to this day. Because in the 1930s the movement was closely associated with Latvian fascism, it was savagely persecuted under Soviet rule. Its ideology today remains intensely nationalist. "We have always believed that Latvia should be only for the Latvians," one of its leaders has said. "God is a Latvian – or at least, our god is."

Its theology maintains the existence of a single godhead who takes different forms. This, however, is a modern construct derived from the real, but now almost forgotten, ancient pagan religion. The Dievturi number only a few hundred, but their past sufferings and the purity of their folksinging gives them a prestige.

A certain holistic, pagan-influenced mysticism, a willingness to see divinity in all the works of nature, has however characterised all three Baltic cultures up to the present day. This is true both of those authors who hark back directly to the ancient traditions, and those, like the Estonian poet Jaan Kaplinski, who render them into wider, universal terms – in his case, neo-Buddhist.

The new attitude to folk-traditions in Europe dates back to the later 18th century and the rise of Romanticism. Baltic folklore played a part in this cultural shift, because a key figure in the movement was the German philosopher Johann Gottfried Herder, who was profoundly moved by Latvian folksongs and stories when a Protestant minister and teacher in Riga in the 1760s. His influence led to generations of research by Baltic German scholars and, in the mid-19th century, the work was taken over by the first generations of native Baltic intelligentsia.

years by the Soviet Air Force) houses hundreds of thousands of examples. These give clues to an ancient tradition: for example, beer-mugs were decorated with "male" symbols, such as suns and horses.

Lithuania has a particularly rich tradition of folk-carving, which is illustrated by the intricately carved wooden crosses to be found outside many villages. Covered with ancient symbols, these crosses resemble pagan totem poles. The carved crosses on the famous Hill of Crosses at Šiauliai is an apotheosis of Catholic piety and of Lithuanian nationalism, but also of ancient pagan symbolism. Another sight to watch out for in the Lithuanian countryside is Rūpintojėlis ("The Thinker"),

Their first task was the recording and codification of this oral history. In Latvia, this process is connected above all with the name of Krišjānis Barons, who assembled the *dainas*, or Latvian folksongs. The 217,996 items form one of the largest collections of oral folklore in the world. Following the formation of the independent states after 1918, the governments and universities also set out to collect folk-art.

The Estonian National Museum in Tartu (now returned after being confiscated for 46

Left, festive crown, Lithuania. Above, Latvian sashes; a wedding knot tied by Lačplēsis's belt.

a mournful figure, now presented as Christ, but much older than Christianity. Removed under Soviet rule, these works of art are now being restored.

However, the task of recovering the meaning of such figures, and the ancient Baltic tradition in general, is an intensely difficult one, both because of the suppressive affect of Christianity, and the effects of modernisation, especially that which took place under Soviet rule. One of the reasons why many Estonians wish to recover the area of Petseri, or Pečory, captured by Estonia from Russia in 1920 and transferred back by Stalin in 1944, is that the small Setu minority who live there have preserved folk traditions which have been lost in Estonia itself.

The first major guide to Estonian folk stories (as opposed to folksongs, which had been published in various collections) was *Old Estonian Fairy-Tales*, first published in 1866. It is still popular in Estonia, and is held to have contributed to the creation of an Estonian prose-style that is independent of the German models it previously imitated.

In 1861, Kreutzwald published the "national epic" *Kalevipoeg* ("Son of Kalev"), a reworking in verse of stories about a giant hero; the work was intended to help build up a national spirit, and prove to a sceptical world that the Estonian folk-tradition was

Latvian republic, the Order of Lāčplēsis was the highest state award, and there are plans to restore this honour. Kangars, the traitor in the epic, has become a generic name for traitors, while Laimdota, Lāčplēsis's beloved, has given her name to boutiques and hairdressers, and Spīdola, the witch, gives her name to ships and yachts.

Pumpurs also gave the ancient Latvians a pantheon of pagan gods, like the classical Olympus – quite unhistorical, but another passport to European respectability in his time. The contemporary habit of giving children "traditional" pagan names, such as Laima or Vytautas (after the Lithuanian medieval Grand Duke), dates from this period.

capable of producing an epic – considered at that time to be the highest form of literature. As with the Finnish *Kalevala*, debate has raged over the merits of the work ever since.

Invented gods: The *Kalevipoeg* is still taught in every Estonian school, but otherwise its influence has progressively diminished. This has been far less the case with the Latvian national epic, *Lāčplēsis* ("The Bear-Slayer"), by Andrējs Pumpurs, in which another mythical hero is made a leader of the medieval Latvian resistance against the German invaders. *Lāčplēsis* has since become the theme of a verse play by Jānis Rainis, a rock-opera and several other works. Under the first

Today, this rich folkloric tradition is threatened from two directions: the first is by Western mass culture, especially influential in countries as poor as the Baltic states have become under Soviet rule. On the other side, there is also a danger that the over-use of folklore on official occasions, in schools and so on, may eventually drain it of the joyous spontaneity which so far has kept Baltic folklore alive and part of Baltic life, and not – as so often in the West – either a museum-piece or an artificially revived hobby.

Above, song festival in Tallinn, an exuberant nationalistic and inspirational event.

THE SINGING TREE

Most traditional musical instruments are common throughout the Baltics and Eastern Europe: the goat-horn, whistle, flute, reed, violin, squeeze-box and zither. Other instruments belong to particular regions: the bagpipe in Estonia and Latvia's Protestant part, the hammer dulcimer in Lithuania and Latvia's Catholic part, and the *hiukannel* or bowed harp in the Estonian islands. But one instrument unique to the Baltic lands is a kind of board zither with between five and 12 iron or natural fibre strings. Its history can be traced with some certainty back at least 3,000 years and its Baltic names have supposedly originated from the proto-Baltic word *kantlēs,* meaning "the singing tree": *kantele* in the Finnish language, *kannel* in Estonian, *kāndla* in Livonian, *kokles* in Latvian and *kanklės* in Lithuanian.

This is a deified instrument and, according to folk beliefs, the tree for its wood must be cut when someone has died but isn't yet buried. In a fairytale a youth helps an old man who turns out to be God and he rewards the good-hearted lad with this particular instrument.

Thus the Apollonic, heavenly aura and the fine, deeply touching tone quality have made *kokles* a symbol of national music for Estonians, Latvians and Lithuanians. Unfortunately the playing of the original instrument has almost died out. In the beginning of the 20th century *kokles* developed into a zither of 25 to 33 strings, like a harp. "Modernisation" during the Soviet time resulted in a soprano, alto, tenor and bass *kokles* family. Folksong arrangements and compositions of questionable musical quality were played and presented as the national music.

A folklore revival in the 1970s and 1980s restored an interest in traditional instruments. Many of them, such as the bagpipe, jew's-harp, whistle, flute, reed, horn, clappers and rattles, are made by enthusiasts and played informally. They are used by both solo performers and folklore groups and it is now hard to imagine a celebration of calendar customs, folk-dance parties or folklore festivals without them.

The most important festivals are the summer and winter solstice celebrations and there are large gatherings at such festivals as the "Baltica", which involves all three Baltic republics and sometimes includes Scandinavian countries, too. More local but no less exciting are "Skamba,

skamba kankliai" in Lithuania, and the children's and young people's folklore festival, "Pulkā eimu, pulkā teku", in Latvia. There are also a number of festivals which are associated with individual towns and villages.

In Lithuania visitors should try to listen to *sutartinės* which is endless sonoric meditation, both vocal and instrumental. For a while it seemed this unique ancient polyphony style had become extinct, but recently it has been revived by folklore groups. The instrumental version of *sutartinės* is played on *kanklės,* pan-pipes, trumpets or horns.

Primitive musical instruments are usually made by the players themselves. The more sophisticated ones such as the *kannel/kokles/kanklės,* bag-

pipes, flutes, violins, accordions and zithers are made by just a few skilled masters. Being in great demand, these instruments are not easy to obtain, though they can be found at fairs and folk-crafts festivals where there is also a good variety of bird, devil and animal-shaped clay whistles, usually played by children.

The most popular musical instruments in the Baltics are the accordion and, of course, the guitar, which are played at family celebrations and informal parties. Catholic and Lutheran churches mostly have organs with distinctive characteristics. The organ of Riga Dom is recognised world-wide, while those in the rural areas can have their own unique charm. ∎

THE CULTURAL INHERITANCE

"Unhappy the land that needs heroes", wrote the radical German poet and playwright Bertolt Brecht. Yet the Baltic states could hardly have survived 50 years of political and cultural subjugation without consolation from folklore and literature. Heroes from old legends embodying the national fate and those from painting, poetry and music generally, offered freedom and a refuge to those who felt the Soviet occupation had snatched away their homeland.

Internal emigration happened almost regardless of formal education. Theatres, opera and ballet performances were packed – and packed with half-hidden national significance, which the censors either ignored or missed. Writers for decades exploited communist subsidy to keep national pride and independent thought alive. They fostered the climate for independence which in the 1980s popular culture – rock music – finally brought to the surface. Banned under communism, it united classical composers, politicians and people in a mass gesture of defiance, thus earning itself a unique place in Baltic history.

Today, the bubble has burst. Without a patron state, the cultural world is struggling financially, as it is in all the former Soviet empire. Suddenly creative artists are no longer waged and need to finance themselves by selling their talents and wares. Painters, given choice studio flats in the Soviet system, have had to look elsewhere for work. Many music publishers can no longer make ends meet. For writers, an irony is that although they can now at last write freely and publish what they want in their own language, they enjoy only a fraction of the market the Russian language used to offer. There is very little money to fund opera and ballet.

The quality of work is also suffering. Right up until independence, there was a reactive energy to be tapped: a well of rage and sadness that could charge talent with creativity and power. Painters and sculptures could deal in allegories; playwrights and song-writers could pit their imaginations against the censors; filmmakers were not short of documentary material; and song-writers were inspired by the challenge of pulling the wool over the censors' eyes.

In the absence of an alternative political structure, people have looked to intellectuals and artists for leadership. Baltic writers, painters, musicians, sculptors, composers and philosophers have long been prime movers in public life. Raimonds Pauls, one of Latvia's better-known pianists and composer of

numerous pop hits, was made first minister of culture. Musicology was no bar to Vytautas Landsbergis becoming president of Lithuania, nor was being a novelist anything but an asset when Lennart Meri became Estonia's first post-war president. In fact, political and artistic achievements are often viewed in conjunction with one another: a musician or artist's popularity frequently depends on their perceived current standing in the national political debate.

Roots of literature: Intellectuals and artists have nurtured the idea of independent nationhood since it first emerged in the early 19th century, when the three languages began

Preceding pages: Rimas-Zigmas Bičiunas, Vilnius painter. Left, Kati Ivaste, Tallinn ballerina. Above, Māra Zalite, Latvian poet.

to be recorded in written form. The freedom to write – and to express a national sentiment in this manner – arrived in a burst of romantic novels and epic verses from which the modern culture took off.

Latvian Andrējs Pumpurs told in *Lāčplēsis* the tale of the bear-slayer drowned in the River Daugava, who, when he regains life, will ensure the eternal freedom of his people. Friedrich Kreuzwald fathered the national Estonian epic, the *Kalevipoeg*. A tsarist ban on printed Baltic languages impeded mid-century development but the lyrics to *Pavarasario balsai* (*Voices of Spring*, 1885), by a Lithuanian priest, perfectly encapsulated national striving and romantic sentiment.

young preacher at the Dom cathedral, while from 1837 to 1838 Richard Wagner managed the German Opera and Drama theatre. Since Russian laws closed Vilnius University from 1832 to 1905, many culturally active Lithuanians also lived in Riga.

Tartu, on Estonian soil, educated Balts of all origins. Students of the 1850s included Latvia's Krišjānis Barons, who first collected the Latvian folk songs called *dainas*, and his friend Krišjānis Valdemārs and Juris Alunāņš, who founded Latvian theatre. Much Latvian effort went into overcoming perceived German colonial condescension. Budding Estonian culture was less confrontational. Many Germans teaching and studying

The priest's involvement was of symbolic significance, for it was generally priests and doctors who established the Baltic written cultures, first in German, then later in Estonian, Latvian and Lithuanian.

The Baltic peoples could boast early of high-quality European centres of learning and a fertile intellectual ambience. In Lithuania the Jesuits created Vilnius University in 1579, and in 1632 the Swedes commanded a university in Tartu. Riga, meanwhile, acquired a cosmopolitan cultural importance. The East-Prussian-born Johann Gottfried Herder (1744–1803), the translator and author of the idea of nationality, was a popular

in enlightened Tartu shared Estonian fascination with the native language and themes. But for young Estonians the birth of their nation was above all romantic. As Kristjan Jaak Peterson (1801–1822), a poet and Tartu graduate living in Riga, declared:

Why should not my country's tongue
Soaring through the gale of song,
Rising to the heights of heaven,
Find its own eternity?

Peterson's question has remained relevant to the present day.

Literature led the emerging 19th-century arts with the novel of social realism. The Lithuanians Jonas Biliūnas, writing under his own name and the rather more familiar assumed names of Julija Žemaitė, Juozas Vaižgantas and Antanas Vienuolis all described peasant life. In Estonia the novelist Eduard Vilde and the playwright August Kitzberg exercised a similar function while the two brothers Kaudzīte wrote the first Latvian novel, *The Times of the Land Surveyors* (1879).

Exiled genius: Then suddenly from Latvia emerged a world-class genius, Jānis Rainis (1865–1929). A complex, multi-talented figure, Rainis was a lyrical poet, dramatist, translator (of *Faust*), political activist and cultural forefather. He wrote his best plays in Switzerland, where he fled after his involve-

this giant figure, while his wife Aspazija (1868–1943), a romantic poet and early feminist, is also revered. Both are remembered in a museum in their Jūrmala home.

Latvian literature, always close to the folk tradition and rustic life, was given a lyrical, inward quality by the terse, philosophical *daina*. The plays of Rūdolfs Blaumanis (1863–1908), also a master short-story writer, also set a high artistic standard. Blaumanis's folk comedy *The Days of the Tailor in Silmači* (1902) is still staged in the open air every midsummer. Affected by his German education and familiarity with the German poets, Jānis Poruks (1871–1911) introduced introspection, melancholy and dreams to

ment in the 1905 Revolution. His fate set a sad precedent for future Baltic novelists. His play *Fire and Night* (1905) is a dramatic statement of the Latvian spirit. *The Sons of Jacob* (1919) deals with Rainis's own conflict between art and politics. Jānis Tilbergs's portrait of Rainis in the Riga art gallery conveys his authority as a national elder and the personal loneliness voiced in his poetry. Modern Latvian literature still rotates around

Left, Jaan Kross, Estonia's premier novelist. **Above**, Monika Biciuniene, Lithuanian painter, with portrait by Vytautas Ciplijauskas; Egilis Straume, saxophonist, at Riga Academy of Music.

Latvian poetry and prose. Kārlis Skalbe (1879–1945), dubbed a Latvian Hans Christian Andersen because of his allegorical tales, was also an exquisite poet and short-story teller. Other notable poets include the symbolist Fricis Barda, Anna Brigadere (1861–1933) and Aleksandrs Čaks (1901–50), whose modern Imagist style burst forth with Latvia's 1918 independence and brushed the realities of urban life in the city of Riga with lyrical excitement.

Lithuanian literature did not develop such early power and variety, which may account for its greater openness to European influences. The literary group Four Winds, formed by Kazys Binkis (1893–1932), was devoted to Futurism; others imitated German Expressionism. Vincas Krėvė-Mickevičius (1882–1954) was, however, a great prose writer and dramatist whose work continued in exile. Krėvė, having briefly become Foreign Minister, fled in 1940. His epic masterpiece *The Sons of Heaven and Earth* remained unfinished after his death.

The Young Estonia (or Noor-Esti) Movement, devoted to raising Estonian literary standards to a European level, flourished from 1905 to the middle of World War I. The prosaist and traveller Friedebert Tuglas (1886–1971) brought the world to Estonian readers through his romantic exotic

stories, and conveyed the problematic existence of the artist. A. H. Tammsaare (1878–1940), author of the hefty novel *Truth and Justice*, and influenced by Dostoevsky, Knut Hamsun and Bernard Shaw, has been called the greatest Estonian prose writer the 20th century. A more radical experimental literary group, Siuru, nurtured the spirits of poets Jaan Oks (1884–1918) and Marie Under (1883–1977). Under, who spent the Soviet period in exile, is still Estonia's most highly regarded poet.

Romance and mysticism: Foreign influences and rural, national life stimulated Baltic visual arts and music. National Romanticism, a style acquired in the 1900s in St Petersburg, replaced old-fashioned academic painting and influenced architecture, taking over from European art nouveau. When that dreamy style became exhausted, the new schools of national painting took over. The Baltic national romantic style incorporates folk heroes and legends and recalls world-class painters from Munch to Beardsley, Klimt to Boecklin and Bakst. In this vein, over Latvia's Rudolfs Perle (1875–1917) and Estonia's Nikolai Triik (1884–1940), towers the Lithuanian mystical painter and musician Mikalojus Konstantinas Čiurlionis (1875–1911), a Baltic William Blake.

In thin, richly-coloured oils Čiurlionis created symbolic landscapes suggesting a mystical universe, with motifs such as the wise serpent from Lithuanian folklore. He conceived many of his memorable paintings as linked musical movements or as cycles of life and death, day and night. They are extraordinary, pantheistic, poetic distillations of human life. Čiurlionis's own nature was rich and varied. He travelled widely, wrote for newspapers and almost single-handedly founded the national cultural life before dying aged 36. His pictures can be seen and his music heard at his own museum in Kaunas.

After Čiurlionis Lithuanian painting, in the hands of the Kaunas-based *Ars* Group, grew into a satisfyingly complex art of landscape and portraiture, well informed on European developments and characterised by a rich, dark palette. Emerald green, dark pink, mauve and a touch of yellow evolved into national colours, and a persistent motif was the inclusion of folkloric wooden figures and toys.

The first Estonian art exhibition was held in Tartu in 1906, out of which emerged Triik and the Expressionist Konrad Magi (1878–1925). Magi co-founded the Pallas art school in Tartu, which produced the highly individual painter Eduard Wiiralt (1898–1954), who is best known for his graphics.

Any Baltic visitor interested in painting should head for Latvia, where professional painting was established when Vilhelms Purvītis (1872–1945), Jānis Rozentāls (1866–1917) and Jānis Valters (1869–1932) combined European Impressionist, Fauve and German Expressionist tendencies with their own distinctive approach to landscape and portraiture. The influence of these artists extended to Lithuania and to future generations of Baltic artists.

Purvītis, founder of the Riga Art Academy, captured the Latvian landscape but most of his work was burned in Jelgava during the war. Valters, who studied in Germany, painted landscapes tinged by subjective mood and represented in stark Fauve colours. Rozentāls's work climaxes in his portraiture. Generally the Latvian portrait tradition is outstanding. Rozentāls's depiction of his mother and the painting by Voldemārs Zeltiņš (1879–1905) of opera singer Pavils Gruzdna, using Purvītis's pale Latvian colours, lead into the later highly coloured avant-garde movement. Artists such as Oto

intensely active year at the Leipzig Conservatoire produced works still recorded today, including the String Quartet in C minor and the first Lithuanian symphonic composition, *In the Forest*. To a modern ear, the symphonic work often recalls the music of Bruckner, Mahler and Sibelius, but Čiurlionis was a very distinct talent in his own right. He later reworked many folksongs, wrote choral pieces and organised national musical life in Vilnius.

From the First National Awakening all the Baltic cultures developed strong traditions in choral singing. The first operas were written on national themes in the early 20th century, establishing opera as a popular but

Skulme, Leo Svemp and Jānis Tīdemanis bring this rich period to life.

The fine arts of the pre-war Baltic nations differ markedly in colour and mood. Rationalism and abstractionism were always present in Estonia, where the 1923 Estonian Artists Group was strongly drawn to Cubism and Bauhaus and art deco; Latvia, however, took a more determined emotional path.

Notable music: Čiurlionis contributed to modern Lithuanian culture not also through his painting but also through his music. An

<u>Left</u>, altar painting, Dundaga, by Jānis Rošentāls.
<u>Above</u>, *Vyties preliudas* by M. K. Čiurlionis.

conservative genre. Baltic symphonic music otherwise evolved from the St Petersburg conservatoire, echoing to the memory of Tchaikovsky and Rimsky-Korsakov. Outstanding composers of the era included Latvia's Emil Darziņš, particularly famous for his *Melancholy Waltz*, which was influenced by Tchaikovsky and Sibelius, and Estonia's Artur Kapp, who wrote symphonies and oratorios. Other notable figures include Latvia's Emils Mangeles. Latvians consider Alfreds Kalninc a musical father-figure for his varied work, both romantic and choral. His son Jānis also became a composer, later well-known in Canada as John Kalniņš.

In all the arts Scandinavian influence between the wars was very strong. An equally strong sense of alienation was felt from the Russian soul – the so-called "asiatic principle". Among the other arts which flourished were ballet, in the Russian tradition. In the applied arts, the Baltic states notably excelled in graphic art and in book publishing and illustration.

The aesthetic spirit: The distinct national characters of three states are perhaps most visible in their architecture. The Lithuanian spirit includes a hankering after lost grandeur, and some Lithuanians would love their Central European capital, with its baroque and neoclassical buildings, to be known as

with many adaptations also from prose. A strong tradition of open-air performances, with real animals on stage, persists in Latvia alongside rather verbose poetic theatre.

After the war alien ideology and the expulsion of several key figures cramped development of arts which were just emerging from an inevitable provincialism. The Latvians Anšlāvs Eglītis, Zenta Maurina and Mārtiņš Zīverts, the Lithuanians Antanas Vaičulaitis and Krėvė and Estonia's Marie Under continued the best pre-war literary traditions of theatre, prose and poetry abroad. But many writers died in the war, or shortly after. A literature of suffering and displacement, recounting the mass deportation

the Athens of the North. The rational Estonians combine their functional buildings with a fairy-tale German Old Town and a skyline outstanding in its aesthetic balance and beauty. Perhaps they have most successfully fitted their national artistic spirit into the modern world. The bourgeois quality of Riga, in Latvia, is much more perplexing, diluted by its proximity to the countryside and modern poverty, and heightened both by the creative arts and the density and mixture of population.

All the Baltic cultures reach out to the larger world through theatre, frequently devoting half their repertoire to world classics,

of artists and intellectuals to Siberia, emerged only in the 1980s, though in 1946 *The Forest of Gods* by Balys Sruoga recounted the experience of Lithuanian intellectuals in a German camp with irony and humour. The Estonian Jaan Kross (born 1920), who was imprisoned by the Nazis, spent nine years in Russian labour camps and his novels and short stories provide poignant accounts of his country's history.

Stalin's Socialist Realism might have destroyed the Baltic arts but they showed latent independence by avoiding the official prescription. Latvia's talented Andres Upits and Vilis Lacis transformed themselves into controversial Soviet apologists, as did the much-appreciated Lithuanian woman poet Salomėja Nėris.

Soviet avant-garde: A new creative generation emerged in the 1960s during the Khrushchev thaw, ready to exploit the easier position of the arts on the fringe of a centralised empire. The Baltics became the home of the Soviet avant-garde, with productions of Becket and Ionesco, and in the mid-1980s the uncensored publication of George Orwell's *Nineteen Eighty-Four*. This relatively liberal climate pre-empted dissident activity. It also produced notable opera singers and ballet dancers, in particular Mikhail Baryshnikov and Boris Godonov

the choral composer Velio Tormis and Lithuanian modernist Osvaldas Balakauskas also enjoy world renown.

The later Soviet period brought more abstractionism into painting, from Jonas Švažas and Dalia Kosčiunaitė in Lithuania to Mari Tabaka in Latvia. Estonia's Mari Kurismaa sought a refuge from absurd, punitive Soviet reality in ideal geometric poise.

Lithuanian theatre, meanwhile, has generated several world-class producers, who are represented most notably today by Jonas Vaitkus and Juozas Nekrošius. Poet Paul-Eerik Rummo's *Cinderella Game* is the best of a flourishing absurdist and fringe Estonian theatre tradition. Estonia is also well-known

from Riga, and a proliferation of bold, popular poetry against the official tide.

Music managed to experiment with atonality and minimalism. Communist Poland, where Baltic composers were allowed to travel, was a rich source of ideas and provided a window on the West. The coincidence of modern ideas with folksong atonality was carefully exploited. Estonian music has since flourished both at home and abroad, due to the work of émigré classical composer Arvo Pärt. The Latvian conductor Mariss Jansons,

Left, Pēteris Plakidis, Latvian composer. **Above**, Leonids Vigners, Latvian conductor.

for its cartoons. Adolfs Šapiro and Pēteris Petersons are active, cosmopolitan figures in Latvian theatre.

Popular present-day writers include Latvia's poet and children's writer Imants Ziedonis and prose-writer Zigmund Skuins and Lithuania's Juozas Aputis, all of whom have at some time in their careers been heavily censored by the Soviets. The novels of Lithuanians Vytautas Bubnys and Vytautas Martinkus, otherwise in quite different styles, show the continuing attraction of folk themes. Estonia's Jaan Kross and the poet Jaan Kaplinski have acquired a high reputation and international following.

A BRIDGE TO THE FUTURE

After the Soviet Union fell apart, Estonians, Latvians and Lithuanians found themselves, for the first time in 50 years, longing for the future. It promised the best that democratic capitalism had to offer: vibrant economies, higher standards of living and responsive government. But these things don't happen overnight and the immediate future hasn't been nearly as good as advertised.

It is true that the economies have been expanding: Estonia's has become one of the fastest growing in Europe. But Baltic observers now believe that the dramatic social and economic changes are still to come. Optimists believe the Baltic states could be new Hong Kongs, dynamic and wealthy. The biggest hope, expressed regularly by Balts even before independence, was that the three countries could become economic bridges between the former Soviet Union and the West.

Already an estimated 85 percent of all trade west of the Ural mountains runs through the Baltics. And of six ice-free ports used by Russia to export its rich supply of raw materials, four are in the Baltic states: Klaipėda in Lithuania and Liepāja, Ventspils and Riga in Latvia. Tallinn in Estonia can be kept open by ice-breakers if necessary in winter. At Latvia's main port, just outside Riga, the harbour cranes are busier than ever before. Despite stiff Russian trade barriers, the upturn has been caused by increased shipments of coal to the West from the resource-rich CIS states. Ironically, this boom has been fuelled by the economic troubles faced by coal mines elsewhere in Europe. As high-cost coal output decreases, producers such as Germany and the United Kingdom are ordering cheaper coal from the East, which means that more coal than ever before is being channelled through Baltic ports.

Maurice Cartwright, a British entrepreneur who founded a joint venture with a Kazak coal mining company, has been using Riga's port since March 1991. He says that his firm, called Kazmin International, is shipping as much as 20,000 tons of coal from

Kazakstan through Riga every month. He is bullish on the prospects for trade through the Latvian port, though it has limited capacity, handling only 700 tons of cargo an hour, compared with a main port like Rotterdam, which can handle 16,000 tons an hour. And though port authority bureaucracy is still maddening, Cartwright says it is not nearly as bad as the bureaucracy he has dealt with elsewhere in the former Soviet Union.

If trade ever booms, as many Western financial experts predict, Estonia is in a

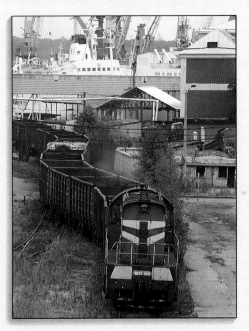

position to benefit, too. It has the most technologically advanced port, Tallinn New Port, which was completed with Soviet funds a few years before it became obvious the empire was going to disintegrate. It has a depth of 60 ft (18 metres).

Baltic highway: The Via Baltica – perhaps the grandest of the Baltic infrastructure projects – best symbolises the gap between wish and reality. The road, according to its backers, will one day be one of Europe's great arterial highways, linking Finland to Germany by way of the Baltic states and Poland. Drivers venturing on to what is a busy and dangerous two-lane winding

Preceding pages: sea traffic, Tallinn. Left, timber terminal, Estonia. Right, Tallinn's port.

country road certainly hope so. And while stopping at any one of the half-dozen infuriatingly slow border crossings, they will have plenty of time to consider the slow pace of change.

Western companies have, however, already been attracted by the economic potential of the inter-Baltic highway, the majority of them from Scandinavia. They have been building and renovating a whole variety of service stations, stores, hotels and restaurants along the road.

The Finnish oil conglomerate Neste was among the first investors, pumping millions of dollars into sleek, Western-style service stations in all three capitals. The Swedish

company Ake Larson Byggare AB also built service stations in Tallinn for the Norwegian oil company Statoil, and it has the largest petrol station in the Baltic states outside Tallinn. The Swedish telecommunications company Eriksson has invested huge sums of money in a mobile telephone system for the Baltic states. Scandinavians have been involved in a number of joint hotel ventures and German and Austrian companies are also looking at Lithuania's tourist potential, particularly in the resorts and backwaters of its unspoilt coast.

The "Baltic bridge" concept doesn't stop with trade and inter-state commerce. Balts also see their countries, like Hong Kong and Taiwan, as financial and business bases for international investors who have an eye on lucrative former Soviet markets. The distinctly European capitals, Tallinn, Riga and Vilnius, should be more comfortable bases for businessmen than, say, Moscow, Kyiv or Tashkent and, if the banking systems improve, the capitals would offer launching points into the East.

The giant cereal-maker Kellogg has already been convinced. It is building a processing plant near Riga to sell its Latvian-made cereals in Latvia. For Kellogg, Latvia is a means to break into the much bigger, potentially far more lucrative Russian market. McDonald's, already established in the world's busiest restaurant in Moscow, has set up a base in the Baltics, in Riga, where it is opening three restaurants, plus a fourth in Tallinn, costing $3 million and employing 300 people.

Sympathetic observers argue that Estonians, Latvians and Lithuanians will serve as ideal mediators for Westerners trying to crack Russian markets. "Balts understand Russians," say the Baltophiles, "and because they are Europeans themselves, they understand the West."

Foot in the door: John Battle, an American investor, has already taken the words to heart. His US-based company has invested hundreds of thousands of dollars in the Baltic states. Its most ambitious project is an office complex for Western businessmen in Tallinn's picturesque old town, despite some objections from local Estonians who fear that Western investors might overrun the country and buy all the best property. Battle admits that bureaucratic obstacles occasionally drive him crazy, but he chides other businessmen for waiting too long to strike at the opportunities here. "Now is the time for Western companies to get their foot in the door and prepare for the future," he says. "In the long run the Baltics will be profitable places to do business."

But there hasn't yet been a full-scale rush to invest. Western businessmen are intrigued about doing business in the Baltic states, but they remain wary about the overall economic situation and about the possibility of political instability.

"They didn't believe that new national currencies could work," cautions one American analyst. "They also don't believe that they can trust Baltic partners. There have been so many stories about people getting burned, businessmen here just don't have enough credibility."

Many international investors also say that the Baltic market, with only 7 million people, isn't worth the effort. If they want to reach the Russian market, many wonder why they shouldn't just skip the Baltic bridge and go straight to Russia.

Most big-name firms have yet to take the plunge or are making token investments. Car-makers such as General Motors, Honda and Mercedes, for instance, have opened dealerships in the Baltic states, but they have

economically precarious Russia has far too much to lose to think about threatening the Baltic states.

Most Balts, however, understand that current hardships have little to do with outside enemies. They realise that what they have to battle against is themselves. As any locally-based businessman understands too well, lackadaisical attitudes to work and rampant incompetence constitute the greatest obstacle to economic success, not the lack of money, equipment or technological know-how. The biggest question is whether Balts can grow out of the debilitating character flaws that developed during the Soviet era. Can they regain the dynamic and hard-

not yet considered building factories. Despite the boast that they can do business with Russia and prosper by it, deep down the Balts do not trust their big eastern neighbour, while Russia, in turn, alleges that Baltic governments are practising discrimination. Russia has imposed stiff customs tariffs on Baltic products to protest against the alleged discrimination of Russian-speakers in Latvia and Estonia. There is an outside chance that they will be locked in disputes in the future, but, for the time being, an

Left, in front of one of Riga's many restaurants.
Above, Vilnius's famed Stikliai hotel/restaurant.

working reputation built up during the years of independence before World War II?

The American investor John Battle believes that it will take one-and-a-half generations before typical Soviet attitudes disappear from the three states. "That's quite a long time," he said. "But on the other hand, it will take three time longer before characters change in Russia and in the rest of the former Soviet Union."

Balts encourage the comparison with the rest of the Soviet Union because they know that it makes them look so much better. They frequently point to their past as evidence that their futures are brighter than Russia's. They take pains to explain that as independent, pro-free-market states in the 1920s, and 1930s' standards of living came close to Western European levels. Estonia's and Latvia's approached Sweden's and Denmark's, and surpassed Finland's.

"We did it before, we can do it again," is a common sentiment. "Unlike the Russians," say the Balts confidently, "we haven't forgotten how to work hard."

Unfortunately, the Balts have forgotten more than they like to admit. As more and more realise, economic conditions today are very different. In the 1920s and 1930s, Europeans needed more butter, milk and cheese and gladly imported it from the agrarian

spreads across all three Baltic states. Sweden and Finland have been buying them up, usually in the form of pulp, which is used to make paper, and Sweden is showing particular interest in local birch, from which high-quality paper is made. A boom in the export of wood resources has made a handful of Baltic mediators very rich. According to one press report in Estonia, middlemen who make deals between local suppliers and foreign buyers are making a profit of up to $400,000 a year. But the foreign demand is also driving up the price of trees beyond the reach of local furniture factories.

There is an existing electronics industry – the world's first miniature camera was made

Baltics. Today, with dairy surpluses spilling out of warehouses throughout Europe, these products are no longer needed. The expected increase in agricultural production will ensure that Balts can always feed themselves, but they can no longer rely on the export market.

Wood products: Economists here say that textiles and wood products, such as furniture and handicrafts, are the Baltics' best export prospects. The quality in these areas is indistinguishable from Western-made goods and they can compete favourably with the West.

With few natural resources, the backbone of the export trade since independence has been trees, cut from the rich forest that

at VEF in Riga – and somewhat overconfident Balts have suggested that, like some poorer Asian countries, they could mass produce high-tech goods for export. The confidence that they can do anything the West can do probably comes from the tendency, even among Western analysts, to overrate Baltic economic potential. It is certainly true that the Baltics are, economically speaking, 10 times better off than the rest of the former Soviet Union. But the more important fact is that they are also 10 times worse off when compared to the rest of the Western world. They don't come close in workmanship, infrastructure, banking and a host of other services. There has also been insufficient training in job skills. For years the Soviets imported Polish workers to renovate the old cities. Now embassies find they have had to bring in builders as well as materials to refurbish their residences, as they cannot find suitably qualified local people to carry out these jobs.

Some politicians are taking a more measured look at the immediate future for the three countries, predicting not a period of fabulous wealth but rather one of stability and consolidation. "The Baltic states will have stable democracies and growth economies after only 15 years," predicted Trivimi Velliste, the Estonian Foreign

in fact many of the fears have proved groundless. There has been no mass unemployment. Some of the big, inefficient firms have lingered on, paying wages out of government subsidies which, however low, are preferable to government benefits.

In an effort to try to smooth out the road to free markets, the World Bank and the IMF have provided loans to the three Baltic states, the largest amount going to Lithuania. The money, which has to be paid back at 7.6 percent interest, will be used to buy such essential imports as heating oil, agricultural chemicals and medical supplies.

Even before world financial institutions arrived on the scene to give the Baltic states

Minister, in the early 1990s. "Only then, will you be able to start talking about prosperous, Western-looking nations."

Inevitable crash: The IMF has also predicted that GNP would fall by at least 20 percent a result primarily of the cut-off of raw materials from Russia and the collapse of Eastern markets. Hundreds of huge, rusting Soviet-style factories as well as smaller businesses would be forced to close down. Some economists predicted a corresponding rate of unemployment at 30 percent or more. But

Left, brewery at Utena, which makes one of Lithuania's main beers. **Above**, trams in Tallinn.

a hand, the three countries had gone a long way toward laying the foundation for free-markets. All three have passed wide-ranging legislation on corporate law, foreign investment and taxation. Estonia was also the first former Soviet republic to introduce its own national currency. Latvia and Lithuania soon followed.

As for privatisation, the process has been fastest and most radical in Lithuania, which has otherwise been generally regarded as the economic slowcoach of the region. The government began selling off apartments and enterprises to private citizens in late 1991. Progress towards privatisation in Estonia and Latvia has been much slower, with parliaments locked in disputes over how to proceed. Estonia's centre-right government has pledged to cut taxes, raise business confidence and, in general, speed up anything that looks like a free-market reform. It has also pledged to cut out several levels of bureaucracy from all ministries and government departments. In contrast, the Lithuanians threw out their more radical government in favour of reformed communist politicians. A government made up of leaders who aren't as actively in favour of capitalism could mean that Lithuania will take smaller, less drastic economic steps in the future.

Although all three states have said they are interested in letting foreigners participate in the purchase of state property during the privatisation period, all three have also expressed the fear that foreigners will buy up everything in sight. "The Soviets came here and took everything," explained one Lithuanian analyst. "Now there is the fear that Westerners are going to come and take everything, too."

Asset-strippers: A main concern of many observers in all three countries is that former bureaucrats and organised criminals will sabotage the future by ripping off all the most valuable state assets. "It will come to the day when all you can do is get shares in a waste treatment plant and maybe keep the lousy apartment you're living in," warns Jüri Estam, a journalist in Tallinn. "That's all that will be left of the privatisation process."

The rise of the post-Soviet rich has not been accompanied by the rise of a stabilising middle class. Nor is it likely to happen soon. More likely will be a sharp increase in the very rich upper class and a corresponding increase in the numbers of poor.

However, it is not all a case of gloom and doom. The signs of change for the better are ever more evident in the Baltic capitals where new shops, restaurants and services start up every day. Western goods, though still too expensive for most Balts, are on shelves everywhere. Kiosks and stalls are continually being erected. Stores seem to be getting cleaner all the time and many have been renovating and expanding. Service in stores has significantly improved, as management feels the heat of competition and employees begin to worry about the prospect of being out of a job.

Even local restaurants, notorious for their poor standards of service during the Soviet era, are beginning to understand the once-alien notion of the customer as king. All are striving to please patrons, and the ubiquitous doorman is a thing of the past. Western restaurateurs have also been moving in to fill a void of top-class eating establishments. Chen Dong, a Belgian-Chinese businessman, opened the Baltic's first Chinese restaurant in Vilnius. Since then, some twenty other Chinese have sprung up, and the city is now home to numerous ethic restaurants.

In Tallinn Old Town, the Indian restaurant Maharaja was once the classiest between the Baltic Sea and Vladivostok. Although the English and Estonian partners have been at loggerheads on questions of business, they still manage to achieve almost world-class food and service. In Vilnius the German-run Idabasar, near the Gates of Dawn, established a good reputation the moment it opened at the end of 1992.

However, most of the changes are just beginning to touch the average Balt. If the craziness of shortages and long queues has ended, prices have gone through the roof. Most people are struggling harder than ever to make ends meet, spending at least half their money a month on such basics as milk, bread and butter. And though unemployment still stands below 10 percent in all three countries, everybody knows that for the first time in their lives their jobs are at risk.

Although the Baltic states long ago abandoned the notion that the West will bail them out economically, moving closer to the West, especially Europe, is the ultimate goal. Politicians say that they would like to join the European Union as quickly as possible, preferably before the year 2010, and the Eurocrats in Brussels talk about "when" the countries join, and not "if". But unless Europe lowers its economic standards or an economic miracle happens in the Baltics, Estonia, Latvia and Lithuania are likely to remain closer to the Third World for a few years yet.

Despite this, most Balts are convinced that prosperity will come sooner or later and that the future, even if it is hard, has to be better than the past.

Right, indications that society may slowly be starting to prosper, at a cafe in Vilnius

In the spring of 1992, an elk was spotted standing in the waters of the River Daugava in the centre of Riga, too frightened to move. Framed by the city skyline and the yawning bridges that connect this industrial capital of nearly a million people, the elk made an appearance on national television before scientists captured it and released it in one of Latvia's many forests. No one knows how such a shy animal ended up in the heart of the Baltic states' largest city, but it apparently felt quite at ease in the Daugava's waters which are so polluted that human swimmers have come out in infections and skin rashes.

Throughout the three countries there is a clash between poorly planned urbanisation and a countryside left to run wild after half a century of communism. One of the problems for visitors now is that much of the resultant pollution is impossible to see or gauge immediately. Six months after the elk came to town, Karl Gustav XVI of Sweden visited the Sloka paper mill nearby on the River Lielupe. The mill pours its hazardous waste into the Daugava and protesters have twice had it closed down. On inspection, the king declared that it did not seem as bad as he had been led to believe.

Coastal hazards: The Lielupe and the Daugava rivers empty themselves in the middle of Riga Bay beside Jūrmala. This has long been regarded as the Baltic Riviera, a high spot on more than 1,000 miles of white sandy coast that stretches from Narva on the Russian border in Estonia to just beyond Nida at the Lithuanian border with Kaliningrad. On a fine day it is often hard to imagine that the Baltic Sea's tempting blue acres, breaking in long, lazy curves over spotless white beaches, are not as pure as driven snow. But into this sea flows the cess and chemical waste of conurbations both within and beyond the Baltic states.

The Sloka mill reopened because the country needed newsprint, but it has since been mooted that it is not the main source of coastal pollution. A study team whose work

was published in *Ecocide in the USSR* blamed the pre-war sewer system in Riga as well as in Jūrmala, where holidaymaking and 219 coal-fired hot-water systems have taken their toll. (Note that tap water in Riga is not clean enough to be drunk.)

There are other water-borne hazards, too. The eastern end of this Riviera, around the mouth of the Daugava, is a good place to look for amber. Children, thinking they are in luck, have picked up small lumps of phosphorus and literally burned their fingers.

The beaches at Jūrmala have, from time to time, been officially closed. But at other times the visitor has no way of knowing if the water is clean. Although a ribbon of green algae along the water's edge is a warning sign, there is no hard and fast rule. Dedicated conservationists would not put a toe in a drop of Baltic water; locals dive in to its potentially most hazardous spots. You are probably quite safe away from the towns, in particular industrial centres such as Klaipėda, Ventspils, Riga, Pärnu, Haapsalu, Tallinn and Narva.

Local people are not oblivious to the problems, but they have had to live with them. Families around Kursių Lagoon in Lithuania

Preceding pages: polluting power plant near Narva, Estonia. Left, moose goes for a paddle in the Daugava, Riga. Above, nesting white storks.

continue to catch and eat lead-contaminated bream, perch, roach and eel because during the Soviet period nobody told them not to, and now they cannot afford to eat anything else. The Nemunas, which brings mercury, phenols, DDT, HCH and phosphorus compounds into the lagoon and Klaipėda's port, is the country's most polluted river. There is, however, no sign of dead fish being constantly washed up on the riverbanks or sea shore, and fish is regularly caught and sold in the markets and eaten at home and in hotels.

Marine life has also suffered as a direct result of Soviet fishing policies. The natural balance has been destroyed by overfishing, and during the 1980s spawning fish in the

The climate is one thing that cannot be blamed on the Soviet occupation. In fact, the years of occupation actually benefited parts of the countryside through its incompetence and wilful neglect. An obsession with secrecy protected the whole coast from development, and for nearly two generations much of it remained out of sight.

For the first time in nearly 50 years people are discovering beautiful beaches, from the Estonian islands to the dune-backed Neringa Spit in Lithuania, all formerly heavily patrolled by the Soviet army. The Kolka peninsula in northwest Latvia, once the preserve of armed, KGB-trained border guards, maintains a degree of protection simply be-

entire Baltic fell by more than 50 percent. Over the past 20 years concentrations of nitrate from improperly treated waste water have trebled and quadrupled during winter months. This has increased organic material on the sea bottom, which has reduced oxygen levels and led to a decline in salt levels. Stocks of whitefish and smelt have dropped and natural cod reproduction has been seriously affected.

Sea life has also suffered from climatic changes. Mild winters have left the coast free of ice, depriving seals of their natural breeding grounds; a number have died when they have been forced to breed ashore.

cause of its poor roads. In its centre is the 27,000-acre (15,000-hectare) Slītere State Reserve, where Western ornithologists come to see the buzzard migration in spring.

The reserve's director, Elmārs Peterhofs, is concerned about its future now that the Soviets have gone. "I have seen what tourists have done to the Finnish islands," he says. "We must stand very firmly against such developments. This territory is only interesting as long as it stays the way it is." Even when fires swept through 7,400 acres (3,000 hectares) of the reserve's dry forest and peat bog in the summer of 1992, he was not pessimistic. "The fire was unique for Western Europe. This territory has not been influenced by man for more than 100 years. We can see how the natural ecosystem responds."

Throughout the Baltic states, naturalists say that Soviet mismanagement has actually saved large tracts of beaches, woodland and wildlife, sustaining habitats that have disappeared forever elsewhere in Europe. Each of the three countries has a long list of natural parks and special areas set aside as being of particular scientific interest. Under the Soviets it was relatively easy to designate territory because the state owned everything. And, although not all areas of special interest have avoided damage and pollution, some 25,000 birds are, for example, thought to live in soggy forests the Soviet administrators tried to drain but actually made wetter.

Furthermore, unlike the rest of Europe, the percentage of rural land has increased since 1940. In Latvia, more than two-thirds of the population lived in the countryside. By the end of the Soviet era, Stalin's mass deportations, emigrations to the West, collectivisation and immigration of Russian labour to work in Soviet factories had shrunk rural populations to less than one-third. Dozens of ruined stone farmhouses can be seen in southern Estonia. In Lithuania 10 percent of the rural population migrated to rural areas every decade from 1950 to 1980.

"The socialists were too lazy to spoil nature," says Valts Vilnitis of the Latvian Environmental Protection Committee. "During the First Independence period 29 percent of the country was forested. Now it's 42 percent. That kind of increase is unique in Europe. Agricultural lands also decreased. It was simply bad management."

Wildlife inhabitants: These habitats have benefited all manner of animals and birds. The coastal wetlands are breeding grounds for ducks, waders, terns and swans, the uplands are scavenged by birds of prey, corncrakes chatter in summer meadows and white storks nest everywhere. City streets are pecked over by the ubiquitous hooded crow. The woods are home to elk, deer, martyn, lynx and boar and the abundant rivers and lakes support beavers and otters.

The World Wide Fund for Nature reports that in Latvia alone there are 400 wolves,

4,000 otters, 50,000 beavers, 400 lynx, 70,000 roe deer and 30,000 boar. Among the 208 bird species to breed or pass through the country is the world's largest colony of black storks. The best chance a visitor has of seeing wildlife is in the Gauja National Park north of Riga, where there are boars, deer, and even bison. Lahemaa National Park east of Tallinn is home to brown bears, lynx, cranes and mink.

Sometimes this wildlife profusion becomes a nuisance. On the Estonian island of Saaremaa, people have purloined 2-ft (60-cm) high metal sheets from an old air base and erected them around potato crops to keep out wild boar, or "forest pigs" as they call them.

The reserves have always provided local licensed hunters with seasonal game, from duck and capercaillie to deer and boar. Now trophy-hunting is on the increase, helping to reduce the number of animals and bringing in much-needed foreign revenue. High on the list are the shy elk, favoured by Germans who also go to Lithuania to hunt wolves. Organised trips bring hunters from as far away as the United States to bag any of these animals as well as lynx and, occasionally, brown bear.

Unofficial hunting does of course go on, and this may now be on the increase as more guns are brought in. Former Soviet army

Left, cement plant in Venta, Lithuania. **Above**, the Ignalina atomic power plant.

weaponry can be bought with reasonable ease in the big markets in the Baltic capitals. At risk, too, are the habitats, now that land may be properly cultivated by the newly returned private farmers. International organisations have already become involved in conservation projects. The World Wide Fund is, for example, working with Latvia to protect the country's previously untouched natural habitats, and 15 percent of the land is to be set aside for this purpose.

There is also concern about the insufficient legislation controlling privatisation of land, which may be used in ways that can cause serious damage to important habitats. IUCN, the World Conservation Union, is

border. Decades of mining have created sharp-tipped slag heaps more than 300 ft (100 metres) high. These black mountains contain toxic heavy metals and organic compounds with large amounts of phenols that are washed into the sea by the rain.

The oil shale burned to produce electricity leaves ash that is mixed with water and pumped to the top of flat sedimentation basins where the alkaline liquid forms bright blue lakes before it evaporates. More than 150 million tons of grey ash have accumulated in these giant, barren fields that stretch for miles. Experts say that if the petrified ash is ever used, it will take more energy to grind it down than was originally generated in

working with each of the states to find ways of dealing with the problem. This should help both the land and the people.

Fuel crises: Forests are already threatened by a burgeoning black market for timber exports, and, with fuel crises, they will increasingly be looked to for heating homes during the long, dark days of winter. Wood and peat currently account for about 4 percent of energy needs.

Energy is a crucial question, and the search for it has been a major contributor to the pollution of the Baltic states to date. Undoubtedly the most evil is the shale oil industry in Estonia based near the Russian

burning the shale oil. Revelations about such industrial vandalism surfaced in the mid-1980s and helped to galvanise the movement towards independence. It was then that a Soviet plan to build a large hydro-electric power station on the Daugava was exposed by Dainis Ivans, a Latvian journalist.

He concluded that the project, which would flood historic villages on a pretty stretch of the river above Daugavpils and turn the river into a series of lakes, would not actually result in enough water to keep a power station working. Ivans and a colleague wrote a critical article, which led to public opposition and, a year later, the cancellation of the plan. Ivans was subsequently elected chairman of the Latvian Popular Front, the first organised opposition to the Communist Party; after independence he became a member of parliament.

Chernobyl also stirred fear in the Baltic states, not only because the 1986 explosion caused fallout across the three countries, but also because a plant of exactly the same design was under construction in Ignalina, Lithuania. No geographic survey or seismic studies had been carried out before it was built. Two reactors are now up and running, but plans for a construction of another two at the same site were halted following demonstrations organised in 1988 by the

Gorbachev's *perestroika* gained momentum, public pressure to halt the mining increased. *Ei Ole Üksi Ükski Maa* ("No Land Stands Alone") became the rallying cry for the Estonian nation. Moscow finally called a halt to further mining in the region.

Now that many of the protesters are in power, they find their hands tied by lack of money. Exploitation of shale oil in Estonia continues. Its thermal power stations produce 52 percent of the country's output, and the country's total output is twice the amount that it needs. It imports gas and oil (27 percent) for heat. The shale oil supplies will run out in the near future and, in spite of Chernobyl, nuclear alternatives are consid-

Lithuanian Greens and the pro-independence Sąjūdis movement. "The protest about the environment was a kind of protest against the government," says Rapolas Liužinas from Lithuania's Environmental Protection Department. "It made people realise they are hosts in their own land and shouldn't accept the dictates of others."

In Estonia there were protests against a phosphate mining enterprise in the north, which would have polluted a large part of the country's ground-water supplies. In 1987, as

Left, hunters on Hiiumaa island, Estonia. **Above**, brown bear and cub.

ered. "Sooner or later we will have to come to that," says a former industry minister, "but opinion has to be created."

In Latvia, Ivans concedes: "I don't like nuclear energy but other kinds of energy are too dirty." The country is completely dependent on outside energy supplies and a large proportion of its electricity comes from its two Baltic neighbours.

Like Estonia, Lithuania has no natural fuel resources and produces twice as much energy as it consumes, both at the Ignalina nuclear station and at a thermo-electric power plant in Elektrėnai near Vilnius. Lithuanian officials don't plan to close down Ignalina but, with the help of Swedish experts, they are trying to increase the reactor's safety.

In the meantime, little has been done to promote heat and light conservation at home. Windows are often badly fitted, buildings poorly insulated, and the anonymous concrete blocks of flats erected in every town have no modern thermostat control. Through central planning, the government can regulate the heat in the blocks of flats, but on previous occasions when fuel crises have prompted governments to lower their temperatures, the occupants have simply turned on their hot-water taps and steamed up their homes. Even when winters are mild, artificial light is necessary for all but four hours of the day.

From air and water: The environment ministries in each of the countries say that waste water treatment systems in many towns are obsolete and in need of repair. Feasibility studies have been carried out, but money remains an obstacle. Riga is particularly bad, and people have been boiling their water there since an outbreak of hepatitis A in 1989. Most rural areas get their drinking water from wells where run-off from agriculture may pollute ground-water supplies. The Lithuanian Environmental Protection Department reports that about 40 percent of all well water is unsuitable for drinking because it contains large amounts of organic substances, oil products, ammonia, pesticides and detergents.

In the countryside, lichen grows abundantly in most of the damp woods – a sign of relatively clean air. Estonia, however, poisons not only its own atmosphere, but Finland's too. Shale-oil-fired thermal power plants near the Russian border emit hundreds of thousands of tons of sulphur dioxide and nitrogen oxide compound annually. Prevailing winds carry it to Finland where it kills forests. "Estonia, with its temperate climate, and Estonians, with their modest temperament, cannot boast many world records," states a report published by the government for the 1992 Earth Summit in Rio de Janeiro. "However, there is no doubt that we hold at least one first in the whole world: production of sulphur dioxide per capita." In 1988 it was 308 lb (140 kg) per person. East Germany ranked second with 275 lb (125 kg).

Elsewhere, Soviet-built industry still sends its foul breath into the air. In cities and industrial areas, metallurgical, chemical, fertiliser, shale oil, cement, cellulose and paper companies are some of the worst offenders. Pollution from across the borders also causes headaches and finger-pointing. In 1990 the River Daugava was poisoned by an organic cyanide spill from a polymer factory in Belarus, while Lithuania's cement plant in Akmenė and an oil refinery and power station in Mažeikiai send air pollution to Latvia. Lithuania itself suffers from Polish industrial pollutants and waste from Kaliningrad that feeds into the River Nemunas.

Since independence, pollution in some areas has dropped off as industrial output has slowed, mainly through a catastrophic shortage of raw materials, which have traditionally been supplied by the former Soviet Union. There is also growing co-operation among all the counties around the Baltic Sea. Several have contributed money and expertise for dealing with pollution and hazardous waste.

But water and air pollution continue to affect everyone's lives. "We don't know what we are eating or drinking," says Valdis Segliņš of the Latvian Environmental Protection Committee. "Everything depends on living standards and where people live. For most people it is not a matter of choice."

Left, marsh plants thrive in the large boggy areas. Right, pristine beaches on Latvia's coast.

114

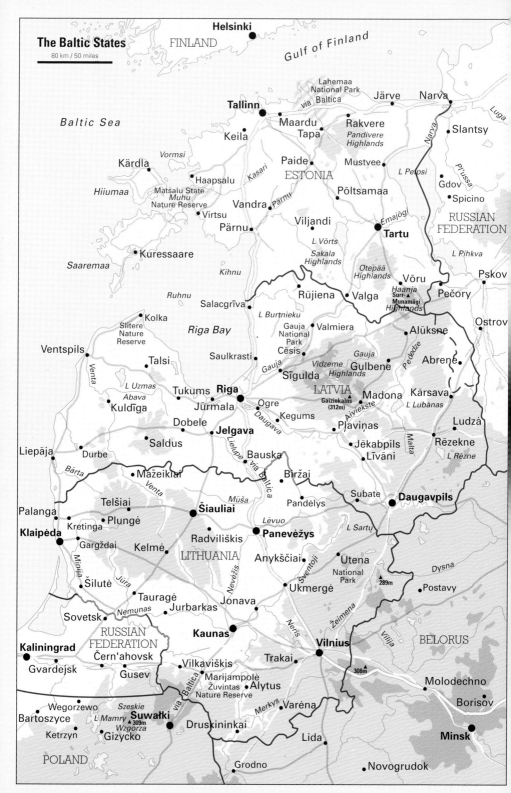

The Baltic States
80 km / 50 miles

FINLAND

Helsinki

Gulf of Finland

Baltic Sea

Lahemaa
National Park
via Baltica
Järve
Narva

Luga

Tallinn
Maardu
Rakvere
*Pandivere
Highlands*
Slantsy

Keila
Tapa

Narva

Vormsi
Paide
Mustvee

Kasari

Kärdla
Haapsalu
ESTONIA
L Peipsi

Gdov

Hiiumaa
Matsalu State
Muhu
Nature Reserve
Vandra
Pärnu
Põltsamaa
Spicino

Virtsu
RUSSIAN
FEDERATION

Pärnu
Viljandi
Emajõgi
Tartu

L Võrts
L Pihkva

Kuressaare
Kihnu
*Sakala
Highlands*

*Otepää
Highlands*
Võru
Pskov

Saaremaa
Rūjiena
Valga
*Haanja
Surr-▲
Munamägi
Highlands*
Pečory

Ruhnu
Salacgrīva
L Burtnieku
Ostrov

Kolka
Riga Bay
Gauja
National
Park
Valmiera
Alūksne

Ventspils
Saulkrasti
Cēsis
Gauja
Abrene

Slitere
Nature
Reserve
Talsi
Gauja
Sīgulda
*Vidzeme
Highlands*
Gulbene

L Uzmas
Tukums
Riga
LATVIA
Madona
Kārsava

Venta
Abava
*Gaizinkalns
(312m)*
L Lubānas

Kuldīga
Jūrmala
Ogre
Aiviekste

Dobele
Kegums
Pļaviņas
Ludza

Daugava

Jelgava
Jēkabpils
Rēzekne

Saldus
Bauska
Līvani
L Rēzne

Liepāja
Durbe
Bārta
Lielupe
via Baltica
Biržai
Malta

Mažeikiai
Subate
Daugavpils

Venta
Mūša
Pandėlys

Telšiai
Šiauliai
Lēvuo

Palanga
Plungė
Radviliškis
Panevėžys

Klaipėda
Kretinga
L Sartų

Gargždai
Kelmė
LITHUANIA
Anykščiai
Utena
Dysna

Minija
Nevėžis
Šventoji
National
Park
289m
Postavy

Šilutė
Jūra
Ukmergė
Žeimena

Tauragė
Jonava
BELORUS

Sovetsk
Nemunas
Jurbarkas
Neris
Vilija

RUSSIAN
FEDERATION
Kaunas
Vilnius

Kaliningrad
Čern'ahovsk
Trakai
308m
Molodechno

Gvardejsk
Gusev
Vilkaviškis
Borisov

Wegorzewo
Szeskie
Marijampolė
*Žuvintas
Nature Reserve*
Alytus
Varėna

Bartoszyce
L Mamry
▲309m
Suwałki
Druskininkai
Merkys
Minsk

Ketrzyn
Wzgorza
Gizycko

POLAND
Lida
Novogrudok

Grodno

118

PLACES

The three Baltic states, each about the same size, sit side by side on the eastern edge of the Baltic Sea between Poland and the Gulf of Finland. Tallinn, the northernmost capital, is on roughly the same latitude as Scotland's Orkney islands and southern Alaska. This means summer days lengthen into light nights and winter days are grey and short. A point in Lithuania marks the centre of Europe, between the Atlantic and the Urals.

Although they have linguistic, cultural and historic differences, the three countries share a similar landscape and coastline. The overwhelming image is one of quiet roads and flat lands, rising in rolling hills towards the east, of myriad small rivers and lakes and of forests of the tallest pines. Scattered through them all are ancient hill forts and occasional boulders, "presents from Scandinavia" left by retreating glaciers. These have frequently been bestowed with magical properties over the years.

The landscape of all three states is essentially rural, with vast tracts of unfenced arable and pasture inherited from the collective system. A few neoclassical manors, built by the former occupying Russians, Swedes, Germans and Poles remain. In the cities it is the legacy of these conquerors that prevails, particularly the Hansa merchants who for centuries monopolised trade in the Baltic Sea.

The "Amber Coast" is a wonder of endless beautiful white pristine beaches backed by dunes and pine forests, which stretch for hundreds of miles. Its rest homes and cure houses, spas and safe swimming beaches have made its resorts popular for millions of Balts, Russians, Belarussians and Poles for more than a century, though post-independence has seen the numbers of holidaymakers fall dramatically.

The Soviet legacy is a mixture of tedious satellite suburbs and conserved city centres unmolested by high-rise buildings. The traditional domestic architecture of two- and three-storey houses built of solid wooden planks is still evident, though many country farms have fallen into disuse, and thatch and wood-shingle roofs have mostly been replaced by corrugated iron. National pride survived the Soviet years, and there are many small museums throughout the three countries, devoted to bee-keeping, folklore, poets and local heroes.

Travelling through the three countries by public transport is slow but not difficult. The roads are not always in good repair but they are relatively empty, and the Baltic highway drives through them all, from Warsaw to St Petersburg. Together the three Baltic nations are the same size as Washington State, and a little larger than England and Wales. A visit to one country can easily include a day or two in part of another.

Preceding pages: commemoration of a celebratory meeting of Estonia, Lithuania and Latvia during the First Independence in 1934.

ESTONIA

The northermost of the three countries is Eesti Vabariik, the Republic of Estonia. It is the smallest, least densely populated and most Westernised of the Baltic states. It was the first independent Soviet state to have its own currency and for many years television sets directed people's attention towards Finland and the West.

The fact that Estonian is a Finno-Ugric language, and the country's conquerors have been Danes and Swedes, has made Estonians feel more a part of Finland than of neighbouring Latvia, with whom they have shared much of their history. Finns, for their part, have long taken advantage of Estonia's relative cheapness, and have taken the ferry over from Helsinki to Tallinn, where a lot of their money is spent on alcohol.

Tallinn, the capital of Estonia, has the prettiest old town in the Baltics, a medieval enclave set on a hillock above its port. Within the remaining old walls and towers, beneath frugal Protestant church spires, are winding cobbled lanes leading to the old square. The city was a showcase in the 1980 Moscow Olympics when, just to the east of it, by Pirita Beach, a new port was built to stage the sailing events in the Games. Sailing around the country's islands is a pleasure waiting to be rediscovered.

Estonia has a second city in Tartu in the south, a distinguished university town that brims with student life. On the Russian borders around Narva there is a high population of Russians working in the shaleoil industry, the basis of the country's wealth and the cause of many environmental concerns. Much of the Russian border is otherwise taken up by Lake Peipsi, the fourth largest lake in Europe.

Nearly 40 percent of the country is forested, with pine, spruce and junipers, and brown bears and beavers are among its inhabitants. Nearly half of the land is made up of marshes and there are around 1,500 lakes. There are also around 1,500 islands. The largest, off the west coast, are Hiiumaa and Saaremaa, rural backwaters where the earliest stone churches in the Baltics are to be found. It is hard to imagine a quieter place in Europe.

Preceding pages: summer country garden in Saska, near Lake Peipsi; Palmsa manor, Lahemaa National Park; Uus Street, Tallinn Old Town. **Left**, Estonia's national dress.

Estonia

32 km / 20 miles

FINLAND

Baltic Sea

Naissaar

Tallin

Väike-Pakri

Paldiski

Suur-Pakri

Osmussaar

Rummu

Keila

Keila

Vormsi

Palivere Risti **R**

Kõpu **Kärdla**

Rohuküla Taebla **Märjamaa**

Suuremõisa Heltermaa **Haapsalu**

Käina *Vigala*

Hiiumaa

Matsalu State *Kasari* Jarva

Kassari Matsalu Bay Vana-

Matsalu Bay Nature Reserve Vigala

Emmaste *Muhu*

Lihula

Saaremaa Orissaare Koguva Pärnu- T

Panga Leisi Angla Virtsu Vatla Kalli Jaagupi

Karja

Mustjala **Sind**

Karrma Valjala

Kihelkonna Viki Karla **Pärnu** Pä

Pühа *Pärnu*

Kuressaare *Bay*

Abruka *Kihnu*

Sääre Ikla

Ruhnu Ainaži

Stai

Salacgrīva

Mazirbe Kolka

Riga Bay *via Baltica*

Dundaga Roja **Limbа**

Ventspils

Valdemārpils Nogale Mērsrags

128

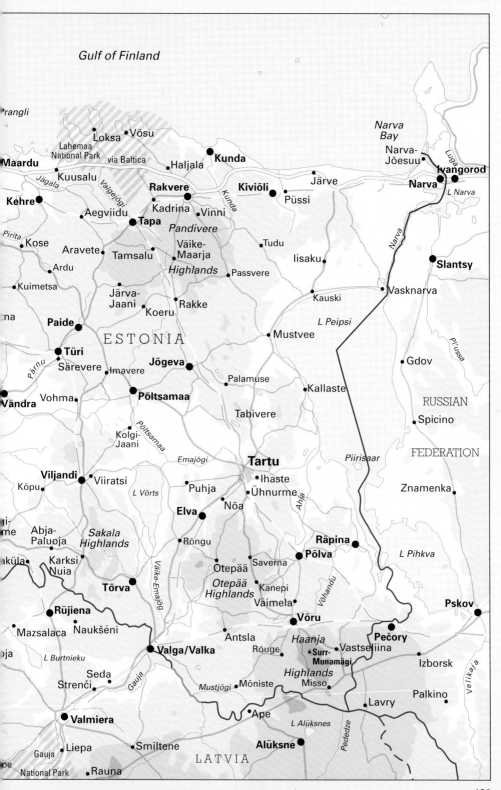

Gulf of Finland

Narva
Bay

Narva-
Jõesuu

Ivangorod

Narva

L Narva

ʼrangli

Loksa Võsu

Lahemaa
National Park   via Baltica

Maardu

Kuusalu

Kehre

Aegviidu

Jägala

Valgejõgi

Haljala

Kunda

Kiviõli

Järve

Püssi

Rakvere

Kadrina

Tapa

Vinni

Pandivere

Kunda

Pirita

Kose

Aravete

Ardu

Tamsalu

Väike-
Maarja

Highlands

Tudu

Iisaku

Slantsy

Passvere

Kuimetsa

Järva-
Jaani

Koeru

Rakke

Kauski

Vasknarva

ⁿa

Paide

Mustvee

L Peipsi

Gdov

Narva

RUSSIAN

Türi

Särevere

Imavere

ESTONIA

Jõgeva

Palamuse

Kallaste

Piʼussa

Pärnu

Vändra

Vohma

Põltsamaa

Tabivere

FEDERATION

Spicino

Kolgi-
Jaani

Põltsamaa

Emajõgi

Tartu

Piirisaar

Viljandi

Viiratsi

L Võrts

Puhja

Ihaste

Ühnurme

Znamenka

Kõpu

Nõa

Ahja

Elva

ji-
me

Abja-
Paluoja

Sakala
Highlands

Rõngu

Räpina

Põlva

L Pihkva

aküla

Karksi
Nuia

Tõrva

Väike-Emajõg

Otepää

Saverna

Otepää
Highlands

Kanepi

Väimela

Võhandu

Rūjiena

Mazsalaca

Naukšēni

Antsla

Haanja

Võru

Pečory

Pskov

oja

L Burtnieku

Valga/Valka

Rõuge

Surr-
Munamägi

Highlands

Vastseliina

Izborsk

Velikaja

Seda

Strenči

Gauja

Mustjõgi

Mõniste

Misso

Lavry

Palkino

Valmiera

Ape

L Alūksne

Pededze

Liepa

Smiltene

Alūksne

Gauja

National Park

Rauna

LATVIA

129

In the days when visitors to Estonia often arrived by sea, the first glimpse of Tallinn, the capital, made a lasting impression. Its ancient ruins and quaint houses with steeply peaked roofs, more Mediterranean than Baltic captivated many visitors. In summer, it might have been the South of France, with early 19th-century Russians making an annual summer pilgrimage from St Petersburg. "I have seen delicate creatures," wrote an English visitor in 1841, "who at first were lifted from the carriage to the bathing-house, restored day by day, and in a fortnight's time bathing with a zest that seemed to renew all their energies."

In the evenings, "a band of military music plays, and restaurants offer ices, chocolate, etc., and you parade about and your friends join you, and you sit down and the gnats sting you; and if you don't like this, you may adjourn to the *salle de danse* close by, where the limbs so late floating listlessly on the waves now twirl round in the hurrying waltz."

Estonia had been a Russian province since 1721, and while the lot of the Estonian peasant had been pathetic for many years (and all ethnic Estonians were peasants) tsarist rule became increasingly repressive in the latter half of the 19th century. There were no more foreign tourists, Russians excepted, and as far as most foreigners were concerned, Estonia ceased to exist.

Surprising new state: A declaration of Estonian independence after World War I caught the world by surprise. Russia, torn apart by revolution, was unable to do much to counter the move. Authors of travel guides rushed in to appraise the reincarnated nation. "The broad visage of the Estonian," wrote one, as if reporting on a newly arrived specimen at a zoo, "has slanting eyes, low forehead, high cheekbones and projecting lower jaw." His conclusion was that Estonian origins were "not of Europe".

Estonian independence lasted only until World War II. It then disappeared under the even heavier hand of communist Russia and was presumed lost for all time. Rather sud-

denly in 1988, extraordinary reports were received in the West of a "Singing Revolution". Tens of thousands apparently spent that summer giving throaty voice to all the old Estonian songs and defiantly waving the long-hidden national flag. Within two years, although not without moments of nail-biting uncertainty, Estonia was independent again.

For all the ravages of a Soviet economic policy which had aimed at turning Estonia into an annex of heavy industry, much of the character which delighted visitors of 150

years ago had survived. Russians were still visiting in droves, but for the "Old European" atmosphere and the food rather than the beaches and swimming, which were prime casualties of environmental vandalism. As for the newly independent Estonians, they seemed to have borne the burden of the previous half-century with fortitude.

The "non-European" physical features of the ethnic Estonians are a reflection of Finno-Ugric ancestry. Because of the similarities between the Estonian and Finnish languages, Estonians had been able to follow Finnish television during the Soviet era. Its terms of reference did not flatter the Soviet system.

Left, 15th-century soldier. **Right,** Konstantin Päts, the country's leader during the First Independence.

Estonia's frontiers have been chopped and changed over the centuries. Their present configuration makes Estonia a country of some 17,000 sq. miles (44,000 sq. km), small enough to be covered by a day's driving in any direction, with a population of less than one-and-a-half million of whom about 65 percent are ethnic Estonians. The remaining 35 percent are predominantly Russians, most of them relatively recent arrivals sent in to man the industries which represented Estonia's role in the Soviet economic scheme. A few people living in the eastern part of the country are the descendants of 17th-century Old Believers, a sect that fled from Russia to escape, among other things, the tax that Peter

13th-century Germans were not the first to arrive, and there were others who followed after them.

Hardy beginnings: The future Finns and Estonians were among the first tribes to drift across Europe from Asia. Leaving the lower slopes of the Urals, they followed the river courses, subsisting mainly on fish and clothing themselves in animal skins. They had already reached the Baltic coast when mentioned by Tacitus in the 1st century AD. "Strangely beast-like and squalidly poor, neither arms nor homes have they. Their food is herbs, their clothing skin, their bed the earth. They trust wholly to their arrows, which, for want of iron, are pointed with

the Great imposed on the beards they traditionally wore. An additional group are the diluted remnants of Estonia's most influential settlers, the Germans. The latter came in two guises: the first were 13th-century Teutonic Knights who arrived ostensibly as bearers of Christianity but also as migrants with an urgent need to find somewhere to live, having recently fallen on hard times in the Holy Land; these people were followed by German craftsmen and merchants who formed the burgher class which ultimately monopolised the towns and cities. To an unusual degree, Estonians have taken a back seat while others have written their history. These

bone… Heedless of men, heedless of gods, they have attained that hardest of results, the not needing so much as a wish."

There seems to have been some pushing and shoving among new arrivals on the Baltic shores, especially when large numbers of Slavs turned up, but eventually the future Finns, Estonians, Latvians and Lithuanians took up positions in more or less the pattern that persists today.

The first conquerors were the Danes under Valdemar II, who arrived with what should have been an invincible armada of 1,000 ships. The Estonians resisted the invasion so fiercely that the Danes were in danger of being routed. They were rescued, so the story goes, by a red banner with a white cross floating down from heaven – the image that was to inspire the future Danish flag. Their spirits up, they took possession of Tallinn.

Some years earlier, in 1200, around 500 heavily-armed German knights had landed farther south in the Gulf of Riga with a commission to spread the Word of God. They did so more efficiently than the Danes, who were themselves recent converts.

In the end, the Danes asked the Teutonic Knights to lend a hand against the Estonian pagans. The knights tackled the task with customary efficiency and declared, in 1227, that the task had been finally accomplished.

1347, the Danish monarchy was desperate for cash. Tallinn, or Reval as it came to be known, was sold off to the efficient and prosperous knights.

A large part of the commercial success of Reval and Narva, Estonia's two ports, was due to a virtual monopoly on trade to and from Russia. When Ivan III seized Narva and made it a Russian port it so alarmed the Baltic Germans that they sought the protection of Sweden. Under Gustavus Adolphus, Sweden was energetically bent on expanding their Baltic holdings, but there was no desire to tamper unnecessarily with a German infrastructure which worked so profitably. Later Swedish kings, particularly

The knights transformed an economy which had previously rested on primitive agriculture and products of the forest into one of the best centers of farming and commerce of the Middle Ages. They constructed castles and founded towns everywhere, filling them with craftsmen and merchants recruited from Germany. Their social system was simple: Germans occupied the positions of noble, burgher and merchant; the Estonians were serfs. This system survived political and religious change for six centuries. In the year

Left, the Danes take Tallinn, 1219. **Above**, the capital as it looked in 1615.

Charles XI, did interfere by taking over German-owned estates and either giving them to Swedes or, increasingly, keeping them for themselves. The dispossessed and disgruntled who had previously turned to Sweden for protection against Russia, decided they now needed protection from Sweden. With perfect impartiality, they turned to Russia. Peter the Great readily agreed to help.

The outcome was the titanic struggle between Peter and the equally legendary Charles XII of Sweden. A Russian force 35,000 strong made for Narva, held by a much smaller Swedish garrison in the castle. Charles, who was not yet 20, hurried to its aid. He arrived with 8,000 men and, in the middle of a snow storm, plunged straight into battle. The Russians were cut to pieces, losing every piece of artillery Peter possessed. Charles's advisers urged him to press on to Moscow, but the young leader had other ideas. "There is no glory in winning victories over the Muscovites," he said breezily, "they can be beaten at any time."

While Charles went off in pursuit of other enemies, Peter laid the foundations of Petersburg and planned a second attack on Narva. He entrusted the command to a Scot named Ogilvie who not only succeeded in overwhelming the garrison but decided, apparently independently, to take no prisoners,

Charles was far from over, however, and in the course of fighting that swept across Europe the Baltic states were utterly devastated, the horror compounded by plague. With the Peace of Nystad in 1721, Sweden finally ceded its Baltic possessions and Estonia, for one, prepared for its first taste of Russian rule.

Like the Swedes, Peter was not inclined to upset the way the German hierarchy ran Estonia, and the Estonians continued, according to one commentator, "to live and die like beasts, happy if they could subsist on dusky bread and water". Nothing much had changed by the middle of the 19th century. "Beyond his strict adherence to his church,"

military or civilian. A terrible massacre was finally stopped by the arrival of Peter the Great in the country. He is said to have stopped the proceedings by cutting down some of the crazed attackers with his own sword. Moreover, he said, there was a perfectly good use for able-bodied Swedish prisoners: the conditions at the Petersburg building site were so bad that the work force was dropping like flies.

With Narva under his belt, Peter turned to Reval and its Swedish garrison. The defenders put up a great fight but ultimately they succumbed to thirst and an outbreak of plague. The Great Northern War between Peter and

it was reported of the Estonian peasant, "we can find but little interesting in his character; nor indeed is it fair to look for any, excepting perhaps that of a servile obedience or cunning evasion, among a people so long oppressed... Provided he can have a pipe in his mouth, and lie sleeping at the bottom of his cart, while his patient wife drives the willing little rough horse... he cares little about an empty stomach. Offer him wages for his labour, and he will tell you, with the dullest bumpkin look, that if he works more he must eat more."

The same source, a Lady Eastlake, moved in privileged circles during her stay, but she kept her eyes open and provides a wonderful insight into conditions. The ruling Tsar Nicholas I was so paranoid about revolutionaries – the insurrections of 1848 were just around the corner – that police surveillance everywhere was oppressive. If nothing else, though, it kept crime figures low. Over a whole year, she reported, there had been only 87 misdemeanours among Reval's 300,000 population, "and five of these consist merely in travelling without a passport".

Most illuminating of all, perhaps, are Lady Eastlake's observations about the cloud that hung over young men in the form of military service in the Russian army. The conscripts were chosen by ballot, No. 1 being the un-

his daily bread by his own exertions for the remainder of his life, or to be chargeable to his parish, who by this time have forgotten that he ever existed, and certainly wish he had never returned."

Impossible choices: The last years of the 19th century saw the emergence of the Young Estonians, a sign of awakening nationalism. The social order as they saw it was still dominated by the German hierarchy, but being anti-German did not make them pro-Russian. They were simply against the status quo, and for people in that mood Marxism was a very reasonable answer. The savage oppression of the St Petersburg uprising in 1905 destroyed any sympathy for the tsar.

lucky number. "From the moment that the peasant of the Baltic provinces draws the fatal lot No. 1, he knows that he is a Russian, and, worse than that, a Russian soldier, and not only himself, but every son from that hour born to him; for, like the executioner's office in Germany, a soldier's life is hereditary… If wars and climate and sickness and hardship spare him, he returns after four-and-twenty years of service – his language scarce remembered, his religion changed, and with not a rouble in his pocket – to seek

Left, Fat Margaret on fire, 1917. **Above**, a 19th-century view of conscription into Russia's army.

For most Estonians, World War I presented an impossible choice between Germany and Russia when, in truth, they would rather have been fighting against both. Nevertheless, tens of thousands found themselves in tsarist uniform, their plea to form their own units under their own officers falling on deaf ears. The Russian Revolution in 1917 simplified the choice, the more so when it was announced that an Estonian national army was to be formed. About 170,000 volunteers immediately joined up, while a not inconsiderable number of Estonians preferred to join the supposedly internationalist ranks of the Bolsheviks. From their various places of exile, members of a provisional Estonian government sent up a cry for independence.

Numerous fierce battles were fought over Tallinn between local Bolsheviks, who were backed by Red Guards, and the nationalist irregulars, who included schoolboys and the Tallinn fire brigade. The tide at first went in favour of the Bolsheviks and by the end of 1918, they held Narva and Tartu, and Russian comrades had advanced to within 20 miles of Tallinn. The struggle amounted to civil war and this was fought with all the savagery associated with such a terrible event.

The tide eventually turned, although not without considerable clandestine help given to the nationalists by the British Navy. The resulted in street fighting in Tallinn. Numerous other disturbances were countered by increasingly authoritarian measures. In the end these amounted to dictatorship and the sad conclusion among Estonia's allies was that the country was not quite ripe for parliamentary democracy.

Regained rights: Prior to the war, more than half of Estonia had belonged to 200 German-Balt families. An Agrarian Reform Law passed after independence took over all baronial and feudal estates, together with those belonging to the church and the former Russian Crown lands. The land was redistributed and 30,000 new farms created. The lot of the previously hapless peasant was further

details are veiled to this day, but it seems to have involved using captured Russian destroyers and a series of raids by torpedo boats which penetrated the naval defences with which Peter the Great had ringed the Russian Baltic ports. The final battle was at Narva, and resulted in the nationalist coalition driving some 18,000 Bolsheviks across the Russian border. One year later, with the Bolsheviks still engaged in heavy fighting elsewhere, Russia renounced its sovereignty over Estonia "voluntarily and for ever".

Communists elsewhere in Estonia were not inclined to accept the new government. There was an attempted putsch in 1924 which improved by the establishment of the right to engage in trade.

Estonia was still struggling to find its feet when any gains were put in jeopardy by the secret protocol of the 1939 Nazi-Soviet Pact. Stalin and Hitler agreed that the Soviet Union would annex Estonia, Finland and Latvia, and Germany could claim Lithuania, although this was later amended to give Lithuania to Russia as well. A blatantly rigged election set the stage for an outright annexation on 6 August 1940, and almost immediately 60,000 Estonians went missing. They had been forcibly conscripted into the Soviet army, deported to labour camps or executed.

The collapse of the Nazi-Soviet Pact naturally changed everything. German forces invaded in July 1941, meeting determined resistance in Estonia where large numbers of Soviet troops were cut off. Estonia had only about 1,000 Jewish families, nothing like the numbers of Latvia and Lithuania, but even so 90 percent of these were murdered as Germany set about incorporating the country in the Third Reich. By the end of the war, however, some 70,000 Estonians had fled to the West, so one way or another the population dropped from its pre-war level of over one million to no more than 850,000. The educated classes did not wait to find out what would happen when the German forces in Tallinn surrendered to the Red Army on 22 September 1944.

Tens of thousands of those who did not flee were consigned to Soviet labour camps. The vacuum was filled by the arrival of comparable numbers of Russians with the dual purpose of manning heavy industry and completing the Russification programme begun by the tsars. There was little Estonians could do except to turn their television aerials towards Finland to see how their Finno-Ugric cousins were getting along.

At home, Soviet policies continued unabated so that during the 1980s the proportion of Russians and other Soviet implants living in the country rose to 40 percent. With virtually the whole of the country's industry under Moscow's remote control, no thought was given to the ecological impact of belching industrial works which in some instances were erected in the middle of established residential areas.

With their stars firmly attached to Moscow's wagon, Estonia's loyal Communist Party members were totally opposed to any sign of a nationalist revival in Estonia. The long-term implications of *glasnost* and *perestroika* were, however, not lost on them, and they took no comfort at all from the 2,000 demonstrators who summoned up enough nerve to mourn the anniversary of the Nazi-Soviet Pact in Tallinn's Hirvepark. In this respect, the party hard-liners and the large Russian minority were as one.

While members of the Estonian Heritage Society went about discreetly restoring national monuments, the radical-chic banner of environmental concern brought the independence movement to life.

The first scent of this potential awakening came with the cancellation of plans for increased open-pit phosphorus mining in the northeast of the country. This was followed by demands for economic self-management and then, most extraordinarily, came the "Singing Revolution".

The extent to which the Estonian establishment fell into line with the new mood was revealed when the Estonian Supreme Soviet defied the USSR Supreme Soviet by endorsing the legitimacy of a declaration of sovereignty. When the independence

movement properly got under way, there were tense moments as the world waited to see whether there would be a repetition of the events in Czechoslovakia in 1968. In the event, the dissolution of the Soviet Union happened so rapidly and on so many fronts that Estonia moved very gratefully to the side-lines.

The Russian connection, which had begun with Peter the Great's victory over Charles XII of Sweden, was finally ended when Estonia was offered – and politely declined – membership of the Commonwealth of Independent States, the hastily contrived successor to the USSR.

Left, a 1930s advertisement for pork products. **Above**, the Russian border at Narva, early 1990s.

TALLINN

Tallinn is a curious city, where the cosmopolitan brushes shoulders with the medieval and a general air of sophistication is veiled by a rundown atmosphere. Only 53 miles (85 km) across the Gulf of Finland from Helsinki and midway between St Petersburg and Stockholm, the city holds a blessed maritime position that has made it a little bit too interesting over the centuries to other nations. Resulting layers of cross-cultural history have given the city its unique flavour.

Estonians were the first to build a stronghold here, in the 10th century, but they were overcome by the seafaring Danes in 1219 and, in 1285, the city, which came to be called Reval right up until the beginning of the 20th century, was enlisted into the Hanseatic League. The Estonians, nonetheless, persisted and eventually, in 1346, the Danes sold the prosperous but rather troublesome town to the Teutonic Knights. A year later it was bought by the Livonian Order. Meanwhile, Tallinn's merchants grew fat, guilds burgeoned and the old part of town was expanded and refined.

In 1561 Tallinn was seized by the Swedes, and all-important trade between Russia and the West was broken off. This did little for urban development, and the economic depression was further burdened by plague. The Swedes remained in control until the end of the Great Northern War in 1710 when the Russians took over and turned Tallinn into a garrison town. Under Russian rule for the next two centuries, Tallinn also began to be industrialised and the city spread outwards rapidly from the medieval centre.

In 1918, after nearly a millennium, the Estonians managed to get their capital back, but in 1940 it was annexed by the Soviet Union. The Soviets added their own touches: large, uniform suburbs and a huge migration of Russian

Preceding pages: Tallinn's skyline. **Left,** a light dusting of snow on the city walls.

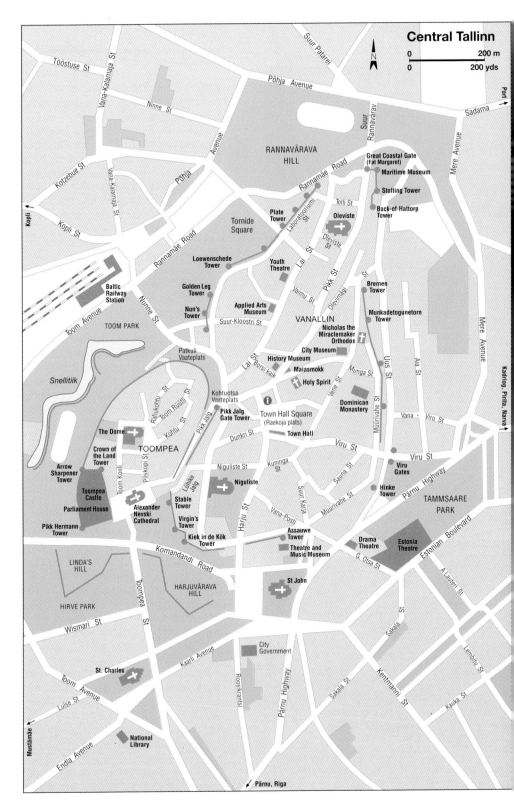

Central Tallinn

0   200 m
0   200 yds

Tööstuse St
Vana-Kalamaja St
Ninne St
Põhja Avenue
Suur Patarei
Põhja Avenue
Port
Sadama
Kotzebue St
Vana-Kalamaja St
Põhja Avenue
Kopli
Kopli St
Avenue
RANNAVÄRAVA HILL
Suur Rannavärav
Mere Avenue
Tornide Square
Rannamäe Road
Great Coastal Gate (Fat Margaret)
Maritime Museum
Stolting Tower
Back-of-Hattorp Tower
Rannamäe Road
Plate Tower
Laboratooriumi St
Tolli St
Oleviste
Oleviste St
Loewenschede Tower
Youth Theatre
Lai St
Baltic Railway Station
Golden Leg Tower
Nun's Tower
Applied Arts Museum
Suur-Kloostri St
Vaimu St
Pikk St
Olevimägi
Bremen Tower
Munkadetogunetorn Tower
VANALLIN
Nicholas the Miraclemaker Orthodox
Toom Avenue
Nunne St
TOOM PARK
Patkuli Vaateplats
Lai St
Borsi käik
History Museum
Maiasmokk
Holy Spirit
City Museum
Munga St
Dominican Monastery
Uus St
Mere Avenue
Kadriog, Pirita, Narva
Ala St
Snellitiik
Rahukohtu St
Toom Rüütli St
Kohtu St
Pikk Jalg
Kohtuotsa Vaateplats
Pikk Jalg Gate Tower
Town Hall Square (Raekoja plats)
Vene St
Müürivahe St
Vana - Viru St
The Dome
TOOMPEA
Dunkri St
Town Hall
Viru St
Viru St
Crown of the Land Tower
Pliiskopi St
Niguliste St
Kuninga St
Sauna St
Viru Gates
Arrow Sharpener Tower
Toom Kooli
Niguliste
Suur Karja
Müürivahe St
Pärnu Highway
Hinke Tower
Toompea Castle
Alexander Nevski Cathedral
Lühike Jalg
Stable Tower
Harju St
Vana-Posti
TAMMSAARE PARK
Parliament House
Virgin's Tower
Assauwe Tower
Drama Theatre
Estonia Theatre
Estonian Boulevard
Pikk Hermann Tower
Kiek in de Kök Tower
Theatre and Music Museum
G. Otsa St
Komandandi Road
LINDA'S HILL
HARJUVÄRAVA HILL
St John
A Lauteri St
HIRVE PARK
Toompea St
Wismari St
City Government
Pärnu Highway
Sakala St
Sakala St
Lembitu St
Kentmanni St
Kauka St
St. Charles
Toom Avenue
Kaarli Avenue
Rooskrantsi
Luise St
Endla Avenue
Mustamäe
National Library
Pärnu, Riga

nationals. In 1990 the Estonians reclaimed their city which, architecturally, can never be called simply "Estonian".

Giant's tombstone: The first place to visit is the Old Town, perched on a low hill by the shore. Set apart from the rest of the city by old fortification walls, this is one of the purest medieval old towns in all of northern Europe.

The upper town, or **Toompea**, site of the original Estonian settlement, crowns the hill at 157 ft (48 metres) above sea level. The lower town spills out over an inclined horseshoe below. As they developed, they each acquired distinct personalities: the ecclesiastical and feudal powers lived above, the merchants and guild members below.

You must pay to bring a car into the Old Town and its beauty is far too detailed to be appreciated by simply driving past. So, to tour it, put on a good pair of walking shoes – although all the local women manage to wear them, high heels are a trial on its worn cobbled streets – and head for the central **Viru Gates**.

These gates (14th-16th century) used to join directly with the old town walls, which can be seen to the north along Müürivahe Street. Walk a little way further down this street past the sweater sellers in the old town walls and turn into the passageway at No. 33, posted with old stone grave-markers. They come from the 13th-century **Dominican monastery**, which is behind the wall now on your right.

The monastery was once a huge maze of churches and dormitories – paid for mostly by the monks' brewery – but a fire in 1531 destroyed almost everything, including the **monastery church**. The small Monastery Museum and Tallinn's only Catholic church can be accessed either from Müürivahe No. 33, or from a courtyard on Vene Street. To see any of the former interior, you must head down Vene Street and then through into another courtyard. There, behind a nearly hidden brown door beside Tallinn's **Catholic church**, is the somewhat small **Monastery Museum**.

Vene Street was named after the many Russian merchants that once lived on it. A little further down is the yellow

Nicholas the Miraclemaker Orthodox Church (1822–27). The **City Museum** lies across the street, at No. 17, in a 14th-century merchant's home. The house was worked on up until the 17th century and still has an early portal and windows; inside is a carved ornamental stairway. The collection centres on objects from bourgeois households in the 19th century.

Snaking around Olevimägi Street will bring you to the **Oleviste church**, first documented in 1267 and now run by Baptists. Its original steeple was 460 ft (140 metres) high, which made the building supposedly one of the tallest in the world, and it doubled as a lighthouse. However, in 1820 the church was devastated by fire and a smaller 394 ft (120 metres) tower was added during restoration work.

The church was named after the Norwegian King Olaf, considered a holy man, but legend has given it another origin. As the story goes, when the church was almost finished no one would consent to build its steeple because of a

Fat Margaret, home of the Military Museum.

curse that whoever did would fall to his death. Finally, a young foreigner named Olev agreed. Sure enough, no sooner had he finished the work than he fell and, as the curse had promised, a snake and a frog crawled from his mouth.

St Olaf's is set between Lai Street and Pikk Street, the main street of the lower town, which connects the upper town with the harbour. Its furthest end is marked by the 15th-century **Great Coastal Gate** and 16th-century **Fat Margaret's Tower**, which supposedly won its name from a vast cannon kept there in the 17th century. It now houses Tallinn's **Maritime Museum**. Just outside Fat Margaret's Tower, facing the harbour, is a huge broken arch erected in memory of the 852 victims of the 1994 Estonia ferry disaster.

Attached to the Great Coastal Gate are the **Stolting Tower** and the **Back-of-Hattorpe Tower**, part of the early fortifications that still stand along this part of the old town. In Laboratooriumi Street there are seven more towers. Outside them, where the moats once were, sprawl handsome municipal parks. Just a couple of blocks down from St Olaf's towards the gate are three attached and nearly identical yellow houses, at Pikk 71. Locals call them the **Three Sisters**. These are mirrored by three narrow houses also from the 15th century at Lai 38–42, dubbed the **Three Brothers**. Lai runs parallel to Pikk and was the lower town's second main street; while Pikk housed the merchants, Lai was the craftsmen's address.

These streets are crowded with fascinating medieval houses. Much has been left untouched – in fact, few of these houses even have modern heating systems or running hot water. In every corner there are architectural treasures left over from the times when individuals took care to put personal stamps on the buildings they lived and worked in.

The most famous guild building on Pikk Street, at No. 26, is the yellow **House of the Brotherhood of the Blackheads**. The odd name of this organisation of unmarried merchants came from their African patron saint, St

Mauritius. Dating from the 15th - 16th century, the building's Renaissance facade is completed by carved stone plates of the Brotherhood's coat of arms on either side of the portico. It is now used for concerts, official receptions and state visits.

Another former guild house stands at Pikk 20, and at No. 25 is the **Peeping Tom Building**, named after a bachelor pharmacist who lived here and was said to peep in on the daughters of the family opposite. His brightly painted stone face spies out from top left of the facade.

The **Great Guild House** (1407–17), at Pikk 17, has been converted into the **History Museum**. Beginning in the back hall, its exhibition traces the history of Estonia, from its origins, and the museum labels – in English, Estonian and Russian – go well beyond just names and dates. The building, which once covered the entire block, is also remarkable. The twin-naved main hall has high-vaulted ceilings and is completely original. **The Dragon Gallery**, which is situated across the street at Pikk 18, is proof that life didn't stop altogether for the Old Town after the Middle Ages. The gallery was built in 1911 with stone dragons and half-naked Egyptian women carved all over its facade; the merchant owner had lived in the east for a number of years. Its downstairs is a contemporary art gallery. Next door houses one of the oldest and most popular cafés in Tallinn, the **Maiasmokk (Sweet Tooth) Kohvik**.

People used to walk in the middle of the street in the Old Town, with traffic moving on either side, and every house had a fine portal with stone benches and steps leading down to the street. Most of these were removed in the 17th century when pavements were introduced.

At Lai 23, however, there is a 15th-century house that still has its front step; the left side is original while the right side is a recent duplicate. The step bears the emblem of the Tallinn's City Theatre (Linnatheater) that now owns the building. The beam coming from its centre was once used to hoist goods to the upper floors.

Up and down hill in the Old Town.

In keeping with its artisan history, Lai Street still houses many types of art organisations and museums. One that is easy to miss but very pleasant is the **Applied Art Museum** at No. 17, tucked away in an old granary in the courtyard. It displays Estonian craftwork from the 1920s to the modern day.

The Borsi Kaik passage leads back to Pikk Street, facing out on Puhuvaimu kirik, or **Holy Spirit church**, first mentioned in 1316. On its facade hangs the oldest street clock (1680) in Tallinn, and its intimate interior is rich with detail ranging through the Gothic to Classical styles. Most valuable is the doubled-winged wooden altar made by Bernt Notke of Lübeck in 1483. The north balcony is decorated with paintings depicting the life of Jesus.

The Church of the Holy Spirit is squeezed in just before the entrance to Saiakang, or White Bread Passage, so-called because it was once lined with bakeries. Although only a few paces long, a crowd of old shops and cafés still manages to squeeze into this narrow alley and it is always one of the busiest places in Tallinn. The smallest building in town, just 4 ft 3 inches (1.3 metres) wide, used to stand at No. 3 and once housed an entire family.

This passage leads out on to the spacious and cobbled **Town Hall Square**. Now a busy thoroughfare of restaurants and shops, with a small blue train and horse-drawn carriages for summer tourists, it goes back in time every June for the week-long "Days of the Old City" festival. Outdoor gatherings are still held here, but it used to be the absolute centre of activity in the lower town. A weigh house functioned in one corner for many centuries but was destroyed in the war.

The sturdy and monumental **Town Hall** (Raekoja) still stands to its south side, erected between the 14th - early 15th century as both a fortification and a storehouse. The weather vane on its church-like steeple – topped by an image of Old Thomas, the town mascot – is baroque, but the rest of the building is unflinchingly Gothic. The stern interior is closed to the public. There is a small

Town Hall Square, an unhurried hub.

City Council Museum with changing exhibitions in the basement.

The **Town Council Apothecary**, at Raekoja 11, near the mouth of White Bread Passage, is another Town Hall Square landmark. This pharmacy was first documented in 1422 but is believed to have existed even earlier; it has been closed several times for restoration but is proclaimed to be the longest continually functioning apothecary in Europe. It was run by the same family for 350 years. In 1583, the Hungarian Johann Burchart started work as a salesman in the apothecary and eventually managed to lease it. After 106 years, his family bought the pharmacy, and thereafter it was handed down from eldest son to eldest son, some of whom also became famous doctors – in 1725 one was summoned to Peter the Great's deathbed. (The tsar died before he arrived.)

The **House of Tourism** curves on to the Town Hall Square at Vanaturu Kael 3, with colourful reliefs of the apostles peering down from its facade. The originals are displayed inside, along with a permanent exhibition of graphic art. Continuing down past it would take you on to Viru Street with its many shops and cafes and back to the Viru Gates.

Harju Street on the opposite corner of the square leads to the **Niguliste church**, built on a monumental scale by merchants in the lower town to vie with the church on Toompea. The first written record of it dates from 1316, but it had to be rebuilt in the 15th century after it was gutted by fire.

Niguliste's several buildings were devastated by World War II and only the church itself has been restored. It is still impressive but has been turned into a museum with the result that although it looks like a church, the interior feels anything but sacred. However, some of its treasures that have survived are well worth seeing. The wooden altarpiece, for example, was made by Hermen Rode of Lübeck in 1482, and there is a fragment from the *Danse Macabre* canvas by Notke. One creepy gravestone to a Dr Johannes Ballivi in 1520 is carved with a skeleton.

Lühike Jalg, or "Short Leg", behind Niguliste, climbs straight up on to Toompea, the upper town. This is where the Estonians first settled and where the Danes built their 13th-century castle, which became known as "the Small Fortress". The rest of Toompea, home to the feudal lords and the Tallinn bishop, was called "the Big Fortress".

Toompea Castle was constantly bombarded over the centuries and was mined in 1944 but, amazingly, much of it still stands. The castle was separated from the town by a 65-ft (20-metre) stone wall and a deep moat, and the western and northern stretches of this wall are intact. The highest of its four towers – the 150-ft (46-metre) **Pikk Hermann Tower** – has survived, as well as the **Crown of the Land Tower** and **Arrow Sharpener Tower**.

The castle itself, however, has been greatly restored and is now fronted by the elaborate **Parliament House** (1870), with gardens on its south side. To see it in its original limestone form, head down Komandandi past Linda's Hill. This hill was the starting point for the **Baltic Chain of Freedom**, which stretched nearly unbroken from here to Vilnius in Lithuania in August 1989. It is crowned with the sad **Statue of Linda**, the widow of Estonia's legendary hero Kalev.

Across the windy castle square is the mustard-yellow **Alexander Nevski Cathedral** (1894–1900), built in the style of Moscow churches of the 17th century. It is not a local favourite and the writer Tuglas Friedeberg once declared: "It looks like a samovar and should be blown up." You cannot ignore it even with your eyes closed, however, for it is topped with 11 bells, including the largest (15 tons) in all of Estonia. The interior has been beautifully restored with a massive iconostasis and several icons, attracting a steady crowd of Russian Orthodox believers.

The **Neitsitorn**, or Virgin's Tower, which was bombed in 1944 but restored and turned into a cafe and wine cellar, is behind the Alexander Nevski. Just below it is the **Kiek in de Kök tower**, built in the 15th century to hold gunpowder.

Parliament building, Upper Town.

The small round holes in its stalwart facade were made to mount guns. It is now used as a **Historical Museum** and a photographers' gallery. From the top floor there is a fine view of the city.

Heading further up from the Castle Square, along the steeply winding Piiskopi Street, you will reach the melancholic, dark-grey **Dome church**. It was first mentioned in 1223 and it has remained a strict and noble embodiment of the Gothic style, except for a baroque tower added in the 18th century.

Many people were buried over the centuries within the church, and their gravestones and burial vaults now dominate its interior. Most were military leaders and noblemen – such as the Swedish Commander-in-Chief Pontus de la Gardie and his wife, the daughter of Swedish King Johann III – with Scandinavians on the left side of the altar and Germans on the right. A few, however, were common folk: in the southwest corner, marked by a big boot, is the epitaph of seven shoemakers. Before leaving Toompea, head towards

Rahukohtu Street and turn into the yard of the house at No. 3. From here, on Patkuli Vaateplats, the view is spectacular, looking out over both Tallinn and Kopli bays. Squeeze down the narrow Linnus Street to Kohtuotsa Vaateplats for another gorgeous view, this time over the Old Town. The steep and cobble-stoned Pikk Jalg (or Long Leg) Street nearby will bring you back into the lower town.

Seaside parks: The Old Town is the tourists' favourite in Tallinn, but on weekends the locals wander in the parks on the east side of Tallinn Bay reached through the Kesklinn, or city centre.

Kadriorg Park was laid out between 1718 and 1725 by the Italian architect Niccolo Michetti under the orders of Peter the Great who named it in honour of his wife, Catherine. It is a woody, informal park, planted with lime, oak, ash, birch and chestnut trees and punctuated by open fields.

One trim garden, nonetheless, stands in its oldest, southern end, with a monument to Estonia's literary giant Friedrich

The Old Town: traditional café life.

SAILING AND THE SEA

Arthur Ransome bought a boat in Tallinn in 1919. "Reval [Tallinn] was built as a fortress on a rock," he wrote, "and from the rock one looks out over a wide bay, with the green wooded island of Nargon on one side of it, a long promontory on the other, and far out beyond the bay a horizon of open sea. I do not believe that a man can look out from that rock and ever be wholly happy until he has got a boat of his own. I could not."

Ransome, English journalist and author of popular children's books, played chess with Lenin and helped to negotiate independence for Estonia. He had a boat designed for him in Tallinn and built in Riga and he spent many months sailing the eastern Baltic, with his wife Evgenia, a former secretary to Trotsky, writing up the experience in *Racundra's First Cruise*.

Sailing around the three countries' waters remains a pleasure, and the coast's many islands give it added spice. The silver grey waters of the Baltic, lacking any discernible

tides, are a gulf of the Atlantic, connected to the North Sea by narrow channels. Fed by rivers such as the Narva, Daugava and Nemunas, the sea has a low salt content and at 163,000 sq. miles (422,000 sq. km) it is the largest area of brackish water in the world. It is also a very shallow sea, with an average depth of 197 ft (60 metres), and it freezes over easily. In 1658 and 1809, it was completely covered with ice.

There are sailing clubs in each of the countries and regattas are a part of the summer scene. In Riga, where boats are still built, there was an annual pre-war race which took yachtsmen from the city castle around the island of Ruhnu in the middle of Riga Bay, which involved one night at sea.

But the smartest club is the Olympic Sports Centre at Pirita just outside Tallinn, built for the 1980 Moscow Games. Optimistic dinghies bob in its calm waters and larger yachts pull in from all parts of the sea. There are few proper marinas on the coast, but island havens, working ports, such as Liepāja in Latvia, or some of the fishing villages on Lithuania's Neringa Spit, are prime targets for development and outside companies are already showing an interest. Larger harbours will have more to offer with the disappearance of the Soviet Fleet.

The hazards of sailing the Baltic waters include half-hidden rocks and promontories: 1,578 miles (2,540 km) of Estonia's 2,350-mile (3,780-km) coast belongs to its 1,500 islands. A particular danger is the strait between the country's west coast and the islands of Hiiumaa and Saaremaa, and on the landward side of the smaller islands of Vormsi and Muhu.

The principal 40-mile (64-km) Muhu Vain channel dodges one way and another between marker buoys, and many vessels have failed to make it from one end to the other. The 30-mile (48-km) long Irbens Strait, between Saaremaa and Latvia, is also navigated with care, round the 7-mile (11-km) shoal that spills down from the island. A hazard of going aground is that there is no tide to lift vessels free.

But the shallow waters make bathing both warm and safe. It is not surprising that the coast, with its spas and sanatoriums, has for more than a century been a popular resort, not just for Balts, but for everyone from here halfway to the Black Sea. ∎

Dinghies at the Pirita Olympic port.

Kreutzwald (1803–82) and a large duck pond. Peter's peach-and-white **Kadriorg Palace** is a bit further in and until recently housed the National Gallery. In front of it is a splendid royal garden and pool. Behind the palace is another baroque-style building in peach: the Estonian presidency identifiable from the massive security surrounding it.

Not far away is the **Song Festival Stage** (1960). The huge amphitheatre looks like the yawning mouth of a great white shark, and it can hold 32,000 singers. The grounds, built for 150,000, were stuffed with more than a quarter of a million for an historic rally of the "Singing Revolution" in 1989.

Kadriorg Park is separated from the water by a wide road. It has a seaside walk on its other side. A small amusement park for children stands at its start and a little further down the road is the beautiful **Russalka Memorial** (1902). It was erected in memory of the 170 Russian sailors who drowned just off Tallinn harbour on the iron-clad *Russalka* ("Mermaid") in 1893. The

granite foundation represents a ship crashing against underwater reefs and the base rises as a sharp cliff. Posed on top is a bronze angel, cross in hand, facing the sea.

The **Maarjamägi Memorial Complex** (1960) is down the road, back on the inland side of the main road. Distinctly Soviet in its austere monumental lines and not very popular locally, it is nevertheless surprisingly moving. It is divided into five sections: an obelisk dedicated to the 1917 revolution; two human-sized palms with a (no longer) eternal flame; a "wounded seagulls" archway representing the resilience of the revolution; a headstone for the Tallinn divisions of the Great Patriotic War in 1944–45; and a grave to a World War II sailor named Yvgeny Nikolov, martyred at the hands of the Nazis.

The road, here called Pirita Tee, leads on to the **Olympic Yachting Centre**, which was built for the sailing events of the 1980 Olympic Games in Moscow but is still used by locals. **Pirita Beach** stretches along the harbour north of

here. In Pirita Harbour, visit the Lembitu, Estonia's pre-war submarine, which was restored and open to visitors.

Pirita convent (1407–36) lies over the bridge and across the road. It was built for the Swedish-based St Bridget's order of nuns and in its time was one of the two largest buildings in Tallinn (the Dominican monastery was the other). The nuns lived on its north side and the priests and their assistants on the south; behind the vestry was a parlatory with a central partition with holes through which they could communicate.

The convent was destroyed in 1577 during the Livonian War but the 115 ft (35 metre) high western facade with its arched portal of flagstones is still quite beautiful and the shell of the rest of the main church is intact. The gravestones strewn over its front yard come from several centuries, for peasants continued to live on the site for a considerable time after its destruction.

One graveyard that simply must be seen is Tallinn's **Forest Cemetery**, situated at Kloostrimetsa, down the road from Pirita. The Balts are fond of their cemeteries and some people say this is the most beautiful place in all of Tallinn; surely, it is one of the most beautiful cemeteries in the world. It looks almost like a national park, with graves running up and down small hills under a deep forest of fir trees. In 1933, the writer Eduard Vilde was the first to be buried here and most of Estonia's stars have since followed suit, including Georg Ots, Lydia Koidula and Konstantin Päts. Rising just to the right of the main gates is the so-called "hill of celebrities".

On the western side of Tallinn and in easy reach of the city is an **Open-Air Museum**. Situated at Rocca al Mare on the Kakumäe Peninsula, it was opened in 1964 and contains more than 60 buildings brought here from all over the country, showing how life has typically been lived in rural Estonia.

Suburban reality: To understand Tallinn fully, you must venture off into one of the residential neighbourhoods. Not far from the Forest Cemetery is **Lasnamäe**, an enormous concrete sea of nearly identical buildings with virtually no landscaping, which was the source of great controversy during the Soviet years. Begun in the late 1970s, it was nicknamed the "suburb of Leningrad" because the housing authorities repeatedly installed new immigrants from Russia in them no matter how long locals had been on the waiting-list. It is now more than 70 percent Russian and is commemorated in a song about a young person "with empty eyes" who comes to live here.

The **Kose District** behind Lasnamäe is very different. Almost all the homes here are one-family, and there are gardens everywhere. Other pretty neighbourhoods of this kind are **Nõmme** and **Merivälja**. The latter is where most ambassadors and the nouveau riche live. Conversely, **Mustamäe** and **Väike-Õismäe** are the other "Russian" districts, built during Soviet times with few parks and monotonous structure. The worst part of town is **Kopli**, near the former Soviet military base where people live in barrack-style housing, and the crime rate is high.

Left, fancy gutter, Tallinn. Right, St Bridget's convent, Pirita.

NARVA AND THE EAST

The skyline of the most Russian of Estonia's cities is dominated by the Russian and Estonian fortresses which face each other across the border that is provided by the River Narva. Estonia's second largest city, **Narva**, is the hub of the country's industry, a position reinforced by the building programme undertaken during the Soviet occupation. The city has a population of just over 73,000. It is closer geographically to Russia's second city, St Petersburg (85 miles/137 km), than to the Estonian capital, Tallinn (131 miles/210 km). With a population that is 98 percent ethnic Russian (few came voluntarily), the questions of citizenship and property ownership are acute political issues.

Narva's name probably derives from a Baltic/Finnish word, *narvaine,* meaning "the threshold". Indeed Narva has been the focus of attention of great or emerging powers since its earliest days. The city was first mentioned in 1240 when it was listed in census records compiled by the Danes who built Fort Narva (once called Herrmannstadt) which they sold to the Teutonic Order in 1347. In 1492, the year Columbus sailed to the New World and the Russians finally repelled the Mongols, Tsar Ivan III built a fort at Ivangorod on "his" side of the river.

The Teutonic Knights responded by enlarging their fort to overlook the Russian construction. The tsar swiftly responded with further building work, but in the rush the engineers forgot to include a church. The story goes that the furious tsar gave the engineers just another 24 hours to construct a church or they would be put to death.

In 1558, after the Russians had taken Narva, the Teutonic Knights asked the Swedes for assistance. However, by the late 1600s, Sweden had appropriated all German properties so the knights turned to their old enemy, the Russians, for help. Peter the Great obliged.

The result was the Northern War which began near Narva in 1700. When the Peace Treaty of Nystad was signed in 1721, the city was once again under Russian control where it remained and flourished for two centuries.

By the late 19th century Narva was an industrial giant and a major seaport, rivalling Tallinn. Its largest company, Kreenholm Textile Manufacturing, employed more than 10,000 people in its factories: Estonia's first strike was organised here in 1872.

During the first republic Narva remained part of Estonia. The city was affected by economic depression during the 1920s and 1930s, and suffered terribly during World War II. On 17 August 1941 the Germans entered Narva and when, in July 1944, they were finally driven out, 98 percent of the city had been destroyed.

After the war, the Russians set about rebuilding Narva. Two hydroelectric plants were constructed on the river with a third plant, powered by oil, situated approximately 5 miles (8 km) west of the town. Together these plants produce most of the energy for

northeastern Estonia and for a region of Russia extending into St Petersburg.

The new and the old: The city has been the last in Estonia to change the old Soviet street names and its Lenin statue was only removed from central Peetri land in the mid-1990s after a long and fierce battle with the local Russian authorities. Peetri land is taken up by the Estonian customs and border installations. On the northern side of the square, slightly set back in a park, there are two adjoining buildings that date from the Swedish period. They once formed part of the old city walls and main gate. The rest of the charming **Old Town** lies between here and the river.

The **Friendship Bridge** is the main crossing between Russia and Estonia and all foreign visitors need a visa to make the 5-minute walk across it to see Ivangorod. Be sure to have a multiple entry visa for Estonia if you want to come back! On the Narva side, all sightseeing, except for the **1872 Kreenholm Strike Memorial**, is north of the castle and easily explored on foot. The memorial is inside the Kreenholm factory and the warden at the entrance will gladly let you have a glimpse of the statue.

Inside the multi-storied **Narva Castle** there is a permanent exhibition of local history. Of particular interest are the photographs showing how Narva looked before it was destroyed during World War II by Russian and German bombing. Other parts are given over to touring exhibits. There is also a small concert hall, and the surrounding countryside can be seen through the small windows on the top floor of **Pik Herrmann** (Long Herman) tower.

Narva's statue of Lenin stands in the grounds of the Castle; it is hidden on the left-hand side of the compound, symbolically facing east across the river towards Russia. The walls around the fort are walkable and photographers should note that in the late afternoon the southwest corner bastion offers superb views of both forts. Or you may want to walk along the river's edge to the beach and then up the headland for pictures of both forts separated by the river.

The Swedish Town Hall in Narva.

The **Old Town Hall**, built by the Swedes, was one of the few buildings that survived World War II. A beamed period ceiling can be seen in the foyer.

Bastions once circled the city, but many were destroyed during World War II, leaving only those along the river. A pleasant stroll along them leads to the **Narva Art Gallery**, on Vestervalli 21, which was built by Peter the Great and was once a palace. It now shows local artists' work and has a permanent collection that was bequeathed by the Lavrezov family of local historical portraits and 18th- and 19th-century Russian genre paintings.

The 9-mile (15-km) drive north along the river to **Narva-Jöesuu** on the coast is a dull, flat one. At intervals there are monuments commemorating the many regional battles dating back to the Northern War, and brides still leave their bouquets as a tribute to fallen heroes.

Peter the Great visited the town when it was called Hungerburg and gave it its present name. Narva-Jöesuu was a popular 19th-century spa town which attracted many Russian artists and writers, but today the factory chimneys are intrusive. The town is, however, still filled with early-20th-century **gingerbread houses**, and one of the most colourful is just off Ranna Street. The **Orthodox Church**, created from rough-hewn logs, is a gem.

To the west, near **Meriküla**, look for the **Shiskin Tree**, festooned with bright ribbons. Couples come here on their wedding day to make a wish, then tie a ribbon on to as high a branch as possible. The higher the ribbon, the greater the chance that the wish will be granted. If the couple wish to start a family soon, then a pink or blue ribbon is also added.

West to Tallinn: Leaving Narva, the M11 runs through industrial suburbs to **Sillamäe**. Just to the south of Sillamäe, however, is the farming community of **Sinimäe**, clustered around the only wooded hill in the area, which has seen innumerable battles since Viking days. During the Northern War, Swedish troops used it as a defensive position. In 1918 the Estonian Nationalists defeated

Left, newly-weds at the Shiskin Tree. Right, house with frills, Narva Jöesuu.

the communists here, while in World War II over 45,000 Russian and 15,000 Germans were casualties on these slopes.

Another Northern War battle site is at **Toila** on the coast between Sillamäe and **Johvi**. There is a large **regional park** here containing over 200 different plants, nature walks and a pebble beach. The park is on the former property of a German baron who had a manor house built here in 1899. Estonia's first president used it as a holiday retreat but it was destroyed in 1943. The **River Saiut** flows through the park and in 1700 Charles XII of Sweden stood on its high western bank, facing his Russian counterpart on the other side.

Between **Johvi** and **Kohtla-Järve** rolling countryside begins, and several **windmills** dot the skyline, all that remain of the hundreds which once covered the landscape. The large mounds visible from the road are slag heaps left from shale oil exploration early this century. Today, underground fires are common and large sinkholes may appear without warning.

The **cliffs** which run for about 18 miles (30 km) between **Martsa** and **Aa** form part of a limestone-based plateau and are best reached via the road to Ontika. Rising 182 ft (56 metres) above the sea, the views from them are terrific.

Purtsee Castle at Purtsee, to the west of Kohtla-Järve, is easily missed, as it stands several hundred yards away from the M11, in the middle of several other buildings. The restored red-roofed edifice dates from the Swedish period, when the town of Purtsee was a freeport. Although the castle was partially destroyed during the Northern War, it was still inhabited until 1938. The keyholders, who now show visitors around, live in a nearby farmhouse.

Kunda, 9 miles (15 km) off the main road on the P18 and beautifully situated on the coast, was for years marred by a fine coating of white dust from the enormous local cement plant. The German/Swedish owners have successfully reduced the early 1990s emission rate of 20 tonnes per hour to only a few kilogrammes per hour.

The castle at Rakvere.

Midway between Narva and Tallinn is **Rakvere**, the country's seventh largest city. The **castle**, which acts as a beacon, was built in 1253 on the site of a wooden one that was destroyed during the Livonian War. There are also the ruins of a **Franciscan monastery** dating from 1515 and several charming streets of late 19th-century buildings

Green lung: After the industry of the east, **Lahemaa National Park** comes as a breath of fresh air, and locals point to the coincidence of wealthy Soviet living in the area when it was created in 1971. Until 1989 permits were required to visit the park which covers 162,500 acres (65,000 hectares) of land, water and off-shore islands between Rakvere and Tallinn. Now it is open to everyone.

More than 75 percent of the park is woodland and the population is less than 20 per square kilometre. There are remains of ancient settlements, freshwater lakes, a few farms and four manor houses. Sheltered bays dip between craggy promontories which jut into the Gulf of Finland. It is an important wildlife area with deer and elk, and during the migration season, for special species such as the black stork. Plant life abounds and among the 850 documented varieties is the rare arctic bramble.

Võsu and **Loksa** are the park's two main towns. Loksa is much larger, with a cargo port, and a mainly Russian population. It is easy to make trips around the park from either town.

Palmse, south of Võsu, is the most famous of Lahemaa's manor houses. In 1286, a group of nuns from the Cistercian Order of St Michael in Tallinn were given the land by King Erik Montvert of Denmark. The pond they built there for their fish farm is still in use today. In 1673, the estate was bought by the Vaan der Pahlen family who built the current manor house in 1785. The Estonian government confiscated it in 1923, and during World War II it was a German command centre until it was destroyed by the Russians in 1944. Renovation lasted between 1972 and 1985, and today the estate is a perfect period piece, filled with Empire furniture.

The **lake** at the rear of the house is inhabited by a family of extremely nasty swans. A **summer house** and a **winter garden** add to the beauty of the grounds. In the orchard are over 30 varieties of fruit trees, many dating from the end of the 19th century.

The nearby church of **Illumäe** was built by and contains the grave of the most illustrious member of the Vaan der Pahlen family, Carl Magnus. He fought against Napoleon Bonaparte, allowed the peasants who worked the farm to use his last name, and in 1823 opened the first school for local children. In front of the church is a **memorial** to those killed during the 20th-century's wars and those who perished in the Gulag.

Vergi, on the coast but east of Vösu, was home to a large Soviet naval base but the last of its occupiers left in 1992. The white building at the tip of the peninsula is a customs house. Beyond Vergi is **Altja**, a living museum of thatched, weather-beaten houses. The nearby headland is dotted with attractive sheds for storing fishing gear.

Sagadi, to the south, is another restored German manor house. Built in 1765, it became a school during Estonia's First Independence. Restoration work was finished in 1986, and although its original elegance remains outside, inside is a **Museum of Forestry** and a mixed bag of furnishings.

On the western side of the park **Kolga manor**, now the administrative centre for a large collective, still remains unrestored. (Plans for its makeover have been indefinitely postponed due to a lack of funds.) The graceful 18th-century building is a cliché of a crumbling pile with falling plaster, peeling wallpaper and a cracked exterior. The owners have turned one of the old stable blocks into a small, very basic **hostel**, and if enthusiasm were the basis for a rating, it would be given 10 out of 10.

Käsmu, the peninsula on the west side of Vösu's bay, has some of the cleanest waters between Tallinn and St Petersburg. The impressive wooden houses were built by smugglers who made illegal vodka and sold it in Fin-

Left, Kolga Manor, prior to restoration. Right, restored Sagadi manor.

land during the early days of the 20th century. The town was once a major ship-building town with an apprentice programme which attracted young men from the entire Baltic region.

Off-shore, towards the end of Käsmu's peninsula, is **Hell Island**, and beyond it is **Mohni Island**, an uninhabited nature reserve. The coastline is noted for the boulders which dot the shallow waters, and many of the largest have been given names. Nearby are large piles of stones and it is customary to add to them: if you put yours on without the others falling, your wish will come true.

At **Viitna**, south of Palmse on the M11, a 17th-century **coaching inn** has been restored and turned into a restaurant for hungry travellers. Tallinn is only about an hour's drive from here; the M11 is a dual carriageway for most of the way and forms part of the Via Baltica highway, which links Tallinn, Riga and Vilnius.

South to Tartu: Just east of **Jöhvi**, look for signs to **Vasknarva**. Travelling south via this old Livonian fortress town on Lake Peipsi is not the most direct route into southern Estonia, but it is the more interesting, and adds less than 25 miles (40 km) to the 115-mile (185-km) journey to Tartu.

Approaching **Kuramäe**, the green domes of the cathedral of Pühtitsa (Estonian for "holy place") convent beckon through a forest of oak and pine. This is the only **Eastern Orthodox nunnery** in the Baltic States, built on a site which has been sacred since the 16th century when a peasant saw a vision of the Virgin Mary on the top of a hill. An icon was found beneath an ancient oak tree near the same spot, and the icon of the Assumption of the Mother of God is still the convent's most prized possession, surrounded by precious gems and mounted on a pillar to the right of the cathedral altar.

The first nun was sent to Pühtitsa in 1888 to establish the convent, and the complex of buildings, circled by a high granite wall, was designed by Mikail Preobrazhensky, a professor at the St Petersburg Academy of Arts.

Communal
dining hall,
Kuramäe
nunnery.

The five-domed, three-aisle **Cathedral of the Assumption,** which can accommodate up to 1,200 worshippers, was finished in 1910. There are five other churches in the complex, including a small one just outside the main walls, which is used for funeral services. The **Church of St Sergius of Radonezh** is located at the apex of the **Holy Mount,** where the first miracle occurred, and is a five-minute walk along a lime-tree shaded path from the convent's central area. Constructed in 1895, the church is dedicated to the patron of the Order, Prince Sergi Shakhovsky, and it contains his family vault.

Under post-war Soviet occupation buildings were allowed to deteriorate and by 1961 it appeared the convent could close. A change in Moscow's attitude towards religion and a new bishop in Tallinn began the convent's physical rejuvenation. Today there are over 100 nuns in residence, ranging in age from 18 to 80-plus. Some 60 acres (24 hectares) of the 187-acre (75-hectare) property is farmed. Cash is

raised from the sale of icons and other religious items made by the nuns. These, plus tapes and records of the convent's choir, can be bought at the small information centre.

Tours are offered between 9am and 5pm. Women are requested to wear skirts that come below the knee; men must wear long trousers, and both sexes must have their upper arms covered. Divine Services are held at 6pm daily and 9am on Sunday. Anyone may attend but, unless of the Orthodox faith, you are asked to remain in the back of the church and refrain from walking around, talking and taking photographs.

Nothing about the small cluster of houses which comprise **Vasknarva** (Estonian for "waterfall") reflects its great past. It was once the guardian of the river route into Narva at the northern end of **Lake Peipsi**, Europe's fourth largest lake which forms a large part of Estonia's eastern border. The town was founded at the beginning of the 12th century as a way-station on the trade route linking the principalities of Novorod and Pskov with Tartu and Tallinn. However, after the decisive Russian victory in the Northern War, the need for a stronghold waned, and Vasknarva began its slide into obscurity. All that remains of the old **Livonian fortress** is part of two walls. Fishing has long been the mainstay of Vasknarva, but with Estonian independence its geography has once again made it part of a trade route. This time the small boats do thriving business transporting contraband Western goods eastward.

The road along the top of Lake Peipsi goes through forests of tall conifers and beside white beaches of bleached oyster shells. There are occasional fishing villages strung along the water's edge, their clapboard houses painted a variety of colours, each fronted by banks of vibrant flowers and backed by greenhouses which are used to extend the short growing season.

Mustvee, 40 miles (65 km) north of Tartu, is Lake Peipsi's largest town. It has two Orthodox churches, a fish processing plant and several inconguous modern apartment blocks.

Left, gathering shells, Lake Peipsi. Right, fishermen at Vasknarva.

TARTU AND THE SOUTH

People often call southern Estonia the "real" Estonia. This is where the percentage of non-Estonians in some towns falls into single-figures, the dialect is deep Finno-Ugric, and the locals have kept up a tradition of hospitality and generosity. The region is split roughly between the undulating Sakala, Otepää and Haanja highlands. Each has its own "metropolitan" focus – Viljandi, Otepää, and Võru – but these cities have a predominately rural feel. For the most part, industrial activity is secondary or subordinate to agriculture.

Brains of Estonia: The largest city in the southern half of Estonia, with around 102,000 residents, is **Tartu**, 116 miles (187 km) southeast of Tallinn. Just as many say the south is the real Estonia, many call Tartu its real capital.

At the very least, Tartu is the intellectual capital. Founded in 1632, **Tartu University** was also a powerhouse for Latvian intellectuals during their National Awakening. It has endured as the main seat of higher education in the humanities and currently has around 10,000 students. It is also endowed with less esoteric institutions: an agricultural and a medical school.

Tartu was first recorded in 1030 as a stronghold built by Grand Duke Yaroslav of Kiev. The city has been razed on several occasions since – by Estonians in 1061, Germans in 1224, the Northern War in 1708 and by fire in 1775 – and most buildings in the Old Town date from the 18th century.

The city has developed in a north-south fashion along the Emajõgi River, with most of the main university buildings sprinkled on the northern end where the Old Town lies. This district is immediately distinguishable by the wide cobbled Raekoja Plats (**Town Hall Square**) in its centre, anchored by a pinkish neoclassical Town Hall (1798) at its head. The grey clock-tower rising from the middle of its roof was added in the 19th century to help the students be on time for classes.

In front of the town hall stands a fountain with a kissing couple under an umbrella. The statue, a symbol of Tartu's student population, was designed by the Estonian artist Marti Karmin in 1999 and has quickly become a local meeting point. Running along the northern side of the square is an unbroken row of pastel-coloured buildings greatly responsible for Tartu's reputation as the neoclassical prima donna of Estonia. The most noticeable of them is **Barclay House** (1793) at No. 18. Erected on a wooden foundation in marshland that later dried up, it leans to the left. Inside is the **Pildigalerii**, whose collection centres on the Pallas Higher Art School that ran in Tartu from 1919 to 1940.

The **University Building** lies just a couple of blocks away, at Ulikooli Street 18, a stately oasis in the cramped and crumbling side streets of the Old Town. Pale yellow with six white columns, the University Building is the most impressive neoclassical structure in Estonia. Completed in 1809, it was designed by the architect Johann Krause.

Further down Jaani Street is the 14th-century brick Gothic **St John's church**. The renovation of the interior, which lasted for many years, is due to be completed at the end of 2000. On the exterior you can admire hundreds of tiny terracotta sculptures. The 15 faces above its pointed portal represent the Last Judgment.

Across the street is a green building (1640–90) that was one of the first sites of the original Swedish-run university. Restored in 1766 and again at the end of the 19th century, it is now the **Tartu Police Station**. Locals call it "the most expensive hotel in town". In 1944, 192 Tartu citizens were rounded up by the communists and murdered in the yard.

The neoclassical rule is further broken on the south side of Town Hall Square. First along Vabaduse Street is the grim brown **market hall** (1937). The **bus station** stands on the next block, and then the **outdoor market**, which is devoted half to foodstuffs and half to dry goods. The river bank is dominated by the modern glass Hansapank office

tower. Across the road on Riia Street is another set of modern buildings comprising the Tartu Department Store and the Hansakeskus (Hansa centre) with the Pallas hotel on its fourth floor.

Ritual heights: The **Vanemuine Theatre** (1977), at Vanemuise 6, and adjacent **University Library** (1980), at W. Struve Street 1, are the final modern touches. Both are white and functional, but the library is distinguished by the students perpetually gathered on its wide fountain-clad plaza for a quick smoke.

It is a short, pleasant walk from here to **Toome Hill**, the park that dominates the Old Town. In the southern side of the park stands the observatory. From the west entrance on Vällikraavi Street turn up under the grey **Kuradisild** (1913) or Devil's Bridge. This is named for a Professor Mannteuffel from Germany who, in the late 19th century, introduced Estonia to the use of rubber gloves in surgical operations, but whose name resembles the German *Teufel* (devil). You will find yourself between the **University Internal Hospital** (1808) and

House in the Soup District.

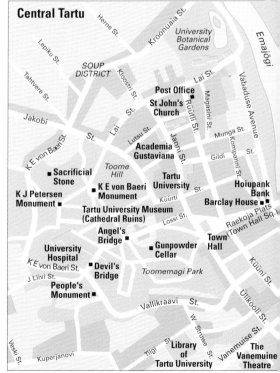

Central Tartu

SOUP DISTRICT

University Botanical Gardens

Emajõgi

Herne St.

Kroonuaia St.

Lepiku St.

Lai St.

Vabaduse Avenue

Tähtvere St.

Kloostri St.

Post Office

St John's Church

Magasini St.

Riiütli St.

Jakobi

Lai St.

Lutsu St.

Janni St.

Munga St.

Kompanii St.

K E von Baeri St.

St.

Academia Gustaviana

Gildi

St.

Toome Hill

Sacrificial Stone

K E von Baeri Monument

Tartu University

St.

Hoiupank Bank

K J Petersen Monument

Küürti

Barclay House

Tartu University Museum (Cathedral Ruins)

Lossi St.

Raekoja Plats (Town Hall Sq.)

Angel's Bridge

Gunpowder Cellar

Town Hall

University Hospital

K E von Baeri St.

Devil's Bridge

Toomemagi Park

Küüni St.

J Liivi St.

People's Monument

Vallikraavi St.

Ülikooli St.

Veski St.

Kuperjanovi

Tiigi St.

W. Struve St.

Library of Tartu University

Vanemuise St.

The Vanemuine Theatre

the **University Maternity Hospital** (1838). Straight ahead is the ochre **Angel's Bridge**, also named as a result of a linguistic confusion: Toomemägi Park was laid out in English style and the locals confused the words "English" and "angel".

Toomemägi is strewn with statues of people connected with Tartu University. In spring biology students traditionally wash the pensive head of Karl Ernst von Baer – a professor linked to Darwin – with champagne and put a tie around him. The monument to the writer Kristjan Jaak Peterson – the first Estonian national to enter the university – is shown erect with a stick in his hand because he is said to have walked the 155 miles (250 km) from Riga to Tartu.

The "Romantic Corner" of the park lies to the left from the statue of Baer. It consists of a stone mound called the **Hill of Kissing** to the top of which bridegrooms must carry their new wives, a low **Bridge of Sighing** with a well-worn cement bench, and **Sacrificial Stone** where the lovelorn can leave a prayer to the ancient gods. Sacred stones are found all over Estonia; people used to gather round them on a Thursday full moon, and leave (non-bloody) sacrifices. Tartu students have continued this ritual by ceremonially burning their notebooks here at midnight on the Thursday before their exams.

The monumental ruins of the **Cathedral church**, for whom the hill is named, loom above this part of the park. Begun in the 13th century, this was once the largest brick Gothic church in the Baltic countries, but the majority of it was destroyed in the Livonian War. The broken wings of 10 flying buttresses give an idea of its former grandeur.

The huge choir on the church's eastern end was completely restored in the early 1800s under the direction of Krause. For a time it served as the university library, but it now contains the **Tartu University Museum**. On each floor are exhibitions of the history of the university, from its opening in 1632 in honour of the Swedish King Gustavus Adolphus to the present day. A lovely

The ruined cathedral.

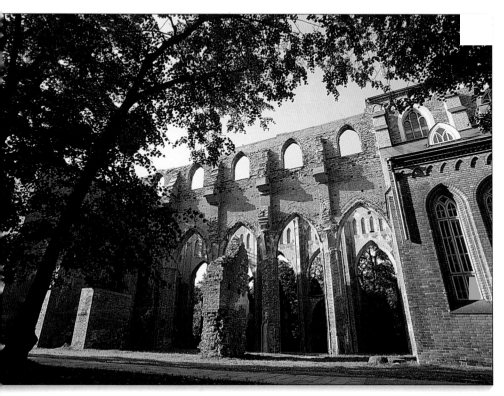

white baroque hall on the second floor is a public concert room with walls lined by cases of antique biological species. On the southeast edge of the park is the Gunpowder Cellar or **Pussirohukelder Restoran** (1778), now a restaurant built into the side of Toome Hill and currently under restoration.

Neighbourhoods with flavour: Tartu is divided into different districts, each with its own name. Lai Street divides the Old Town from **Suppilinn**, or Soup Town, so called because its streets are called after soup ingredients like Bean and Potato. The industrial area south of the Old Town is the **Ropka District**, and the attractive **Karlova District** has cut-corner wooden houses built during the Estonian Republic as boarding houses. The area of stately homes behind Toomemägi Park – and very popular with university professors – is the **Tähtvere District**.

Some of the most curious buildings in Tartu are ordinary houses. The weathered house at 65 Marta Street, beside the wooded park in which the dilapidated **Karlova manor** stands, for example, is a marvel of wood and stone edging work.

At Riia 27, **St Paul's church** (1919) was designed by the Finnish architect Eliel Saarinen. Created in red brick with a square tower, it looks a bit like a fire station. One wing has been transformed into Tartu's **Sports Museum**. Architecture buffs will also want to have a look at the constructivist Tammekann Villa, built by Finnish architect Alvar Aalto in 1932 on Kreutzwaldi 6.

Westward: The small city of **Viljandi**, 48 miles (77 km) west on the P57, clings to the slopes of a primeval valley plumbed by **Lake Viljandi**. Now the capital of the **Sakala upland**, with about 22,000 inhabitants, the site has been settled since AD 1000, but the Old Town is tiny; one small grid between Tallinna and Tartu streets and the **Castle Park**. Its appeal depends on its lovely lakeside setting and the ruined castle perched on a series of hills above the water.

A good place to start a tour of the town is the **Viljandi Local History**

Dancers in Viljandi.

Museum (1779–80) at Kindral Laidoneri Square 12, in the Old Town. This square used to be the market place, and its central fountain covers the town well. The museum is downstairs in Viljandi's third-oldest building and contains a model of the former castle. It also houses many painstakingly decorated old objects of daily use, such as tankards and horse yokes. There are also regular exhibitions of continuing local handicraft and artwork.

Two houses down, at No. 8, is the **Cultural College**. Viljandi has contributed substantially to Estonia's cultural history, and the town now has three well-known choirs: the Koit Merited Mixed Choir, the Sakala Male Choir and the Eha Female Choir. A professional drama company is housed in one of the town's few contemporary buildings, the **Ugala Theatre** (1981), beside the Valuoja River.

Initially a grand hotel, the Cultural College building was occupied during World War II by the Nazis, who called it "the hospital". It is presumed to have been a site of human experimentation. At dawn, a truck would cart corpses away. The 18th-century **Town Hall** stands one block away from here on Linnu Street.

The entrance to the Castle Park is just down Lossi Street, over a long wooden footbridge. Begun in 1223, the **Order Fortress of Viljandi** is presumed to have been the largest fortress in the Baltics, designed to stretch over three adjacent hills, with its only entrance on the first hill, occupied by servants. The second fold, once split between servants and horses, is now a field edged with bits of old wall. A dog show is held here every summer and in June there is a midsummer bonfire. If you climb (carefully) up on the stone by the edge, you will get a great view over a long and narrow lake. The third hill supported the castle, the church and the prison. This final section has more ruins than the other two and they stand out starkly against the sky.

A bright red-and-white **suspension bridge** leads from this end of the castle

The view from Big Egg, near Võru.

grounds into the rest of the park. Built in 1879, the bridge was brought to the town from Riga in 1931 by a German count whose favourite daughter, the story goes, had persisted in using it for racing her horse across.

The 15th-century church of the former Franciscan monastery, **St John's**, has its own wooden footbridge, at the head of Castle Park just off Pikk Street. It is used primarily for concerts. The town's main Lutheran church, **St Paul's** (1863–66), lies outside the park across Vaksali Road. Red brick with stone inlay, it has an industrial-age Gothic veneer.

By the lake's shore Viljandi has a different feel – it is considerably sportier, happier and younger. At one end are tennis courts and a town stadium, and there is also an **athlete's hotel** and a **waterside restaurant**. Boats and pedalos can be rented from the pier beside the restaurant. **Viljandi Lake** is supposedly not polluted, but it is advisable to row out to the centre if you want to jump in because the bottom of the lake is so muddy.

Winter resort: Estonia's entire southern region is dotted with pretty lakes, many of which are swimmable (though it is always best to check with a local). The largest, at 105 sq. miles (270 sq. km), is **Vorts Lake**. It is, however, only 20 ft (6 metres) at its deepest.

The lakes of **Otepää** in the **Otepää Highlands** help make this cosy town not just one of Estonia's most popular winter resorts but also a gracious rest spot during the summer months. Otepää is only a short drive southwest from Tartu, but in its tranquillity it could be a million miles away from the city. Its population doubles in winter to around 5,000; only around 30 of the town's residents are non-Estonian.

The main employment here is in the local sausage factory and the Otepää Truck Repair Garage. Resort facilities include a ski jump, cross-country ski paths, a scattering of downhill slopes, a public beach and a few hotels. The biggest event is a 37-mile (60-km) cross-country marathon that draws about 12,000 skiers every February.

The town and its surroundings have been designated a "protected area". Building above three storeys is forbidden, salt cannot be used against ice on the roads, and motorboating on Otepää's lakes and hunting and camping in its woods are prohibited.

The town clusters up against these woods, and the centre has a pleasantly closed-in feeling, accentuated by a narrow triangular central park. The **Tourist Information Centre** is based here, at Lipuväljak 9, and the **Otepää Theatre**, home to an amateur theatre company and most town gatherings.

The oldest building in town is **Otepää church**. Opened in 1608, it was built by Estonian peasants so that they wouldn't have to attend the church of the German population. The folklorist Jakob Hurt was its first Estonian pastor, from 1872 to 1880. The current steeple was added in 1860 and is 168 ft (52 metres) high.

When the Estonian Students Co-operative was forbidden from consecrating their flag in Tartu in 1884, they defiantly brought it to the Otepää church. Stone reliefs on the front doors that

A miller takes a break.

depicted this momentous nationalistic event were destroyed by the Soviets, but the locals replaced them with bronze casts in 1990. The **Monument to the 54** in front of the church, dedicated to the soldiers from Otepää who died in the War of Independence, was also blown up by the Soviets – once in the 1950s, and again in the early 1980s – but each time it was stubbornly replaced by the people of Otepää.

Linnamägi, former site of a 10th–11th century wooden stronghold and a bishop's 13th-century stone castle, is a small tree-covered hill a short walk south from the church past a municipal garden. The first level of the hill is marked with a large stone monument dated 1116, the year when Otepää first appears in the records. Locals use this spot for their midsummer celebrations. The excavated ruins of the castle stand on the shelf above. The expansive vista from here makes it easy to imagine why ancient warriors fought for the site.

Dryad magic: In ancient times Estonians gathered under oaks whenever they had to make important decisions. The most famous oak – the one that decorates the two-krone bank note – is a couple of miles outside the centre of Otepää centre. Standing wide and noble between a cow pasture, vegetable patch and Püha Lake, the **Pühajärv Oak** is 65 ft (20 metres) tall. Five people linking arms can reach around it and it is believed to be the biggest and oldest tree in the country. Its popular name is "the Sojatamm", or War Tree, because of its part in independence history. In 1841, a local German landlord tried to force the Estonian peasants on his land to use heavier equipment than they felt their horses could draw. They refused, which resulted in a battle beneath the oak. The peasants lost, but their act became a legend of Estonian solidarity.

Neitsijärv, or Virgin's Lake, which you pass on the way from the town to the War Tree, derives its name from the Middle Ages when brides had to spend their first married night in the bed of the Pühajärv landlord. One young girl left her wedding for the manor and never

Neighbours, Mehikoorma, Lake Peipsi.

appeared. In the morning, they found her bridal dress beside this lake, where she had drowned herself. The largest lake in the area is **Lake Püha**. It is alluring, but swimmers should beware hidden springs. Most summers someone drowns in it, suffering from cramp caused by the unexpected ice-cold water. The public beach here is safe: there is a lifeguard all summer, and boats can be rented out.

The Soviet dissidents Andrei Sakarov and Alexander Solzhenitsyn both used to spend quiet weeks by Lake Püha and, if you ask, locals will show you where the prime minister of Estonia during the Soviet era kept his holiday home. (He alone was allowed to use a motorboat here.) His house is now a guest house owned by Tartu University.

English paean: About 13 miles (20 km) south from here is **Sangaste manor** (1874–81) built for Count Friedrich Georg Magnus von Berg as a small-scale copy of Windsor Castle. It is a particularly incongruous-looking orange-brick mansion set back amid acres of agricultural plains. The manor was seized in the 1930s and most of the family fled to Finland. Sangaste has passed through many hands since, even housing hay and a tractor in its octagonal, multi-vaulted ballroom after World War II. In the 1970s, it was used as a Young Pioneers' Camp. These days it is a hotel and a conference centre.

Wide pastureland separates Sangaste from **Valga**, the southernmost city in Estonia, straddling the border with Latvia where it becomes Valka. Many non-Estonians live here, and unlike other southern towns it is not in the hills and it is industrially developed. The city has an enormous animal feed factory and a wine distillery.

If you edge down along the border for a while, you will eventually reach one of Estonia's largest forests. The **Mõniste Outdoor Museum** here contains a reconstruction a 19th-century southern Estonian farmhouse.

About 30 miles (50 km) southeast of Võru is the peaceful hamlet of **Rõuge**. A picture of southern harmony, Rõuge

Vastseliina castle.

curls in around seven clear lakes. One, called **Rõuge Suurjärv**, or Rõuge's Big Lake, is the deepest in Estonia (125 ft/ 38 metres). The Rõuge church (1730), with its white exterior and red-roofed bell-tower, is delightful. Its organ was built by the local Kriisa Brother organ-makers. Behind the church lies the **Valley of Nightingales** which attracts hundreds of these birds in spring.

Further east is the centre of the **Haanja Highland**. Haanja is slightly higher than the Otepää and Sakala uplands and its forests are deeper, but it has also been widely tamed by potato fields and pastureland. Its summit is **Suur-Munamägi**, or Big Egg Hill: the highest peak in Estonia, reaching 1,044 ft (318 metres) above sea level. A 115-ft (35-metre) observation tower has been added to its summit, and the result is a view that is truly heavenly. On the clearest days, you can see all the way to Russia and Latvia.

It may also be possible to glimpse the ruins of **Vastseliina Castle**. To reach it, head east towards the "new" Vastseliina

village, whose cultural centre is in an 18th-century manor house.

The "old" village, called Vahtseliina, was built in the 14th century around the castle, but not much is left of either. The red and beige brick castle has been reduced to two towers and one section of wall, lost in an overgrown section of field. The 19th-century Vahtseliina **coach stop**, where a tsar once stayed, has been turned into a restaurant.

The folds of Haanja were created during the Ice Age, and the landscape is smooth and unending. Gentle pastures are edged by lone farmhouses and tiny lakes which appear then fade.

The **A. S. Etas Ski Area**, which is located 7 miles (12 km) south of Võru, has only one small car-park and ski lodge, at the crest of a sudden bowl, 230 ft (70 metres) high and 4 miles (7 km) long, that falls into a tree-lined valley floating in mist. The lift equipment is being updated and there is no equipment for making artificial snow. You can cross-country ski or sled, and the surrounding woods are filled with game.

Three for the road.

You may well encounter a deer bounding gracefully across the road.

The most popular place for fishing in the area is **Verijärv**, or Blood Lake, a bit closer to Võru and filled with perch and pike. Large and picturesque, at the base of another steep forested valley, it got its name because a servant supposedly once drove a cruel lord of the manor into its waters.

Võru, the urban centre for the Haanja highlands, sprawls around the biggest lake in the town, **Tamulajärv**. Along with agriculture, Võru depends on furniture-making and dairy production. The population is about 19,000 of whom about 90 percent are Estonian.

The town was officially established in 1784, and both the small yellow Orthodox church and the St Katarina church were built soon after.

The most famous 18th-century structure in Võru is the **Friedrich Reinhold Kreutzwald Museum** (1793), on Kreutzwald Street 31, where the Estonian writer and doctor lived for most of his life. Kreutzwald was born in the Rakvere region in 1803 and studied in Tartu from 1826 to 1833. However, he spent the next 44 years practising medicine in Võru where he compiled *Kalevipoeg*, the Estonian national epic.

The museum is divided between three houses. The first is where the small home of Kreutzwald's Estonian mother stood; she couldn't live in the same house as Kreutzwald's wife, Maria, who was from a wealthy German family in Tartu. This house has an exhibition of his life and many publications.

His own home has been kept as much as possible as it was when he lived there and it includes portraits of the family, who, ironically, spoke only German at home. Maria couldn't understand why her husband bothered with Estonian. On the walls of the low building at the back of the yard are interpretations of the *Kalevipoeg* from a panorama of artists, including some of Estonia's best-known, such as Erik Haamer, Juri Arrak and Kristjan Raud. **Kreutzwald Park** runs towards the lake down Katariina Street to a statue of Kreutzwald. Võru's **Regional Museum** stands at the start of the park.

The drive from Võru back up to Tartu on the P64 gradually becomes less hilly but the forests remain. Tucked into one that has been protected by the state as a "gene bank", just beyond Põlva on the right, is the **Kiidjärve Mill**. Constructed in 1914, it is impressive, with careful brick trimming on orange brick. It is the largest functioning watermill in Europe.

The **Karilatsi Outdoor Museum** lies on the other side of the Tartu road, just beyond Kiidjärve. One section displays farm equipment in sheds that look very unsteady. The other section is home to an old schoolhouse that is still set for lessons, a windmill that you can enter and an overgrown garden that was designed to be a map of the region.

Just outside Tartu is a better maintained outdoor museum of agricultural history, the **Ülenurme Museum**. Fittingly, the surrounding landscape is anchored by far-flung farms, many of which have been renovated. It is a sign that the south is ploughing on, refusing to be shaken by the north's vagaries.

Left, Võru house of the writer Kreutzwald. **Right**, the town's oral traditions.

PÄRNU AND THE WEST COAST

The spas of Estonia's western shore used to be favoured by Russian tsars, and even under Soviet rule Russians flocked here for their summer holidays. Only in the last few years have the spa resorts gradually begun to emerge from years of neglect and a growing number of hotels have been refurbished to attract new Western – and in particular Finnish – visitors.

The hardest hit town during the lean years has, naturally, been the most developed resort. **Pärnu**, 80 miles (130 km) due south of Tallinn on the M12, was reknowned for its long sandy beach and four sanatoriums. As Russian tourists dropped off in number, it began taken on a rather sad, forlorn air.

Pärnu, with a population of 51,000, is one of the few places outside of Tallinn where people traditionally know how to deal with a tourist. The town has undergone something of a revival in the 1990s. The majestic Rannahotel overlooking the beach, was refurbished by the Scandic Hotel in an attempt to bring the city back to its former glory. The Ammende Villa recently reopened, a four-star gem in Pärnu.

Once again holidaymaker have a reason to come to Estonia's prime spa resort. The long beachfront and numerous parks are restorative places to stroll, and the **Old Town** is ripe with structural curiosities. Younger Estonians particularly like Pärnu; every July there is a large jazz festival, and all summer the bar and cafés are hopping.

The city proper, which was first noted in 1251, is divided by the Pärnu River. Rather confusingly, the Old Town lies on the south bank within what the locals refer to as the "new" city. The "old" city, north of the river, is where the majority of newer buildings are located. The reason for this is linked to Pärnu's complex history. During the 14th century, the area where the Old Town stands was occupied by a castle and fortification. But when the Swedes took power in 1617, they began to build

across the river instead. The castle fell into decay and was finally destroyed during the Northern War. This made the section on the north bank the oldest part of the city when, in subsequent centuries, development began to spill back over to the former castle area. This "old city" was, however, flattened during the last war, putting the area with the oldest buildings, or the "old town", back on the south side of the river.

Touring Pärnu's Old Town is far less complicated. For one thing, it isn't very large. Visiting would take only a couple of hours, if so many of the most eye-catching buildings didn't also contain enticing bars and cafés.

Pühavaimo Street, running through the Old Town's centre, is one example. First on the block is a delicate yellow building (1670), fronted by an imposing balcony that bears four small lions' heads. Squeezed in next to it is an odd red and mustard-coloured house (1877) that mixes everything from Corinthian columns to a flowery grey trim. It in turn merges into a green baroque structure

(1674) trimmed with courtly white and crowned with an old street lamp.

Generally, however, the Old Town isn't so old; most buildings date from the 19th century. But it does have two intact 18th-century churches, which are perhaps most remarkable for their physical proximity but absolute disparity. **Ekaterina's** (1765–68) is a weird Orthodox conglomeration of knobs and ledges, with green roofing and unevenly soaring spires. The interior is almost lunatic in its iconography; silver shield-like icons crowd the white walls. Meanwhile, the faded white Lutheran church, **St Elisabeth's** (1747), at Nikolai 22 a few blocks away, is the ultimate in architectural austerity.

There are also two remnants of the original 14th-century fortifications. One is the peach-coloured "**Red Tower**", saved during the Swedish era to house prisoners. Tucked down a small alley off Hommiku Street, it is easy to miss but the exhibition of excavated objects – such as the only remaining stones from the castle and cannonballs from the 15th–16th century – in its downstairs level is worth seeing. There is also a sketch of how the town used to look in the 15th century. Upstairs is a shop selling local art.

The other piece left of the ancient walls is the **Tallinn Gate**. Sky-blue with tall green doors, it doubles as a bar; **Baar Tallinn Värav** has been carved into the earthworks above it.

Passing through the gate, you find yourself on a lovely, long, tree-lined walk beside a finger of the Pärnu River curled inwards to create a duck-filled pond. This is the beginning of the lush parks that surround the sanatoriums in a rather awesome silence.

The sanatoriums still offer a wide variety of treatments. Most popular are the **Mud Baths**, housed in a neoclassical building (1926) at the end of Supeluse Street. You might want to think twice about sampling them yourself – the mud comes from Haapsalu on the far side of the Matsalu Nature Reserve to the north, and most of the sanatoriums there have been shut.

Left, Pärnu Town Hall. Right, starting school.

The mauve **Beach Salon**, next door at Mere Avenue 22, functions as a cultural centre with a bandstand behind it. Its front pavilion, facing the beach, is an elaborate maze of ornamental wicker arches and fountains.

These two buildings stand by the northwest edge of the **Pärnu Beach**, beginning with the **Women's Beach** where only women and small children are allowed so that they can sunbathe nude in peace. You can walk for miles from here south along the tree-lined promenade that parallels the beach, eventually leaving the sanatorium area but continuing past former beach pavilions, dogwalkers, tennis courts and football fields, and finally fields of dank, waving reed.

The Old Town has its own walks, the most famous of which is the triangular **Lydia Koidula Park**. The poetess Koidula (1843–86) was born in a village outside Pärnu but she lived in the city from the age of seven until, at 20, she moved with her family to Tartu. At 30, she married a Latvian doctor in Kronstadt. She died there 12 years later of breast cancer.

Many consider Koidula's collection of verse, *The Nightingale of Emajõgi*, to be the foremost work of Estonia's period of National Awakening, and the pen-name Koidula, given to her by a fellow artist, means literally "singer of the dawn". Her real maiden name was Jannsen, and the modest wooden school-house where her family lived is on Jannseni Street. The house itself is now the **Lydia Koidula Museum**, but for those who don't speak Estonian it is a bit dull since the contents are mostly cases of her poetry, books and writings.

The **Pärnu Museum**, on the other hand, is surprisingly rewarding. Located in a dim, Soviet-style building, its appearance is dreary but, after a first room of taxidermal examples of local fauna, the artifacts become more interesting. Archaeological finds date from as early as 8000 BC. A 13th-century woman's costume, a 16th-century Gothic chalice and embossed-leather Bible, and 19th-century furniture are also on display.

North into Läänemaa: The P74 northwest from Pärnu leads to the small town of **Lihula** which has a huge, Soviet-built **cultural centre**, an orange plaster-and-stone **Orthodox church**, and a point-spired cream and red **Lutheran church**. From Lihula, the P38 heads directly north into the **Matsalu State Nature Reserve**. Matsalu Bay has a range of habitats including reed-beds, water-meadows, hay-meadows and coastal pastures. It was already noted for its birdlife fauna back in 1870. Among the species found here today are the avocet, the sandwich tern, the mute swan, the greylag goose and the bittern. There are also some white-tailed eagles. Ruffs perform their special mating dance in its waters every spring.

The reserve itself was formed from 98,000 acres (39,700 hectares) of the bay area in 1957. It can be visited by car or, since water covers some 65,000 acres (26,300 hectares) of this same area, by boat. Either way, it's best to notify the reserve office ahead of time if you plan to visit.

Matsalu Bay lies in the southern part of the coastal district of **Läänemaa**. One of the flattest sections of the already rather flat Estonia, it is also low in arable land but the overall impression is certainly pastoral. The quietude is a bit misleading: this is the one area of the Baltics that has seismic activity.

The main town is **Haapsalu** whcih has close to 15,000 inhabitants. The large military base and fishery established here under the Soviets expains why the population is 30 percent Russians. Although the entire district has been under either Russian or Soviet control since 1710 (except for the 20 years of the republic), the locals identify strictly with the Swedes, who ruled over them for 129 years from 1581 to 1710.

Still, it was under the Russians that Haapsalu became a spa of great repute and it was to satisfy Russian demands that many of its fanciest buildings were constructed. It was also under the Russians – and then the Soviets – that these ornate structures were allowed slowly to fall apart and for Haapsalu's **Tori house farm.**

highly touted curative mud to become too polluted to recommend.

The town originally centred around the **Haapsalu Episcopal Castle**, which dates from 1279. Little of the castle itself remains, but its Romano-Gothic **cathedral** is one of only three functioning cathedrals in Estonia.

Single-naved and towerless, Haapsalu cathedral was built to double-up as a fortress, and its immense facade still looks stubbornly impenetrable. Inside, the tall white walls and high vaulted ceiling are almost bare.

In a side chapel is a baptismal font from 1634, with Adam, Eve and the serpent etched into its bowl; a vivid reminder of original sin to be washed away. Against its wall leans a sad wooden sculpture of a woman holding a child; a memorial to the people from Läänemaa deported to Siberia. The box beneath it, marked "1949–1989", contains Siberian soil.

Farmyard life.

Directly above this memorial is the **window of the white lady**, focus of Haapsalu's favourite local legend. As the story goes, a monk from the castle cloister fell in love with a sweet village girl and managed to bring her into the castle disguised as a boy. But when she began to sing in the choir, their treachery was discovered. As punishment, she was built into the walls and he was thrown into the cellar.

Every August, at the time of the full moon, the poor girl returns, and there are few villagers who do not claim to have seen her white reflection in the aforementioned window. She is not timid; she will appear before even a large crowd, and during this time, in fact, Haapsalu holds a "White Lady Festival" of varied cultural events that climaxes with the audience walking around en masse to the southwest side of the cathedral where this window stands. Locals absolutely promise the white lady will appear – as long as it doesn't rain. The only thing that scares her away is a sky heavy with rain clouds.

Directly in front of the castle entrance is the large square that used to house the town market and just to the left (or west)

Farmyard life.

is the space that served as the Swedish market. It now encloses a very pleasant **cafe**. On the square's east side is the salmon-coloured **Town Museum**, within what used to be the Town Hall. Many of the artefacts inside come from the castle and there are exhibitions about the region's old farms and Haapsalu's days as a summer resort.

You can see the ghosts of Haapsalu's spa days by walking down to the "**African Beach**", so called because there used to be, along with little bathing houses, statues of wild animals set in the water. Although the water isn't swimmable any more, locals are still fond of strolling along its seaside **promenade**. The former **Casino**, built in the 1900s, is now a shell of chipped, green-painted wood and lacy cut-out porticos, but concerts are still held in the bandstand beside it.

Of interest here are a sundial and a set of steps by the artist R. Haavamägi, who was born in Haapsalu, and the **Tchaikovsky Bench**. Tchaikovsky used to favour Haapsalu for his holidays and even used a motif from a traditional Estonian song in his *6th Symphony*. The bench – decorated with the composer's likeness and some notes from the *6th* – stands where he came every evening to watch the sunset.

Continuing further down Sadama Road from this point will bring you to the **Haapsalu Yacht Club**, which continues to thrive. The 1991 World Ice Yachting Championships were held in the bay here, and since its official opening to the public in the summer of 1992 the club has received yachts from all over the Baltic.

Town activity has moved away from the castle and beach down the lengthy **Posti Street**. However, if you wander the quaint back streets or the curious and creepy overgrown **Old Town Graveyard** – which lies on Posti Street opposite the very comfortable **Haapsalu Hotel** – you will find it easy to understand the appeal that Haapsalu has held for artists.

Ilon Wikland, for example, illustrator of the Pippi Longstocking books, was

Flowers for teacher as autumn term begins.

188

born in Haapsalu and, although she fled with her family to Sweden at the age of 14, has depicted the town and the small house on Rüütli Street beside the Adventist church where her father was minister in many drawings. Some original works hang in the **Pippi Boarding House**.

The town has also been rich in handicraft artists, and the "Haapsalu Shawl", created of such fine wool that it can be drawn through a ring, is known throughout Estonia. A couple of shops specialise in local crafts, most notably the **Amadeus Shop** at Jaama Street 7 beside the **town market**. At the end of this street is the once splendid **railway station**, built in 1905 to receive Tsar Nicholas II on his summer holiday.

Heading out of town back towards Tallinn will take you past the home of Ants Laikmaa, an influential early 20th-century Estonian painter. Laikmaa was an eccentric man, and the home he designed for himself, which has now been turned into the **Ants Laikmaa Museum**, is a very peculiar blend of red-and-white piping with a steep moss-covered roof that has to be seen to be believed.

A small sign points towards a bumpy road leading through the woods. The house stands at its very end, in a large yard pecked by chickens. Begun in 1923, it was changed in design so many times that it was never finished during Laikmaa's lifetime.

Laikmaa was immensely popular in Haapsalu, but it was probably useful he had such a private area for his daily life. Known for using carriages long after the advent of the car, his handsome moustaches, and appearing in costume when the mood struck him, the artist was the host of many unusual house parties. To get an idea, note the two small caricatures, signed "E.B" that hang upstairs. From here Tallinn is about an hour's drive northeast. If you feel that you have not yet truly experienced the sea, head west. At **Rohuküla**, about 5 miles (8 km) west, you can catch a ferry to the islands of **Vormsi** or **Hiiumaa** where the water is cleaner and tourists are few and far between.

Gone fishing, Haapsalu.

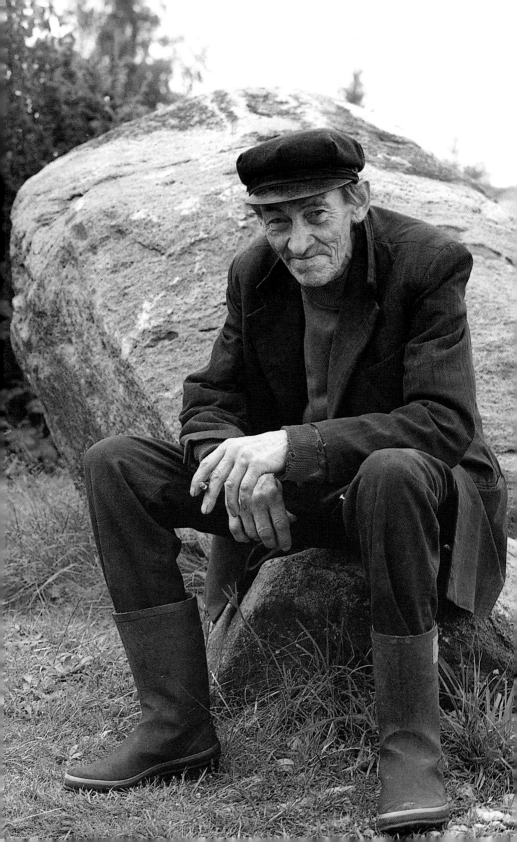

THE ISLANDS

Most of the 1500 or so islands off the coast of Estonia are mere hiccups, but two are so sizeable that island acreage ultimately accounts for some 10 percent of Estonia's total land territory. These larger islands, **Saaremaa** and **Hiiumaa**, are perhaps the most unspoilt and attractive corners of the country.

Ironically, their unspoilt condition is due partly to the Soviet occupation. Clustered off the western shore, these islands were (rightly) considered likely points of escape to the West as well as strategic security posts. They were therefore kept for the most part incommunicado from the rest of the Union. Meanwhile, since they clearly were impractical for any industrial projects, military personnel were virtually the only people to be brought in.

The islanders have continued to require most arrivals from the mainland to present visitor cards, even after independence. They say that this is the reason their islands have remained so peaceful and crime-free – which they certainly are. In the 13th century the islands were divided between the Oesel-Wiek (Saare-Laane) bishopric and the Livonian Order. Three centuries later, Saaremaa (Oesel) reverted to Denmark while Sweden took Hiiumaa. In 1645, Saaremaa also was assigned to the Swedes and from then on they were destined to share Estonia's fate.

Somehow, the islanders stubbornly retained a distinct way of life. They also began to stockpile impressive monuments left behind by the parade of conquering egos. The 13th-century churches and 18th-century manor houses that decorate their shores have now been mostly repaired, but they also are as blissfully free from disfiguring reconstruction and commercialisation as the islands themselves.

Across the sea: To reach Saaremaa, the largest of all the Estonian islands, it is necessary first to cross Muhu, where the ferry from Virtsu on the mainland docks. Estonia's third largest island, Muhu is only 78 sq. miles (201 sq. km) and, along with about 500 smaller islands, belongs to the greater Saaremaa County. It hasn't developed any tourist trade of its own, and its accommodation is strictly for permanent and summer-long residents, but it does have at least one sight worth stopping to see.

The area around the **Koguva Outdoor Museum** is thought to have been settled back in the late Iron Age, but this still-inhabited fishing village was first documented in 1532. Of the 105 buildings still standing, parts of three date from the early and mid-18th century, making it the oldest preserved conglomerate of peasant architecture on the islands.

Koguva is not far from the **causeway** that leads to Saaremaa. It is a beautiful road, and terribly romantic. The water on either side is filled by a beckoning green carpet of swaying reeds. In spring, it changes to white as thousands of swans come here to mate.

Saaremaa is, at some 1,030 sq. miles (2,668 sq. km), a spacious, quiet and

unassuming place. Much of its land has been cultivated, and the simple island roads are laced by field after field of livestock grazing and wheat, interrupted only by patches of thick forest. Industry is at a minimum, and those inhabitants who aren't at work on the land tend to be connected to the sea.

There is only one town of real consequence, **Kuressaare** on the south side of the island, where 17,000 of Saaremaa County's 41,000 inhabitants live. Kuressaare is said to have been particularly popular with party officials during the Soviet regime (this might perhaps explain how the town received the funds for the renovation of its centre), and it certainly is extremely handsome. Indeed, if it weren't so unselfconscious – and low on tourists – it would be a classic tourist trap.

Most of the buildings in the centre are gems of late 18th – early 19th-century neoclassicism, with pretty wooden houses and gardens mixed in beside them. Side streets reveal an ancient hand-pump for water or a freshly painted home with a paint-can tied proudly to its wooden gate. On Kaevu Street, an old **windmill** has been transformed into the posh **Veski bar and restaurant**.

Activity focuses around the triangular plaza where Tallinna Street turns into Lossi Street. At this junction are the **market**, the **administrative halls** and, after 9pm, the main spot for local youths to see and be seen. The yellow **Town Hall** (1654–70) lies along the hypotenuse of this triangle, its entrance protected by stone lions. To its left, an 18th-century fire station of burnt-brown wood has a new lease of life as a **tourist information centre**.

Opposite it is the **Weigh House** (1663), with a stepped gable. Now a dingy food store, the House encloses one side of the tiny **Market Square** where, in addition to jars of gooseberries in season and packets of foreign cigarettes, you will find a range of distinctively patterned, hand-made woollen sweaters and mittens for sale. Sometimes there will also be a table or two piled high with slippery black

Kuressaare, capital of Saaremaa.

Koguva Farm Village in Muhu.

mounds of the expensive Saaremaa speciality, eel. Some claim that it was this and the locally brewed beer, considered by many to be the finest in Estonia, that made Kuressaare so popular with Soviet party officials.

A second, smaller piazza, lies a few steps down Lossi Street. This has the **County Seat** and a **Monument for the Fallen in the War of Liberation**. This is actually the third such monument erected here; twice the Soviets tore it down only for the locals to re-erect it.

Continuing down Lossi from here will take you past the **Apostolic Orthodox St Nicholas church** (1790). Its fancy front gate tied with large silver-painted bows is unmistakable and its white exterior is topped with rounded green spires. The interior echoes this colour scheme, and treads between neoclassical and Byzantine styles.

Kuressaare's main tourist attraction and its original *raison d'être* is at the end of the street. The **Kuressaare Episcopal Castle** was built as the bishop of Oesel-Wiek's foothold on Saaremaa,

and the earliest record of its existence dates back to 1384. It is the only entirely preserved medieval stone castle in all of the Baltic nations.

Ringed by a large and beautiful public **park**, a moat and imposing bastions erected during the mid-17th century, the castle is in the unyielding, geometric, late-Gothic style, made of white-grey dolomite quarried in Saaremaa. Each corner is crowned by a tower with an orange turret and at the heart of the castle is a tiny, symmetrical courtyard.

From the courtyard, stone steps lead down to basement rooms coated with soot and up to a narrow, vaulted cloister. The former refectory lies on the west, and to the north are the austere former living quarters of the bishop. Ten elaborate wooden epitaphs from the 17th century represent coats of arms of noblemen in Saaremaa and their individual occupations. One has oars, another tools, a third stags and arrows.

Climbing the towers is worthwhile but requires fortitude; the watch-tower in the southeast corner of the convent

building is connected by a drawbridge suspended 30 ft (9 metres) above the ground, and the defence tower is honeycombed with stone stairways.

Some upper rooms have been devoted to exhibition halls of modern Estonian art, and a few house the **Saaremaa Regional Museum**. This rich collection traces the inhabitants of Saaremaa from the 4th millennium BC and has the oldest preserved wooden sculpture in Estonia: "Seated Madonna with the Infant" (1280–90). The labelling is in Estonian and Russian, but there are lengthy plaques in English.

From the castle, it is a pleasant walk down to the small **harbour** and the dilapidated wooden building that served as a local yacht club during the years of the Estonian republic. In the 1970s this was a favourite place for bathing. Swimmers now must head south of the town to the **Mandjala-Järve beach**.

Island road trip: Other spots to visit in Kuressaare include the still-functioning **Sanatorium**, specialising in baths of curative sea mud since 1876 – although the smell of the mud is so evil it is hard to imagine anyone's health could be improved by soaking in it – and the **Linnakodaniku museum**, exhibiting early-20th-century objects from the island. But be sure to leave time to tour the rest of the island.

Travelling to **Kihelkonna** in the west, and following the coast up to **Leisi** in the north, then back south to Kuressaare will take you past many of Saaremaa's interesting sites. First stop is the **Mihkli Farm Museum**, near the town of Viki. Although small, this open-air museum exactly preserves a farm typical to western Saaremaa. The main dwelling house (1834) stands with most of the other buildings in a circle enclosing a yard and a quaint little flower garden. Most of the roofs are covered with reed, and the walls are of dolomite or wood. Original objects from the farmstead include household equipment cut with the Mihkli family emblem.

Turning at Kihelkonna north towards **Mustjala**, you will first catch a glimpse of the pointed red bell-tower of the

Island fishermen.

medieval **Kihelkonna church** and then the ancient, weathered-grey **Pidula watermill**. From here it is a short drive to the **Panga Scarp**.

This steep limestone scarp is one of the highest points on the island and one of the loveliest. The water below is almost olive green but so clear you can easily make out the thousands of pebbles that line the sea floor. In the distance, the horizon stretches blue and seemingly endlessly, except for the tiny shadow of Hiiumaa Island. In summer the sound of crickets fills the air.

Unsurprisingly, this very magical place has played a central role in island superstitions. In pre-Christian times, locals would throw one baby boy, born the winter before, off the cliff into the water every spring; this was an offering to the Sea God with the prayer that he send back a lot of fish. In later times, they threw a ram instead.

Island brides have continued the long-established tradition of scarp pitching to this day. On the eve of their wedding they often write their maiden name on a piece of paper, put it into a bottle and toss it off the cliff.

Turning east from here takes you to **Leisi**, an attractive rural town, from where you will turn south. A few miles down the road are the **Angla windmills**. In the mid-19th century, there were about 800 windmills on Saaremaa. Only a small proportion have survived, but at Angla there are still five left, sticking up suddenly on a slight swell amid wind-swept wheat fields.

Nestled behind a moss-covered stone wall on a sloping lawn across from fields of cattle a mile (2km) from here is one of Saaremaa's greatest treasures: the 14th-century **Karja church**. Saaremaa is packed with some of the earliest churches in the Baltics but no other has such marvellous stone sculptures still intact.

These sculptures tell a thousand tales. A relief on the first left buttress upon entering, for example, depicts village life. A woman listens to another with a pig on her back, symbolising gossip, while the man beside her has a rose

behind his ear, representing silence. This is on the northern and thus colder side of the church, the side where the women sat because they were considered to be stronger. St Katherine of Alexandria, to whom the church is dedicated, is carved into the northern arch before the altar. This 14th-century beauty, the legend goes, was wooed by King Maxentius of Egypt, although he was already married. She refused him and, enraged, he had her arrested and torn to pieces. The sculpture shows her with Maxentius's wife on her left, clinging to her skirt, St Peter on her right and the evil king crushed beneath her feet.

Directly opposite is St Nicholas, the protector of seamen and on his left are three village girls who were too poor to marry until he became their benefactor.

Painted on to the ceiling above the altar is an interesting table of Christian and pagan marks: the Star of Bethlehem and the symbol of Unity, both drawn with endless lines; the three-legged symbol of the sun; the "leg" devil; and two pentagons, symbols of gloom, which locals gleefully point out were also symbols of the Soviet Union.

The church still holds services two Sundays a month. At other times, except Mondays and Tuesdays, an old woman caretaker will unlock the doors with a big metal key and let you in.

If you head south again, turning right at the **Liiva-Putla** fork, you will reach the tiny hamlet of **Kaarma**, site of another medieval church. Work began on **Kaarma church** in the latter half of the 13th century but it was rearranged over subsequent centuries and is strikingly large. Its artefacts are more varied than those of Karja. The christening stone, for example, dates from the 13th century, the wooden "Joseph" supporting the pulpit is from around 1450, and the elaborate Renaissance pulpit was finished in 1645. Current restoration work has exposed fragments of early mural painting.

Other 13th and 14th-century churches in the area worth visiting include **Valjala church** and **Püha church** situated east of Kuressaare. The latter most clearly

Left, crab fisherman. Right, windmill keeper.

shows how these churches were built not just to be religious centres but also to serve as defensive strongholds.

If you turn left at the Liiva-Putla fork, you reach a much older landmark. The **Kaali meteoric craters** are not beautiful – the largest one, behind the Kaali Elementary School, is referred to as **Lake Kaali** and it looks like a big opaque green puddle – but it is remarkable to think that the bowl surrounding it was carved out by part of a 1,000-ton meteor that hit the earth here nearly 3,000 years ago. Eight smaller craters, made from other chips of the meteor, dot the woods surrounding it.

A wilder cousin: For spots of natural beauty, **Hiiumaa Island** is perhaps more rewarding. At 382 sq. miles (989 sq. km), it is Estonia's second largest island but only has 11,000 inhabitants, 4,000 of them in the capital of **Kärdla** on the north coast. There is virtually no settlement in its heart where there is a peat moor (peat bogs growing directly on sand) and swamp – and almost all agriculture focuses on the southern and western edge. Some yet to be cultivated areas in the south contain another natural oddity, "wooded meadows", and the rest of the island is overwhelmed by pines and junipers. There are so few cars on the road that inhabitants typically drive on either the left or right according to whim. Less than 5 percent of the population is non-Estonian; during the Soviet regime, it was the only area in Estonia without a single Russian-language school.

Fishing is the most important industry, although until the late 1980s barbed-wire was wrapped along the shore from Kärdla in the north to **Emmaste** in the far south. The coast is also notoriously treacherous to approach because of the shallow waters of endless shoals and rocks. This means that you have to walk out quite a way over pebbles simply to get your stomach wet, but unlike the coastal waters of most of Estonia, these are clean enough to swim in.

The eastern harbour of **Heltermaa** has been slightly dug out, and it is to here that the ferry from the mainland, at

Family home, Saaremaa.

Rohuküla by Haapsalu, arrives. Just inland is the historical hamlet of **Suuremõisa**. Hiiumaa once had around 25 stately 16th- to 19th-century manor houses, but most now have either been destroyed or have irreparably deteriorated. The **Suuremõisa manor** is one exception. Built by a Swedish family called Stenbock in 1772, then bought in 1790 by O.R.L. v. Ungern-Sternberg – for decades Hiiumaa's richest and most powerful landowner – this manor still has its main building, stable master's home and stables, several outbuildings and cellars, and expansive front and back lawns. Inside the main building are 64 rooms, some with original painted ceilings and ceramic fireplaces. The bottom floor is currently used for aerobics classes and the local "cinema", and the top floor houses an agricultural school. Under the trees at the back there are grave stones for the family's much-feared guard dogs.

Just down the road is **Püha church**. First built of wood in the mid-13th century, then replaced with stone in 1770, its tall white bell-tower, topped by a hexagonal brown roof, has been extended three times since then. Turned into a cellar by the Soviets, the church resumed offering services on Christmas Eve 1990.

On its south side stands a rather squat white chapel containing the tomb of Ebba Margarethe Gräfin Stenbock, Suuremõisa manor's first owner. On its north side, strewn amid alders, are a tumble of other old graves. Around the northeast corner is a log inset in the church wall; this is the spot through which the priest used to hand out bread to the poor and needy.

At **Hagaste** – 3 pebbly miles (5 km) down the road – island authorities have assembled a traditional Hiiumaa farmstead. The yard is surrounded by the slanting basketweave (*korendusaed*) fence particular to both Hiiumaa and Saaremaa. A small windmill (1925) stands in the foreground; the resident caretaker will demonstrate how it works. His home is an old storage-hut, built during the Swedish period and roofed

Farmer's daughter, Hiiumaa.

with stones. There is also an apiary, an old sauna and a *paargu*, an outdoor kitchen to be used in summer that looks like a teepee built of stout tree branches.

Back up the coast in the main town of Kärdla, **the Rannapaargu Café**, in front of the grassy **Kärdla Beach**, has been named after this same special type of kitchen. To reach the café, you must walk down Lubjaahju Street past yet another Hiiumaa peculiarity, the giant swing. Found in villages all over the island, the swings are the traditional meeting places for young people, and they are particularly busy on Midsummer's Eve.

Some of Hiiumaa's most interesting structures are the lighthouses that twinkle along the shore. The most remarkable is the **Kõpu Lighthouse**, halfway out along the thickly forested **Kõpu peninsula**, on the windswept western wing of the island. This soaring four-cornered and red-crested white lighthouse looks like a cross between a space rocket and a pyramid. First lit in 1531, it is considered to be the third oldest con-tinuously operating lighthouse in the world. Be careful not to bump your head climbing up the old stairway. There is wonderful view from the top; the world below spreads into a sea of dark-green pine and endless water.

One of the few patches of cultivated land is at nearby **Ulendi Village**, a modest collection of steep-roofed, wooden houses, farm plots and weather-beaten outbuildings. The sheep pasture immediately on the right upon entering the settlement contains a **burial site** dating from 4000 BC.

Artists' retreat: Understandably, many of Estonia's best-known artists and writers keep summer retreats on Hiiumaa; conductor Eri Klas, for example, has his on Kõpu. But the most popular spot for summer cottages is **Kassari**, just southwest of Heltermaa.

Kassari is one of between 200 – 400 islands that cling to the coast of Hiiumaa (the number of islands depends on the water level). But it curves in so close to the shore by the town of **Kaina** that it has been incorporated into the larger

island with two short bridges. The bay between them, **Kainu Bay**, used to be rich in curative sea mud but it is now too polluted. Nevertheless, birds like it, including golden eagles and other rare species. You may even see an eagle or two flying over the road. These birds, in turn – along with the island breezes and the sea – are responsible for the richness of flora all over Hiiumaa. In fact, the island has about 975 different species of plant, some of them, such as the orchids, also quite rare.

Kassari, however, is richest in junipers, whose berries and bark might be called the island staple. Still used variously – the wood for butter knives that keep butter from turning rancid; the branches for sauna switches to perk up the kidney; the berries for a vodka spice, a source of vitamin C and other medicinal purposes – this scraggy dark bush has even been wrangled into furniture.

Junipers crowd the pebbly projection of **Saaretirp** with special determination. This mile-long promontory is a favourite place to picnic or ponder for

the Kassari residents. Like many beauty spots, Saaretirp has several local legends. Leiger, the island hero and a very big man, is said to have built it one summer as a bridge for Suur Toll (Saaremaa's hero and also a giant) to come to eat apples with him the following autumn. Accordingly, it stretches out south towards Saaremaa, ever narrowing as more and more land slips under the sea. At the end of the headland nothing remains but a needle point and a large heap of stones: if you find a pebble with a hole in it, make a wish and place it on the pile, and your wish should come true.

Kassari's sheltered position makes the water warm, and beside it the apples crop early. The last owner of the former **Kassari manor house**, Baron Edvard Stackelberg, had an especially large apple orchard, though neither it nor his home still remains. But the small servants' house directly opposite where it stood is in good shape and houses the **Hiiumaa Koduloomuuseum** of local culture. The museum contains a huge light reflector from the 19th-century Tahkuna lighthouse, maps of island history and traditional fishing tools.

Down one more pebble-laden lane is the **Kassari chapel**, the only stone chapel still surviving in Estonia with a roof of thatched reed. Carefully restored in 1990, it has been kept without electricity and is illuminated by a simple central candelabra and candles burned into the end of each old blue pew. The walls are decorated only with ancient oak-leaf wreaths, taken from funerals in the surrounding graveyard.

A graveyard spills out around the church, darkened by shivering trees. Baron Stackelberg's is next to a swineherd's, to show that in front of God all people are equal.

One final church to note on Hiiumaa just inland from Kassari is the **Kaina Kirik**, built between 1492 and 1515. Although heavily bombed during World War II, it is still a very moving spot with wind rushing through the limestone shell and over the old tombs set directly into its floor. During the summer a song festival is held here.

Left, typical island architecture, Sore farm museum, Hiiumaa. Right, Saaretirp, where Hiiumaa fades into the sea.

202

LATVIA

The main highway of the Baltics has been the 640-mile (1,030-km) River Daugava. "Its banks are silver and its bed is gold," said Ivan the Terrible, who failed to get his hands on it. Others were more successful, starting with the German crusaders who arrived in Riga, near the river's estuary, which they made their base for the conquest of the Baltic peoples. Today, Riga is the most exciting city in the Baltics. It is rich with the architecture of the Hansa merchants, with their gabled homes and store-houses dating back to the 15th century. In the expanded 19th-century city there are exquisite art nouveau buildings, many designed by Mikhail Eisenstein, the father of Sergei Eisenstein, who was also born here.

With a population of a million, Riga seems too large for its own country, which has a total population of around two-and-a-half million. Riga and Latvia's industrialisation has been accompanied by Russian immigration. They are in the majority in its five largest towns, and Riga's seaside, Jūrmala, the "Baltic Riviera", attracted a large number of retired Soviet officers.

A secondary highway is the River Gauja, which is the centre of a fine national park. To the east are the more remote blue-lake lands of Latgale, which fell into Catholic hands under Polish rule. To the west is Kurzeme, the former territory of the Lutheran Duchy of Courland, where tall pines became masts in Duke Jēkabs's shipyards at Ventspils. Too grand for a duke, but lacking the power of a king, he built an empire with toeholds in the Caribbean and in Africa. War has erased most signs of the Duke's presence here.

One building belonging to a Courland duke which has survived is Rundāle palace, the most spectacular piece of civic architecture in the Baltics. It was built by Rastrelli, architect of the Winter Palace in St Petersburg, for Johannes Ernst Birons, a lover of the empress Anna Ivanovna and briefly regent of Russia.

The soul of Latvia and the Latvians lies in the countryside among its magic oaks and ancient hill forts. To find these places, visitors should head for Lāčplēsis on the banks of the Daugava, where they can see the hero's magic belt, woven with symbols, that can foretell the future of the whole nation.

Preceding pages: Eisenstein facade, Elisabetes Street, Riga; birch forest; Jūrmala beach. Left, sweet peas and gypsophila, Riga market.

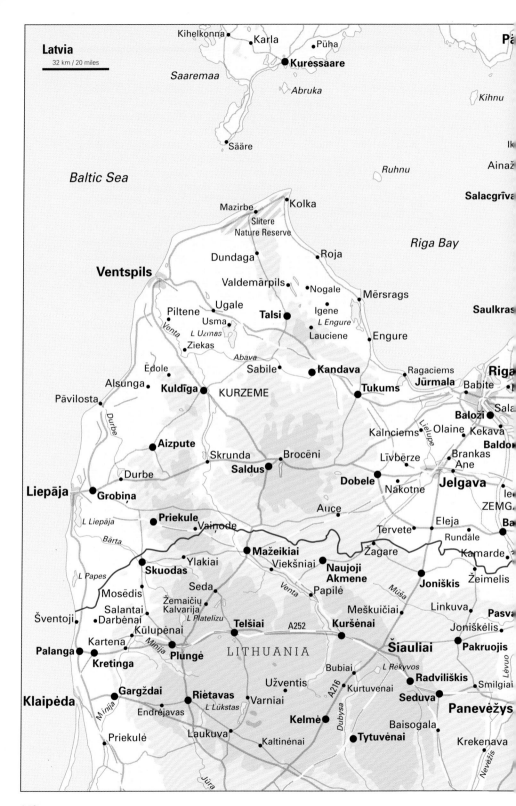

Latvia

32 km / 20 miles

Kihelkonna• •Karla •Püha

●Kuressaare

Saaremaa

◌\Abruka

Kihnu

Baltic Sea

◌Sääre

Ik

Ruhnu

Ainaž

Ruhnu

Salacgrīva

Mazirbe• •Kolka

Slitere
Nature Reserve

Riga Bay

Dundaga•

•Roja

Ventspils

Valdemārpils•

•Nogale

Mērsrags

Piltene• Ugale
Usma•

Talsi●

Igene
L Engure

Saulkras

Venta

L Uzmas

Ziekas

Lauciene

•Engure

Abava

Ēdole

Sabile•

Kandava

Ragaciems

Rīga

Alsunga•

Kuldīga●

KURZEME

Tukums

Jūrmala Babite

Pāvilosta•

Durbe

Baloži

Sal

●Aizpute

Skrunda•

•Brocēni

Kalnciems•

Olaine• Kekava

Baldo

Durbe•

Saldus●

Līvbērze•

Brankas
Ane

Liepāja

Grobiņa

Dobele

Nakotne

Jelgava

L Liepāja

Priekule

•Vaiņode

Auce•

Eleja•

Tervete•

ZEMG

Bārta

Mažeikiai

Žagare•

Rundāle

Ba

L Papes

Skuodas

Ylakiai•

Viekšniai•

**Naujoji
Akmene**

Kamarde

Mosēdis•

Seda•

Joniškis

Žeimelis

Šventoji•

Salantai•
•Darbėnai

Žemaičių
Kalvarija

Venta

Papilė•

Mūša

Meškuičiai•

Linkuva•

Pasv

Kūlupėnai

L Platelizu

Telšiai•

A252

Kuršėnai

Joniškėlis•

Kartena•

Minija

Šiauliai

Pakruojis

Palanga●

Kretinga

Plungė•

LITHUANIA

Bubiai•

L Rēkyvos

Lėvuo

Radviliškis

Smilgiai

Gargždai

Riėtavas

Užventis•

A216

Kurtuvėnai•

Seduva

Klaipėda

Minija

L Lūkstas

•Varniai

Panevėžys

Endrėjavas•

Kelmė●

Dubysa

Baisogala•

Priekulė•

Laukuva•

•Kaltinėnai

Tytuvėnai

Krekenava

Jūra

Nevėžis

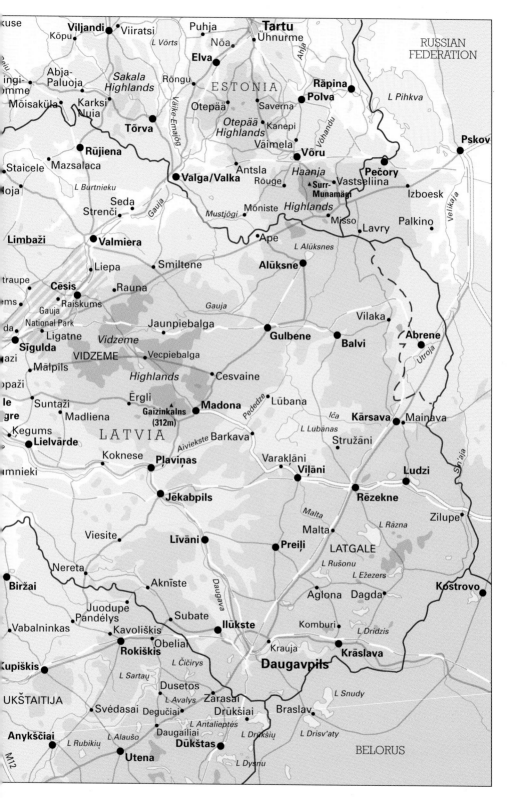

kuse
Viljandi Viiratsi Puhja **Tartu**
Kõpu L Võrts Nõa Ühnurme
Elva
RUSSIAN
FEDERATION

ingi- Abja-
omme Paluoja *Sakala* Rõngu E S T O N I A **Räpina** L Pihkva
Môisaküla *Highlands* Otepää Saverna **Polva**
Karksi
Nuia
Tõrva *Otepää* Kanepi
Highlands Vāimela **Pskov**
Rūjiena Võru

Staicele Mazsalaca Antsla **Pečory**
L Burtnieku Valga/Valka Rõuge *Haanja* **Surr- Vastseliina**
oja Seda **Munamägi** Izboesk
Strenči Mõniste *Highlands* Misso
Mustjõgi Lavry Palkino
Limbaži **Valmiera** Ape L Alüksnes

Liepa Smiltene **Alüksne**
traupe **Cēsis** Rauna
ms Raiskums *Gauja*
Gauja Vilaka
da National Park **Abrene**
Ligatne *Vidzeme* **Gulbene** **Balvi**
Sīgulda VIDZEME Vecpiebalga
azi Mālpils
paži *Highlands* Cesvaine
le Ērgli
gre Suntaži ▲ **Madona** Lūbana Iča **Kārsava** Mainava
Madliena Gaizinkalns L Lubānas
Ķegums (312m) Stružāni
Lielvārde L A T V I A Aiviekste Barkava
Koknese Varakļāni
imnieki **Pļaviņas** **Viļāni** **Ludzi**

Jēkabpils **Rēzekne**
Malta Zilupe
Viesite Malta L Räzna
Līvāni **Preiļi** LATGALE
Nereta L Rušonu
L Ežezers
Biržai Aknīste Agłona Dagda **Kostrovo**
Juodupe
Pandėlys Subate Komburi L Dridzis
Vabalninkas Kavoliškis **Ilūkste**
Obelia Krauja **Krāslava**
Rokiškis
upiškis L Čičirys **Daugavpils**
L Sartai
Dusetos L Snudy
UKŠTAITIJA Zārasai
Svėdasai Degučiai Drūkšiai Braslav
L Avalys
L Antalieptės
Anykščiai L Alaušo Daugailiai L Drūkšiu L Drisv'aty
L Rubikiu **Dūkštas**
Utena L Dysnu BELORUS

LATVIA: A SHORT HISTORY

When Latvian independence was self-proclaimed in 1918, the country had to be assembled like a jigsaw puzzle out of territory inhabited by Lett-speakers. This amounted to the southern half of what had previously been Livonia together with Latgale and the Duchy of Courland. To complicate matters, the city of Riga, Latvia's capital, had hitherto been for all practical purposes an independent city-state with an overwhelmingly foreign population. It was a German city from the day the crusaders landed, and it had remained a predominantly German city through all the vagaries of Polish, Swedish and Russian rule. At the outbreak of World War I, the non-Latvian element was as high as 90 percent.

The Latvians managed to restore themselves to a majority of something like 75 percent over the country as a whole between the world wars, but independence was then snuffed out by Soviet annexation. The combined effect of mass deportations and Russian immigration inexorably reversed the trend, so that by 1989 the Latvians were reduced to the barest majority of 52 percent. Against the backdrop of massive impending change in Eastern Europe and the Soviet Union, Latvians knew they were in a private race against time. It had been the Kremlin's intention all along to obliterate the 1918 frontiers so that Latvia, like Estonia and Lithuania, was in effect an unbroken extension of Russia itself. The struggle which ensued was a replay of events leading up to World War I, the reincarnation of the land of the Latvians.

Beginnings: Curious events had led to the arrival of the German crusaders in 1200. Almost 1,000 years after Christianity had been adopted as the official religion in Armenia and then Rome, it had still not reached the eastern shores of the Baltic, and there was rather a rush among the Pope and various Christian princes to make up for lost time.

To this end, a number of missionary monks were despatched. The area around the

mouth of the River Daugava fell to a certain Meinhard of Bremen. He arrived in 1180 and persuaded Latvians to be baptised in the river in such satisfactory numbers that he was made a bishop. The real test came when he informed his converts that the price of salvation was the payment of a tithe. They not only abandoned the faith en masse but put the good bishop in fear of his life. He implored Pope Clement III to send help.

The Pope had other problems. The crusade in the Holy Land had gone disastrously

wrong and large numbers of crusaders, expelled from their strongholds, were homeless. Among these were the Knights of the Sword under Bishop Albrecht von Buxhoerden and they were dispatched to the Daugava where they went about their business with Teutonic efficiency. "All the places and roads were red with blood," wrote a chronicler of the Knights of the Sword.

Almost at once, Riga had a defensive wall, a fortress and at least one church. By 1211, Bishop Albrecht was ready to start building a cathedral. Word was sent to the Pope that the Daugava mission had been accomplished and that a contingent of knights was

Left, the Reformation arrives in Riga, as shown by a stained-glass window in the Dom. Right, a 12th-century knight of the Livonian Order.

being sent north – to Estonia – where the Danes were experiencing similar difficulties with truculent pagans.

The Knights of the Sword were in due course amalgamated with other orders; these came to be known collectively as the Teutonic Order. Having discharged their divine duties, they tackled the secular task of creating a city-state for themselves with immense zeal. They imported fellow Germans not merely to build the city and port but also to organise agriculture. The Latvians were excluded from the process except as labourers.

The military power of the Teutonic Order was eclipsed in the 15th century, but by then the German economic and land-owning oli-

garchy was thoroughly entrenched in Latvia. It was safe as long as Russia was kept out of contention by the Mongol empire. With the demise of the latter, however, an alarming threat materialised in the person of Ivan the Terrible. The only recourse was to seek the protection of Poland-Lithuania, and then there was a price to be paid. Lutheranism had made inroads in Latvia under the German influence and Poland was uncompromisingly Catholic. The Jesuits were to be given a licence to bring Latvians back into the fold.

The way the Jesuits went about their task revived memories of the Teutonic Order, and this was coupled with a rigid Polish feudal order harder on the peasants than anything previously experienced. The country was sharply divided on the desirability of Polish protection. Riga profited enormously by being elevated to the role of Poland's principal port, so the merchants had no complaints. The landed gentry and the peasants, however, were paying the price and became increasingly desperate for protection against the protectors. Protestant Sweden seemed the most likely candidate. The resulting Swedish-Polish war saw the Swedes repulsed but Latvia was left a wreck. It was followed by the bitter winter of 1601 in which 40,000 peasants died from hunger and cold.

Gustavus Adolphus tried to topple the ruling order again 20 years later and this time a Poland much weakened by events elsewhere succumbed. The Swedes rebuilt Riga castle, added barracks outside the Swedish Gate and built castles on the River Daugava. Poland remained in charge of Latgale in the east and, in the south and west, the Duchy of Courland and Semigallia. In 1561 this small slice of Latvia had belonged to Gotthard Kettlers, the last Grand Master of the Teutonic Order, who had submitted to Poland, and had been granted a degree of independence. Its importance grew under Duke Jēkabs, who became a prince of the Holy Roman Empire.

A duke's empire: Though Protestant, the Kettlers had been friends of the English Stuart kings and Jēkabs (James) had been named after his godfather, James I. He had been a great shipbuilder, and at Ventspils he built an impressive navy, turning out 24 men-of-war for France and 62 for Britain. With unbounded ambition he acquired territory for the duchy in the Gambia and Tobago and he devoted much of his long rule to attempting to colonise them.

The duchy brought a degree of stability to the south of the country. In the north there had been few tears when the Jesuits were sent packing by the Swedes. The barons, however, were horrified when their estates were expropriated and given to the Swedish aristocracy. Hoping to be third time lucky, they looked again for a more sympathetic protector: their choice this time was Russia.

The Great Northern War of Sweden versus Russia was a titanic struggle which swept across the entire breadth of Europe. In and around Latvia, the Swedish crown sought to finance the war by taking 80 percent of the estates, dispossessing both the Swedish barons, who had only just been given them, as well as the remaining Germans. These lands were squeezed for all they were worth and reached the point where they were providing the Swedish crown with more revenue than all other sources put together. Latvia then produced someone who proposed to take matters into his own hands: Johan Reinhold von Patkul.

Patkul, a German land-owner, sent word to Charles XII that the Teutonic Knights had conquered Latvia and converted it to Christianity long before he or his ancestors came

sion of Latvia. Patkul was taken aback, on arriving in Moscow in September 1699, to find that the Swedish ambassador had just negotiated a new 30-year peace treaty with Peter the Great. His fears were allayed when he noticed that Peter did not seal the agreement with a kiss on the Cross. Peter had got wind of Patkul's proposal and thought it was excellent, but he wanted to modify the division of the spoils. Russia would take Estonia, Augustus could have the rest of Livonia, and Denmark could help itself to what was left, including Sweden itself.

Augustus launched the scheme in 1700 with an invasion that got as far as Riga before it was halted. Peter was called on for help,

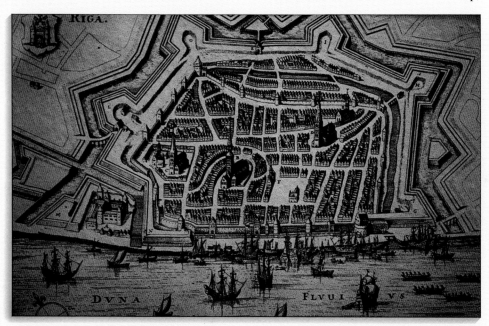

on the scene. Therefore, the descendants of those knights, among whom he numbered himself, had an inexpungable right to rule. Charles's reply to this tirade was to sentence Patkul to death. He specified that both his head and right hand should be cut off.

With this sentence hanging over him, Patkul approached Augustus II, the odious Elector of Saxony, who prevailed upon him to include Russia in his scheme in return for a promise that there would be none of the "usual barbarities" in the event of an inva-

Left, Jēkabs Kettlers, the famous Duke of Courland. Above, Riga in the 6th century.

but his forces were tied down at Narva in Estonia. In the event, the Russians suffered a shock defeat at Narva and the victorious Charles turned his attention on Augustus. The Elector of Saxony was in no position to resist, and the terms of his surrender included handing over the wretched Patkul. The earlier death sentence still stood, but Charles specified an amendment. Patkul would still have to lose his head but he could keep his right hand. Instead, the beheading was to be preceded by torture.

Sweden was not destined to hold on to Latvia or its neighbours for much longer. Peter the Great's ultimate victory in his duel with Charles XII opened the way to realising his dream of Russian control of the Eastern Baltic. By then he had another, purely personal, interest in the region. Some years earlier, he had been struck by a woman called Martha who had arrived at court on the arm of first one and then another of his ministers, the second being Prince Menshikov. She was a waitress, the daughter of a Lithuanian slave, who had been employed by a Protestant pastor in Latvia before marrying a Swedish army officer. The marriage had failed and Martha was pursuing other interests among the Russian nobility.

Menshikov loyally relinquished the lovely Martha and she became Peter's mis- indigenous culture in order to break out of a rigidly-tiered system. The result was that the Lett language and everything that went with it was pushed farther and farther into rural backwaters. As these conditions applied for seven centuries, it is amazing that there was anything left to rescue in 1918.

Catherine I died after a reign of only two years, but the Latvian connection with the Russian crown was renewed when Peter's niece Anna acceded to the throne. While Catherine was undoubtedly fast, Anna was downright debauched. More to the point, she was the dowager Duchess of Courland, and she brought German Balts from Jelgava, Riga and elsewhere to the Russian court en

tress. On embracing the Orthodox faith, she changed her name to Catherine and after eight years of companionship he married her. Peter changed the law to allow him personally to crown her Empress in 1724.

On Peter's death, Catherine was proclaimed empress in her own right. The accession to the Russian throne of a Latvian peasant was all the more extraordinary because there was practically no social or economic mobility in Latvia: ethnic Latvians weren't even allowed to own property in their own capital. Martha's change of name and religion is an indication of the way in which ambitious Latvians had to leave behind the masse. Jelgava, then called Mitau, was the capital of Courland. Anna's father-in-law was Duke Jēkabs's son, and he had introduced French opera and ballet into its social milieu. Anna granted the first Russian constitution in Jelgava in 1731, but it was her chamberlain and lover, Johannes Ernst Birons, who has left the greatest mark. An opportunist and a scoundrel, he became the Duke of Courland after Anna's husband died and was a power behind the throne. He managed to find enough money to bring in Bartolomeo Rastrelli, architect of St Petersburg's Winter Palace, to build him the sumptuous palace at Rundāle. He was also responsible for sending some 20,000 to Siberia. When Anna died he became Regent of Russia, but was eventually himself sent to Siberia for a brief term of banishment.

The German Balts in Russia's courts used their influence to restore the port of Riga after the depredations of the Russo-Swedish wars. This care did not extend to other parts of the country. They ignored a countryside that was devastated and stricken by plague. It was said that, Riga apart, Latvia was ruled by wolves for a century afterwards.

Neglect and ghastly conditions led in 1802 to a peasant uprising led by "Poor Conrad" who, reflecting the revolutionary mood in France, was called "the Lettish Bonaparte".

Sweden, to dislodge it. To rebellious 19th-century peasants, the Lutheran church was a symbol of German domination. The Russian Orthodox church hastened to exploit anti-Lutheran feelings. The Orthodox catechism was translated into Lettish and given away free in large numbers. German land-owners retaliated by refusing to make any more land available for Orthodox churches. German-Russian rivalry took on a life of its own, and the role of the German Balts sparked a furious row between Tsar Alexander III and Bismarck. Lutheran pastors were locked up or sent to Siberia, and as many as 30,000 of their flock were formally advised that they were henceforth Orthodox.

The revolt was put down ruthlessly and Poor Conrad died an excruciating death. There was a repetition in 1840, with the peasants directing their fury at the Lutheran church.

Four centuries after the demise of the Teutonic Order, the Latvian establishment was still dominated by German aristocrats and burghers. The country had subsequently been ruled by Poland, Sweden and Russia, but the old German system had somehow endured in spite of the efforts, particularly by

Left, the 1905 Revolution breaks out in Latvia. **Above**, Valdemārs (second left) and other key figures of Latvia's National Awakening.

The Latvian peasant derived some benefits as the region was drawn into the Russian economic sphere to counteract German influence. The Russian railways were extended to the Baltic coast, and Riga handled a large share of Russia's trade. At the same time there was a remarkable sprouting of literary activity in Lett. The rich Germans held on to their positions, but the lower rungs had to make room for Latvians. All of this increased Latvian political awareness, but satisfaction at overcoming the old German obstacles did not necessarily make organisations like the Young Letts pro-Russian. Political sympathies on the workshop floor in Riga were more inclined towards Karl Marx.

The Baltic Revolution of 1905, which coincided with the St Petersburg uprising, was aimed with equal venom at everything German and Russian. Order was restored in Riga only by the intervention of the Imperial Guard. The tsar had no qualms about letting the outraged German barons take their revenge, and when they had done so he rewarded them with concessions, such as granting permission to re-open five German public schools. One way or another, the German element clung on and at the onset of World War I, the population of Riga was still at least 50 percent Baltic-German.

The wounds of the rebellion had not yet healed when World War I broke out. The country was at first occupied by a defensive Russian army. In 1915, and not without Russian misgivings, the Latvians were permitted to raise a national army. When the Russians were withdrew in confusion after the Bolshevik revolution, the Latvians put up a spirited defence of Riga against the advancing Germans at the cost of some 32,000 casualties. When the Germans took Riga, it was not the prize they were hoping for. The port was inactive, the machinery having been stripped and shipped to Russia.

A secret national organisation bent on Latvian independence was formed within the first months of German occupation and was in contact with refugees in Russia and exiles who had fled after the 1905 rebellion. Events took a curious turn in April 1918 when the tottering German emperor, of all people, was offered the Baltic crown. Moreover, he accepted. The Latvian nationalists' argument was that some kind of autonomy would be possible as part of the German empire, whereas no Russian party would countenance any degree of independence.

The Allied victory in November 1918 simplified matters. A state council simply proclaimed independence and offered citizenship to all residents apart from Bolsheviks and German Unionists. The fly in the ointment was that 45,000 German troops still occupied Riga and there were as many again scattered about the rest of the country. When they withdrew, the Bolsheviks arrived and there was no organised force to stop them. They declared Latvia a Soviet republic. The situation was rescued by Estonia which drove the Bolsheviks off its soil and then crossed the border to help the Latvians do likewise.

Independent Latvia was in a sorry state. The population was a third below pre-war levels, industrial output was virtually nil, and many children had never been to school. A land reform programme expropriated the German baronial estates and redistributed them in parcels to Latvian peasants.

The Bolsheviks professed an end to tsarist imperialism, but in reality they were as determined as Peter the Great had ever been to hold on to the Baltic coast. To make matters worse, Latvia almost went to war with its erstwhile ally Estonia over title to the border town of Valka.

Hanging by a thread, independent Latvia nevertheless went ahead. Agrarian reform was supplemented by a take-over of industry and commerce, or what was left of them. The Latvian language was of course given official status, and there was a general revival of Latvian culture. Perhaps the most significant statistics were the changing population ratios. By 1939, Latvians were in a commanding majority, as high as 75 percent.

Progress came to a jarring halt in 1939. The Bolshevik undertaking to respect the independence of the Baltic states "voluntarily and for ever" vanished with the

Nazi-Soviet Pact of 1939. A Soviet invasion was followed by annexation, although not one that was ever recognised by the Western powers. The Nazi-Soviet Pact was short-lived, and in June 1941 the German army drove out the Soviet forces. Latvia, together with Estonia and Lithuania, was made part of Hitler's Ostland, a welcome development as far as many of the ethnic German population were concerned. The consequences for Latvia's 100,000 Jews were horrific: 90 percent were murdered.

Riga was reconquered by the Soviet Army on 8 August 1944, and with that the NKVD set about restoring order in its customary manner. An estimated 320,000 people out of a population of just 2 million were deported to the east; most never returned. Active guerrilla resistance to the Soviet regime continued until as late as 1951, but very little news of it leaked out to the West.

More executions and deportations followed in the purge of so-called bourgeoisie nationalists in 1949–53, and all the time Russians were surging in ostensibly to man the industrial machinery of the Five-Year Plans. Khrushchev purged 2,000 influential locals who raised their voices in protest, replacing them either with Russians or so-called Latovichi, Russians who purported to be Latvians on the strength of a few years' residence in the country. Notorious Latovichi such as Arvids Pelse and Augusts Voss enforced Russification policies with a severity that at least matched anything attempted by the tsars. Even such mundane activities as folk-singing were driven underground. Signs of a quiet revival surfaced in the 1980s. It began with the unobtrusive restoration of derelict churches and the odd historical monument. Poets and folk groups also performed discreetly.

The principal catalyst that brought protest out into the open was the Green Movement. Environmental concern served as cover for the formation of nationalist pressure groups, and before very long the underground press was addressing such taboo subjects as the activities of the secret police and human rights violations. The breakthrough occurred in 1986, when public protest managed to stop the construction of a hydro-electric scheme on the River Daugava.

With this victory in hand, and a softer line on public protest coming from Moscow, the resistance movement began to talk of national sovereignty within a Soviet Federation. The National Independence Movement of Latvia (NIML), founded in June 1988 largely by victims of earlier purges, was more radical in its aims. They maintained that the illegal annexation of 1940 invalidated the Soviet regime and all its works. A census taken in 1989 revealed that Latvians were on the brink of becoming a minority in their own country – they represented a mere 52 percent of the total

population – and this lent an air of sudden urgency to the campaign. The Russian minority rallied in opposition forming an organisation called Interfront.

The Soviet Union eventually collapsed so quickly and so passively that it is all too easy to forget how bravely Latvians demanded "total political and economic independence" and, specifically, a free market economy and a multi-party political system. Nor will Latvia forget the five killed by Soviets at the Ministry of the Interior in January 1991. Elections gave the nationalists a two-thirds majority, and the country was renamed the "Republic of Latvia".

Left, the Black Brotherhood building, a casualty of World War II, has now been rebuilt. **Above**, Latvian soldiers.

RIGA

Riga is the largest and most exciting city in the Baltic states. With a population of approximately a million people, it almost seems too big for the country it occupies: just over twice that number live in the whole of Latvia. It is also the least ethnic of all the Baltic capitals, for the Russification of this cosmopolitan city was swift after the war, and by the time of independence a full 70 percent of the population was Russian.

The city lies some 5 miles (8 km) from the great sagging dip of Riga Bay and for some 3,000 years its warm waters have provided both a gateway and an outlet for the continental heartlands by way of the River Daugava on which Riga stands. Like Tallinn in Estonia, its skyline is an impressive collection of towers and spires.

Riga's former prosperity can be seen in its churches, its guild halls and in one of the largest collections of *Jugendstil* buildings in Europe. In the 1970s the city was earmarked for restoration and Polish craftsmen have spent the intervening decades working amongst its decay: there is still an incalculable amount to be done. A final blessing for Riga's citizens is Jūrmala, the lovely sandy beach at the mouth of the Daugava, which has been favoured by generations of holidaymakers from all over the former Soviet empire.

The Old Town: Riga is not a difficult town to get around and nearly everything of merit or note can be reached on foot. The dead-straight main street, Brīvības iela (Freedom Street), heads down to the riverfront past the former Intourist high-rise hotel, the **Latvija**, around the Freedom monument and dives into the cobbled streets of the old city where it is renamed Kaļķu Street.

Continue down Kaļķu Street past the Hotel de Rome, the smart, German-run establishment on the edge of the Old

Preceding pages: panoramic view across Riga. **Left,** St Peter's shadow falls beside St John's church.

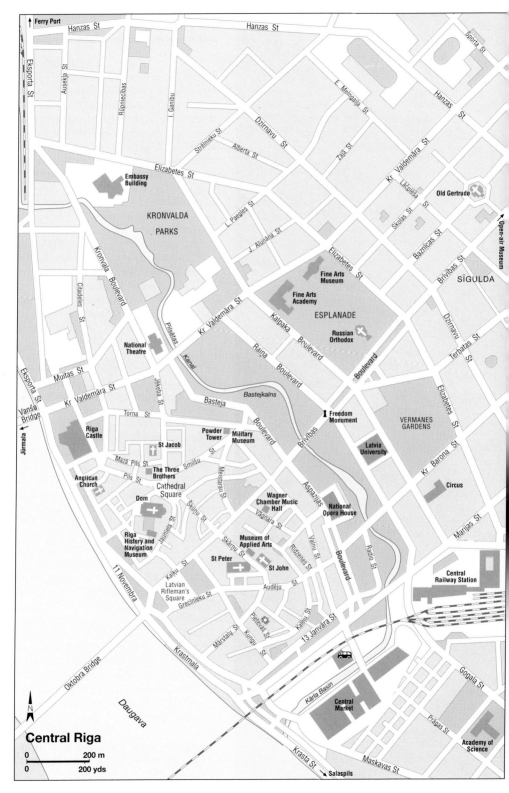

Central Riga

0   200 m
0   200 yds

Ferry Port
Hanzas St
Hanzas St
Sporta St
Eksporta St
Auseka St
Rūpniecibas
I. Ganibu
Strēlnieku St
Alberta St
Dzirnavu St
Zaļā St
E. Meingaila St
Hanzas St
Elizabetes St
Kr. Valdemāra St
Lāčplēša
Embassy Building
Old Gertrude
KRONVALDA
PARKS
L. Paegles St
Skolas St
Baznīcas St
Brīvibas St
J. Alunāna St
Elizabetes St
SĪGULDA
Open-air Museum
Kronvalda Boulevard
Fine Arts Museum
Fine Arts Academy
ESPLANADE
Citadeles St
Plīsētas
Kr. Valdemāra St
Kalpaka
Boulevard
Russian Orthodox
Boulevard
Dzirnavu
Terbatas St
National Theatre
Kanal
Jēkaba St
Raina
Boulevard
Muitas St
Eksporta St
Vanšu Bridge
Kr. Valdemāra St
Basteja
Bastejkalns
Boulevard
Freedom Monument
VERMANES GARDENS
Elizabetes St
Jūrmala
Torna St
Brīvibas
Riga Castle
Powder Tower
Military Museum
Latvia University
Kr. Barona St
St Jacob
Maza Pils St
Smilšu
Mestaru St
Aspazijas
Circus
Anglican Church
Pils St
The Three Brothers
Cathedral Square
Škūnu St
Wagner Chamber Music Hall
National Opera House
Marijas St
Dom
Jauniela St
Vagnara St
Vaļnu St
Ridzenes St
Radio St
11 Novembra
Riga History and Navigation Museum
Škārnu St
Museum of Applied Arts
St Peter
St John
Boulevard
Central Railway Station
Kaļķu
Latvian Rifleman's Square
Grecinieku St
Audēju St
Kaļeju
13 Janvāra St
Mārstaļu St
Pieļevas St
Kungu St
Krastmala
Oktobra Bridge
Gogaļa St
Kārļa Basin
Central Market
Prāgas St
Daugava
Academy of Science
Krasta St
Maskavas St
Salaspils

226

Town, down to Ratslaukums (Town Hall Square) after the fifth crossroads. Ratslaukums encapsulates all of Latvia's history and in its centre stands the **Blackhead Brotherhood house**. This historic gem was heavily damaged during World War II. The remains were destroyed by the Soviets in after the war and the 17th-century guild house was rebuilt with private donations and opened its doors to the public in 1999. The building will soon house a tourist information centre and is a good place to start a tour of the city. Founded in the 13th century, the brotherhood organised the city's social life and the house became a meeting place for bachelor merchants arriving from abroad. One of the community's patron saints was Saint Mauritius, who was black and gave the brotherhood its name. The historic **Town Hall** opposite is also set to be rebuilt in the near future.

Adjoining the Blackhead Brotherhood house is an ugly black building, the former Museum of the Latvian Riflemen, home to the excellent and chilling **Occupation Museum**. The museum retraces Latvia's plight under the Soviet and Nazi occupations from 1939 – 1991 with explanations in English, German and Russian. The museum is a must for anybody interested in recent Latvian history. The moving exhibit depicts the life of Latvians deported to Siberia and those who fought in the forests against Soviet aggression.

In front of the Occupation Museum, facing Akmens bridge is Strēlnieku laukums (Latvian Riflemen Square) with a red granite monument to the **Latvian Red Riflemen**, the local unit, which was chosen as Lenin's guard, in its centre. In this land of dramatically changing fortunes, the Latvian Riflemen remain heroes today – because after all they were valiant Latvians.

Facing the rebuild Blackheads' house is the elegant steeple of the **Church of St Peter's**, Riga's patron saint. A lift glides heavenwards to a viewing platform 236 ft (72 metres) up in the 380-ft (122-metre) steeple, which has been resurrected since its destruction during World War II.

The first church here, made of wood, was built by the city's craftsmen in 1209. Two centuries later it was rebuilt in stone. In 1709, 15 years after the steeple was completed, the city fell to the Russians and Peter the Great took a special delight in climbing to the top of the tower, then the tallest wooden structure in Europe. When it was struck by lightening in 1721, he personally helped to put out the fire.

In the corner of the square at Grēcinieku Street 18, is the half-timbered **Mentzendorff House** which offers a good idea of what life was like in a prosperous German's home in the 17th and 18th centuries, though the building itself dates back 300 years. Among its former owners was Andreas Helm, head of the Small Guild, and Rheinhold Schlevgt, master of the Order of the Blackheads who established a pharmacist's on the premises. Its interior, which was restored between 1982 and 1991, features *trompe l'oeil* wall decoration and painted ceilings inspired by Jean-Antoine Watteau. The rooms

Snow scene from the top of the Latvija Hotel.

have been furnished with period pieces from the Museum of the History of Riga and Navigation.

For nearly 100 years before Peter I's arrival, the city had been under the control of the Swedes, who had rebuilt its **Castle**, the flag-topped citadel to the north just by Vanšu bridge. Riga had been the largest city in their empire, bigger even than Stockholm. But after they had been driven out in a nine-month siege by Peter's Russian army, the city was in no great shape, and two-thirds of the population had died. Among them were many Latvians who were barred from living within the city walls, where they could not own property. Since the arrival of the German crusaders and the construction of the city in stone, they had been relegated to the lands beyond the city walls, and to Pārdaugava on the river's far bank, where they lived in buildings that had to be built out of wood. Each time the city was threatened, as it had been by the Russians, they had to burn their property and accept the protection of the city walls.

The eighth and last time this happened was in 1812 when an eagle-eyed watchman on St Peter's belfry spotted a distant cloud of dust heralding the French invasion. Four churches, 705 houses, 35 public buildings and hundreds of acres of vegetable plots were torched before it became clear the dust was caused by a herd of cows. Napoleon crossed Latvia via a different route.

Facing St Peter's on the north side are two other important churches. **St George's** now houses the **Museum of Applied Arts** and it should be visited if only to see the building's interior. This was the original church in the city, founded by the crusading Bishop Albrecht of Bremen in 1204 as a chapel for the Sword-Bearer's Order. It stood beside the castle complex which launched the first crusades against the Baltic people. Rebuilt after a rebellion in 1297, it was the first stone building in the city and it remains the only example of Romanesque. It has not been used as a church since the Reformation when it was turned into a storehouse.

Left, Milda. **Right**, the Dom, St Peter's and the English church.

Next to St George's, the redbricked **St John's** is distinguished by a steeply stepped Gothic pediment. The church started life in 1234 as the chapel of a Dominican abbey. In 1330 it was enlarged and its buttresses became the dividing walls of the new side altars. It was taken from the Dominicans during the Reformation and in 1582 a divine service in Latvian was held here for the first time. On the south wall, facing St Peter's, is a grille covering a cross-shaped window behind which two monks were cemented up during the building of the church and for the rest of their lives they were fed through the small gap. Between St George's and St John's is Jāṇa sēta, a small square abutting part of the old red-brick city wall, whose upkeep was the responsibility of the city's guilds.

Rīdzenes Street, running parallel, marks the former small river of Rīdziņa which ran into the Daugava, and it was around here that the earliest Liv and Latgalian fishing and trading settlements were established.

As you wander round the streets and lanes of this area, where some of the remaining two dozen ancient storehouses are still being restored, look out for the **house of John Rheuttern** at Mārstaļu Street 2/4, where exhibitions are often held. It was built by this rich German merchant in 1685, during the Swedish occupation, and beneath the roof is a frieze showing the Swedish lion devouring the Russian bear. At No. 21 is another baroque mansion which was built in 1696 for Rheuttern's son-in-law, a burgher named Dannenstern. Both have fine portals by the local stonemason Hans Schmiesel, who was responsible for the handsome if rather out of place portal on St Peter's church. Just past it on the left is Peitavas Street where a **Jewish synagogue** has been beautifully restored both inside and out. It should not be passed by without taking the opportunity to look in.

To the north, off Kaļķu Street, is Vāgnera Street which has both the sumptuous **Wagner Chamber Music Hall** where recitals are regularly held in its

Mentzendorff House Museum.

FEARLESS FILM-MAKER

There was a tangible anxiety in Latvia after Juris Podnieks was reported missing on 23 June 1992. Everyone was concerned for the man who had so many times risked his life making films that challenged and antagonised the status quo in Latvia. He was a man of creative talent and complete dedication, whose charisma, courtesy and kindness touched everybody he met.

The police were called out and divers were sent to Lake Zvigzde just west of Kuldīga in Kurzeme where he had last been seen. Psychics and mystics tried to divine where he might be. It was eight days before his body was brought up from the lake. It was hard to believe that this heroic 41-year-old film-maker had died in a silly scuba diving accident, after he had so often tempted a much more dramatic fate.

Podnieks was born in Riga, a city with a film tradition that goes back to Sergei Eisenstein, who was born here in 1898. He trained at the Moscow Film School before being apprenticed at the Riga Film Studios in 1968. In 1982 he made his first major documentary about the last surviving members of Latvia's famous Riflemen who had been Lenin's guard.

On the eve of *glasnost*, he was in the right place to explain to the West what it was like to be living in different parts of the Soviet Union. *Is It Easy To Be Young?*, made in 1987, included interviews with disillusioned veterans from the Afghanistan war. It was the first time people had queued to see a documentary at the cinema. It received awards and accolades abroad.

The following year the nuclear power station at Chernobyl erupted and Podnieks was the only cameraman to capture it from the air and from the ground. "The world had to know," he said simply when asked why he had taken such risks. He used the footage in his film about life in the Soviet Union called *Hello, Do You Hear Us?*, which won the 1989 Prix d'Italia.

His news footage was regularly used in the West and his documentaries continued to mirror the changes taking place in Latvia and the Baltics, and also to hurry them on. On 13 January 1991, he was in Vilnius in neighbouring Lithuania when Soviet soldiers shot and beat up unarmed civilians, killing 14 people. His images were on news programmes around the world. A week later the Soviet special police turned their attention on Riga. On 20 January, Soviet black berets began an assault on the Interior Ministry and shots whistled around Bastejkalns Park, the tranquil haven between the Freedom Monument and the Art Museum.

Podnieks was immediately in the thick of it, with his teenage son and cameramen Gvido Zvaigzne and Andris Slapiņš. The pink, smooth-topped stones in the park are memorials to the five men killed that night including both cameramen. Slapiņš, a friend as well as a colleague, insisted Podnieks pick up his blood-stained camera and record his dying words. "Keep filming…" he said.

Podnieks used this footage and Slapiņš' last words became famous in *Homeland*, a hymn to Latvia which included a moving record of the 1990 Song Festival. Slapiņš left an unfinished film of his own, *The Baltic Saga*, about the 20th-century killing fields of Kurzeme and, among other projects, Podnieks was engaged in finishing the work when he died. ■

Podnieks: a sympathetic eye in a dangerous world.

elegant surroundings, and, at No. 15, a pharmacist's which is the only rococo building in the city.

Cathedral and citadel: The "newer" part of the Old Town lies on the north side of Kaļķu Street, which goes down to the river and crosses it at Akmens bridge. Immediately evident is the yellow art nouveau **House of Cats**, with splendid black cats on its turrets and, opposite, the **Great and Small Guild Halls**. The House of Cats is supposed to have been built by a Latvian aggrieved that his nationality disqualified him from membership of the Big Guild, and he topped its two towers with black cats with their backsides pointing at the Guild building. A court case ensued, the cats were turned round and the Latvian was admitted to the Guild.

Traditionally only Germans were allowed to belong to the Great Guild of St John's, a merchants' guild founded in 1384. The building was last redesigned in 1866 by the city architect J. D. Felsko and today it is the home of the Philharmonic Orchestra. The Small Guild of St Mary's was for artisans and was started in the mid-14th century. Both functioned until the 1860s but they were not finally dissolved until the 1930s.

All streets here lead to the **cathedral square**, the cobbled focal point of the old city, where buskers provide constant entertainment for the pavement cafés. The square was in fact only created in 1936 when Kārlis Ulmanis, the first and last prime minister under the first independence, had a number of buildings demolished so people could gather to hear him speak on the balcony of the bank building on the corner. The building is now leased to Radio Latvia.

St Mary's Cathedral, the Dom, is a magnificent red-brick structure, with a gable like a Hanseatic merchant's house and a bulbous dome of northern Gothic solemnity. Steps lead down to the north door because the city's constant rebuilding has meant the ground level has actually risen over the years.

The cathedral was begun by Bishop Albrecht just after St George's, in 1211, and he is buried in the crypt. The plaques,

Pavement café.

tombs and headstones decorating the interior show just how German the city remained, no matter who owned it. Especially notable is the **6,768-pipe organ** – if there is a concert, it should not be missed; tickets are sold at the Wagner Concert Hall or at the entrance one hour prior to the start of the concert.

The cloister gardens are surrounded by a 118 metre-long vaulted gallery, one of the most outstanding examples of north-European medieval construction work. Enter through the **Museum of the History of Riga and Navigation** on Palasta Street 4. This is an eclectic collection of historical items and memorabilia, and doesn't have too much to do with the sea. Its scope is very wide and it is the best museum in the city, reflecting the wealth of its merchants. It was the first public museum in the Baltics when it opened in 1773 and it was based on the collection of Nicolaus von Himsel, a medical practitioner who died nine years earlier at the age of 35.

Pils iela (Castle Street) leads off the Dom square in front of a large, elegant, green art nouveau building with ruched curtains that give it something of the air of a boudoir. This was and is once again the city's **stock exchange.**

In the corner of Anglikāņu Street off Castle Street is a smart brown Renaissance-style building, which belongs to the **Danish Embassy**. It was originally built as the British Club for expatriates, merchants and sundry travellers (Napoleon called Riga "a suburb of London"), and every brick and detail of the **Anglican church** behind it was brought here from Britain, including a shipload of earth to provide the foundations. Wives and other women were allowed in the club once a year.

Pils Street arrives at the **castle** or citadel the Swedes designed in 1652. The first castle was built here in 1330 by the Livonian Order, who later decamped to Cēsis. In 1481, in one of many internecine wars within the city, it was razed by the townspeople, but the Livonian Order returned to besiege the town 34 years later and it was rebuilt. Today it houses three museums: **History of**

Left, merchants' store-houses in the Old Town. Right, Swedish Gate.

Latvia, History of Literature and Art, and Foreign Art.
Opposite the castle, Mazā Pils Street dives into the narrow lanes of the Old Town again. The most attractive group of buildings here are the three buildings known as **The Three Brothers**. These are the oldest residences in the city, merchants' homes of almost doll's house proportions dating from the 15th century. They have been colourfully restored, and they show how the families would live on the lower floors while leaving the upper areas for storage. One of them is home to the city's small Museum of Architecture.

Nearby is the red-brick **St Jacob's**, the principal Catholic church. Its 240-ft (73-metre) thin green spire, topped by a gold cockerel, is one of the three sky-pricking steeples that shape the city's skyline. In 1522 it became the first church in Latvia to hold a Lutheran service, but 60 years later, when the Polish king Stephen Bathory took the city for a brief spell, it was handed to the Catholics who have kept faith here ever since. In front of it is the peach-coloured **residence of the archbishop** and on the north side is the **parliament building** on Jēkaba Street which was blockaded against Soviet attack in 1991.

Turn right along Troksnu Street, leading directly to the grey **Swedish Gate**. Built in 1698, this is the only gate left in the city walls and through it the condemned were led to their fate. The executioner lived in the apartment over the gate; he would place a red rose on his window-ledge on any morning he had to perform.

The street on the far side of the gate is lined by the yellow Jēkaba kazarmas (Jacob Barracks), erected for the occupying Swedes. Turn right up Torņa Street past the old houses built against the city wall. Some of the red-brick wall has been restored and a café is proposed in the battlements. At the end of the street is Pulvertornis, the **Gunpowder Tower**, the last of 18 city towers. Its round red-brick walls and concave, conical roof, topping 85 ft (26 metres), are reminiscent of Lübeck, Queen of the Hansa.

The lofty naves of St Peter's.

CITY OF ART NOUVEAU

Art nouveau, the architectural style which brings such an unexpectedly decadent air to Riga's streets, celebrated the triumph of the bourgeoisie at the turn of the century. From Edinburgh to Brussels, Vienna to St Petersburg, and in highly-developed Riga more than in any Russian city, the new urban middle classes found prosperity. A new wave of architects jumped at the task of designing residential blocks, academies, schools, department stores, libraries, banks, restaurants and factories. Around forty percent of the boulevard city which grew up in the 1900s is what the French refer to as *art nouveau*, and the Germans call *Jugendstil*.

Riga hosted a mixture of new, often decorative approaches to building. The residential houses in Alberta Street, built by civil engineer Mikhail Osipovich Eisenstein, father of the great Russian film-maker, are saturated in finishing details. Inside the entrance hall to 2a Alberta Street the exterior decoration evolves into a turquoise

hall of columns, embroidered with leaves and curves.

Eisenstein's "decoratively eclectic art nouveau", a staggering synthesis of rationality and ornament, is shared by other contemporary Riga architects including the Baltic Germans Friedrich Scheffel, Heinrich Scheel and Reinhold Schmaeling. All studied in St Petersburg, where art nouveau flourished. The entrance hall to Scheel and Sheffel's residential block with shops at 8 Smilšu Street shows a characteristic affinity with the Arts and Crafts Movement. That thread takes the curious visitor back to one of Riga's most important architects, the Baltic German Wilhelm Bockslaff. Bockslaff built the graceful turreted brick Stock Exchange (1905), on Kalpaka Boulevard. Since 1919 the building has housed the Latvian Art Academy. The pastel-painted assembly hall, its ceiling embroidered after William Morris, is a treasury of stained glass, and the whole building is a fine monument to the eclecticism of art nouveau.

The houses, shops and banks on Brīvības Street and in nearby Gertrūdes and A. Čaka streets employ the perpendicular to express the solidity and the excitement of town life. Architects of this so-called rational art nouveau from the mid-1900s include Latvians Jānis Alksnis, Eižens Laube and Paul Mandelstamm and Konstantins Pēkšēns.

Mandelstamm, Laube, Pēkšēns and Aleksandrs Vanags, though in touch with St Petersburg trends, all graduated from the Riga Polytechnical Institute, which encouraged them to develop a more specific modern Latvian style from 1905 to 1911. A general heaviness, in some cases as if the building had been poured out of a mould, in others as if it were a test-run for many different building materials, including stucco, wood, stone, brick and plaster, characterises this national romanticism. It incorporated stylised ethnographic ornaments and the natural materials used in an urban setting, together with tapered window recesses and steep roofs, suggested a continued link with rural life.

The individual features of scores of unmodified, unmodernised buildings make a walk round Riga a joy, particularly in winter when no foliage obscures one of architecture's happiest testaments to high-spirited urban living. ■

Sumptuous facade on the corner of Alberta and Strelnieku streets.

234

Russian cannonballs feature on the walls; a **Museum of War** is housed inside.

The Sand Road, Smilšu Street, leads past the tower back to the cathedral. This was the main road out of town across marshes and through the forests towards St Petersburg. At one time it was the only proper road from the city.

Parks and art: To say that the old city is an island is rather fanciful, but it is entirely surrounded by water. The old moat that encircles it on the landward side is now a small canal running through a series of attractive parks from the ferry terminal in the north on the far side of the castle, to the railway station and market in the south. To the north, on Kr Valdemāra Street, is the **National Theatre**. To the south, between Brīvības and Kr Barona Street, is the fine 19th-century **Opera House**, formerly known as the German Theatre, which has been lovingly renovated with money donated by exiled Latvians. Richard Wagner was director for a year here in 1837.

In the park just to the north of Brīvības is **Bastejkalns,** the high spot of the city and not much more than a hiccup with little waterfalls and pleasant summer terraces by the canal. Nearby are five inscribed stones which commemorate the film cameramen and policemen killed during the Soviet attack around the modern Park Hotel Rīdzene in January 1991. The bullet holes, which used to stud the lobby staircase, were finally removed when the hotel was renovated in 1999.

The rallying point for the nation is the **Statue of Liberty** on Brīvības, the elegant lady locally known as **Milda**, who holds aloft three golden stars representing the three regions of Latvia: Kurzeme, Vidzeme and Latgale. She was designed by K. Zāle and erected in 1935. Somehow she managed to survive the occupation of the Soviets who officially described her as a memorial to the Soviet saviours of the city. The first post-war public demonstration was held here, in June 1987.

Rai a Boulevard runs along the top side of these parks: this was the diplomatic street of embassies during

Cheese stall, Riga market.

the years of independence, some of which have returned. Brīvības continues up past the Post Office and Sakta souvenir shop, opening into a boulevard dominated by the Latvija Hotel.

On the left is the **Russian Orthodox Church**, now reclaimed from its Soviet use as a planetarium. The Esplanade park behind it leads to the 19th-century **Arts Academy** and the **Fine Arts Museum**, which contains the best of Latvian artists' works and is well worth a visit.

Elizabetes Street at the top of the park should be followed for a while to appreciate its **art nouveau** and **romantic nationalism buildings** (*see page 234*). Nos. 10 and 33 were designed by Michael Eisenstein, father of Riga's most famous film-maker, Sergei Eisenstein. But most of his work can be seen in Alberta Street (second right and first left after Kr Valdemāra) where he was responsible for the houses up to No. 8, plus No. 13 opposite. After years of neglect and vandalism by tourists, most of the beautifully tiled entrances of many a Jugendstil building are now closed to

visitors. At the end of the street is Strēlnieku Street, with another Eisenstein masterpiece at 4a, which has his typical bright blue touch. On the corner of the two streets was the house the Latvian architect Konstantins Pēkšēns built for himself. Two other famous people lived there: the writer Rūdolfs Blaumanis (1863–1908) and the artist Jānis Rozentāls (1866–1916). A museum on the top floors contains their respective study and studio.

Rozentāls' work can also be seen on the facade of the former **Latvian Society building** near the university on the opposite side of Brīvības in Merķela Street. This street continues across Kr Barona, one of the main shopping streets, and down past the seasonal **circus**. After independence the circus could not survive, and while the animals languish in cages out the back, discos have been put on in its arena.

The market: Beyond the railway station are the humps of the five 39-ft (35-metre) high Zeppelin hangars, which were brought here in the 1930s to house the market – one of the real wonders of Riga. It used to be Europe's largest market, and must still be a contender for the title. It is built over a large underground storage system, and each hangar has its speciality: meat, dairy products, vegetables. Cream is sold in plastic bags, there are barrels of sauerkraut, fancy cakes, pickled garlic, dried herbs and mushrooms, smoked fish and whole stalls selling nothing but tins of sardines. On the way in via the station there are baskets of kittens and puppies, and wooden kiosks and stalls surround the hangars. Down by the waterfront the old flea-market spreads itself over acres of pavement. It is open every day, and is at its busiest on Fridays and Saturdays.

Beyond the market is the squat, brown, Empire-State building replica belonging to the **Academy of Science** and just beyond, in Jesusbaznīcas Street, is a fascinating octagonal wooden **Lutheran Church of Jesus** made of solid boards a foot wide. Built in 1822, it is the seat of the Lutheran bishop of the Commonwealth of Independent States.

Left, accordion player by the old city wall. **Right,** the view upriver beyond the market's Zeppelin hangars to the TV tower.

AROUND RIGA

Beyond the Old Town and the centre of Riga there are several attractions that can only be accessed by means of public transport or a car. These attractions are so diverse it is difficult to think that a visitor would be interested in all of them; however, there should be something in this list for everybody.

Perhaps of greatest general appeal is **Brīvdabas Muzejs**, the **open-air ethnographic museum**, which is located at Berģi, 6 miles (10 km) northeast along Brīvības Street. More than 100 buildings are set out in a 250 acres (100 hectares) of woodland beside Lake Jugla. (If you would like a swim the lake at Bergi is recommended in preference to use of public swimming pools in Riga.) The idea for the museum arose in the wake of the desolation of the countryside after World War I, and work began on it in 1924.

The most impressive building here is the 18th-century Lutheran church just to the left of the entrance. The whole building, including its figurative wood carvings, was made with an axe. There is a special higly decorated seat beside the altar for the local German landlord, and the front pews were reserved for imported German workers. Church was obligatory for all workers at that time and those caught skiving were put in the stocks or the pillory exhibited outside. Before the 19th-century organ was installed, the only music would have been an accompanying drum.

The museum display is divided into Latvia's ancient regions and it shows the contrasts between the rich Kurzeme farmers and those of poorer Latgale. By and large the farmsteads were built solely for the family unit, which usually meant three generations. In the museum, costumed figures populate the village and a blacksmith, potter and spoonmaker often perform. There are occasional folk gatherings here and a major craft fare is held on the first week in June – it's very entertaining and should not be missed if you are in the area.

In the same direction as this museum is the **Motor Museum**. Smerʒa Street leads down to it from Brīvības, passing by the city's large **film studios**, which operate an open-door policy. Just beyond the film studios, the street forks right into Sergei Eizenštein Street where the Motor Museum's glistening facade stands out like a brand new Rolls-Royce radiator grille.

Riga has been a key player in motor manufacturing in Eastern Europe: its Russo-Balt factory, for example, presented Russia with its first car and tank. However, the fruits of its labours are rather poorly represented in this museum. The high spots are waxwork figures of the famous with their vehicles: Stalin in his 7.3-tonne bullet-proof car which had hydraulic glass-windows 3 inches (8 cm) thick; Maxim Gorky with his 1934 Lincoln; Brezhnev at the moment of impact when he crashed his 1966 Rolls-Royce, together with the subsequent press cuttings saying that his non-appearance was due to a "sudden bad cold".

The Forest Park: To the north of Brīvības is **Mežaparks** (Forest Park), a suburb of formerly upmarket wooden villas and houses occupied by many Germans before 1939 when Hitler demanded they went back home. This is where the city **zoo** was founded in 1912 to show off all the animals of Latvia, though some of them, such as the beaver and wolf, are long since gone. In all there are 350 kinds of animals, including an elephant and the largest herd of Tibetan wild asses (*kiangs*) in captivity. There are about 50 of them, all descended from a pair given to the zoo by China in the early 1960s.

The main **open-air concert stadium** is also in Mežaparks, and it is here that choirs gather in their thousands. Just to the south are the three great cemeteries of the city: the **Cemetery of Heroes** for the seemingly infinite casualties of 20th-century wars, but particularly from World War I and the War of Independence; **Raiņa Cemetery** for the great and the good of Latvian literati; and **Meža Kapi**, the old forest cemetery.

High times: On the opposite side of the city is the **television tower** rising above the Daugava to the south. This is built on the upstream end of an island called **Zaķusala**, and is reached over Salu bridge. On the north side of the island is a modern office block where the Latvian State Television company operates from. At 907 ft (368 metres), the tower is the 10th highest building in the world, as the guide will tell you as you are whisked by lift to the viewing-room halfway up. From a restaurant on the same level you can see Riga Bay.

Opposite the tower, the only gold dome in the city peeks out from the skyline in a clump of lime trees in Riga's **Moscow District**. This is the place of worship for the **Old Believers**, a sect expelled from Russia during the 17th century, and this church now has the largest parish of the faith in the world, with a congregation of approximately 25,000 people. The church has a unique collection of 17th- and 18th-century icons, and a very rich and contemplative atmosphere that is broken only by the

Old mansion house in Mežaparks.

rather incongruous chimes of a grandfather clock. Services are held at 8am and 5pm every day and there are four-hour services on Saturday evenings and Sunday mornings.

The Moscow road, the A215, follows the right bank of the Daugava for 10 miles (16km) to **Salaspils** where the Livonian Order built its first palace, in the 14th century, and in 1412 signed an important agreement with the Bishop of Riga, establishing shared rule over the capital. On this site in 1605 the Swedes suffered a crushing defeat by the Poles who then ruled Lithuania. An atomic power station was built here in 1979. But Salaspils is destined to go down in the history books primarily as the site of a nightmarish World War II concentration camp where 53,000 died.

A 100-acre (40-hectare) **memorial park** was opened in 1967, centred on a long sloping, concrete building inscribed: "The earth moans beyond this gate". On the far side are half a dozen monumental statues and a lengthy, low black box where wreaths are placed. It emits a continuous and eerie ticking noise, supposed to represent a beating heart. The sites of the former barracks are marked and an inscribed stone marks the place of the gallows. There were 7,000 children killed among the Latvians, Belarussians, Poles, Czechs, Austrians, Dutch and Germans who died here. On the opposite side of the highway is a memorial to 47,000 Soviet prisoners of war who perished under the Nazis.

The seaside: The word *jūrmala* in Latvian simply means seaside, and this is the name given to the Baltics' most famous resort. Jūrmala, the playground of Riga, stretches along a narrow strip of land, pressed against the beach by Latvia's second largest river, the Lielupe, which follows the coast for about 5 miles (8 km) before emptying itself into Riga Bay just west of the mouth of the Daugava. People do swim here, but it is not recommended. If you are desperate for a dip it is generally a better idea to head further away from the city than here.

◄Memorial to Nazi victims at Salaspils.

There is a good road to Jūrmala from Riga, which leaves the city over the distinctive suspension bridge, nick-named "**Voss's guitar**" after a local political party boss who had it built, it is said, so he could get to his seaside home more quickly. This road was also nicknamed "ten minutes in America" as it was used as a set in Soviet movies about the America capitalist enemy. Anyone driving to the resort, or even through it, needs to buy a permit for the day from the roadside offices on its outskirts. A ferry service runs every summer from Riga to Lielupe.

This is the place to look for amber, especially after a storm. In its raw state, battered by the elements, it will look like dull stones scattered on the beach. Here, in pine woods behind the sand dunes that so typify the whole Baltic coast, there are some beautiful Edwardian wooden villas, with stained-glass windows and fancy duckboards still intact. Apart from the wooden homes, a whole Soviet holiday structure was built up. Factories and unions provided rest homes and apartments (some only for workers, without their families) and they included places for mud, peat and spa-water cures.

Jūrmala has long been a popular bathing spot. Peggie Benton, an English diplomat's wife, was in Riga at the outbreak of World War II and like many people from the city rented a villa at Jūrmala for the summer. "The Latvians kept up the delightful Russian custom of bathing naked," she wrote in *Baltic Countdown.* "One soon learned not to worry and got used to strolling up to a policeman, tightly buttoned into his uniform, to ask how much longer until the red flag went up and we had to put our clothes on again." Parts of the beaches in all three Baltic countries still have single-sex areas for those seeking all-over tans.

Although independence has resulted in a dramatic drop in tourism from the former Soviet interior, in high season Jūrmala seems quite full enough. The crowd swells at weekends as well as on summer weekday evenings, since the train from Riga takes only approximately 30 minutes.

There are a dozen train stops to choose from between **Lielupe** and **Kemeri**, a spa town set back from the sea. In its heyday the grand Kemeri hotel had a cosmopolitan air, hosting international chess championships and social events. **Majori** is the central stop, and the main pedestrian road, Jomas Street, has nu-merous cafes, restaurants, souvenir shops and an outdoor concert hall, all within easy reach of the rail station.

The cultural high point of Majori is the attractive wooden house once lived in by the poet Jānis Rainis in a street called J. Pliekšāna iela, which was Rainis' real name. He lived here during his last three years, from 1926 to 1929, and a museum preserves his effects. His wife, the poet Aspazija, is also commemorated at the house.

There is an abundance of seaside enter-tainment to enjoy, but just strolling around brings rewarding sights such as the renovated Lutheran church in **Dubulti** and the bright blue wooden Orthodox church nearby.

Left, Russian church, Bulduri. **Right**, statue to Rainis and Aspazija, Jūrmala.

KURZEME

Kurzeme is the westernmost region of Latvia, a healthy agricultural area half surrounded by sea. It was once known as Courland (Kurland in German), named after the Curi or Kuri, the amber-rich seafaring people who dominated the coast before the arrival of the German crusaders. In 1561, after the break-up of Livonia, Courland came into its own. It became a duchy under the sovereignty of Poland, and included the region of Zemgale (formerly Semigallia) to the south of Riga, plus a small corner of modern Lithuania.

Its dukes enjoyed a degree of independence, building castles for themselves and Lutheran churches for the people. Many became rich and powerful, notably Jēkabs Kettlers (1642–82), who went empire-building and collected a couple of outposts, one in Gambia, West Africa, the other the Caribbean island of Tobago.

Kettler amased his fortune largely from the pines that grow exceptionally tall and straight. The most impressive forests are in the Slītere Nature Reserve (*see page 110*) and along the sandy coastal region, which was once below the sea. Trees grow to around 110 feet (35 metres) and some are up to 500 years old.

Kurzeme's thriving shipbuilding and trading activities were conducted at the two important ice-free ports of Ventspils and Liepāja, though neither of these modern industrial centres bears any sign of those years of greatness today.

The coast around Kurzeme is a continuous white sandy beach, from just north of the major Lithuanian resort of Palanga up to the Kolka peninsula and down to the fishing village of Mērsrags and Lake Engure in the Bay of Riga. Beyond this is Jūrmala, Latvia's riviera, and Zemgale, or the Central Region. For 45 years, until 1991, most of this coast was used by the military and was therefore inaccessible: today, even in the heat of summer, much of it remains completely deserted. Between

the coastal lowland in the west and Riga Bay in the northeast, towns, villages, churches and estates are tucked in the valleys and wooded corners of a landscape that rolls between rivers and hills. Kuldīga and Talsi are the principal inland provincial towns.

The town of **Kuldīga** is 100 miles (160 km) west of Riga, and is a good centre for exploring the region. A castle was first built here in 1242, and in 1561 the town was made the capital of Courland by the first duke, Gottard Kettlers. The castle was built beside the River Venta, which was navigable all the way to Ventspils and the sea.

The city declined after the Great Northern War and the castle was reduced to little more than a ruin: a park remains where it once stood. The churches are worth exploring: the Baptist church has a striking clock-tower, St Catherine's Lutheran church has a fine wooden altar and pulpit from 1660, and there is a grand view over the town from the top of its 85-ft (25-metre) tower. The altar of the Holy Trinity Catholic Church

in Raiņa Street also has an impressive altar, which was donated by Tsar Alexander I in 1820.

Part of the town's charm is derived from the Alekšupīte, a tributary to the River Venta, which runs by a mill and between wooden houses that date back to the 16th century. Most of the old buildings are centred around the square overlooked by the 19th-century town hall, but the main street today is Liepājas, which runs back from Raiņa Street (try the fresh raspberry cakes at the cafe on the corner) a few streets back. This street, with a wooden building that looks as if it might be a Wild West saloon, leads to the main modern square and the modern Kursa hotel.

At the old bridge over the Venta, which is now closed to traffic, you can see the **Kuldīgas rumba**, a shallow waterfall that runs the 360-ft (110-metre) width of the river. Grooms carry their brides across it for luck. In the fast-flowing waters beneath the bridge, people try to catch fish in their hands.

Around Kuldīga there are plenty of excursions to be made. The countryside is riven with streams and small lakes. The River Venta, which rises in Lake Venis in Lithuania and twists down to the sea at Ventspils, is particularly popular for watersports.

A pleasant drive leads northeast of Kuldīga, to **Sabile** and **Kandava**, towards **Tukums** in the Vidzeme region (*see page 269*). These villages are known for their gypsy population. Vina Kalns, **Wine Hill**, in Sabile is in the record books as the most northern place in Europe where vines are grown.

Between Kuldīga and Ventspils is the small town of **Piltene**, the seat of a bishopric that retained its independence from 1234 to 1583. The remains of its castle of the Livonian Order lie behind the church, built in 1792. Overlooking the lake are the original church and nunnery dating from 1254.

At the end of the Livonian Wars, when the rest of western Latvia became the new Duchy of Courland, the lands of the Bishop of Piltene and Oesel (the old name for the island of Saaremaa, now

Sand dunes by the beach, Liepāja.

Estonia) were not included in the sale, and the bishop, Johann von Munchhausen, sold them in 1559 to Frederick II of Denmark. Frederick then gave them to his brother Magnus, who married the sister of Ivan the Terrible. The tsar crowned him "King of Livonia", a dubious title which he relinquished in 1578. He then retired to Piltene, where he founded Latvia's second school. He was buried in the castle, but in 1640 his remains were returned to Denmark.

Ancient churches: Danish craftsmen were imported via Piltene and art historians detect their hand on the robust folk carvings of the altars and pulpits of local churches. But the principal carvings at Piltene, which have not survived, were by the 18th-century master carvers from Ventspils, Nicolas Soeffrens the older and younger, ship carvers who turned their skills to church work.

Among other local churches with fine carving is **Zlēkas**, between Piltene and Kuldīga. This is the largest church in Courland and it has a fine black and gold baroque pulpit and altar which were carved by local Latvians. At **Ēdole** on the opposite side of the main Ventspils road and about 12 miles (20 km) northwest of Kuldīga, there is a church that dates from the 17th century. It also has a recently restored 13th-century castle. The keys of both the church and castle are to be found at a nearby house called Saules Lejas.

One of the most interesting churches is at **Ugāle**, directly north of Kuldīga on the road between Tukums and Ventspils. Built in 1697, its organ was installed four years later, making it not only the oldest in the Baltics, but also unique in Europe. Is has 28 stops, including the only surviving baroque register. It was built by Cornelius Rhaneus from Kuldīga, who may have been Dutch.

The beautiful, unpainted lime wood carvings by Michael Markwart from Ventspils include stars that once revolved and angels' wings designed to flap. Jānis Kalni špastor, the charismatic Lutheran pastor, is a musician and master organ restorer and he gives guided tours which are likely to include a few tunes

Good and bad women, Zlekas pew.

(tel: 71475). The neighbouring village of **Usma** is the origin of the 18th-century Lutheran church in Riga's open-air ethnography museum.

The Piltene bishops were not intolerant and they attracted a prosperous Jewish population. **Aizpute**, a town to the south, was known as "Klein Danzig" by the Jews, who had their own municipality, citizens' guard and uniform. The town makes a pleasant stop and has a church dating back to 1254.

Aizpute is on the main road from Riga to Liepāja and was a centre of military activity under the Soviets. Just north of **Skrunda** was the USSR's most westerly, and therefore most important tracking station, which was deserted and dynamited in the mid 1990s. In Embute there is a Lutheran church dating from 1792. The key is with the little nearby shop. One of the German barons from the family for whom it was built is depicted in the stained-glass window of 1902, designed by a local Latvian artist.

Around Talsi: The region northeast of Kuldīga is Talsi, centred on the town of the same name. Like a painting on a chocolate box, it is a pretty, tranquil idyll tucked under hills beside a large pond. Not surprisingly, it has long been an artists' haunt.

The oldest wooden church in the Baltics is 10 miles (16 km) northeast of Talsi at **Iğene**. It has been a working church since 1555, though most of it dates from 1752. The altar, however is original. It was moved here from a nearby plague-stricken village. Approach it from Vandzene along a gravel road, taking the first left after the village pond. There is a ruined wooden church of a similar age just to the south, at **Lauciene**.

North of Talsi is a series of former large country house estates. The palace at **Nogale** is a particularly good example. It was built in 1880 for Baron von Firks as a summer residence and hunting lodge, and from 1920 to 1980 it was a school. It has now been restored. The ceiling paintings in the bedrooms, allegories of music and dance, are intact and an attractive conservatory has been repaired. The two-storey neoclassical

The country town of Kuldiga.

building, overlooks a lake and 170 acres (70 hectares) of parkland. It has plans to become a cultural and residential centre and is presently open to the public. The adjacent village has a public sauna and a stone windmill with a church-steeple style roof.

The neighbouring village to the west is **Valdemarpils**, where the main estate is still in the process of reconstruction. It takes its name from Krišjānis Valdemārs, one of the leading lights of the National Awakening, who was born in nearby **Cīruli** in 1825. He became enchanted by the sea near here at Roja and went on to found Latvia's first seamen's school at Ainaži, right up by the Estonian border.

Outside his country manor in Valdemarpils is one of the oldest elm trees in the country, a huge and crippled beast that is in need of support. **Lake Sasmaka** is nearby and the village has a church dating from 1646 and a small museum of local history in Statcijas Street.

The largest estate in the whole of the Baltics was **Dundaga**, the northernmost village of any size on this cape. In the 18th century the castle's lands stretched for 270 sq. miles (700 sq. km), and today some attempts are being made to restore some of its former glory. The crozier and sword, symbols of the Church and the Sword Bearers, are inscribed on its entranceway and the main door inside the courtyard is guarded by a statue of a bishop and a crusader. The estate belonged to the bishops of Courland, the last of whom was Herzog of Holstein, brother of Germany's Frederich II.

There are seven coats-of-arms on the castle, belonging to owners going back to 1245, and they include those of the von Bülows and the Osten-Sachens, the subsequent inheritors of the **estate**. Today the building is a weekly boarding-house for schoolchildren who live too far away to bus in daily. In a first-floor bathroom still in use is a bath supposedly used by Duke Jēkabs, but it isn't particularly impressive.

Like all Latvian castles, Dundaga is surrounded by stories of devils and

Neoclassical Nogales.

ghosts: it was built on a magic grey stone, and the sister of a local baron is rumoured to walk here whenever there is a full moon. There is an attractively sited open-air concert venue in the grounds behind.

The local church, which is dated 1766, has wood carvings by Soeffrens and an altar painting by Latvia's great 20th-century artist, Jānis Rozentāls. The confessional possesses a definite Scandinavian flavour (the keys are available from Inta Biezbarde, tel: 42231). Memorials to several members of the Osten-Sachens family are scattered in the church grounds.

Secret coast of the Livs: On the Riga Bay side of the cape, the road from Jūrmala continues through pine trees of extraordinary stature, which once provided masts for many western ships throughout the ages. A barrier, now abandoned, marks the point where the Soviet army held sway. People living in these small villages were heavily vetted, and as on the rest of the coast fishing was simply banned.

The tarmac runs out at **Roja**, and is replaced with a bright carpet of white stones. All around this peninsula, which encircles the carefully controlled **Slītere Nature Reserve**, there is scarcely any sign of life.

At the top of the peninsula, just beyond Kolka, is a point where the waters of Riga Bay meet the Baltic Sea. It is a fabled sight, which Latvians had heard about but until recently never seen. The marked line where the seas meet runs out past the half washed-away lighthouse to the horizon, and when the wind blows, the waters are whipped up into a great crashing wall.

Continuing down the western, Baltic side of the coast are a further series of former fishing communities. Typical is **Mazirbe**, where farmlands stretch back from the dunes of the bleached sand which is strewn with small cockle and mussel shells. A white wooden hall has recently been built, with help from neighbouring Estonia, as a meeting-place for the last of the Livs.

Latvians are very proud of this pure,

Café and chat in Aizpute.

all-but-lost tribe who have inhabited this coast since prehistory, and who were the first settlers of Riga. Being Finno-Ugric by origin, their language is more like Estonian than Latvian and they have their own ancient flag, which is green, white and blue. Estonians and Finns contribute funds to help ensure their continued well-being.

There are scarcely more than 100 Livs left, scattered throughout the country and the world. In fact, only one old woman in Mazirbe speaks Liv and their leader lives just down the coast, at **Mikelbāka**. A small museum containing exhibits of Liv life is being prepared in an ancient barn in Mazirbe.

The heyday for **Ventspils** was under Duke Jēkabs who launched his ships for the Caribbean and West Africa from here. But, after his death, Ventspils went into decline and was reduced to just seven families after the plague of 1710. It enjoyed a cultural renaissance during the years of independence, however, and after the war the Soviet Union built it up as an industrial centre. It was the main terminal for Soviet oil exports and the late Armand Hammer's Occidental Petroleum has chemical factories here.

Controls, however, were lax, and though there is no visible evidence of pollution, towards the end of the Soviet era it was so bad that children went to school wearing masks. It is an industrial town, certainly, and the river mouth is filled with shipping activity, though some rather high walls and furtive, dead-end alleys frustratingly obstruct views of the river and wharfs.

The Old Town has the kind of run-down feeling often associated with ports: its wooden houses are in bad repair and its four-storey **castle**, much billeted and little loved, has recently been abandoned and is now just a tip.

But walk down Pils Street from the castle towards the 18th-century town hall and see the brighter side of the place: the architecture of the lowly houses and the touches of art nouveau give a hint of a rather grand little port. Here, with a lighthouse-sized lantern, is a sparklingly clean Lutheran church

dated 1833 and dedicated, in German, to God and the Kaiser. In the nearby **Regional Museum** all is revealed: photos of the swish port at the beginning of the 20th century; the swank Royal Hotel; emblems from the Norwegian and Swiss embassies from the 1920s and '30s; a bourgeois drawing-room. There are also Liv national costumes and customs, and a general feeling of far more prosperous and happy times.

A **Maritime Museum** in the modern part of town consists of an open-air exhibition of the coast and its fishing industry, with examples of pitch-black boats dating back 300 years. There are also beach houses and drying huts. It was not until the 19th century that fishing moved away from the river and on to the sea, and it was not until 1863 that peasants were allowed to own land.

The other significant port on this coast is **Liepāja**, which is located 80 miles (130 km) south of Ventspils and has more than twice its population (114,900). Liepāja is a centre of metal smelting and was once a major Soviet military base

with submarine pens. Trawlers, which travel as far as West Africa, are moored in its harbour, and commercial traffic is beginning to come back again. On the dockside in front of the old customs house in 1919, the British navy formerly recognised the state of Latvia when it disembarked Prime Minister Ulmanis, escaping from Riga.

The Old Town is spread out and tidy and its green, two-storey wood buildings, though in need of paint, sit attractively in the lanes of lime trees that give the town its name. The cafés and bars from the pre-war years are run down, but they have not been destroyed and a pedestrian mall has been added, based on Moscow's Arbut Street. A large neoclassical building in front of the Hotel Liva is one of the country's principal teacher-training colleges.

The town has two sturdy churches, Catholic **St Joseph's** from the 17th century and, behind the attractive market, Catholic **St Anne's**, with an altar carved by Nicolas Soeffrens.

Past the yellow former British consulate where Kārlis Ulmanis was hidden for a while in a garden shed, Kurmajas Prospekts leads down to the sea. On the right is an unusual **Art Gallery and Museum**, with a garden full of sculptures. The house was built by Hakels Nelsons, a wood carver, in 1901 and it has beautiful panelled ceilings and patterned parquet floors as well as fine carvings. It passed to Nelsons' daughter on his death, but she hanged herself here, and her widower, a compulsive gambler, lost the home in a card game. The state took it over in 1935.

At the bottom of the boulevard, perched on the dunes, is a monument dedicated to the sea. For a mile or two to the south, a pleasant shady park rests among the trees with a few scattered grand old villas and an amusement park for children.

To the south, the immaculate beach continues its drift towards distant Lithuania, passing eroded sandbanks and the highest dune on the coast (125 feet/35 metres) near Nica before crossing the border and arriving at the next large resort, **Palanga**.

Left, the pulpit in Ugale church. **Right**, a carving on its rare organ.

ZEMGALE AND RUNDALE PALACE

The region of Zemgale was for a time linked with Courland, and it borders the modern region of Kurzeme from Lithuania in the south to Lake Engure halfway up the west side of Riga Bay. Skirting Riga, it then slips below the River Daugava and slides along the length of the Lithuanian border tailing away to the far southeast. Apart from the northerly area around Tukums, most of Zemgale is characterised by a dead flat, fertile plain, part of the central lowlands that in places actually sink below sea level. This is considered to be the breadbasket of Latvia.

There are comparatively few lakes, and the main river is the Leilupe, which flows through the ancient towns of Bauska and Jelgava, Zemgale's capital, which the dukes of Courland and Semigallia made their home. There are a number of large 18th- and 19th-century estates in the region, but this was the front line in World War I, and many were burnt by the retreating Russian army. One that has been restored is the castle at Rundāle near Bauska, the finest palace in the Baltics. All of these places are within easy striking distance of Riga.

A step west: The region of Tukums lies to the west of Riga and Jūrmala, and is a stepping-stone into Kurzeme and the Baltic coast. Heading west from the capital, the A218 passes through scenes of World War I conflict, notably at **Ložmētejkalns**, site of an heroic attack by the Latvian Riflemen on a strong German position in 1918.

Tukums is the first town of any size on this road. It has a castle mound and was originally a Liv settlement. On the outskirts are a military airport and large animal feed factory, and it is an important centre for furniture manufacture. It has a pleasant old centre, and a tradition of ceramics which is carried on in the factory in Talsa Street. In Darzau Street is the **regional museum** which has a collection of works by the most important 20th-century Latvian artists, including Rozentāls and Svemps. The Lutheran church dates from 1670. Just to the north of the town is **Milzkalne**, the highest spot in the region, which has a view over Riga Bay.

A few miles past Tukums on the Ventspils road is **Jaunmokaspils**, a newly refurbished hunting lodge. It was built in 1901 by Wilhelm Bockslaff, who designed the Art Society building in Riga, for George Armitstead, who owned the hippodrome in the capital. Its most striking features are its ceramic stoves, built by the firm of Celms & Bems, especially one imprinted with old postcards of Riga from the city's 700th anniversary celebrations in 1901. On the first floor is a **Museum of the Forests of Latvia** and it includes a collection of around 40 different animal horns from all over the world. The lodge provides facilities for hunters' holidays in the area.

From here the road continues to the attractive towns of **Kandava** and **Sabile** on the way to Kuldīga (*see page 249*).

From **Lapmežciems** to **Bērzciems**, most of the communities on the coast

have names ending with -*ciems*, meaning village. There attractive farm buildings stand near the sea and lurk in the wood. Just beyond the new buildings at **Ragaciems** is a well-established campsite. The **Engure lake and nature reserve** lie beyond the thatched church tower roof at the little port of Engure. Some 50,000 birds visit this long (12-mile/18-km), shallow lake every year. An ornithologist from Salaspils is the only resident and it is closed to the public, though licenced hunters and fishermen come here from September to April. Camps have been organised here for exiled Latvians who have not known their grandparents.

South of Tukums, on the road to **Dobele**, is **Jaunpils,** a village with a lakeside manorial castle and church dating back to the 16th century. This was the estate of one Baron Reke, whose coat of arms is over the church altar. The manor at Dobele was built for a Swiss, Jānis Berlics, in 1820.

Dukes' domain: south of Riga, the only town of any size is **Jelgava**, home of RAF, makers of the Latvija minibus. Though you would not know it to look at it, Jelgava is an historic town, formerly called Mitau, that once rivalled Riga. The history of the town, and of the 11 dukes of Courland and Semigallia, the Kettlers, the Madems and Herzogs who were friends of the Russian Romanovs and influential at court in St Petersburg, is laid out in the **History and Art Museum**. This is housed in the Academia Petrina, built in 1775 and once an important educational and scientific centre. It lies just behind the landmark tower of the ruined Holy Trinity church. Most of the exhibits, which include gold and silver ducats minted here, and a waxwork of Duke Jēkabs at home, have full explanations in German. Also in the old part of town is **St Ann's church**, from 1619, which has an altar painting by Jānis Rozentāls.

The wide, slow Lielupe, which slips north into Riga Bay, has always carried river traffic. Today pleasure-boats ply the waters and there are small craft for hire on the left of the bridge that brings

Left, arcaded corridor. **Right**, the Gilded Hall.

the road in from Riga. On the right is **Rastrelli Palace**, a large and solid Italianate building on the site of the town's original **castle** (1265). Since 1957 this three-storey, brick-red and cream building set around a square has housed an agricultural college. It is an impersonal resting-place for the dukes of Courland and Semigallia.

Frederick-Wilhelm, the penultimate of the Kettlers dynasty of dukes, altered the family's fortunes when he married Ivan V's daughter Anna Ivanova, in St Petersburg in 1710. The 17-year-old newlyweds had just started back to the young duke's palace in Jelgava when he became ill and died. Reluctantly Anna was obliged to continue her life in Jelgava. Bored and confined in what to her must have seemed something of a backwater of wooden homes and flat farmlands, she began an affair with Johannes Ernst Birons, an ambitious Courlander on the palace staff.

In 1727 Anna became Empress Anne of Russia, peopling her court with German Balts and making Birons a count.

Within nine years he was wealthy enough to employ Bartholomeo Rastrelli (1700–71), the architect of St Petersburg's Hermitage or Winter Palace, to build a manor for himself at Rundāle, to the south of Jelgava.

Rundāle Palace is an imposing, well-restored palace of 138 rooms, approached through a grand drive flanked by twin semi-circular stables. Above the east wing a double-headed German eagle rises over the motto: "Faithfulness and Jealousy". At the height of its construction between 1736 and 1768 it employed 1,500 labourers and artisans. Work on the building and grounds, which still have to be restored, was interrupted first in 1738, after Birons had achieved his ambition of becoming Duke of Courland and diverted Rastrelli into turning Jelgava Castle into Rastrelli Palace. The second interruption was more serious when, after becoming regent of Russia for a year following the empress's death, Birons was banished to Siberia for 23 years.

Privately owned until 1920, Rundāle

was damaged and fell into disrepair after World War I and has been under reconstruction since 1972. Its stairways, galleries, landings, rooms and halls are gracious and well decorated. The wall paintings are by the Italians Francesco Martini and Carlo Zucchi and the exquisite decorative moulding is by Michael Graff from Berlin. His oval **Porcelain Study** is particularly striking. On the ground floor there is a collection of period furniture and ornaments, including a guitar made from wood taken from the ruined palace by Andris Kārkliņš, who emigrated to America and became a flamenco player. The finest rooms are upstairs, where some interesting Dutch, Flemish and Spanish paintings from the 17th and 18th centuries are hung.

The dukes' throne stood in the **Gold Hall**, which is matched in magnificence by the **White Hall** or ballroom where the intricate stucco work includes a delicate heron's nest on the ceiling. In 1992 royalty returned when the Queen of Denmark was entertained here.

At the entrance to the palace is an exhibition of Ventspils **church wood carvings** by Nicolas Soeffrens, whom Peter the Great invited to work on his ships. The pieces are all carved from ships' timbers.

Rundāle was the apogee of the fusion of German and Russian society which came together and flourished in the region in the 18th and 19th centuries. A number of important manors were built in this accessible area. The one at **Mežotne**, which was given by Tsar Paul I to his children's governess, Charlotte von Lieven, in 1797, has been restored, but like Rastrelli Palace it has become an uninspired-looking institution. One of the grandest houses otherwise was at **Eleja**, due south of Jelgava on the main road to Vilnius, but it is now just a forlorn ruin.

Semigallian roots: The flatlands of Zemgale were originally inhabited by the Semigallians, who in the 13th century produced one of the greatest Latvian leaders, Viesturs. The centre of his domains was to the west of Rundāle in **Tērvete**, but the tribe was pushed south by the German crusaders who built a castle on the site of their stronghold, some of which still remains. Nearby is the **Meža Ainavu Park** which has a museum to a children's writer, Anna Brigadere, who lived here from 1922 to 1933. The park has Latvia's tallest tree.

To the east of Rundāle is **Bauska**. On arrival there is a car-park just beyond the bridge over the River Mūsa. The river shortly converges with the Mēmele, helping to form half a moat for the **Livonian Order's castle** which did not survive the Great Northern War. Climb the tower: there is a good view from the top. Bauska itself is a pleasant little rural textile town. Several German painters settled here in the late 17th century, including Joachim Henning, Niklaus Tabin and Dietrich Seitz, who became mayor in 1706. Some of their work can be seen in **St Anne's church**.

From Bauska the road leads directly north back to Riga, past Brencis, a high-class hotel, restaurant and garage, just beyond **Iecava**, which is best known for its large chicken factory.

Left, an ornament from Jelgava Castle. Right, Bauska's old castle.

VIDZEME

Lying to the east of Riga, Vidzeme is the largest of the country's four regions. In the north it stretches from the Bay of Riga all along the Estonian border, and in the south it lies beside the right bank of the Daugava from the capital to the eastern region of Latgale. Beside the river's banks, there are scattered castles and remains of ancient settlements, pointers to a powerful past.

At the heart of the region is another river route which, though less exalted, is just as ancient and rather more beguiling. This is the River Gauja, which runs through a deep gorge at the centre of the Gauja National Park. It is Latvia's showcase rural attraction, rich in wildlife, full of prehistoric hill forts and containing one of the most important archaeological sites. They call it "little Switzerland", and have installed a bobsled run, but "little" is the key word. The Baltics' highest point is in Vidzeme: it is just 1,025 ft (312 metres).

The **Gauja National Park** begins at **Sigulda**, 30 miles (50 km) northeast of Riga and is an easy day-trip from the capital by road (A212) or by public transport. On the roadside just before Sigulda is one of the country's best known restaurants, the Sēnīte (Little Mushroom), where a canteen and smarter restaurant have a reputation which is considerably more attractive than the dull Soviet slab they inhabit.

From Sigulda the park extends north through **Cēsis**, the main centre for excursions, to **Valmiera**. It covers around 350 sq. miles (900 sq. km) along more than 60 miles (100 km) of river, and is divided into sections with varying degrees of access. Boating is popular on the river, and organised parties embark in inflatables for overnight camps, taking three days to travel from Valmiera to Sigulda. Logging on the river was ended when the area was designated a national park in 1973.

Cultural retreat: There is something rather sedate about Sigulda: it is a pristine and airy little town which hides its affluent past beneath a film of cleanliness. It became popular during the National Awakening, as a place where Latvians from Riga could discover their rural roots. It has more recently become a winter sports centre, with a bobsled run and ski slopes on the far side of the railway crossing, to the left. The **castle** is through the town on the right.

The deeply moated castle, which included a convent, is now a crumbled ruin. It was built by the Crusaders' Order of Sword Bearers who came here as soon as they arrived in Latvia in 1207. They used large boulders and stuck them together with mortar mixed with eggs and honey. Today, there is a open-air concert hall in its midst.

The large and not particularly attractive country house beside it is the modern "castle" built in 1878. Artists and writers of the Awakening used to come for inspiration, and Rozentāls and other painters used to like to hike up to **Gleznotāju kalns**, Painters' Hill, just to the east, which has one of the best views over the Gauja (walk from the car-park

Preceding pages: fir forest near Sigulda. **Left,** Straupe church and estate. **Right,** narrow-gauge railway from Alūksne to Gulbene.

on the far side of the old castle). Kronvaldu Atis (1837–75), a teacher of Latvian, is remembered by a statue outside the new castle, and some of the stained glass produced during his lifetime is still *in situ* in what is now a sanatorium. The town also has an information centre, near the white Lutheran church. Even if it looks closed, walk in and ask for whatever advice you need. It has a room full of stuffed animals culled from the park, including wild boar, beaver and various deer, from roe to elk.

One of the best places to see wildlife and natural scenery, with possibilities of sighting at least a deer, is just beyond Sigulda in **Līgatne**. There are also some rare plants here, such as Lady's Slipper orchids, Linnaea and woodland tulips, and in spring it is carpeted with lily-of-the-valley. Turn left to Līgatne through **Auglīšgatne** on the Sigulda to Cēsis main road, turning left again just before the river, where there are two parking spots and day tickets to the parks can be bought. Nature trails are mapped out,

and a ferry takes cars over the river. From Sigulda there are two ways across the Gauja. The road goes over a bridge, and every 30 minutes a cable car swings alongside it, 135 ft (40 metres) above the river, taking 3½ minutes to cover the half-mile (1 km) distance. On the far side, the road falls away to the right to reach the side of the river where day tickets to the park can be bought in the car-park.

Castles and caves: The banks of the Gauja are characterised by red sandstone cliffs and caves, the deepest of which is **Gūtmanis' Cave**, found opposite the car park. Scratched by graffiti more than 300 years old, it is 35 ft (14 metres) deep and the fresh spring water that wore it away still bubbles up into it, tasting strongly of iron. The cave is named after a healer called Gūtmanis who first used the water as a cure.

Some 10 minutes' walk further up the road is **Turaida castle**, a fort of red bricks and a single remaining round tower which breaks up through the forest heights. At the foot of the maple- **Picnic above the River Gauja.**

lined approach is a stable with some fine horses for hire. Alternatively, you can hire a horse and carriage to take you up to the castle.

In the language of the ancient Livs who first settled this valley, Turaida means the Garden of the Gods. Inside the castle there is a gallery and a small museum charting its history. On the path from the stable is a Lutheran church (1750), and a small restaurant in an old drying kiln which serves grey peas and other good local dishes. A few yards away, beneath a large elm tree, a black marble slab marks the grave of Maija, the Turaida Rose who was killed in Gūtmanis' Cave in 1620. This 19-year-old local girl was in love with a castle gardener, and when a Polish officer approached her in the cave, she devised a scheme whereby he would kill her rather than submit her to a fate worse than death. She had a magic scarf, she said, and he could have it if he promised to leave her alone: to prove the scarf's effectiveness, she put it around her neck and told him to try to cut off her head.

From Turaida the road continues to **Inciems** where it meets up with the road to Valmiera. The next small town along this road is **Straupe**, where there is something familiar about the old castle. The square tower which rises in a dark dome and lantern, and the scrolled and stepped gable of the building below, are reminiscent of the cathedral in Riga. It dates from 1263. The castle is in a pleasant setting beside a large pond and near the Brasla river, and today it is used as a clinic for rehabilitating alcoholics. Knock on the door to get shown round. There is not much to see in the castle itself, except for some wood panelling and several grand ceramic stoves. Parties may be shown up the main tower.

In the grounds is a bell-tower and a **Lutheran church** which has some interesting 17th-century painted panels. Tombstones and tablets mark the passing of generations of the von Rosen family, owners of the castle and fierce protectors of the German Baltic way of life. The present generation is scattered, though some have helped in its restora-

tion. It has an organ made in Riga in 1856 by the firm of Martin, and the acoustics make it a good recital venue.

Another German monument is nearby at **Ungurmuiža**, on the way to Cēsis. This belonged to the von Campenhausens who had it built in 1751. In 1938 it became a school, and money is currently being sought for its restoration. Many of the fine wall paintings have disappeared, though paintings of Tsar Alexander guarding the baron's bedroom are still there. In the grounds is a tea-room folly and a school the baron had built for local children, which has been used as a kitchen for the people of the local collective.

Between Ungurmuiža and Cēsis is **Raiskums**, beside a lake of the same name, where there is threshing barn, school house and curious wood and stone chapel from the 19th century.

Excursion centre: Cēsis is a pleasant, wide-open town which was a popular cultural centre during both the National Awakening and First Independence. Its attractive yellow-and-white, two- and three-storey buildings date back several centuries, and a Lutheran church, St John's, was started in 1281. There are several hotels and good places to eat including Saieta nams and the more expensive Pie Raunas Vārtiem.

Cēsis has certainly seen its fair share of bloodshed. The place was a walled town and a member of the Hanseatic League and its history is very well documented in a good **museum** in the building next to the old **castle**. The castle is a chalky-white fortified convent which served as a power base for the Livonian Order. The old red-brick factory nearby is a brewery.

Cēsis was inhabited by Baltic Finns until the Letgallians moved in around the 6th century, and it has provided much archaeological information. But the most impressive digs have been in the **Āraišu** area of the park just to the south. It was here that Letgallians built a large lake fortress in the 9th century, and its excavation has been one of the most important finds of this kind in northern Europe. Burial barrows have

Milk seller.

been uncovered as well as graves, and a scheme has begun to reconstruct some of the ancient buildings on the lake. A stone castle built by the Livonian Order has also been excavated.

Beyond Cēsis is **Valmiera**, which also has an ancient castle and was once a member of the Hanseatic League. An observation tower near the castle gives a good view of the valley. North of the town up towards **Strenči**, is one of the most picturesque stretches of the River Gauja. To the northwest is **Mazsalaca**, an attractive, out-of-the-way resort on the River Salaca.

Coastal route: The Gauja was strategically important as the main route to Tallinn and St Petersburg. Today, the most pleasant way to drive to Tallinn is up the scenic coast, around the eastern edge of Riga Bay, which allows views of the Baltic sea through the pines. Unlike the rest of Latvia's coast, its sandy beaches are scattered with boulders and stones. From Riga the M12 goes up past summer villas up to **Saulkrasti**, beyond which lie small com-

munities, such as **Kumrags**, which has some fine views and a good beach.

Salacgrīva provides a convenient stopping-point, and between here and **Ainaži**, the coast takes on a different aspect as meadows push out into the sea. Ainaži is right up by the border, and was out on the map as the port Krišjānis Valdemārs chose to base Latvia's Maritime Academy in 1864. Ainaži flourished for a while as a port and shipbuilding centre, but now it has returned to being a backwater, with a small museum charting its moment of seafaring glory.

Along the Daugava: To the southeast of Riga the Moscow Road, the A215, follows the north bank of the Daugava, leaving Riga through the **Moscow District** with its Old Believers and traditional Russian community, a district that was pulled down and rebuilt in the 1960s. Just beyond it is **Rumbula**, where the big weekend market draws people for miles around. Bigger than Riga's market, it is the main place for buying and selling cars – which are often stolen.

Gauja Park deer.

The road continues towards the big textile town of **Ogre**, past **Ikškile**, which in the Liv language was called Üxküll Ykescola. This is an island on the Daugava, inaccessible to the passing traveller, and it bears the remains of the oldest stone church in Latvia, built in 1186. The riverbank here is a good picnic spot and a stone monument gives a brief history of the church so frustratingly just out of reach.

At **Ķegums**, the country's first hydro-electric scheme, built between the wars, has pushed back the river's banks and created a long lake. The change of landscape is a source of regret to the historians and traditionalists who converge at its centre, around **Lāčplēsis**.

Magic belt: Lāčplēsis is the home of a Latvian legend, from a 19th-century epic written by Andrējs Pumpurs who used the names of real places for his characters. Lāčplēsis was brought up by a bear and on one occasion tore apart a rogue bear with his hands, giving him the name "bear-slayer". He was last seen in a fatal struggle with the Black Soldier of Death, but he will return, it is said, to throw the enemy into the sea and make the land free again.

The father of Lāčplēsis was **Lielvārdis** (named after the neighbouring village), who possessed a magic belt decorated with symbols which could tell personal fortunes. A copy of this belt is kept in the **Andrejs Pumpurs Museum** at Lāčplēsis, a village steeped in history. There was a Liv settlement here 3,000 years ago and the site is on a hill next to the museum overlooking the river. A sacred oak is at **Kaibala** nearby.

The museum, begun in 1970 under Edgars Kauliņš, the last, enlightened boss of the local Lāčplēsis collective farm, has an exhibition dedicated to Pumpurs, who was an officer in the Russian army. It also gives an introduction to the literature of the National Awakening, to which Vidzeme's sons made a considerable contribution.

Lielvārdis' belt, some 15 ft (5 metres) long, is brought out mainly on weekends when children and newly married couples come to Lāčplēsis to be blessed.

Folk-dancers in Cēsis.

A hand passing over it may come upon a warm spot, and when the symbols here are read they may reveal something of the person's destiny.

Before the Moscow road turns north to Madona, away from the Daugava river, it is worth noting the Swedish castle at **Koknese**. Following the river downstream past a white Lutheran church set on a wide sweep in the river, the road comes to the ruins of the two-storey castle, where the Perse meets the Daugava, a point appreciated by teenagers who dive in to the green waters off the old walls. A Swedish grave from the Northern Wars lies in the surrounding woods.

Madona, is the next town of any size, a quiet spot with a renovated inn from the 16th-century Swedish days. Just north of Madona is **Cesvaine**. Its late 19th-century "castle", a mix of neo-Gothic with an art nouveau interior, was the hunting lodge of Baron Adolf von Wolf, who had no fewer than 99 estates in the Baltics. A hybrid statue has the tail of a fox, the mane of a lion and the face of a wolf, while another statue of a wolf has its tail pointed towards Gulbene, whose baron Wolf had argued with. The estate has a 60-acre (25-hectare) park which supposedly sustains 200 animal species. A squat tower to the left of a summer house is all that remains of a 14th-century **Bishop's Palace**.

Just outside Cesvaine, is **Gaizinš**, the highest hill in the Baltics, a stunningly low 1,025 ft (312 metres). In case you might miss it, a 15-storey red-brick look-out tower of graphic ugliness has been built on top of it. Its summit provides a 360-degree view of the lakes, pasture-land and the acres of deep green forest. There is resort at **Mežezers**, a lakeside complex of boating and camping facilities with A-frame cabins in the woods, which is sorely in need of holidaymakers.

North of Madona is **Gulbene** where a manor house with a fine portico lies in ruins: bullet holes still pepper its facade. In 1944 the Germans blew up the church tower before the advancing Russians to deprive them of a viewing platform: it

irst-aid for
veteran
ehicle.

fell on the church, destroying the roof. Beside it is the only statue of Martin Luther in the Baltics.

Just north of Gulbene at **Ate** there is a small **open-air museum** of around a dozen buildings. It is a popular place for weddings and a room is devoted to famous sons and daughters of Vidzeme. There are also souvenirs on display from the family of Baron Wolf, the man of many mansions.

From Gulbene a narrow-gauge railway runs up to the attractive town of **Alūksne**, which has one of the most pleasant hotels in Latvia. The town is centred on a ruined 14th-century Livonian castle on a lake. It sits on an island reached across a small wooden bridge and is devoted today to sports activities. Follies dedicated to Greek gods are scattered in what is now the cemetery in the surrounding woods. These were put up by the Nietinghoff family to honour the dead of the Great Northern War.

One of the town's main claims to fame is that its pastor, Ernst Glück,

adopted the daughter of a Lithuanian grave-digger, Martha Skavronska, who went on to marry Peter the Great and become Catherine I of Russia. Glück also produced the first Latvian translation of the Bible, in 1689, and a copy of it, one of only a dozen left in the world, is kept along with many others in the **Bible Museum**. The earliest Latvian religious tract, *God's Word*, dates from 1654 and is also in the museum.

When Glück first arrived in Alūksne, he lived in the castle, but he later moved to a single-storey wood manse behind the Lutheran church, and his plantation of oaks is still standing.

Literary trail: Between these eastern towns and the Gauja National Park, a number of Latvian literary figures are remembered in a pastoral setting that can have changed little since they knew it more than 100 years ago. Beneath shady trees are several wood barns, cottage gardens and small platforms for the delivery vehicles to collect and return milk-churns.

Beside **Lake Alauksts** is the **Skalbe Museum,** which contains local painted furniture. Kārlis Skalbe (1879–1945), a writer of fairy-tales, died in Sweden where he had emigrated. His remains were returned in 1992 and buried beneath a stone overlooking the lake.

The museum at the nearby village of **Vecpiebalga** celebrates the Kaudzītes brothers, Reinis and Matīss, who jointly wrote Latvia's first major novel, *The Time of the Land Surveyors* (1879). Vēcpiebalga also has a museum dedicated to the writer Jānis Subrabkalns and the composer Emils Darzins, with an exhibition of writers and composers who have emigrated.

At **Ērgļi** there is a museum where the playwright Rūdolfs Blaumanis was born. **Indrāni** nearby is the setting of his most famous play.

Between Ērgli and Sigulda is **Malpils**, a clay manor house rebuilt just after it was set alight in 1905. It is now used as a school and houses a **Museum of Agriculture and Irrigation**. On display are some rather fine paintings and the first map of Latvia, from 1688, drawn by Swedish engineers.

Left, sledge-happy. Right, Lutheran church, Alūksne.

276

LATGALE AND THE BLUE LAKES

Latvia's easternmost region is "The Land of the Blue Lakes". A mass of deciduous trees makes it not just bluer, but greener, too. It is the poorest and the most remote of the regions. Its people, who speak a dialect some regard as a separate language, have larger families and are more gregarious. They sometimes like to think of themselves as the Irish of Latvia. If there is any festival or gathering here it is bound to be lively. Traditionally, the people of Latgale had homesteads adjoining each other, rather than isolated country homes as in the rest of Latvia. They continue their established crafts, especially ceramics, making big, chunky jugs and candelabra which are thickly glazed, and seen everywhere in the country.

Rubbing up against Russia, Belarus and Lithuania, Latgale's geography has given it a different history, too. While Kurzeme and Zemgale were being recruited to the Lutheran cause by the dukes of Courland, the Swedes in Riga and Vidzeme were banishing practising Catholics, and many of them came to Latgale, where Catholic Poland held sway. They left their mark in the baroque Jesuit style of their grand churches: St Peter's in Daugavpils, St Ludwig in Krāslava, the Holy Cross of Pasien and the huge, white, country church at Aglona, where Catholics from all over Europe gather on Ascension Day.

But among these slightly distant lands is Daugavpils, Latvia's second largest city, a cosmopolitan place tucked in the far southeast 140 miles (224 km) from Riga, and the best part of a day's train ride away.

River road: The town of Pļaviņas is the last on the A215 Moscow Road from Riga before Latgale. Here the River Daugava has a serious reputation, especially at Lāčbedre (the Bear's Den) where men and boats have disappeared into the maw of a particularly voracious whirlpool. Just beyond Pļaviņas as the A215 turns inland to Madona. Taking the right fork, the road follows the

Daugava upriver to **Jēkabpils**, named after the Courland duke. Beside the road on this north bank is **Krustpils castle**, occupied by the army but with plans to open for tourists.

The town of Jēkabpils, marked by the dome of a Russian Orthodox church of 1887, lies on the far bank of the river and is one of the three sugar manufacturing towns in Latvia. "Three spoons of sugar in your coffee," people used urge: "One for Liepāja, one for Jelgava and one for Jēkabpils." There is a Regional Museum in the town and the Maritime School is a sign that it has been a stop on the river route to the hinterland since Viking times.

The town is famous as the birthplace of Jānis Rainis (1865–1929) the most important literary figure of the National Awakening. His father was an estate overseer and he built Tadenava, the house where Jānis was born. The building is now the **Rainis Museum** containing the family's household items.

A bustling country market is held at weekends and everything from car boots

full of piglets to tsarist gold roubles are offered for sale.

Līvāni, the next town upstream, is on the map because of the cheap glass-fibre two-storey houses made here which bear the town's name. They have a reputation for catching fire and burning to the ground in 10 minutes flat, which is what happened to the one belonging to the chess grandmaster Anatol Karpov, near Plavinas. The Party immediately rebuilt it. In post-Soviet times they have been sold off to their occupants for as little as a few hundred pounds.

Daugavpils, near the Lithuanian and Belarus borders, is at a crossroads between the Baltic to Black Sea route, and the road and railway from Warsaw to Moscow. This former capital of the Duchy of Pārdaugava, known as "Polish Livonia", has a sprinkling of 18th – 19th century mansions and the odd bright splash of art nouveau. Around the town, doors, shutters and whole wooden houses painted bright blue are signs of Russians in residence. In its streets and in its markets, Latvian is rarely heard.

The city has been attracting "foreigners" for many centuries, from the Old Believers, the sect exiled from Moscow in the 18th century, to others just coming to this relatively prosperous town to find work.

It is an industrial town, a textile town, and Russification under the Soviets was intense. Prior to World War II one-third of the 40,000 population was Russian or Polish. Now there are 120,000 inhabitants, only 12 percent of whom are Latvian. The industries that the Soviets built up – textiles, bicycle manufacture and locomotive repair sheds – have suffered a depressing slump in the aftermath of independence.

Like other large towns in Latvia, Daugavpils is bereft of road signs, and drivers may take a while to find the centre of this drawn-out conurbation. The rump of the church spires are scattered over an area away from the centre, which is set around the Hotel Latvija (a mini-version of its namesake in Riga) and the stunning white Catholic **Church of St Peter's** behind. This mid-18th

Left, Feast of the Assumption, Aglona. Right, festival in Rēzekne.

century former monastery building is an example of a fortress church and its twin-towered facade is a mark of the Jesuit baroque which was brought in from Lithuania. It is a basilica with three naves, the middle one rising to an impressive tunnel vault.

Beside it, an attractive tree-lined shopping boulevard, formerly called Lenin Street, runs up to the station, with little bookshops and the lively Darts café. On the corner of the big square in front of the Latvija is the main shopping store, worth checking out for ceramics, Latvian linen and Russian hats. In the same street in the opposite direction, just beyond the gloomy grey culture centre, is a small **town museum** which has contemporary exhibitions of art and crafts. In Gogola Street nearby there is a dashing example of art nouveau, and a café that has delicious cakes.

Some 30 miles (45 km) east of Daugavpils is the town of **Krāslava**, and in its centre is **Krāslavas pilsmuiža**, a fine old Polish house under restoration. It also has a distinguished church in St

Ludwig's, built in 1673 and radically altered into its present towerless baroque form in 1763.

The stretch of river between the two towns is particularly enchanting, and it was here that the Soviets wanted to install a hydro-electric power station, causing protests that helped to fuel calls for independence. Since independence, the lack of a sufficient power supply in the country has led to the question tentatively being broached again. What is certain is that a petrochemical plant just over the border in Belarus has been polluting the Daugava for some years.

Lakeland: Rolling lands of rivers and lakes spread north from Krāslava, towards **Rēzekne**, Latgale's capital. Just above Krāslava, lying next to the Hill of the Sun, **Sauleskalns**, is **Dridzis**, probably the most beautiful and certainly the deepest of Latvia's lakes at 313 ft (65 metres). Its resort at **Kombuļi** has been a favourite for tourists from the former USSR.

Ežezers (hedgehog) lake, full of little islands, is to the northeast, and used to

Land of the
Blue Lakes.

have a fine school nearby. **Rāzna**, just south of Rēzekne, is the country's largest lake at 21 sq. miles (56 sq. km), and there is a camp-site, though camp-site in the Baltics means solid buildings rather than tents. Until the Soviets drained half of it and ruined an important stork habitat, Latvia's largest lake used to be **Lake Lubāns,** northwest of Rēzekne.

The traditional wooden architecture in this part of the region is particularly attractive, with splashes of colour and embellishments on doors and window shutters. Small sauna sheds are stuck out in all the gardens which are planted with fruit trees and bushes and beds of bright flowers.

Pilgrims' progress: Northeast of Daugavpils, down stony tracks on the east side of the road to Rēzekne, is the village of **Aglona** which is much too small for its grand baroque church to which thousands of pilgrims make their way every year. During the Reformation, when the Dom in Riga was taken over by the Lutherans, it became the country's principal Catholic church, a role it resumed under the Soviet system when the Dom was used as a concert hall. But whatever the vicissitudes of history, pilgrims have continued to come here on the Feast of the Assumption (15 August) each year, on foot, by gypsy cart, car and charabanc.

The object of their veneration is a picture of the Virgin Mary, kept behind the altar, which is said to have healing powers. The picture is reported to have been presented by Manuel of Byzantium to Lithuania's Vytautas the Great some time between 1325 and 1340. In 1700 the picture was copied and either the copy or the original, depending on which camp you follow, remained in Lithuania while the other came here to Aglona the year that the church was founded. Money came from Jeta-Justine Sastodicka, a local Polish aristocrat, whose portrait hangs on the present basilica's west wall.

The church was built to accommodate Dominicans from Lithuania whom Sastodicka invited to teach, heal and convert. This is the second church on **Filming time.**

the site. The first one was made of wood and built just to the north of the current church's site. In 1787 it burnt down and the present shining white, two-towered Italianate creation rose up around the original organ, which was saved. A monastery and cloister are attached to the church: Dominicans lived here for 150 years until the tsar forbade people from becoming involved in the church.

In 1992, when a visit by the Pope to Aglona was announced, five Lithuanian-trained Latvian novices took up residence, while the grounds in front of the church were completely levelled to pave the way, literally, for the hullaballoo of a papal visit.

Rēzekne, 38 miles (60 km) north of Daugavpils, is a good centre for exploration. Although its population of 42,900 is about one-third that of Daugavpils, Rēzekne is the capital of Latgale. The **Regional Museum** is just up from the trio of churches in the main street. The statue in the middle of the road was erected for the third time on this spot in 1992, amid celebration by costume-clad Latgalians. The Rēzna restaurant in the old Soviet eating-house block just beyond it has been pleasantly refurbished with a jolly mural of a country wedding. The food is good and the staff know how to smile.

Rēzekne is one of many ceramics centres in the region. Some families – the Paulāns, the Ušpelis – have been working potters here for up to eight generations. The first pottery owned by the Ušpelis family, who have been in the business for six generations, is in Riga's Open-Air Ethnography Museum.

To the east of Rēzekne is **Ludza**, another good base for exploring the blue lakes of the region. From here the road goes east to Russia at **Zilupe**. To the south is the fourth of Latgale's great Catholic churches. **Pasiena Church** echoes that of Daugavpils, a twin-towered wedding cake built in 1761, 67 years after a Dominican mission was founded. From here there is a magnificent view across the plains of Russia.

To the north is the region of **Abrene,** which Russia still claims.

Feeding time.

The largest of the three republics is a Catholic country, a fact that is impossible to miss. Vilnius, its capital, owes its splendid baroque flavour to the Jesuits who built its fine university as well as many of its churches. Throughout the country are roadside wooden shrines, and the Hill of Crosses just north of Šiauliai is an extraordinary symbol of a nation of believers. The shrines are part of a folk tradition of wood carving, which can be seen all over the country from the Witches' Park on the Neringa Spit to the monuments to the victims of World War II's genocide: Vilnius had a vibrant Jewish community and was a centre of Yiddish publishing.

Like Latvians, Lithuanians are originally Indo-Europeans and speak a Baltic language. In spite of their dedicated Catholicism, they were the last nation in Europe to convert to Christianity. At the height of their glorious history their Grand Duchy stretched from the Baltic to the Black Sea. Such grandeur can be glimpsed at the dukes' principal residence, the restored red-brick castle of Trakai set in the natural moat of Lake Galvė, west of Vilnius. For some time the Grand Duchy's southern border was along the River Nemunas, where many castles were built.

Lithuania's second city is Kaunas, which was a temporary capital between the wars. This is a business centre, and it also has the museum of Lithuania's towering artistic figure, M. K. Čiurlionis. From Kaunas the River Nemunas runs down to a lagoon kept from the sea by the Neringa Spit. This exceptional sand bar of small fishing villages stretches down into Lithuania Minor, formerly Königsberg, where the kings of Prussia were crowned. It is now the Russian enclave of Kaliningrad.

German can be heard in many of the shops on the spit's southernmost resort town of Nida. Though the coast is shorter than those of its Baltic state neighbours, like them Lithuania has rest homes, bath houses and sanatoriums, chiefly to the north around the bustling resort of Palanga.

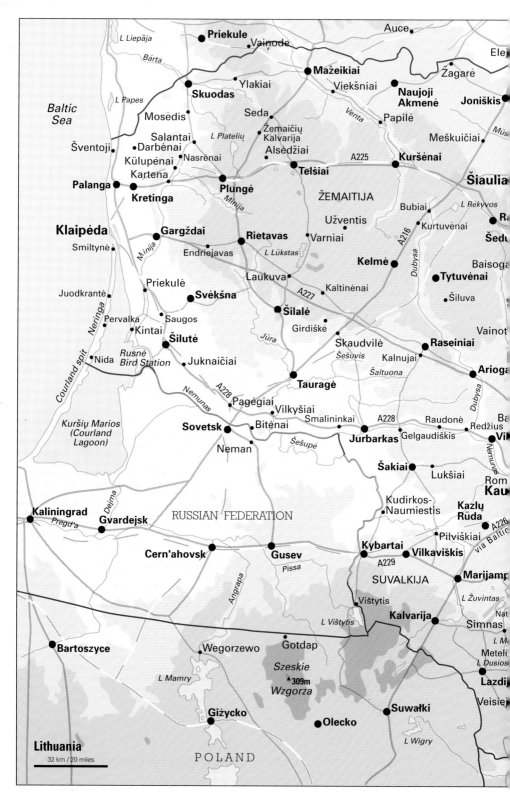

Baltic
Sea

L Liepāja

Bārta

L Papes

Priekule

Vainode

Auce

Elei

Žagarė

Mažeikiai

Ylakiai

Skuodas

Viekšniai

Naujoji
Akmenė

Joniškis

Mosēdis

Seda

Venta

Papilė

Salantai

L Platelių

Kalvarija

Žemaičių

Meškuičiai

Mūs

Šventoji

Darbėnai

Nasrėnai

Alsėdžiai

A225

Kuršėnai

Külupėnai

Kartena

Telšiai

Šiaulia

Palanga

Plungė

Kretinga

Minija

ŽEMAITIJA

Bubiai

L Rėkyvos

Ra

Užventis

Kurtuvėnai

Klaipėda

Gargždai

Rietavas

Varniai

A216

Šedu

Smiltynė

Minija

Endriejavas

L Lūkstas

Kelmė

Dubysa

Baisoga

Laukuva

Tytuvėnai

Juodkrantė

Priekulė

Svėkšna

A227

Kaltinėnai

Šiluva

Neringa

Pervalka

Saugos

Šilalė

Kintai

Girdiškė

Vainot

Šilutė

Jūra

Skaudvilė

Raseiniai

Nida

Rusnė
Bird Station

Juknaičiai

Šešuvis

Kalnujai

Arioga

Šaltuona

Dubysa

Tauragė

Kuršių Marios
(Courland
Lagoon)

Courland spit

Nemunas

A228

Pagėgiai

Vilkyšiai

Smalininkai

A228

Raudonė

Redžius

Ba

Sovetsk

Bitėnai

Šešupė

Jurbarkas

Gelgaudiškis

Vil

Neman

Šakiai

Lukšiai

Nemunas

Rom

Kau

Dejma

Kudirkos-
Naumiestis

Kazlų
Rūda

Kaliningrad

Gvardejsk

RUSSIAN FEDERATION

Pregd'a

Pilviškiai

A226

Cern'ahovsk

Gusev

Kybartai

Vilkaviškis

via Baltic

Pissa

A229

SUVALKIJA

Marijamp

Vištytis

L Žuvintas

L Vištytis

Kalvarija

Nat

Simnas

L M

Bartoszyce

Wegorzewo

Gotdap

Meteli

L Dusios

Szeskie

L Mamry

▲309m
Wzgorza

Lazdij

Veisie

Giżycko

Suwałki

Olecko

L Wigry

Lithuania

32 km / 20 miles

POLAND

294

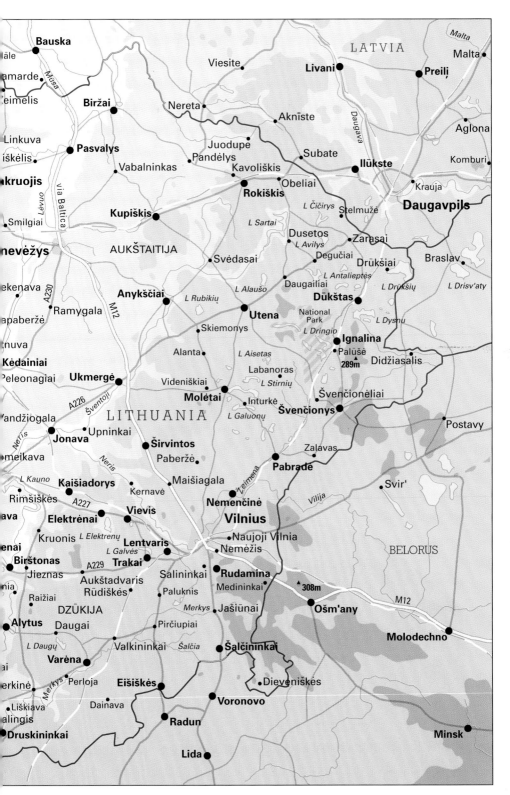

Bauska
āle
amarde
eimelis
Viesite
Livani
Malta
Malta
Preiļ
Biržai
Nereta
Aknīste
Aglona
Linkuva
iškėlis
Pasvalys
Juodupė
Pandėlys
Kavoliškis
Subate
Ilūkste
Komburi
kruojis
Vabalninkas
Obeliai
Krauja
Rokiškis
L Čičirys
Stelmužė
Daugavpils
Smilgiai
Kupiškis
L Sartai
Dusetos
Zarasai
Degučiai
nevėžys
AUKŠTAITIJA
Svėdasai
L Avilys
Drūkšiai
Braslav
ekenava
Daugailiai
L Antalieptės
L Drūkšių
L Drisv'aty
Anykščiai
L Rubikių
L Alaušo
Dūkštas
apaberžė
Ramygala
Utena
National
Park
L Dysnų
nuva
Skiemonys
L Dringio
Kėdainiai
Alanta
L Aisetas
Ignalina
Palūšė
289m
Didžiasalis
Peleonagiai
Ukmergė
Videniškiai
Labanoras
L Stirnių
Švenčionėliai
andžiogala
Molėtai
Inturkė
Švenčionys
LITHUANIA
L Galuonų
Upninkai
Jonava
Zalavas
Postavy
meikava
Širvintos
Paberžė
Pabradė
L Kauno
Kaišiadorys
Maišiagala
Svir'
Rimšiškės
Kernavė
Vilija
ava
Vievis
Nemenčinė
Elektrėnai
Vilnius
BELORUS
Kruonis
L Elektrenų
Lentvaris
Naujoji Vilnia
enai
L Galvės
Nemėžis
Birštonas
Trakai
Jieznas
Rudamina
Aukštadvaris
Šalininkai
Medininkai
308m
nia
Rūdiškės
Paluknis
M12
Raižiai
Merkys
Jašiūnai
Ošm'any
Molodechno
DZŪKIJA
Pirčiupiai
Alytus
Daugai
L Daugų
Šalčia
Šalčininkai
Valkininkai
Varėna
ai
erkinė
Perloja
Eišiškės
Dieveniškės
Liškiava
Dainava
Voronovo
alingis
Radun
Minsk
Druskininkai
Lida

LATVIA
Daugava

Neris
Šventoji
A226
A230
M12
via Baltica
Lėvuo
Mūsa
A227
A229
Neris
Žeimena
Merkys

LITHUANIA: A SHORT HISTORY

Lithuania is now a country of 25,000 sq. miles (64,750 sq. km) with a population of 3.5 million, its very existence snatched back during 1989–91 from the jaws of the Soviet Union. It is a country which has experienced unbelievable swings of fortune.

With hindsight, the turning-point was in 1385 when 11-year-old Princess Jadviga of Poland was due to marry young Wilhem von Habsburg, whom she had known and been betrothed to since infancy. The wedding was to take place in Cracow, then capital of Poland, and the prisoners were released from the city dungeons as part of the celebrations welcoming Wilhem's arrival at the castle to claim his bride. The festivities were in full swing when, unexpectedly, a delegation of Lithuanian nobles arrived in Cracow and went into urgent conference with their Polish counterparts. The outcome was the archbishop going to the castle with unsettling news for little Jadviga. The wedding was called off and she was going to marry another man instead.

For the Polish nobility, if not for Jadviga, the proposal just put forward by the Lithuanian delegation made more sense than her marrying a Habsburg. A conjugal union between Poland and Lithuania with its huge, albeit rather ramshackle, empire would create a force capable of seeing off the Teutonic Knights, who were grabbing ever more of the Baltic lands.

Jadviga must have seen things differently; at least the Habsburgs were Christians. The Lithuanian Grand Prince she was now supposed to marry was an outright pagan. The Lithuanians had resisted every attempt to convert them to Christianity, beginning with Bishop Adalbert of Prague in 997 who was murdered for his trouble. Moreover, Prince Jogaila was three times her age and it was known that he had already murdered a number of close relatives. Little Jadviga watched helplessly as the Castellan of Cracow entered the castle, seized the downcast von Habsburg and banished him from the kingdom.

Left, Grand Duke Vytautas, symbol of an empire. **Right**, the new parliament.

For his part, Jogaila had no more love for the Poles than he did for their religion. The Lithuanians were proud to be pagans. Their warrior elite claimed descent from Perkūnas, the god of thunder. Jogaila had distinguished antecedents including Mindaugas, the first to unite the peoples of Lithuania in 1230. He joined with the neighbouring Letts in attacks on the German crusaders and briefly decided to become Christian so that Pope Innocent would crown him king. Afterwards, he cynically sacrificed a Christian princess to

Perkūnas, and attacked the knights again. The next strong leader to emerge was Gediminas (1316–41), the founder of the Gediminaičai or Jogaillian (Jogailaičai) dynasty that ruled Lithuania and Poland for the next 250 years. He founded Vilnius, where he built his hilltop castle overlooking the Neris and Vilnia rivers. Though he remained pagan he brought in Dominican and Franciscan teachers and he encouraged immigration of artists and craftsmen.

By the time he died, Gediminas had so successfully fought against the Tatars of the east that the Lithuanian empire reached down as far as Kiev and the Black Sea. In the west, the coast around Klaipėda (Memel in German) had been seized by Knights of the Livonian Order in 1225. Before the orders merged they had to fight the Teutonic knights of the southern lands that became Prussia, as well as Lithuania's dukes.

One of Gediminas's grandsons was Jogaila. He had become embroiled in a bloody family feud and was as vulnerable to the acquisitive Teutonic Knights as Poland itself was. The Lithuanian nobles had calculated the strength of a dynastic union with Poland, hence the delegation's trip to Cracow to seek out Jadviga.

Poland was very much Rome's champion and the marriage was not agreed without

alas, did not have a fairy-tale ending. Jadviga hated her husband from beginning to end and sought consolation in burying herself in good works for the poor. She died childless at 24, pointedly leaving her fortune to the educational establishment which later became the Jogaillian University.

King Ladislaus V – Jogaila's full title – fulfilled one of his contractual obligations by going straight to Vilnius and smashing Perkūnas's statue. What followed was the usual fusion of old pagan beliefs and new-fangled Christianity. Perkūnas's mother was transformed into the Lithuanian Madonna. A bishop was appointed and mass baptisms were organised at which converts were pre-

conditions. First Jogaila would have to become a Christian. Second, he would have to convert his whole empire to Christianity. The terms of the marriage also required Lithuania to make some territorial concessions to Poland and release all Polish prisoners and slaves.

On 15 February 1386, Jogaila bowed his head for a splash of baptismal water, assumed the Christian name Ladislaus (the Poles afterwards called him Władysław-Jagiełło), and three days later he married a still confused and unhappy Jadviga. The following month they assumed the crowns of both Poland and Lithuania. The marriage,

sented with a white smock and given a Christian name. Vilnius itself was given a new name, Christianised as well as Polonised into "Wilno".

The new king's previous position as Grand Prince of Lithuania *per se* was given to his cousin Vytautas, another grandson of Gediminas, who showed every inclination to preserve the greatest degree possible of Lithuanian independence within the dynastic union. The rivalry between the cousins focused on retaining the support of the Lithuanian nobility. The Polish nobility then enjoyed a considerably better living standard than their Lithuanian counterparts, and it was extending the Polish rights to the Lithuanians that brought triumph for the king. Vytautas was compensated by being made Grand Duke of Lithuania for his lifetime.

Vytautas was the last of the great Lithuanian rulers. He built the impressive red-brick island castle at Trakai after the nearby castle of his father, Kęstutis, had been attacked once too often by the German crusaders. He drove back the Turks and mustered a bodyguard of Turkic Karaites whose descendants live by the castle today. In 1410 he and Jogaila decisively defeated the German crusaders at Grünwald (Tannenberg) and under Vytautas's rule the Grand Duchy became one of the largest states in Europe, occupy-

"Lithuanian Statutes" and finally written down in constitutional form agreed in 1569 at the Union of Lublin. The two countries were to share a king and a two-tiered government, but Lithuania kept a separate administration and its name.

Although Lithuania was territorially the larger of the two partners, Poland exerted the greater cultural influence. The Lithuanian nobility were Polonised and spoke Latin at court and Polish at other times. For the other social strata, the effects of the union were more painfully felt. The Polish social order was rigorously imposed throughout the joint empire. Unlike the nobility, the Lithuanian bourgeoisie did not assume the status of their

ing Belarus and the Ukraine. Even with shared privileges, the rivalry between the Polish and Lithuanian nobilities see-sawed for many years. The union, which came perilously close to falling apart, was considerably strengthened by Jogaila's son Casimir (by a later wife), who held the position of both King of Poland and Grand Duke of Lithuania. There were times when the titles again went to different individuals, but the union was solidified by two sets of

Left, the German knights vanquished at Tannenberg, or Grünwald. **Above**, confirmation of the Polish-Lithuanian union, 1569.

Polish counterparts. They were summarily demoted, disenfranchised and lost the right to own land.

The Lithuanian peasant had even more reason to rue the Polish take-over. "Common cruelty was an established feature of social life," argues the distinguished historian Norman Davies. "Faced with the congenital idleness, drunkenness and pilfering of the peasantry, the nobleman frequently replied with ferocious impositions and punishments. The lash and the knout were the accepted symbols of noble authority. The serfs were beaten for leaving the estate without permission, for brawls and misdemeanours, and for non-observance of religious practices. A dungeon, together with chains, shackles, stocks, hooks and instruments of torture, were part of the regular inventory."

The history of Lithuania right up to the partition of the union by Prussia, Russia and Austria at the end of the 18th century is therefore tied to Poland's. Lithuania's separate identity had grown progressively weaker, and the partitions made matters worse. "Little Lithuania" or "Lithuania Minor", which included Kaliningrad and the coast, was detached and given to Prussia; Russia took the rest. Tsar Alexander I toyed with the idea of reconstituting the Grand

Russia. The Russian administration responded by decreeing that only Orthodox subjects were to be employed by the state, even in the most menial capacity.

From 1864 onwards, the tsars did their utmost to Russify their Lithuanian holdings, and it was the declared policy of Muraviev, the Russian governor, to eradicate the traces of ancient Lithuania once and for all. That generally took the form of imposing Russian Orthodoxy. Non-Orthodox nobles were not allowed to buy property. They were permitted to rent it, but only for 12 years. Peasants could not buy land without a "certificate of patriotism", for which one of the qualifications was that they were

Duchy – with himself as Grand Duke – but was prevented from pursuing his idea by Napoleon's invasion.

To begin with, it was the Lithuanian nobility and educated classes who fretted under the Russian yoke. They joined the Polish uprising of 1831, and paid dearly. Next time round, about 30 years later, it was a stirring among the peasants, which the Russian government quelled with reforms giving peasants the right to hold up to 120 acres of land each. This satisfied some of them, but others were firmly under the thumb of the Roman Catholic clergy and could not accept with good grace anything on offer from Orthodox

Orthodox. An otherwise qualified landowner could lose his privileges simply by taking a non-Orthodox wife. Land for Jews was completely out of the question.

The programme of Russification reached its extreme in education. The university was closed down and only Russians were admitted to schools above elementary level. The use of the Lithuanian language was banned for all official purposes, and the Latin alphabet, in which Lithuanian was customarily written, was also prohibited. It became a punishable offence to be in possession of a prayer book that was written in Latin characters.

The Russian Revolution of 1905 gave the Lithuanians a chance to reclaim some of their dignity, if not their independence. Resolutions were passed demanding the creation of an autonomous state with a "Seim", or National Assembly, with Vilnius as the capital. Threatened with a campaign of passive resistance, concessions were made such as the reintroduction of the Lithuanian language in schools. National literature sprouted with amazing rapidity, but the great symbolic victory was that Vilnius, effectively part of Poland for five centuries, was restored as the Lithuanian capital. Just as it seemed that the country might be breaking out of its shackles, World War I broke out.

when, having occupied Vilnius, the German Military Governor announced that the city would be returned to Poland. He called it "the Pearl of the Polish Kingdom". Germany's subsequent defeat meant all its plans for Lithuania were shelved, and the question of the country's future was transferred to the Paris peace conference.

The various claims submitted to the conference by a Lithuanian delegation were made to look irrelevant as the Russian revolutionary war, not to mention the activities of a renegade German force under General Bermondt, overflowed into Lithuania. A combined force of Estonians, Poles and Lithuanians managed to repel a Bolshevik

Driven out of East Prussia, the Russian army rampaged through Lithuania, burning, plundering and taking away all Lithuanian men of military age. The German troops in pursuit were received almost as liberators, but it was quickly apparent that Germany also considered Lithuania a source of cheap labour. Any remaining hopes of independence were dashed when it emerged that longer-term German policy was to re-integrate Lithuania into occupied Poland. The cruellest blow fell in September 1915

invasion, but while they were thus engaged another Polish force made a run to seize Vilnius. They held on to it even as the Bolsheviks swept towards Warsaw. In the end they surrendered it to the Bolsheviks rather than to Lithuania, and Kaunas became the capital. It was a small compensation when Lithuania reclaimed Klaipėda (Memel) and the coast from Germany in 1923.

The possession of Wilno-Vilnius bedevilled relations between Poland and Lithuania. The city was undoubtedly the ancient capital of Lithuania, but over the course of 500 years it had become overwhelmingly Polish in every other respect, or so Poland claimed. A

Left, Vilnius in the 16th century. **Above**, Vilnius's Great Synagogue in 1944.

Russian census in 1910 broke down the population as 97,800 Poles, 75,500 Jews and only 2,200 Lithuanians.

The argument centred on the issue of whether language determines nationality. After five centuries of Polonisation and Russification, the Lithuanian language tended to be spoken only in rural areas and among peasants. The national revival did not take off until the first quarter of the 20th century. In any case, the transfer of Vilnius to Lithuania by the Red Army in 1940 was mourned in Poland as a national tragedy.

The Red Army occupied Lithuania in 1940 under the terms of the secret Nazi-Soviet Pact. "Whether you agree or not is

irrelevant," Molotov told the Lithuanian government, "because the Red Army is going in tomorrow anyway." The invading troops had an approved "government" trailing in their wake. The existing parties were dissolved, and those leaders who had not already fled were sent to Siberia.

The Soviet propaganda machine then went into action. The previous government, it said, was "indifferent to the real interests of the people, has led the country into an impasse in the fields of both domestic and foreign policy. The vital interests of the Lithuanian people have been sacrificed to the mercenary interests of a handful of ex-

ploiters and rich people. The only thing left to working people in the towns and in the country has been unemployment, insecurity, hunger, indigence and national oppression." Lithuanians steadfastly denounced the Soviet annexation as illegal.

Lithuania, together with Latvia and Estonia, was occupied by the Germans in June 1941. The 150,000 Jews in Lithuania – Vilnius was then the Jewish capital of Eastern Europe, as the statistics quoted above imply – all but vanished in Hitler's grim "final solution". In common with all the Baltic areas reoccupied by the Red Army in 1944, Lithuania lost another 200,000 people to Stalin's deportation orders. By 1950 Lithuania itself had all but vanished as an incorporated unit of the Soviet Union.

The three Baltic states moved almost in unison out of Soviet control in the late 1980s. In Lithuania, the lead was taken by the Sajudis, a breakaway movement drawn largely from the Institute of Philosophy of the Lithuanian Academy of Sciences. Its objective was full independence. There was no need to consult the Soviet Union, it said cheekily, because no one had ever recognised the 1940 annexation. This was too provocative even for the easy-going Gorbachev and, on the day that the parliament voted for unilateral independence, Soviet tanks drew up outside. Despite the freezing temperatures, thousands found themselves on the streets, and there were shootings at the TV tower in Vilnius where 14 were killed and 700 injured. It appeared that once again Lithuania's future was to be decided by a powerful neighbour. Western television viewers saw Vytautas Landsbergis, a musician who had been elected president, appear increasingly fatalistic.

Within weeks, however, it was apparent that the Soviet Union was beset by greater priorities. The threat to Lithuania's long-delayed independence passed, and Landsbergis could get on with his job. But it was not an easy one, particularly on the economic front, and in the elections of 1992 Landsbergis and the Sąjūdis were voted out of office by the Democratic Labour Party, heirs to the pro-independence wing of the former Communist Party.

Left, victims of Soviet Army, 1991. Right, painting in the parliament shows a 1991 rally in Vilnius.

VILNIUS

Lithuania's capital lies rather inconveniently in the far southeastern corner of the country only a couple of dozen miles from Belarus. It grew up on a hill beside the River Neris, near the point where it is met by the smaller River Vilnia. It was a stronghold against first the German Teutonic Knights and then the Crimean Tatars.

The Neris flows westwards to Kaunas, Lithuania's capital during the period in the 20th century when Vilnius and the surrounding area belonged to Poland. For 17 years the two countries were not on speaking terms. Poland and Lithuania were joined by marriage in 1397; in 1795 Vilnius was swallowed into the Russian empire. Russification followed Polonisation and many of the churches the Jesuits had so elaborately built, evolving a local baroque style which peaked in the 18th century, were given over to the Russian Orthodox belief.

In spite of many decades of neglect, Vilnius has one of the largest old towns in Eastern Europe, bristling with the confident and robust baroque towers of churches that seem too large and too numerous for the half a million population. Today they are mainly Catholic and since independence money and missionaries have been pouring in to reclaim the buildings for the faithful.

About half the population is Lithuanian, while 20 percent is Russian and 19 percent Polish. Before the war Vilnius was one of the great Jewish cities of Europe, and the centre of Yiddish publishing. New streets and buildings in its centre mark the site of their ghetto: 150,000 were killed by the Nazis.

Apart from the imposing architecture Vilnius has a couple of interesting museums, from the cellars of the former KGB building to the recently uncovered priceless Cathedral treasure. Most pleasure is to be had from inspecting the churches and simply walking the cob-

Preceding pages: panoramic view of Vilnius. **Left**, Pilies Street, heart of the Old Town.

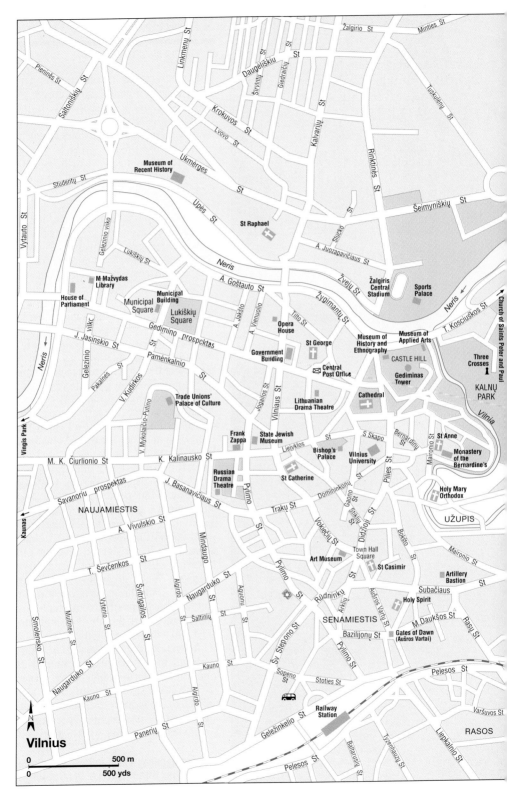

Vilnius

0 ───── 500 m
0 ───── 500 yds

308

bled streets. These are brightened by antiques shops, restaurants, bars and cafes. There are several outstanding restaurants such as the Stikliai, (the first to be privatised and popular even during Soviet times) and the beer bars, often cavernous cellars, are a speciality.

The best place to start a tour of the city is from the top of the **Gediminas Tower**, overlooking the red-tiled roofs and the church towers of the Old Town, the cathedral, the administrative buildings along the main avenue, Gediminas prospektas and the modern housing blocks on the right bank of the Neris stretching from the Lietuva Hotel to the television tower in the Lazdynai district and beyond.

The castle on **Castle Hill**, the oldest settlement of Vilnius, was built by Grand Duke Gediminas (1316–41) at the confluence of the Neris and Vilnia rivers. It was to this spot that he invited merchants, artisans and friars. According to legend, Gediminas dreamt of a powerful iron wolf howling from a hill at the mouth of the Vilnia, a dream which signified that at this spot a magnificent fort and a town would arise.

Today only the ruins of the southern part and the western defence tower (Gediminas Tower) are left. The 14th-century, three-storey octagonal brick tower houses a small exhibit of archaeological findings and the history of the castle, which is one of the symbols of Lithuania's independence. The independence movement scored its first victory when the old Lithuanian yellow, green and red tricolour was raised on the observation platform on 7 October 1988.

On the nearby **Hill of Three Crosses** are the symbols of Lithuanian mourning and hope which were rebuilt and unveiled on 14 June 1989. The first crosses were erected on the hill in the 17th century in memory of martyred Franciscan monks. During Stalin's time they were removed and buried.

At the foot of Castle Hill lies the **Lower Castle** which was constructed in the 16th century. The palace built in the reign of Zygmunt August was levelled in the end of the 18th century to make way for a market, and only the drawings

of P. Smugliewicz are left as a reminder of its beauty. Excavations at the Lower Castle, which later served as the city's law courts and a prison, are currently being undertaken.

The settlement's original church, which became the **cathedral** was commissioned in 1387 by Grand Duke Jogaila (Jagiello). It was built to mark Lithuania's conversion to Catholicism. It occupied the northern part of the Lower Castle and it was rebuilt 11 times.

The present white neoclassical building by Laurynas Stuoka-Gucevičius dates back to 1777–1801 when it was given its dominating portico of six doric columns topped with the imposing renovated statues of Sts Helen, Stanislas and Casimir. The façade has large baroque statues depicting Abraham, Moses and the four evangelists. The interior has three naves of equal height divided by two rows of massive pillars. The main altar is classical and there are several interesting chapels on the right, especially the baroque chapel of St Casimir (1623–36), which now contains the

Gediminas Tower, a high point of the city.

mausoleum of kings Alexander Jagiellon and Vladislav IV.

In the Soviet era the cathedral served as a picture gallery. As a symbol of national revival, it was the first church to be reconsecrated, on 5 February 1989. The 170-ft (52-metre) **belfry** which stands to the front and to the right of the cathedral was originally part of the Lower Castle's defence walls. Although closed to visitors, it is a distinctive landmark and a good meeting-point.

On the left of the cathedral is the **Museum of Lithuania's State Culture and History**, the country's biggest museum. It was founded in 1855, closed by the tsarist authorities and reopened in 1968. Its 270,000 exhibits illustrate the history of the people of Lithuania from the Stone Age to 1940, with re-created interiors of houses from different regions. Further round the hill on the right at No. 2 Arsenalo is the **Museum of Applied Arts**, home to the outstanding cathedral treasure. Some 250 religious gold and silver items had been hidden under the Cathedral since 1655

prior to the Russian army's attack. The treasure was briefly uncovered in the mid-1980s but the men who found it concealed it to avoid the priceless treasure being carted off to Moscow. Only in the late 1990s did they finally reveal the existence of the treasure.

The Old Town: Covering 665 acres (269 hectares), Vilnius's Old Town is one of the largest in Eastern Europe. The main artery running through the medieval city was Pilies (Castle) Street, which begins at the southeast corner of Cathedral Square and runs into Didžioji (Big) Street, past Town Hall Square to the **Gates of Dawn**, the only remaining gates of the town fortifications built against the Tatar invasions in the early 16th century. Only a few parts of the **town wall** remain in Bokšto, the street with the **Artillery Bastion** which is open to visitors.

On the cobble-stoned Pilies Street lie numerous historical buildings and from the balcony at No. 26 Lithuania's independence was declared in 1918. It is well worth venturing into the side streets

Left, votive offerings. **Right,** Altar of the Sacred Heart in the cathedral.

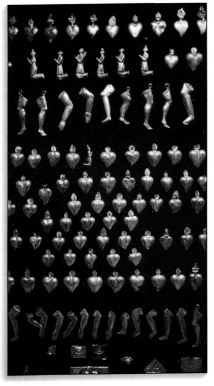

and courtyards for a glimpse of the 19th-century city. There are a number of antique shops, cafés and cellar bars tucked away down these quiet lanes.

Bernardinų Street at the northern end of Pilies leads to **St Anne's church**, one of the best examples of Gothic architecture in Lithuania. Its western facade is patterned with 33 different varieties of bricks, making it amazingly graceful and harmonious. The original chapel was built in the 16th century during the reign of the Jogaillian king Zygmunt August (1520–72). Built without any foundations, the church rests on alder logs. The original interior was destroyed by fires and is of little interest. Napoleon Bonaparte is said to have been so enraptured by St Anne's that he exclaimed his desire to bring the church back to France in the palm of his hand and set it down next to Notre Dame.

Napoleon stayed in Vilnius on the way to Moscow in 1812, at the **Bishop's Palace** in Daukantas Square behind the university. Stendhal was in charge of food and provisions and it was in Vilnius,

he said, that he learned to drink like a Russian. The euphoria that greeted the French army's arrival evaporated on their retreat when the city was plundered by the hungry troops. The palace was built for merchants in the 16th century and redesigned at the end of the 18th century by Laurynas Stuoka-Gucevičius, whose monument stands nearby. In tsarist times it was the residence of the governor general, and under the Soviets it was the Palace of the Art Workers. Today it is the official residence of the President of Lithuania.

Next to St Anne's is the **monastery of the Bernardines** who came here from Poland in 1469. It has a Gothic roof and a baroque belfry, and being built on the edge of the town it was fortified with gun ports. The nearby statue represents the Polish-Lithuanian writer Adam Mickiewicz (1798–1859), born in Lithuania and educated at Vilnius University, who wrote the brilliant epic *Pan Tadeusz* about Lithuanian society.

Across the River Vilnia from here lies **Užupis**, the first "suburb" outside the

fortified city walls. This old and shabby district has become the Montmartre of Vilnius with a decidedly arty population.

Facing St Anne's is **St Michael's church**, built between 1594 and 1625 in the style of the Lublin Renaissance as a family mausoleum for Leo Sapieha, Chancellor of Lithuania. The interior, burnt and desecrated by Cossacks in 1655, is light and spacious. To the left of the altar is the funerary monument of Sapieha and his two wives, while in the catacombs are the mummified members of the Sapieha family.

The many churches in the old town are signs of Vilnius's geographical situation on the border of Catholicism and Orthodoxy. The **Orthodox Church of Paraskovila Piatnickaya** on Didžioji Street was constructed for the first wife of Grand Duke Algirdas in the 14th century, and Peter the Great baptised Alexander Pushkin's grandfather here. Further up the street, in the former Slav quarter, the **Orthodox Church of the Holy Mother of God** belonged to Algirdas's second wife.

Town Hall Square was the political, cultural and economic centre of Vilnius. The original 15th-century town hall didn't survive, and the present one, which was designed by Stuoka-Gucevičius, the architect of the city's cathedral, was completed in 1799. In the 19th century it was frequently used for cultural events, and it became the first town theatre in 1845. In 1940 it was turned into the **Art Museum** and its two floors of galleries house a fine collection of Lithuanian paintings and sculptures from the 19th and early 20th centuries.

Past the Town Hall square up Didžioji Street lies **St Casimir's**, the oldest baroque church in Vilnius, built in 1604–15 and named after the patron saint of Lithuania. The saint, who was the son of King Casimir IV of Poland, is buried here and the crown on the church roof represents its royal connections. The church has long been an object of persecution. Under the tsars it was converted into the Orthodox Church of St Nicholas and the crown of St Casimir was replaced by an onion dome; during World **View from the university tower.**

War I the German occupation regime turned it into a Protestant church and the Soviets made it the Museum of Atheism and History of Religion. St Casimir's was reopened for public worship in 1989.

Didžioji Street leads into Aušros Vartų Street The 1902 **Philharmonic Concert Hall** is at No. 69. The street rises to the only remaining city gate, the **Gates of Dawn** (Aušros Vartai; Ostra Brama in Polish). In 1671 Carmelites from neighbouring **St Theresa's** built a chapel above the gates to house a holy image of the Virgin Mary, the **Black Madonna**, said to have miraculous powers. Its artist is unknown and it has been encased in gold and silver by local goldsmiths, leaving only the head and hands uncovered. The chapel's interior was refurbished in the neoclassical style in 1829, and the pilgrims can be seen from the street below singing and praying in front of the Virgin. Thousands of votive offerings decorate the walls and many pilgrims come to pray, queuing up on the stairs which were installed in the 18th century to connect the chapel to the

adjacent Church of St Theresa. Mass is said in both Polish and Lithuanian.

On the way up to the Gates of Dawn, in the courtyard of the only **Russian monastery** to operate during the Soviet era, stands Vilnius's most important Orthodox church, the **Church of the Holy Spirit**. It was built in the 17th century to serve the Russian Orthodox community, and it bears similarities to Catholic architecture. Before the altar stands a glass case containing the well-preserved bodies of saints Anthony, Ivan and Eustachius, martyred in 1347 because of their faith at the behest of Grand Duke Algirdas. The three saints are clothed in white during Christmas period, black during Lent and red on all other occasions.

Seat of learning: A tour of the Old Town should include a visit to the **university**, founded in 1570 by the Jesuits and one of the most important centres of the Counter-Reformation. For almost 200 years the Jesuits' college was the source of enlightenment, science and culture. It was closed under the

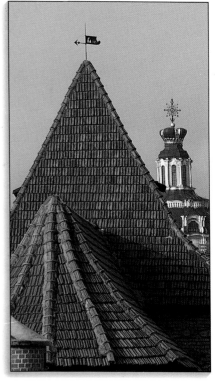

tsarist regime in the 19th century. Today some 16,000 students study at its 15 faculties. The four-storey building with an **observatory tower** dates back to 1569 and its windows are rococo. The **library** contains nearly 5 million volumes, making it the richest collection of Lithuanian books, as well as 180,000 manuscripts from the 13th – 16th centuries. Soon after it was founded, it became one of the best-known libraries in Eastern Europe.

Through the university courtyard a flight of stairs leads into St John's courtyard. Building began at **St John's church** soon after Lithuania's conversion to Catholicism in 1387. It was granted to the Jesuits in 1571 and transferred to the university following the abolition of the Jesuit Order in 1773. The present, late baroque church dates from restoration work carried out after a fire in 1737. Converted into the Museum of Scientific Thought during the Soviet occupation, St John's was re-opened to public worship in 1991. Portraits of famous academics, part of the former museum's collection, adorn the walls. The 225-ft (68-metre) **belfry**, added in the 16th century, is still one of the tallest buildings in the Old Town. The oldest of the university courtyards is the courtyard of the small **observatory**, built in the mid-18th century, when it ranked third in importance in Europe after those at Greenwich, London and the Sorbonne, Paris. The top of the facade is crowned with the signs of the zodiac.

The Jewish city: An essential part of pre-war Vilnius was the Jewish ghetto and the Jewish population which made up nearly half of the city. Today nothing remains of the "Jerusalem of Lithuania", as Vilnius was once called. As a centre of Jewish culture Vilnius had 96 synagogues stretching from Gaono to Pylimo streets and Trakų to Rūdninkų streets, all of which were razed during the war.

In 1941 some 50,000 Jews were herded into two ghettos. The small ghetto around Stiklių Street lasted for 43 days from 9 June to 29 October. Its 15,000 inhabitants were sent to labour and con-

Pilgrims's goal, the Gates of Dawn.

centration camps. The bigger ghetto, established on 6 September around Žemaitijos and Rūdninkų streets, was liquidated two years later. Most of the 50,000 Jews were killed in **Paneriai,** southeast of Vilnius. In the eerie forest you can still see the holes in the trees where men and women were shot and burned by Germans and local Nazis.

The **Great Synagogue** and the **Schulhoyf,** the traditional centre of Jewish culture around Vokiečių, Žydų and Antokolskio streets, suffered heavy damage during the war. The ruins of the synagogue, which dated back to 1661, remained for some years before the Soviet authorities decided to dynamite what was left of the synagogue to make way for a kindergarten and a basketball field. The Jewish cemetery was levelled to build a concert and sports hall, the Palace of Concert and Sport. Its gravestones were subsequently used to make the steps leading up to the white Trade Union House on Taurakalnis Street.

The **synagogue** at Pylimo Street 63, near **Halė,** the main food and flower market, was situated outside the ghetto, and is the only remaining prayer house for the small surviving Jewish community, which today numbers about 5,000, most of whom hope to start a new life in Israel. The recently opened **Jewish State Museum** at 12 Pamėnkalnio tells the tragic story of the community in Vilnius and is the only Jewish museum in the former USSR.

Commercial Street: New Vilnius unfolds along the central avenue Gedimino prospektas, opposite the cathedral. This is where most of the administrative buildings are and it is also the main shopping area. The **Opera House** is at the lower end on the right in Vienuolio Street. The government is housed in the former building of the Central Committee of the Lithuanian Communist Party on Savivaldybės Square. The cells of the hated former KGB building on Lukiškių Square were transformed into a museum and can be visited. There is a moving exhibition on the Lithuanian resistance against the Soviet occupation. Several thousand Vilnius residents went

Concert-bound kettle-drums.

through these cells before being shipped to labour camps in Siberia.

The mile-long (1.5-km) avenue ends at the modern **parliament building**, which was surrounded by barricades for years after the Soviets attempted to storm the building in 1991. The great concrete blocks, flowers and graffiti that regularly featured here were a constant reminder of the struggle for independence.

Vilnius has shed its Soviet symbols. The statues of Stalin, Lenin and Kapsukas, the local communist leader, are now exposed with all other Lithuanian Soviet monuments in the tiny village of Grūtas near Druskininkai. A new icon has now arrived: Vilnius is the only city in the world to boast a monument to the late American singer Frank Zappa. The life-sized bust was executed in the mid-1990s by Lithuanian sculptor Konstantinas Bogdanas, who is known for his many Soviet realist statues.

The new grey housing districts on the outskirts are also the work of Soviet-Lithuanian architects. In 1974 the designers of the new **Lazdynai District** received the Order of Lenin for their grey pre-fabricated ferro-concrete housing blocks. The **Karoliniškės District** to the west of the city is dominated by the **television tower**, which has become infamous for the massacre in the night of 12–13 January 1991 when the Soviet tanks crushed and shot 14 unarmed civilians who were defending the building. The memory of the **"defenders of freedom"** is preserved in a small hall of fame at the foot of the tower as well as in the Lithuanian State Museum.

The 1,070-ft (326-metre) television tower is the tallest structure in Lithuania and has a restaurant halfway up from where there is a breathtaking view of the capital below.

Around Vilnius: One church outside the Old Town but worth making the effort to reach is the **Church of Saints Peter and Paul** which lies beyond the cathedral on the far side of Kalnų Park. It is the best example of baroque architecture in the city and was commissioned in 1668 by Michael Casimir Pac, a Lithuanian army commander. His tomb-

Verkiai Palace, just outside the city.

stone, inscribed *Hic jacet peccator* ("Here lies a sinner"), is embedded in the wall to the right of the entrance. Despite a deceptively plain facade, the baroque interior is breathtakingly beautiful with more than 2,000 undecorated stuccoed figures crowding the vaults, representing mythological, biblical and battle scenes.

Beyond this church to the northeast of the city is the **Antakalnis Cemetery** which symbolises Vilnius's tormented history. In the Soldiers' Cemetery German, Polish, Russian and Lithuanian soldiers lie side by side. In a clearing at the back four giant Soviet granite soldiers guard the eternal flame next to a hall of fame where the dignitaries of Soviet Lithuania are buried. In the centre of the cemetery lie the graves of the seven border guards and the civilians killed during the fight for independence by the same Soviet army.

Further out of town in the same direction is the **Verkiai Palace**, a singular neoclassical manor house now used by the scientific community.

The other major cemetery is to the southwest of the city. **Rasų Cemetery**, founded in 1801, is known as the "Pantheon of the famous". Prominent politicians, academics (Joachim Lelewel), poets (Ludvik Kondratowicz), and painters (Franciszek Smuglewicz, 1745–1807) are among those buried here. Of particular interest are the graves of the artist and composer Mikalojus Konstantinas Čiurlionis (1875–1911), the writer Balys Sruoga and author Jonas Basanavičius (1851–1927).

The adjacent **Military Cemetery** is dedicated to Polish Marshal Piłsudski, whose heart rests here under a black granite slab.

Just out of town to the southeast, on the far side of the Markučiai District, is the **Pushkin Memorial Museum** in the home of Alexander Pushkin's son, built in 1867. One room contains the poet's possessions, and you can also see its 47-acre (19-hectare) grounds where the antitsarist uprising of 1863 was hatched.

To the west of the city along the meandering Neris river is **Vingis Park**,

Summer at Trakai.

which dates back to the 16th century when it was part of the aristocratic Radvilos (Radziwell) estate. It is reported that Tsar Alexander I was at a ball in Vingis when he received the news of Napoleon's invasion in 1812. The first National Song Festival took place here in 1947 and a special stage was built in 1960 to absorb the 20,000 singers, dancers and musicians who still flock here every five years to take part in one of the country's great celebrations.

Trakai: The former capital of the Grand Duchy of Lithuania, 18 miles (27 km) to the west of Vilnius, is a favourite place for an outing. The resort village is surrounded by five lakes up to 158 ft (48 metres) deep. In summer people swim and sail in the lakes around **Trakai Castle**, on a peninsula in Lake Galvė.

Lithuania's most photographed castle was the heart of the Grand Duchy until 1323, when Grand Duke Gediminas moved the capital to Vilnius. The five-storey, red-brick fortifications were constructed by Vytautas and have been undergoing reconstruction since 1952.

The **Trakai Castle Museum** in the rooms around the internal courtyard offers an exhibition on prehistoric discoveries and the splendour of Lithuania's Grand Duchy, which extended from the Baltic to the Black Sea. In the outer buildings are antiques from the feudal houses of later centuries. The ruins of the dukes' earlier castle can be seen in the town park.

In the 14th century Grand Duke Vytautas invited his bodyguard of Tatars from Crimea to come to Trakai, where they settled around the castle. Their descendants, the Karaites (a Turkish ethnic group) still give the royal town its distinctive touch. With only 200 people, the Karaites are the smallest ethnic minority in Lithuania.

The traditional Karaites' food is the *kibinai*, a meat-stuffed pastry served in the **Kibininė restaurant**, a traditional wooden Karaite house. A **Kinessa,** a prayer house of this fundamentalist Judaic sect, which, strangely, celebrates Easter, is at Karaimų 30, the main street.

Right, crossing the moat, Trakai Castle.

KAUNAS

Kaunas is the heart of Lithuania. More than any other city it has preserved its Lithuanian identity: 87 percent of its 415,800 inhabitants are ethnic Lithuanians, and Russians account for under 9 percent. It was relatively unscathed by World War II and large parts of the old city remain untouched, in spite of the grand designs of Soviet planners who had their hearts set on an eight-lane highway through the Old Town.

The country's second largest city has a long-lasting rivalry with Vilnius dating back to 1920 when it became the "provisional capital" after Vilnius fell to Poland. During its two decades as Lithuania's interim capital it developed rapidly from a Russian garrison town to a European city and many of the elegant buildings from that period remain. It is the major commercial centre of the country, manufacturing textiles and food products, and if Vilnius now provides the country with intellectuals, Kaunas provides it with traders and businessmen. The two cities are connected by the River Neris which at Kaunas joins Lithuania's great river, the Nemunas. This river, once Lithuania's southern border, was on the German traders' route and Kaunas became a Hansa town. Today, the river is dammed on the east side of the city, turning it into a recreational area, and pleasure-boats are still able to make the journey from Kaunas to Klaipėda and the seaside.

Around the cobbled square: The city was first mentioned in 1361 and its historical heart is **Town Hall Square** (Rotušės aikste), surrounded by numerous 16th-century German merchant houses. In the middle of the cobblestoned open area is the Town Hall, known as "The White Swan" for its elegance and 175-ft (53-metre) tower. Designed in the late baroque and early classical style, the Town Hall was begun in 1542 as a one-storey building. The second floor and the tower were only added at the end of the 16th century. The Gothic vaulted cellar of the tower served as a prison and a warehouse, the ground floor was reserved for traders and prison guards, and the first floor housed the magistrate's office, the treasury and the town archives.

Part of the building was destroyed during the Swedish-Russian war (1655–60). After reconstruction in 1771 it housed the local government. In 1824, under the tsarist regime, an Orthodox church was established there and later it became the warehouse of the artillery. It served as the provisional residence of the tsar (1837) and as a theatre (1865–69). Under the Soviet regime it was used by the engineering department of Kaunas polytechnic (1951–60). Renovated between 1969 and 1973, it now serves as the "wedding palace", and happy couples and their entourages often line up for photographs in the square outside.

Some 30 percent of the 545 houses in the Old Town have so far been renovated. The 16th-century **warehouse and pharmacy** (Rotušės 2) has a Gothic facade and vaults, and is a unique example of a Kaunas apartment house. The

Preceding pages: Maironis Museum, Town Hall Square. Left, best man at the wedding. Right, pedestrian mall and the former Russian church (now the catholic cathedral).

Gildija House (No. 3), built in the 16th century, is the oldest on the square. Today it is the **Gildija restaurant**, an airy place with high-backed baronial chairs and a beer bar in the cellar which formerly served as a warehouse.

The Jesuits started to buy land and buildings in Kaunas in the early 17th century. The construction of the **St Franziskus Xavier church** and the **Jesuit residence** was finished in the middle of the 18th century. After 1812 it served as a hospital and in 1824 it became the residence of the bishop. In 1924 it was returned to the Jesuits who used it for a boys' school. The church, which has a basilica layout, fine marble altars and wood carvings, was built in 1666 and was frequently destroyed by fires. In 1825 it became the Alexander Nevski Orthodox church and under the Soviets it was transformed into a vocational school. In 1990 it was returned to the church.

The house at 10 Rotušės, which has a Renaissance facade, was once a hunters' inn. A statue for the great Lithuanian poet and priest J. Mačiulis-Maironis has been erected in front of No. 13, where he lived from 1910 until his death in 1932. In 1936 the **Maironis Museum of Lithuanian Literature** was set up here. On display are his study and living rooms as well as an exhibition on other Lithuanian writers. The baroque building from the late 16th century served as a military hospital in 1812. During the 1861 uprising against Russia its cellars were used as prisons.

In the northwest corner of the square is the **Bernardine monastery**. Renaissance with Gothic elements, it dates back to the late 16th century, when the first house was bought by nuns. Its church, **Holy Trinity** (1668) was rebuilt in baroque style. In the 19th century it possessed nine wooden altars but these were lost during World War I. In 1978 it was given back to the Catholic seminary.

In 1933–34, the late-Renaissance belfry was incorporated into the seminary which is located between the church and the belfry. The building was given back to the seminary in 1982.

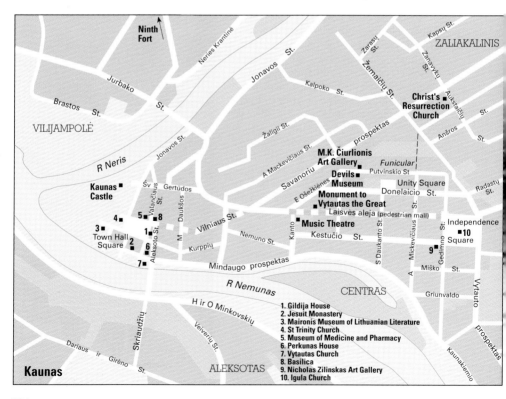

1. Gildija House
2. Jesuit Monastery
3. Maironis Museum of Lithuanian Literature
4. St Trinity Church
5. Museum of Medicine and Pharmacy
6. Perkunas House
7. Vytautas Church
8. Basilica
9. Nicholas Zilinskas Art Gallery
10. Igula Church

The **Museum of Medicine and Pharmacy**, a 17th-century building which used to house a pharmacy, is at Rotušės 28. On display are old instruments and a reconstructed interior of a Lithuanian pharmacy at the beginning of the 20th century.

To the river: From Town Hall Square walk down Aleksoto Street to the banks of the Nemunas. At Aleksoto Street 6 is **Perkūnas House**. Historians cannot agree if the original purpose of this picturesque 15th-century Gothic brick building was a chapel or the Hansa office. The more romantically-minded maintain it was the temple of Perkūnas, the god of thunder, since during renovation in 1818 workers found an 11-inch (27-cm) statue in the building of a town and temples with three fishes which came to symbolise the rivers Nemunas, Neris and the god Perkūnas. The statue was lost but the name remained.

Similar to St Anne's church in Vilnius, the Perkūnas House is one of the most original examples of late Gothic in Lithuania and its rich architecture is a monument to the economic power of the Hansa and Germany. After reconstruction in the early 19th century it served as a school and in 1844 the first Kaunas Drama Theatre was established there. After 1863 the house fell into ruins. Renovated in the end of the 19th century it served as a religious school, and returned to the Jesuits. It now houses the **Museum of Ceramics**.

On the banks of the River Nemunas stands **Vytautas church**, built in the beginning of the 15th century for the Franciscan monks. Here foreign merchants celebrated Mass. It was built in the Gothic style and a tower was added at the end of the 15th century. French troops used it to store their ammunition in 1812, and in 1915, when the German army occupied Kaunas, it was used as a potato warehouse. In 1990 the church, with its sober white interior, was reopened for worship. The grave of priest and writer J. Tumas Vaižgantas (1869–1933), who organised the renovation of the church in 1920, is in the outer walls on the left.

Town Hall Square.

A pathway leads to the confluence of the Neris and the Nemunas rivers. From the bank where they meet there is a good view of the Old Town spires, the Town Hall and the Jesuit and Vytautas churches. Midsummer Eve (St John's) on 23 June is celebrated every year on this piece of ground.

On the banks of the Neris lies **Kaunas Castle**. First mentioned in the 13th century, it was the earliest stone castle in Lithuania. The surrounding walls, 7 ft (2 metres) wide and 43 ft (13 metres) high, could not fend off the crusaders who destroyed the castle in 1362 after a three-week siege. Six years later a stronger castle was built with walls 12 ft (3.5 metre) thick and four towers. Nevertheless, over the centuries it was washed away by the Neris and the northern walls with the towers collapsed. Today, only part of the castle remains.

Through Valančiaus Street walk back to the Town Hall Square and turn left into Vilniaus Street at the **basilica,** which towers 138 ft (42 metres) above the corner. The first church was built here in the early 15th century but its original shape is unknown. The naves were added in the 15th – 16th centuries and the construction was completed in 1655. Of particular interest are the baroque high altar of 1775 and the neo-Gothic chapel to the right. It belonged to Augustine monks until 1895 when it became a **cathedral**. It was elevated to the rank of basilica in 1921.

Little Champs-Elysées: Continue along Vilniaus Street to Birštono Street on the left. In a small yard is the **Prezidentūra**, the residence of the Lithuanian president during the inter-war period. The one-storey building now serves as a teachers' residence.

Vilniaus Street leads into **Laisvės alėja (Freedom Avenue)**, the main thoroughfare of the New Town often optimistically compared to the Champs-Elysées in Paris or Unter den Linden in Berlin. Kaunas residents love to stroll along the mile-long (1.6-km) pedestrian street, designed in the late 19th century. In 1982 it was closed to traffic and the central tree-lined pathway was

Flowers of peace from the Lithuanian army.

dotted with numerous benches. Reposing and green in the summer, it can be quite grey and depressing in winter. Between the wars a number of administrative buildings were put up along this classy avenue now lined with shops.

At the crossing of Sapiegos Street stands the **Monument to Vytautas the Great.** The bronze statue of "the creator of Lithuanian power" stands proudly over four defeated soldiers: a Russian, a Pole, a Tatar and a German crusader holding a broken sword, symbolising the defeat of the Teutonic Knights. A bronze plaque shows a map of medieval Lithuania extending from the Black Sea to the Baltic Sea.

In the park facing the statue in front of the **Music Theatre** lies a small granite slab, marking the spot where the 19-year-old student Romas Kalanta immolated himself on 14 May 1972 in protest against the Soviet system.

The large pedestrian mall ends in Independence Square (Nepriklausomybės aikštė) which is dominated the central **Įgulos (Saints Peter and Paul) church**.

The imposing blue neo-Byzantine building was built in 1893 by Russian architects as the Orthodox church for the army at Kaunas Castle. It was closed in 1960 and transformed into a permanent exhibition of stained glass and sculpture, but after independence it reopened to public worship. Inside are several interesting frescoes of the evangelists and Orthodox saints and the stained glass represents the Assumption. In autumn, which is the favourite time for weddings in Lithuania, couples queue up outside the church to be married.

On the right-hand side of the square is the modern building of the **Mykolo Žilinsko Dailės Galerija (Michael Žilinskas Art Gallery)**. The avant-garde glass-and-granite building houses 1,670 works of art donated by Lithuanian-born Žilinsko (1904–92), a former head of security in East Berlin. It has Chinese, German and Dutch porcelain, Italian paintings of the 16th and 18th centuries, including Rubens, Rafael and Tiepolo, and an interesting collection of 20th-century Belgian art.

Left, city phone booths. **Right**, windmill at Rumšiškes Open-Air Museum.

Museums: Kaunas has the country's best museums. Parallel to Laisvės Street on Donelaičio Street lies Unity Square (Vienybės aikštė), where the symbols of Lithuanian statehood have recently been re-erected. A **hall of fame** with the portraits of famous Lithuanian politicians and writers leads from the **Liberty monument** to the **eternal flame**, flanked by traditional **wooden crosses** remembering those who died for Lithuania's independence.

The entrance to the **Military Museum of Vytautas the Great** is on Unity Square. Lithuania is shown through the ages from prehistoric times to the present day. There is the wreck of the *Lituanica*, the plane in which Steponas Darius and Stasys Girėnas attempted in 1933 to fly non-stop from New York to Kaunas (*see page 338*). Other exhibits show the history of the **Vytautas Magnus University** founded in 1922, closed in 1940 and only reopened in 1990.

The **M.K. Čiurlionis Art Gallery** is situated in the adjoining building and has its entrance at 55 Putvinskio. Built in 1936, the gallery has some 360 works of the outstanding Lithuanian painter and composer, and it should not be missed. The mystic and modernist Čiurlionis (1875–1911) saw nature as an inexhaustible source of beauty. Of his musical poem *In the Forest,* he wrote: "It begins with soft and wide chords, as soft and wide as the sighing of our Lithuanian pines."

Čiurlionis wrote some 20 preludes, canons and fugues for organ and harmonised around 60 folk-songs. In a special listening hall, visitors can hear some of his symphonies and orchestral works. (Concerts are also sometimes put on in his former home, now a museum, in the spa town of Druskininkai, 77 miles/124 km to the south.) The museum also has an exhibition of Lithuanian crosses and spinning implements.

A few houses away, at 64 Putvinskio, is the A. Žmuidzinavičius Collection, better known as the **Devils Museum** for its impressive number of wooden devil statues that the folk-artist amassed during his lifetime (1876–1966). It has grown over the years as new foreign devils have been added, and there are now more than 1,700, including Hitler and Stalin dancing over Lithuania.

From Putvinskio you can either take the **funicular** or climb 231 steps up to the Žaliakalnis District which offers a splendid view of the city. One of the most interesting architectural monuments is the **Church of Christ's Resurrection** at 4 Aukštaičių. It was started in 1932 but never completed. With the annexation by the USSR in 1940, the unfinished church, rising to 205 ft (63 metres) was confiscated and in 1952 it was incorporated into the Banga radio plant and a workshop was installed. In 1988 the building was given back to the Catholic church and restoration began. Being one of the symbols of national rebirth and liberation, it will eventually house a chapel for those who died in the struggle for independence.

Outside the town: A visit to Kaunas is not complete without a tour of the **Ninth Fort**, situated on the road to Klaipėda. It was built at the end of the 19th century as part of the outer town defences on the

Pažaislis monastery, a baroque treasure just outside Kaunas.

orders of Tsar Alexander II to fortify the western border of the Russian empire. It became infamous as a concentration camp during the Nazi occupation.

In the fort you can visit the former prison cells where Jews from all over Europe were herded together awaiting execution. A silent reminder of the horrors are the inscriptions preserved on the walls of the cell. "We are 500 French" (*Nous sommes 500 Français*), wrote Abraham Wechsler from the French town of Limoges before being killed.

The **Way of Death** (Mirties kelias) leads to the place where some 30,000 Jews were shot. A monumental concrete statue overlooks the mass graves where most of the inhabitants of the Kaunas ghetto were buried.

The **museum** housed in a concrete hall near the fort describes the deportations of Lithuanians by the NKVD (the predecessor of the KGB), the Nazi and the Stalinist terror, and the resistance fighters under the Soviet occupation who fought on until 1952.

To the east of the town, above the dam, is the **Pažaislis monastery**, one of Lithuania's architectural gems. Isolated in the countryside, it was built in the 17th century with orchards and gardens which are still cultivated. Entrance is through the Holy Gate and the church has a fine 150-ft (45-metre) cupola which on the inside has a painting of the Virgin Mary. The marble and oak interior is enriched with frescoes which are in the process of being restored under the aegis of the Čiurlionis Gallery which became responsible for it in 1966.

Before the war the monastery was run by nuns from Chicago, but the houses they inhabited in the grounds no longer exist. Restoration work is continuing, and the sacristy and refectory have already been completed.

Nearby, between the dam and the A227, 8 miles (12 km) east of Kaunas, is **Rumšiškes**, the site of Lithuania's main **open-air museum**. This makes a good half-day out, with collections of old buildings from all over the country. One of the large barns has been turned into an excellent café and restaurant.

The Ninth Fort, a vivid reminder of Nazi atrocities.

AUKŠTAITIJA AND THE NORTH

The northern part of Lithuania, which lies above Kaunas and Vilnius, between the Nemunas and Neris rivers and the Latvian border is called Aukštaitija, a name first recorded in the 13th century. In the west it borders Žemaitija (*see page 357*) and it is higher than the coastal region. The communities of Aukštaitija grew up around uniform, one-street villages and the small homesteads were created as land has been divided up among the owners' descendants.

The region was once known for growing flax and still has the largest flax mill in the Baltics. Aukštaičiai cultivate their land by the calendar, working together when necessary. A traditional breakfast will be pancakes made of flour or potato starch, lunch will be hearty and supper something light and dairy-based. The people have a reputation for being talkative, friendly and fond of songs, and the women are known for flax spinning and ornament-making.

Aukštaitija has two distinct regions: a rather flat western region, accessible from Kaunas, and a hilly eastern region which has the greatest snowfall in the country and is best approached from the direction of Vilnius.

The Castle Road: The willow-lined banks on the right-hand side of the A228 Castle Road, which follows the River Nemunas from Kaunas to the coast, are dotted with red-brick fortified manor houses looking out over the wide valley towards Lithuania's southern neighbours. Just beyond Jurbarkas the river forms the border with Kaliningrad. Castles were originally built all along here when the river marked the border between the Grand Duchy and the lands of the Teutonic Order. From the 17th century, merchants and aristocrats made their castle homes here.

The castle at **Raudondvaris** at the start of the castle road on the outskirts of Kaunas was built in the 17th century and remodelled in the 19th century by the Tiškevičiai family who embellished it with a picture collection and a fine library. In the park there is an old manor and the town is a centre for agricultural research. The 19th-century church was built by Lorenco Anichini, who is buried here, and the interior statuary is by Lorenco Pompaloni.

At **Seredžius** there is a hill fort named after a legendary hero, Duke Palemonas, who is supposed to have been descended from Roman nobility. Nearby is the old Belveder manor on a high slope, but it has been rather neglected, as has the park which it lies in. To the north of the manor there is a plain that served as an airfield during World War II. Many of the aeroplanes that took off from here never returned.

Veliuona is a small town high on the river bank with a park and two hill forts: the Castle Mountain and the Gediminas Grave – it is thought that Lithuania's Grand Duke died here in 1341. The town has a 17th-century Renaissance church restored at the turn of the century and this is the burial place of Juozas Radavičius (1857–1911), a famous organ master, and Antanas and Jonas

Juška, Lithuanian folklorists whose remains were brought back here from Kazan in Russia in 1990.

A few miles further on is **Raudonė**, a town in a similarly elevated position. Its park is full of ancient oaks. The 17th-century red-brick palace, a mix of Renaissance and neo-Gothic, was built for a merchant, Krispin Kirschenstein. It was rebuilt in the 19th century and today it houses a school. There is a wonderful view from its tower.

The 17th-century **Vytėnai Castle** was also built by a merchant, Janush Eperjesh, who came from Hungary. It is sometimes called Gelgaudai Castle after its 19th-century owner. There is a park featuring several ponds near the castle; the latter is currently being restored.

Beyond **Skirsnemunė**, (which used to be called Christmemel by the Germans) is **Jurbarkas**, which has hotel and garage facilities. It has a population of 15,000 and the biggest employers are the gravel extraction company, a ship repair yard, a logging concern and a flax mill. There is an interesting 19th-century part of the town and the local park has a farmstead museum which is devoted to the distinguished Lithuanian sculptor Juozas Grybas, who lived here from 1926 to 1941.

Kaunas to Latvia: The Žemaičiai road leaves Kaunas past the Ninth Fort (*see pages 328–29*). After a few miles, at the Cinkiškis crossroads, the A230 turn-off leads up to **Kėdainiai**, an administrative centre with chemical works and a sugar industry.

The Old Town is comparatively large and dates back to the 15th century when it was owned by the dukes of Radvilos. Under their patronage industry expanded, schools and publishing houses grew up and Lutheran, Roman Catholic and Reformed churches and a synagogue, all still standing, were built. The Kėdainiai estate with a manor and park, together with a local museum, tell the story of the town.

From Kėdainiai the road travels north in two directions: the 127 to the west goes up through **Pakruojis** to the border; the A230, running almost parallel **Golden teeth, silver smiles.**

to the east passes through Panevėžys, eventually joining the M12.

The 127 road continues northwards through a land of farmers and artisans, past undulating plains, small brooks and villages. At **Dotnuva** a 17th-century abbey is being restored and the local manor, which before World War I belonged to the Russian minister Piotr Stolypin, is now an agricultural research centre. Similarly, the Komarai manor in **Baisogala**, 37 miles (60 km) north, is now used as a centre for research into livestock farming.

A few miles further on the road meets the Panevėžys-Šiauliai road next to **Šeduva**. This is a small town with an old-fashioned air. There is a local museum and a church dating back to the 17th century. A couple of miles (5 km) to the west is a rest place on **Lake Arimaičiai**. On the eastern side of Šeduva is the notable restored Raudond-varis manor, which belonged to the powerful local landlord, Theodor von Ropp in the 19th century. Three miles (5 km) further on is another manor,

currently being restored, called Burbiškis. Von Ropp also had a country estate in **Pakruojis**, the region's administrative centre to the north. The manor house is still in good repair and there are a number of outbuildings, including a windmill and an arcaded bridge. **Linkuva**, between Pakruojis and the border, had a notable landlord in the noble Karpiai family, who in the 19th century had a reputation for caring for the land, cultivating it and keeping it well-drained. The town has a typical 19th-century layout and the architectural ensemble of church and Carmelite monastery is intact. **Žeimelis** up by the border dates back earlier, and has a number of distinctive pubs.

Up the Via Baltica: From Kėdainiai the A230 is the right-hand of the two roads leading north. Just before Panevėžys it picks up the M12 and the Via Baltica continues on its way to Riga. **Panevėžys** is Lithuania's fifth largest city with a population of 120,000. It dates from the middle of the 16th century when there was a community and a manor house on

the River Nevėžis where a park is laid out today. Its rapid expansion as an industrial centre, including the Baltics' largest textile mill turning flax into linen, has not improved its attractiveness. Since the 1960s its name has been linked with the Panevėžys Drama Theatre, which has built up an impressive reputation. There are usually a number of exhibitions on in the city and the local museum has a collection of butterflies and insects.

The karst region around **Pasvalys**, situated 24 miles (38 km) north of Panevėžys, has underground caverns and in the town park there are signs where some of these have caved in. Southwest of Pasvalys on Road 142 is **Joniškėlis** where the Karpiai family had another manor, which lies in a park. Branching off the M12, road 59 leads up to **Likėnai** and **Biržai** where the landscape is pockmarked with small lakes and holes caused by the karst.

The old town of Biržai was built up around an artificial lake created in the 16th century at the confluence of the Apasčia and the Širvena. The castle that stood here was destroyed in the 18th century but restored in the 1980s and there is a small museum inside. In the 19th century, under the rich and influential Tiškevičius counts, the Catholic and Evangelical Reformed churches were erected. There is a monument in the town to a local poet, Julius Janonis (1896–1917). Also beside the lake is the Astravas manor with a palace and park now used by a textile enterprise. Biržai is famous for its beer.

Kaunas to Rokiškis: This route goes through the eastern edge of the Aukštaitija plains, following the River Šventoji. It leaves Kaunas on the A226, the former Warsaw-St Petersburg postroad which was paved in the early 19th century. It is a straight road, lined with old trees and a few of the old posthouses are still standing.

Jonava on the River Neris is an industrial town producing fertiliser and furniture. The 17th-century church in the old Skaruliai district has been marred by industry, but the main church is of interest, built in the 19th century by the

The manor house at Biržai.

distinguished Vilnius architect Laurynas Stuoka-Gucevičius. The turrets were added in 1935.

As the road enters **Ukmergė** there is a neoclassical post-house built in 1835 on the right. On the south side of the town at **Vaitkuškis** is the former country home of the Koskovskiai family, arts patrons with a taste for literature who corresponded with Balzac.

At **Anykščiai**, where wine is blended from imported grapes and made from cherries, apples and black currants, there is also a literary tradition. On the outskirts is the farmstead of the writer Antanas Vienuolis (1882–1957). The most famous work from the town was a lyric poem written by Antanas Baranauskas (1835–1902) in response to the felling by the tsar of Anykščių Šilelis, the 700 sq. miles (1,812 sq. km) pine forest 3 miles (5 km) to the south. It became a milestone in the idea of conservation and the countryside. In the forest is the **Puntukas boulder**, one of the largest in the country, weighing 265 tonnes. These big rocks, brought by glacial drift, are scattered throughout the Baltics, and are sometimes called "presents from Scandinavia". The sculptor Bronius Pundzius turned one boulder into a monument to the transatlantic flyers Darius and Girėnas in 1943 (*see following page*).

To the north of Anykščiai is the old village of **Niūroniai** and the memorial farmstead of the writer Jonas Biliūnas (1879–1907), who is buried at the nearby Liūdiškiai hill fort. The village also has a small track for horse races, a stable with horses to rent and a huge barn housing a collection of carriages and other horse-drawn vehicles.

From **Svedasai** beside a lake 15 miles (24 km) further on, Road 62 goes northwest to **Kupiškis**, which is surrounded by manor houses, windmills and rural churches. Continuing 20 miles (33 km) on road 67 is **Rokiškis**, a regional centre with a hotel. Beside the main square is a country estate dating back to the 17th century and now housing a museum of wooden sculpture by a local master, Lionginas Šepka, and nearby is a former

Left, rich woodland. **Right**, Juozas Puzinas, folk artist.

Basketball High-Flyer

The game at which Lithuania excels is basketball. It long provided the best players for the Soviet team and the Kaunas team Žalgiris has twice been USSR champions. Seven Lithuanians have Olympic gold medals and the national team took home a bronze in Barcelona in 1992. A few are top players in the US, including Šarūnas Marčiulionis, who has put his money into a successful small hotel in Vilnius.

The history of the game here begins with one of the country's great heroes, Steponas Darius. The village of Rubiškė on the coast where he was born in 1896 has since changed its name to Darius. With his mother and step-father in 1907, he emigrated to the US and as a student he excelled at baseball and football as well as basketball. He signed up for the army in 1917 and fought in France where he was wounded and he returned to the US with two decorations.

In 1920 he was one of the US volunteers for the Lithuanian army and as a pilot he took part in the liberation of occupied Klaipėda. He was a champion sportsman in his native country where he introduced basketball and laid down a sporting tradition that has continued ever since.

He returned to the US in 1927 and worked in civil aviation, founding a Lithuanian flying club, called Vytis. Five years later he and a colleague and mechanic, Stasys Girėnas, set out to bring fame and glory to their newly independent nation by embarking on an epic flight from New York to Lithuania. They had great trouble scraping together the money, but eventually had enough to buy an old plane they called *Lituanica*. There was no money left over to buy any radio equipment.

The plane left New York on 15 July 1933 and flew across the Atlantic, covering 3,984 miles (6,411 km) in 37 hours 11 minutes. Nobody knows exactly why but it never reached Lithuania and crashed at Soldin in Germany. At the time there was friction between the two countries, and rumours that the plane might have deliberately been brought down did not improve international relations. Their bodies were brought to Kaunas, then the provisional capital, and 60,000 turned out for their funeral.

Their death was not in vain: many felt the flight had put Lithuania on the map. The duo's portraits appeared on postage stamps and 300 streets, 18 bridges and eight schools were named after them; many of these survived the Soviet period.

One of the most popular monuments to the heroes is near Anykščiai on a huge boulder called Puntukas. This is one of the country's mythical stones which has been a landmark from time immemorial. In 1943 a Lithuanian sculptor, Bronius Pundzius, was in the countryside hiding from the Germans and he made himself a shelter beside the boulder. To while away his vigil, he sculpted a relief of the faces of the two pilots into the stone, adding the text of their will which had been written before they embarked on the historic flight.

Remnants of the aeroplane and some personal effects are on display in the Historical Military Museum in Kaunas, in the same building as the M.K. Čiurlionis Art Gallery. On the main road from Klaipėda, there is a signpost marked "S. Darius tėviškė" leading 6 miles (9 km) to the village of Darius and a new memorial museum.

Darius immortalised in the village that has taken his name.

338

school for organists. The 19th-century church on the opposite side of the square is richly decorated thanks to the Tyzenhaus family.

The Aukštaitija Uplands: The main M12 highway which runs out of Vilnius towards Riga and Tallinn is a recent construction and it bypasses towns until it reaches Panevėžys. On its western side, on the banks of the Neris 20 miles (32 km) from Vilnius, is the town of **Kernavė**. Forming a triangle with Vilnius and Trakai, this was the capital and the major trading centre of Lithuania in the 13th and 14th centuries. Now a village of just 200, the site includes four hillfort earthworks built to repel the crusaders. There is a beautiful view over the Neris valley from here.

On the eastern side of the M12, the Molėtai highway (Road 1) heads due north through the **Green Lakes**, a popular, hilly area of summer homes, where the deep lake waters, tinted green, are a place for people from Vilnius to cool off. After 16 miles (26 km) up the main road there is a signpost directing you 300 yards (300 metres) down a dirt track, then by foot up a hill, over a bridge and through a wheat field to a black granite stone. You are now standing at longitude 25° 19', latitude 50° 54', which is calculated to be the **centre of Europe**.

Molėtai itself is a base for exploration in all directions. To the west is **Videniškiai** where a richly decorated 17th-century church was built for the Giedraičiai, a rich local family who gave their name to a small town directly to the south. Road 42 northwest to Anykščiai is picturesque, passing through the pleasing villages of **Alanta** and **Skiemonys**. To the east is a landscape of forests and lakes. **Inturkė** has an 18th-century wooden church and near **Mindūnai**, on Road 40, there is a chain of comfortable places to stay.

The wooden village of **Labanoras** has authentic folk architecture and the Labanoras Dūda, a wind instrument played like the bagpipes, comes from here. On 8 September there used to be a colourful church festival in the village.

Crowns of rue and daisies.

Traditionally the people have not been rich. "If it weren't for mushrooms and berries," the saying goes, "Labanoras girls would have nothing to wear."

To the north of Molėtai, at **Virinta**, there is a signposted turn-off to the right to the **Observatory and Museum of Astronomy,** which is worth a visit. **Utena** is a light industrial town which has a Coca-Cola plant and the most-widely sold beer in Lithuania. There is also a 19th-century church and museum.

At **Daugailiai** a left-turn up Road 57 leads through attractive countryside, passing **Antalieptė**, a village completely hidden in the **Šventoji valley,** where there is an 18th-century church and abbey and an old stone watermill by the river. The road leads along the banks of **Lake Sartai** (432 sq. miles or 1,117 sq. km), shaped like a back-to-front E. The surrounding forests are a nature reserve and the lake attracts people from all over the country every February when horse races are held on the ice.

Continuing past Daugailiai to **Degučiai**, on the opposite side of the road, is another resort area of lakes, around **Salakas**, some of which were created when the Antalieptė dam was installed in 1959. Beyond Degučiai the road rises to a high point from which rivulets flow south to feed the Nemunas and north to feed Latvia's Daugava. The road then falls as it nears **Zarasai**, a town of broad streets and wide squares surrounded by lakes. There is a local museum, 19th-century church and a cemetery for German soldiers who died during World War I.

The road to **Smalsai**, southeast of Zarasai, passes through a wonderful hilly land of lakes, while to the north Road 52 goes to **Avilys**, **Čičirys** and **Stelmužė** on the border. Stelmužė has the largest oak in Lithuania, 66 ft (20 metres) high and 33 ft (10 metres) in circumference and supposedly 1,000 years old. There is also an 18th-century manor and 17th-century wooden church with original artwork inside.

Napoleon's Route: Road 2 runs from Vilnius up the eastern borders of Lithuania, and this is the route Napoleon and

Farm work for sun-seekers.

his army took into Russia in 1812. From the capital the road winds through pine forests to **Nemenčinė**, an area full of summer houses on allotments still called "collective gardens". Each one measures 6,480 sq. ft (600 sq. metres) and their commodious and comfortable self-built shacks and houses, many of them made of brick, have been turned into second homes.

From **Pabradė**, with its rather neglected 18th-century coaching inn by the river, the road heads east to **Pavoverė**, where there is a wooden belfry and church with artworks, dating from 1769. The next village, **Zalavas**, is the birthplace of Poland's patriot and pre-war president, Józef Piłsudski (1867–1935). The road continues through the old villages of **Miežionys** and **Modžiūnai**. **Švenčionys** is in a glacial valley and the original settlement was near the hill fort. Down the centuries Tatars, Russians, Belarussians and Poles have settled here.

From Švenčionys a pleasant detour north can be made via **Švenčionėliai** in the west, though even here there is memory of war, with the graves of several thousand local Jews from the region who were murdered by the fascists and buried on the edge of the Labanoras Wood found here.

Road 51 continues north into the **Ignalina National Park**, an area of 1,750 sq. miles (4,530 sq. km) of which 15 percent is lakes. Most of the land is forested and there is a great diversity of flora and fauna, with more than 700 species of plants, 100 species of mammals and 78 species of fish. The park's administrative centres are at **Meironys** and the more interesting **Palūšė**, where there is a 19th-century wooden church and belfry. Boats can be hired here for a better view of the lakes. **Ginučiai**, **Šuminai**, **Strazdai** and **Salos** are all pleasant villages and at **Stripeikiai** there is a bee-keeping exhibition.

Ignalina itself is not far from the park and the Švenčionys Uplands on its eastern side are an attractive hilly area. It snows more in Ignalina than anywhere else in the country and the snow stays

Messing
about in
boats.

longer, which make it a popular centre for winter sports.

Some 17 miles (27 km) further north on Road 2 is the new town of **Dūkštas**. The old town, sometimes called Pažemiškis, is on the far side of the adjacent Lake Dūkštas (sometimes called Lake Pažemiškas), but the places of interest here, the 18th-century buildings, are neglected, and the burnt-out church with a graveyard of noblemen has not been renovated. The local manor house is used for agricultural research. Road 47 east of Dūkštas leads to **Rojus** (Paradise), a farm museum and garden of the scientist and gardener Adam Hrebnicki (1857–1941).

To the north is Sniečkas, which in 1992 changed its name to **Visaginas**. Most of the 33,700 who live here are Slavs. The town itself is situated in a picturesque area of pine forests near a lake, but to the east is the **Ignalina Atomic Power Plant** on the south bank of Lake Drākšiai. It was built in 1974, to the same design as Chernobyl, and has been the subject of some controversy

(*see Environment chapter, page 113*). Two of the four reactors are operating.

On Belarus's border: Vilnius is only 15 miles (24 km) from the Belarus border. There are several places of interest in between, and the roads can be followed into the neighbouring country. The M12 has been the main highway to the east since the Middle Ages, and it goes to the Belarus capital of Minsk. **Nemėžzis** is the first village on the road, settled by Tatars in Vytautas's time, and they have their own chapel and cemetery here. On the opposite side of the valley are the remains of a 19th-century country estate and park. A few miles further, on the right, is **Boreikiškės**, where a manor belonging to the Tiškevičius family was rented by the writer and Vilnius publicist Vladislav Sirokomla (1823–62). Today it houses a museum.

The road is now in the **Medininkai Uplands**, an area of wide valleys, fewer depressions and fewer forests, formed in an earlier glacial age than other uplands in the country. The customs post at the frontier here is still fresh in local people's minds as the place where seven young Lithuanian border guards were massacred in July 1991. Just before the border an old track goes down to the right to Medininkai and the remains of **Medininkai Castle**, a stone defence work from the 14th century which is being restored. A museum documents the castle's history.

Just over a mile (3 km) to the south there is a signpost to **Juozapinės Mountain**, the highest point in Lithuania above sea level, at a meagre 963 ft 4 inches (293.7 metres). The A234 runs due south from Vilnius. Just beyond **Jašiūnai** at the River Merkys, an 18th-century classical palace and grounds are being restored. It belonged to the distinguished Balinski and the Sniadecki scientific families, and many eminent scientists from Vilnius University are buried here.

Just over the border there are castles of ancient Lithuania at **Lyda**, and at **Navagrudak** (Naugardukas in Lithuanian), where there is an exhibition about the history of the two countries. The poet Adam Mickiewicz was born here in 1798.

Left, carved figure at a bee museum, Stripeikiai. Right, country picnic.

THE SOUTH

South of Kaunas and Vilnius, the country is split in two by the River Nemunas which flows down the middle from the Belarus border. To the west, up to the river's southern bank, is **Suvalkija**. To the east, up to the southern bank of the Neris, is **Dzūkija**. Suvalkija was the land of the Sūduva and Jotvingiai tribes until it was joined to the Grand Duchy of Lithuania after the Teutonic Order was crushed in 1410. In the following years of peace, people from Žemaitija and other neighbouring regions came to settle here, but the main villages and townships were not founded until the 17th – 18th century.

From 1867 to 1915 the area was part of the Russian province of Suvalkai and although the region still bears the name, the town of Suvalkai is in Poland today and the capital of the province is now Marijampolė. After serfdom was abolished in the 19th century, peasants settled in farmsteads and a great number educated their own children. Their standards were so high that the local dialect became the basis of the modern Lithuanian literary language.

People of Suvalkija have a reputation of being stingy and thrifty. They are used to working hard, waking early to a hearty breakfast of meat and soup, lunching on the warmed-up left-overs and having a light supper. "It would be better if father fell off the roof than a grain or a drop be lost!" is how a local joke sums up their attitude.

The Suvalkija plain: The first town in Lithuania encountered on the A226 from Poland is **Kalvarija**, on the Šešupė river. The old part is attractive with a post-house (1820) and the remains of a large jail built in 1810 to contain 1,000 prisoners. The classical-style church was built in 1840 and rebuilt in 1908 and it has some good paintings inside. A large Jewish community settled here in the 17th century but most were exterminated by the Nazis. Their burial place is near Orija Square. **Marijampolė** (pop. 40,000), the principal town, lies in a rather dull plain relieved only by the Šešupe, the region's main river. The town manufactures car parts and woollen fabrics, canned vegetables, milk, sugar and mixed feed. It takes its name from an 18th-century monastery of the Marian Fathers and in the 19th century it was a centre of enlightenment. There is a good local museum and the 19th-century church is well known for its fine paintings.

From Marijampolė the A229 leads 94 miles (150 km) eastwards to Vilnius. To the north is one of the most fertile plains in the country. After 31 miles (50 km) on the A226 towards Kaunas you reach **Sasnava**, marked by the belfry of its 1938 church. On the left of the road lies the forest of **Kazlų Rūda** and the town of the same name. Sulvakija is a land of farms on clay soil: forests are left where the soil is light. Further on is **Veiveriai**, which has a post-house and 19th-century teachers' training college.

To the west of Marijampolė, the A229 leads to the border, passing through **Vilkaviškis**, a local centre which was

burnt to the ground in World War II. Nearer the frontier is the **Paežeriai manor**, a 18th–19th century palace set in a park with a lake. Beyond it is **Kiršai**, birthplace of a famous Lithuanian poet, Salomėja Nėris (1904–45).

To the south is a hilly, attractive corner of the country. In the southwest corner on Road 95 is **Vištytis**, a border town by a large lake (70 sq. miles/180 sq. km) of the same name. Vincas Kudirka (1858–1899) author of the Lithuanian national anthem, was born and buried in **Kudirkos Naumiestis**, which is off Road 89.

Suduva land: The southern part of Suvalkija, often called Sūduva, is a picturesque region of lakes and hills. Near the border with Poland is **Lazdijai**, the centre of the district, which has a 19th-century church. Road 82 continues for 11 miles (18 km) towards hills, forests, valleys and a lovely labyrinth of lakes around **Veisiejai**, which has a number of pleasant corners to stop for a rest. The old part of the town has a beautiful park and an early 19th-century church. Lazar

Zamenhof (1859–1917), the Bialystok-born physician who devised Esperanto, lived here in 1886–87.

The A233 goes to **Leipalingis** and on through pleasant countryside towards Druskininkai in the neighbouring province of Dzūkija (*see page 351*). From Lazdijai the 75 heads north towards Alytus and Vilnius, passing through **Šventežeris,** where Evangelical Lutherans settled. The present church, with interesting paintings, was built in the 19th century.

Next is the small town of **Seirijai**, with an Evangelical Reformed church built in the 17th century when the Electors of Brandenburg became owners of the town. The German settlers made their living by spinning and commerce. Today the town has a woollen and yarn industry and many sewing workshops.

North from Seirijai, road 77 goes through forests and around the largest lakes in the region. The biggest of these is the 50 sq. mile (139 sq. km) **Lake Metelys,** which has clear water up to 50-ft (15-metres) deep and is teeming

Why do farmers seldom smile?

with fish. **Meteliai**, near the lake, has a 19th-century church with good interior decoration, as does the 16th-century church in nearby **Simnas**. To the north is **Lake Žuvintas**, which is 40 sq. miles (100 sq. km) in size and is surrounded by a large **nature reserve**, a boggy area which supports more than 600 species of plants and more than 250 species of birds. A natural history museum has details of what can be seen.

Alytus is 15 miles (24 km) east of Simnas on road 76. It lies in a deep valley of the Nemunas, surrounded by dry forests and deciduous woods on the heights above. Its attractive position has led to the development of good hotels and visitors' facilities.

Because the ancient town straddled the river, it developed slowly. Half of it belonged to the province of Suvalkai and half to Vilnius, and in the late 19th century the Russians turned it into a frontier fortress. Today it has a population of 70,000 and up-to-date industries in building materials, machinery, textiles and food process-ing. It is also the cultural centre of Dzūkija. There is a local museum, two 18th and 19th century churches and a third being built. In **Vidugiris**, a forest in the southern part of the city, a monument has been erected to 35,000 Nazi victims. The bridge over the Nemunas is called after Antanas Juozapavičius, an officer killed here during the battle for independence in 1919. During World War II a French airforce squadron, Normandy-Neman, was stationed nearby.

Sūduva to Vilnius: From Alytus the 108 leads 38 miles (60 km) north to Kaunas. Just outside the town, two bridges cross the Nemunas, one going south to Druskininkai (A231) and the other east to Varėna (23), passing through a picturesque landscape and the small town of **Daugai**, an old settlement with a neo-Gothic stone church.

The A231 north of Alytus leads to Vilnius across hilly, wooded country. After 6 miles (10 km) on the right is **Raižiai**, a small village of 100 Tatars. These Turkic-speaking Asian people began to settle in Lithuania in the 14th

Rural living.

century after serving Grand Duke Vytautas who gave them privileges.

On the opposite side of the road is **Punia**, a village built on a precipice. The impressive hill fort here, called **Margiris Mountain**, is often identified with the legendary Pilėnai, which was defended by Duke Margiris against the crusaders in 1336. The fort was finally burnt, along with all who were in it when they refused to surrender. The church was reconstructed in the 19th century with some older sculptures. The pine forest of **Punia**, which is almost completely surrounded by a meander in the Nemunas river, is a most valuable **nature reserve**.

To the north, on the far side of the River Verknė, is **Jieznas**. In the 17th century this town was owned by the Pacai family who built a sumptuous palace based on the calendar, with 12 halls, 52 rooms and 365 windows. Only a few remains can be seen in the park. The church at Jieznas is a wonderful 18th-century baroque monument, with interior decoration and paintings by

Nikodemas Silvanavičius (1834–1919). The picture on the high altar of the Archangel Nicholas is a copy of a work by the Italian master Guido Reni.

To the west of Jieznas is **Birštonas**. Surrounded by forests, this 15th-century town is a holiday resort, and its 3,000 population is temporarily increased by nearly 100,000 visitors a year. It became famous because of its mineral-water springs on the banks of the Nemunas. There is a park, a hill fort called **Vytautas's Mountain** and several comfortable places to stay.

From here the River Nemunas makes its longest loop, winding round 37 miles (59 km). At the far side of it stands **Prienai** where German craftsmen settled in the 18th century, establishing a cotton mill; some of their buildings remain. There is a monument to Grand Duke Kęstutis, which was built in 1937, destroyed in 1954 and restored in 1989. The 18th-century wooden church is decorated by Nikodemas Silvanavičius, the town's distinguished local son, who decorated the churches at Punia and Jieznas. At nearby **Pociūnai** there is a flying club.

East from Jieznas, the A229 to Vilnius goes through some interesting places, among them **Stakliškės**, which has an attractive 18th-century baroque church and an old brewery where they make mead. The town used to be a resort, with mineral water sources, but it has never fully recovered from a fire which devastated it in 1857.

Further down the road is **Lapelioniai (Napoleon) Mound**, though the emperor never visited the place. Fortified settlements or castle hills are called *piliakalniai* in Lithuanian, and they used to be inhabited by local people who could defend themselves against a common enemy. The word for citizen in Lithuanian, *pilietis*, comes from *pilis*, the word for castle.

Aukštadvaris, the next town, lies among several lakes, and has a trout-fishing industry and agriculture school. There is also a hill fort, the remains of a manor house and an interesting church. **Strėva**, another small settlement among the lakes, is good place for a stop.

Carving along Čiurlionis Way, representing the composer's father and mother.

From here the road leads to the magnificent castle at Trakai (*see page 318*) and the capital.

Dzūkija's forests: The woodland of Dzūkija is often called Dainava (from *dainuoti*, meaning to sing). The Dzūkai who live here are known for their cheerfulness and their great singing voices, as well as for an ability to scratch a living out of poor soil. They used to be said to have no saws, only axes; no bricks, only clay. But one saying is "A Dzūkas is a kind man – as long as he is poor."

The A231, which leads up from Warsaw via Grodno in Belarus, enters the country through the broad **Raigardas valley** of the Nemunas river. The bottom of this valley is approximately 200 ft (60 metres) below the road and it is filled with meadows and groves and with little lakes where the river used to run. The disappearance of the town of Raigardas, swallowed by the earth and replaced by a swamp, is told in an old legend. M.K. Čiurlionis used to come here, and his visits inspired him to paint a triptych called *Raigardas*.

Čiurlionis's town: Lithuania's best known artist and composer, Mikalojus Konstantinas Čiurlionis (1875–1911), grew up in **Druskininkai**, the first main town on this road, 96 miles (150 km) south of Vilnius. It is a spa town and resort of wide boulevards and old and new villas, attracting around 100,000 people a year, many of them Poles. Visitors have dropped off since independence however, and smart restaurants like the Astra marble emporium are not as crowded as they once were.

The spa began in 1832 when salty mineral water was first used for treatment: the name Druskininkai comes from *druska* meaning salt. Every litre of water contains 3 grams of minerals and it arrives at the surface, both tepid and hot, from a depth of 235 ft (72 metres) There are several parks, and treatments are offered in the **Remedial Gymnastics and Climatotherapy Park**, where visitors queue up with their special cups to sample the waters in doses often prescribed by their doctors. Near the health park is a wonderful riverside walk,

Raigardas National Reserve.

the **Sun Path**, which traces the Ratnyčia river for 4 miles (7 km) past carved seats and follies inscribed with poems and sayings. At one point the river is wide and deep enough to swim.

The middle of the town has a 20th-century neo-Gothic church and nearby is a memorial to Čiurlionis. His family came here when he was three and until the age of 14 he lived in the family home in the street named after him (No. 41) to the south of the town. This timbered, single-storey house is now preserved as a museum and concerts are held around the piano in the sitting room, while the audience sits outside in the shade of the pretty garden.

Tucked in the woodlands around Druskininkai, which are abundant with mushrooms in autumn, there are some ancient farmsteads: at **Latežeris**, for example, and **Grūtas**, which is also home to Lithuania's Soviet sculpture park. Upstream is **Liškiava**, a 15th-century hill fort with the remains of a castle and an 18th-century church, monastery and manor.

Merkinė, 17 miles (27 km) to the north, is at the confluence of the rivers Nemunas and Merkys. Russia's Peter I stayed here and Vladislav Vaza, the king of Poland, fell ill and died here in 1648. Though a little off the tourist track, Merkinė is worth visiting. It has a hill fort and 17th-century church which amalgamates Gothic and baroque. The local museum is in the Orthodox church where the town hall used to stand. In 1989 a memorial for the victims of Stalin was set up with wooden crosses decorated in typical Dzūkai style.

Lying just north of Merkinė, is the village of **Subartoniai**, which has a memorial museum to Vincas Krėvė-Mickevičius (1882–1954), the classical Lithuanian writer.

Forests cover the light plains on both sides of the road from Druskininkai. The route, lined with more than 20 traditional wooden sculptures, is called the **Čiurlionis Way**, since it leads 31 miles (50 km) from the family home to **Varėna**, the artist's birthplace. The sculptures, by various local masters,

Mother and daughter.

were erected on the centenary of his birth, in 1975. Before Varėna, in woodland beside the Merkys river, is the small town of **Perloja** (pop. 100), a place of independent-minded people. It declared itself the Perloja Republic in 1918, a status it stubbornly maintained for five years, with a government and an armed guard of 50 men, defiant against Russians, Poles, Germans and both red and white Lithuanian factions.

In the centre of the town square is a hugely patriotic statue to Vytautas, Grand Duke of Lithuania, which was sculpted by Petras Tarabilda in 1930. The interior of the town's neo-Gothic church was painted in 1943 by professor Jerzy Hoppen and his students.

The old town of **Varėna**, also on the Merkys river, was burnt down during World War II, and a church is now being built to mark its site. The modern town, the administrative centre of this woodland area, is 2 miles (5 km) to the south. From Varėna roads lead to the farmsteads of **Dainava** and to the **Čepkeliai Nature Reserve**.

Heading towards Vilnius, the road passes more hilly, sandy woodland and the village of **Akmuo**, with an 18th-century wooden church and separate belfry. After 15 miles (25 km) it reaches **Valkininkai**. There are signs of the town's ancient layout and a 19th-century stone church. A little way beyond, at the resurrected village of **Pirčiupiai**, is a monument called the **Sad Mother**, by the sculptor Gediminas Jokūbonis. It was installed in remembrance of the village which was totally burnt, along with all 119 inhabitants, on 3 June 1944 by the Nazis. The memorial is inscribed with each of the victims' names and the village has since been restored.

The road continues through **Paluknis**, past a sports airfield where gliders can be hired for $25–$30 an hour, on the right. Just before hitting the main Vilnius–Trakai road is the manor of the powerful local Tiškevičiai family, called Trakų Vokė, with a palace and a park designed by the French architect Eduard André. For some time the building has been used by an agricultural institute.

<u>Left</u>, Liškiava church, near Druskininkai. <u>Right</u>, the spa town's lake.

ŽEMAITIJA AND THE COAST

The province of Žemaitija (pronounced *jam-i-tee-yer*), which includes all the coast, covers about a quarter of Lithuania and roughly corresponds with the Žemaitija Upland. Although the ancient tribes probably took their names from the places they came from, the Žemaičiai lived not in the Upland but around the mouth of the Nemunas, trading with the Aukštaičiai towards the river's source. On this coast there is also archaeological evidence of Romans and Vikings, and of Bronze-age trade with Britain and the Mediterranean.

For 200 years the Žemaičiai had a running battle with the German crusaders of the Livonian Order who had established their Baltic base in Riga, and with the Teutonic Order who harried them from the west. Between 1382 and 1404 the Dukes of Lithuania ceded Žemaitija to the Order, but in the 15th century it became a self-governing district and duchy, known in the west as Samogitia. To outsiders it long seemed a rather mysterious, wild and pagan land, an image enforced by Prosper Mérimée's novel *Lokis*, and reinforced by the modern novel *Samogitia* by the French writer Charles Pichel.

The Žemaičiai maintain a strong regional dialect and keep their links with the past. Inhabited by men of few words, this is not a land of songs. Most of the countryside is rather severe, and the western slope of the Upland is windier, foggier and wetter than elsewhere. The trees are mostly firs and once-sacred oaks, and the landscape is dotted with old wooden crucifixes in roadside shrines and cemeteries. Three main arteries cross the region: the A225 goes over the top leaving the M12 at Panevėžys; from Kaunas the A228 follows the Nemunas valley to the sea; but the main road runs between the two, from Vilnius to Klaipėda, the main town on the coast.

The Žemaičiai highway: The A227 from Vilnius via Kaunas to the coast is a breezy, uninterrupted 133 miles (214 km). It was completed in 1987 and replaced the old road 159, built in 1939, which stops at all towns en route. The first of these that falls within the Žemaitija region is **Raseiniai**, 53 miles (86 km) west of Kaunas. It is an old city with a 17th-century church and abbey.

Ten miles (17 km) beyond Raseiniai is **Šiluva**, which has a beautiful church and chapel to the Virgin of Šiluva. Just to the north is **Tytuvėnai**, set around an 18th-century church and abbey which has a number of valuable paintings. The surrounding forests and lakes are popular recreational areas.

Westwards from Raseiniai the old road (159) continues for another 20 miles (32 km) to the A216 at Kryžkalnis. Not far from here is a sign on the road: **"Bijotai – Baubliai Museum of D. Poška"**. In 1812 a local worthy cut down a number of huge dry oaks and in their rotten insides he created a museum reflecting pagan Lithuanians' traditions of worship.

A few miles further west is **Girdiškėš** which has a church with unusual wooden

altars. Just beyond it is **Upyna,** which has a 19th-century wooden church and a rich country-life museum. Further along is **Vytogana,** where the transatlantic pilot Stasys Girėnas was born. Every July on the anniversary of the fatal crash that ended his 1933 transatlantic bid, people gather at a farmstead in the village.

This is now approaching the highest point of the highway, marked with a roadside stone where it reaches 590 ft (180 metres) above sea level. There are pleasant settlements in the hills around here, such as **Kaltinėnai** on the northern side of the highway, which has cosy farmsteads and a newly rebuilt church.

Laukuva is 9 miles (15 km) further on, with a typical 19th-century stone church and square. The road north from here leads after 11 miles (18 km) to **Varniai**, an ancient regional town with a population of 2,000. It has a wooden church and an 18th-century cathedral and priest seminary. Nearby is a picturesque resort at **Lake Lūkstas**. On the opposite side of the highway is **Šilalė**,

an administrative centre with a petrol station and hotel.

A more interesting detour is **Rietavas**, the next town on the right. This ancient settlement (pop. 4,000) is centred around an old square. But the main attraction is the manor house and estate of the Oginskiai family. From 1812 to 1909 they ruled over their own autonomous domain, with their own laws and even their own currency. In 1835 they granted civil rights to their peasants, organised agricultural exhibitions, promoted Lithuanian culture and written language, and started publishing the Lithuanian calendar. They established a music school in the town and in 1872 mustered a famous brass band.

They helped introduce electricity and the telephone system to the town of Plungė, to the north, (*see North Žemaitija, page 365*) and it was Irenejus Oginskis who in 1951 started building the main Žemaičiai road. In 1874 a beautiful church in the Venetian style was built on their orders by the German architect Friedrich Augustus Stüler. To-

Ablinga memorial carvings.

day the manor is an agricultural college. Back on the road is the village named after Lithuania's great 20th-century hero, **Steponas Darius,** who was born in 1896 (*see page 338*). He left a small library on sports training and a museum has recently opened.

The road continues through 30 miles (50 km) of uninhabited forests. At **Endriejavas** there is a small lake and 4 miles (6 km) to the north is the former village of **Ablinga**. On 23 July 1941, it was burnt to the ground by the Nazis, killing its 41 inhabitants. In recent years research has been undertaken on those who died, and large wooden sculptures have been made to portray every one of them. The next town of **Gargždai** was also completely destroyed in the war.

Klaipeda and the coast: The coastal plain, Pajūūris, is 10–13 miles (15–20 km) wide and rises to around 132 ft (40 metres). The landscape is diverse, consisting of fertile clay soils, dunes, sandy forests and wet bogs. In the south is the swampy Nemunas delta and the 618-sq. mile (1,600-sq. km) and 13-ft (4-metre) deep Kuršių marios (Courland Lagoon). The coastline has urbanised resorts, around Palanga in the north, and in Neringa along the Kuršių nerija, or Courland spit, (Kurische Nehrung in German). Neringa is not actually a town, but an administrative area with its capital at Nida, near the border with Russia at the southern end of the spit. The area has many miles of empty beaches and some nature reserves.

Klaipėda is the main town on the coast, situated at the mouth of the Danė river on the Kuršių marios lagoon. It suffered heavy damage during World War II when it was used by the Germans as a submarine base. Since the 1970s when investment was ploughed into local industry, its population has dramatically grown to 202,000, making it the third largest city in Lithuania.

In 1252 the Livonian Order built a castle here, called Memelburg, and the city became known as Memel in German. Klaipėda otherwise finds its etymology in the words *klaips*, meaning loaf of bread, and the verb *ėda* to eat. It

Art nouveau, Klaipėda.

THE AMBER COAST

There is amber everywhere in the Baltics. At any opportunity, stalls are set up to sell bargain bracelets, necklaces, earrings, keyrings and brooches made from this ancient mineral. In its raw state, buffeted by tides and exposed to the elements, these are dull stones, scattered like pebbles the length of the beaches. People are always on the lookout for them, particularly after storms, though most of the amber bought today will have been dug out of the ground by excavators in Kaliningrad.

Amber is not in fact a stone, but fossilised resin of primeval pine trees. The amber deposit, dating back 40 million years, forms a seam 2–3 ft (60–90 cm) thick beneath the clay surface of the seabed. The jagged bottom of icebergs are thought to plough up the seabed and chunks of amber then become caught up in seaweed which is ripped out and dragged ashore by storms. In spring, fishermen in waders used to comb the beaches with what look like large shrimping nets to pull in flotsam that might contain

amber. The Kuršių Lagoon was also a great source of it and in the 19th century Juodkrantė was known as Amber Cove: the Stantien and Becker company used to dredge up to 85 tons of it here every year.

The stone's peculiarity is that, while it was sticky resin, insects were attracted to it, and it often solidified while they were trapped by its surface. The result is that you can often hold an opaque, polished stone to the light and see flies, mosquitoes, gnats and other insects perfectly preserved inside. They intrigued the 18th-century English poet Alexander Pope, who wrote:

Pretty! in amber, to observe the forms
Of hairs, or straws, or dirt, or grubs or
worms;
The things, we know, are neither rich
nor rare,
But wonder how the devil they got there.

Amber gave the Baltics their first taste of wealth. It was a commodity with which the earliest tribes could easily trade and barter: according to Tacitus the price it fetched astonished them. It travelled far. Some has been found in the tombs of the Mycenae and the Egyptian pharoahs: Tutankhamun's treasure included an amber necklace. The Baltic shoreline was first called the Amber Coast by the ancient Greek poet Homer, who was probably thinking of the material when he described the brilliant "electron" on his warriors' shields.

The best place to see amber in the Baltics is at the **Amber Museum** in Palanga. A local legend tells how "Lithuanian gold" was created. There was once a queen of the Baltic named Jūratė who lived in a submarine palace made out of amber. She was to be the bride of the god of water, Patrimpas, but she fell for a mortal fisherman called Kastytis whom she visited in his hut on the banks of the Nemunas near Klaipėda at sunset every night for a year. The liaison eventually came to the attention of Perkūnas, the god of thunder, and in a rage he threw down bolts of lightning, one of which killed Jūratė and shattered her amber palace into 10,000 pieces. Perkūnas then punished Kastytis by binding him to a rock on the seabed.

Now when the west wind blows Kastytis can be heard moaning for his love, and when the wind dies down the shore is strewn with fragments of Jūratė's palace. ∎

A beachcomber's dream: Lithuanian gold.

was a Hansa port and it had a flourishing shipbuilding industry from the 18th century. Today it has a modest fishing fleet, and ferries serve German and other Baltic harbours.

What is left of the old town is strung out along a couple of cobbled streets running along the left bank of the Danė, where there are some attractive bars and a floating restaurant, the three-masted *Meridianas*. There are a few remaining half-timbered (*Fachwerk*) buildings. The old post office, rebuilt with German bells in 1987, is now a concert venue. The city also has two theatres (Hitler spoke from the balcony of the one in Theatre Square), a university and a museum devoted to the history of Lithuania Minor.

The northern coast: 25 miles (40 km) north of Klaipėda on the A223 are the two popular resorts of **Palanga** and **Šventoji**. An old settlement of fishermen and amber-gatherers, Palanga became popular in the early 19th century when it developed as a spa and health resort. Today, it is still popular and at a

sign marked "Leidimų Įsigijimas" motorists must pay a toll to drive in.

There are a number of sanatoriums still in use and the old Kurhaus, a fine wooden structure with elegant balustrades which was the resort's social centre, remains unchanged. Restaurants, cafes and ice-cream parlours serve a variety of needs, and there is altogether the bustling air of a seaside town. On summer evenings its wide boulevards are full of strolling holidaymakers, ducking into cafés or buying bottles of beer and portions of garlic toast. Most will head for the short wooden pier that projects into the sea just below the women-only bathing beach, hoping for a glimpse of the "green sky", a momentary phenomenon that sometimes lights the horizon at sundown.

The pier's builder and benefactor was Count Tiškevičius, who owned the 495-acre (200-hectare) Tiškevičius Park, a formal country estate in the centre of the resort. Its large stately home houses the **Amber Museum**, and this is the best place to see the pine-resin fossils and to

learn about the story of the Amber Coast. The park, which includes Birutė's Hill where rituals were performed in pagan times, holds concerts and exhibitions throughout the summer.

A quieter resort is **Šventoji**, 12 miles (18 km) north on the A223. On the mouth of the small River Šventoji, it is also famous for its sand dunes, beach and bogs. It is mentioned on Hansa maps and it became a resort at the beginning of this century, with good places to rest and recuperate, small cottages and simple houses. Accommodation is better than at either Palanga or Klaipėda.

The Courland Spit: The spit, which is called **Kuršių Nerija** in Lithuanian, is named after the Curi who came here from Latvia. It was formed about 5,000 years ago and geologically it is the youngest part of the country. It has no rivers, a few lagoons and along its shore lies a chain of man-made beaches and dunes. A bird's eye-view is a wonderful picture of white, sandy hills against a dark blue background, and it was the sight of these extraordinary dunes that inspired the German naturalist Alexander von Humboldt to write in 1809: "Courland Spit is such a peculiar place as Italy or Spain. One must see it to give pleasure to one's soul."

Winds formed the long, narrow coastal spit no more than a mile wide and 200 ft (60 metres) high. It runs 60 miles (98 km) from just north of Klaipėda down to Kaliningrad; 32 miles (51 km) of the spit are in Lithuania. The lagoon on the inland side is formed by the mouth of the Nemunas.

On the tip of the spit opposite Klaipėda is **Smiltynė**, reached by regular ferries from the port. This is a popular spot, centred on **Kopgalis Castle** where seals glide round the moat. This is a **marine world** and **sea museum** and dolphins give regular shows. Nearby is **Klaipėda Yacht Club** where members sailed the Atlantic in 1989 as part of the Columbus celebrations, and every June a traditional sea festival takes place.

But most of the peninsula lies to the south, where tourist traffic is curtailed by a toll. All the little villages along here

Making a splash in a safe sea.

face the lagoon Until 1992, the white sandy coast, now deserted, was occupied by the Soviet army. **Juodkrantė** is a typical fishing village with 15 old houses and a harbour once known as Amber Cove because of the amount of the material that was dredged up for the local industry.

Shifting sands have meant many of the villages have constantly been on the move. During the 18th and 19th centuries more than a dozen were affected, some of them covered over by sand. **Pervalka** and **Preila** are typical shoreside communities. **Raganų Kalnas**, **Witches' Hill**, is a sculpture park filled with fabled figures, such as the main pagan god, Perkūnas, and Neringa, a local girl who became a giant and helped sailors in trouble.

At the southern end of the spit, just before the border with Russian Kaliningrad, is **Nida**, which has moved several times to escape the mobile sand. This is the largest of the resorts (pop. 1,500, rising to more than 10,000 in summer), with the best facilities. It is the sunniest

and most famous place on the Lithuanian part of the peninsula.

Nida has a distinctive landscape, created by the wind and the sea. White sand dunes stretch away like a desert to the south, and trunks of trees show where ancient forests once flourished. The town has a statue to David Gotlieb Kuvert, who first began plantations to protect the dunes. In an old fisherman's cottage is a **museum of fishermen's life;** the house where Thomas Mann lived from 1930 to 1932 can also be visited.

The Nemunas delta: From Klaipėda the A228 runs southeast through **Šilutė** and **Pagėgiai,** following the north bank of the Nemunas all the way to Kaunas. From the typical small town of **Priekulė** road 221 goes south, past the fishing village of **Kinta,** ending at the tip of the **Ventės Ragas peninsula**, marked by a lighthouse built in 1863. The main reason for coming to this backwater is the wildlife. An important **bird ringing station**, which keeps track of the many coastal migrants, has been operating here since 1929. Some 8 miles (12 km) east of the

The Neringa Spit's extraordinary sands.

A228, beyond **Saugos** on road 183, is the small town of **Švėkšna**. Its impressive neo-Gothic church contains valuable paintings and it has a memorial park and mansion now used as a college. A mile (2 km) outside town is another manor with a park, at **Vilkėnas**.

From Saugos the A228 falls down into the Nemunas delta plain, passing through **Šilutė** on the River Šyša. A town with a population of 2,000 and good tourist services, it was called Heyde Krug until 1923. In the 17th century there was just one inn in the area, which was run by Richard Kant, grandfather of the philosopher. There is a memorial museum to the German dramatist and novelist Hermann Sudermann, who was born in the former manor house of Macikai in 1857. In World War II there was a concentration camp in Macikai, and up until 1954 it was used by the KGB for imprisoning dissident Lithuanians.

Just west of Šilutė in the Nemunas delta is the 17 sq. mile (45 sq. km) **Rusnė Island** which rises just 5 ft (1.5 metres) above sea level. It has a community of around 3,000 who earn a living by fishing and breeding cattle .

The next town of any size on the A228 is **Pagėgiai**, 22 miles (38 km) beyond Šilutė. During World War II, in the forest to the west behind a tangle of barbed-wire, the Germans kept prisoners of war under the open sky: 10,000 of them died. The ground is very hilly because the prisoners tried to bury themselves to escape the cold.

From Pagėgiai the A216 goes 20 miles (32 km) northeast to the turn-off to **Tauragė**, which gave its name to the Tauragė Convention, signed in 1812 between General Yorch for Prussia and General Diebitsch for Russia in Požėronys mill: a monument records the event.

Back on the A228, just beyond the turn-off to Tauragė, is **Bitėnai**. The Lithuanian enlightener Martynas Jankus (1858–1946) was born, lived and worked in the town. He made a notable contribution when there was a ban on printing Lithuanian books. In 1991, the remains

Left, Witches' Museum, Neringa. Right, domestic architecture.

of Lithuania Minor's great philosopher, Vydūnas, were brought back from Germany and re-buried here.

The next village is **Vilkyšiai**, set on a hill. There are a few hill forts just to the south. In the 18th century, after an outbreak of the plague in Europe, a number of Scots and Austrians from Salzburg settled in Vilkyšiai, but the surviving buildings from that time have been rather neglected.

At **Viešvilė** on a river of the same name there is a water mill, pond, park and manor house, and in the past the town had a wood trade. The road and river then close around **Smalininkai**, where there was once a port for river traffic. The river's oldest hydrometric station still functions here. Six miles (10 km) further on is **Jurbarkas**, which has a hotel. The road follows the river another 54 miles (86 km) to Kaunas.

North Žemaitija: The northern part of Žemaitija can be explored around the A225 which runs 85 miles (137 km) from **Kretinga** near Palanga on the coast, to Šiauliai, 99 miles (159 km) north of Kaunas. Industrial Kretinga has many 18th-century buildings including a Catholic church and Minorite abbey. There are interesting chapels in the cemetery, a watermill and a manor house in a park still in good repair. In the 19th century this was cultivated by the Tiškevičiai family who built up a valuable art collection and were substantial benefactors to the town. There is a museum of local folklore.

Between Kretinga and the next main town of **Plungė** is **Kartena** in the beautiful valley of the Minija. It has a 19th-century wooden church and an 18th-century inn. Plungė is a little larger than Kretinga and a centre of light industry and administration, with a long tradition of folk-art. It became rich after the Oginskiai family arrived to buy up the local manor. They enlarged and cultivated the 18th-century "Thunder Oak" park and in 1879 entrusted the architect Karl Lorens with the building of a neo-Renaissance palace imitating the 15th-century Palazzo Vecchio in Florence. In 1889 they also sponsored the education

Dead wood in the Kuršių.

of the great Lithuanian painter and musician M. K. Čiurlionis.

To the north, on road 226, is **Salantai,** a typical Žemaitija town famous for its historical layout, neo-Gothic church and park. Nearby is the **Museum of Nonsense** at the **Orvidai farmhouse**, though overseas visitors are charged a high entry price. All around this area are roadside shrines, wooden sculptures mounted on crosses and on roofed poles.

Mosėdis, 8 miles (12 km) north of Salantai on road 101, is a curious town dominated by the enthusiasm of a local doctor, Vaclovas Intas. He has spent his life collecting boulders and stones. They line the road leading past the 17th-century church to his house, where there is a sunken stone garden and rockery. All shapes and sizes, the boulders lie everywhere around the town, and some huge ones are scattered over the garden at the back of an attractive watermill which is a restaurant and hotel.

Due east of **Salantai** is **Plateliai**, the heart of the **Žemaitija National Park**. Though 480 ft (146 metres) above sea level, there is a large lake beside it: Lake Plateliai is nearly 5 sq. miles (12 sq. km) in size and 150 ft (46 metres) deep and it has seven islands. There are boating facilities on its western side near the town, where there is an 18th-century wooden church and a ruined manor. The owners of the manor were French, called Choiseul de Gouffier, and some of their heritage is in Alka Museum in Telšiai. Other attractive small towns in this region, which is rich with festivals and calendar customs, include **Žemaičių, Kalvarija**, **Alsėdžiai** and **Seda**.

Telšiai is an industrial town with a population of 30,000, but before the war it was an important religious and cultural centre with a bishop's see and seminaries for priest and Jewish teachers. It still has a school of applied art and the **Alka Museum of Žemaitija Culture**. The 18th –19th-century classical cathedral, where a number of well-known Lithuanians are buried, was designed by Fulgent Rimgaila a century after the Bernardine abbey was built.

On the southeast of the town is **Rainiai forest** where 73 people were executed by the KGB in 1941; 50 years later a chapel was built in their remembrance. East from here is **Luokė**, famous for its folklore festivals, and **Lake Germantas**, where there are holiday facilities and an airfield for pleasure flights.

Place of pilgrimage: There is little reason to stop between here and **Šiauliai**, Lithuania's fourth largest town. This is an industrial centre, of shoes, textiles and, notably, bicycles and there is a **Bicycle Museum**. There is a also a museum of photography and radio. To the south are picturesque hills and lakes around **Bubiai** and **Kurtuvėnai**.

Šiauliai is most famous for the **Hill of Crosses**, which lies in the countryside about 9 miles (14 km) to the northeast on the A216. Nobody is sure of its origins, but for centuries it has been a religious site. People come from all over the world to add their crosses to the thousands already here. The hill itself is only a small hump and it used to be much larger. This is because the Soviets bulldozed it three times. Each time the crosses reappeared.

Left, street corner, Šiauliai. **Right**, the Hill of Crosses just to the north of the city. **Overpage:** Dundaga Castle in Latvia.

INSIGHT GUIDES

TRAVEL TIPS

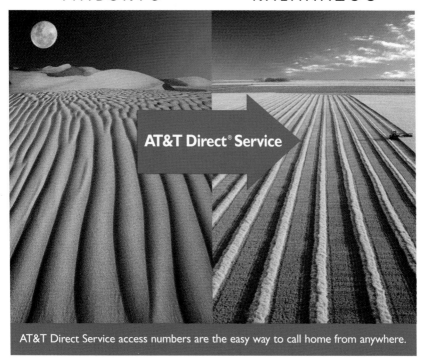

Global
connection
with the AT&T
Network

AT&T
direct
service

The best way to keep in touch when you're traveling overseas is with **AT&T Direct®** Service. It's the easy way to call your loved ones back home from just about anywhere in the world. Just cut out the wallet card below and use it wherever your travels take you.

For a list of AT&T Access Numbers, cut out the attached wallet guide.

AT&T

Israel 1-800-94-94-949	Portugal ▲.........800-800-128
Italy ●. 172-1011	Saudi Arabia ▲ 1-800-10
Jamaica ● 1-800-USA-ATT1	Singapore 800-0111-111
Japan ● ▲ 005-39-111	South Africa 0800-99-0123
Korea, Republic ● ...0072-911	Spain 900-99-00-11
Mexico ▽ ● ..01-800-288-2872	Sweden.............020-799-111
Netherlands ● ..0800-022-9111	Switzerland● 0800-89-0011
Neth.Ant. ▲☺001-800-USA-ATT1	Taiwan............0080-10288-0
New Zealand ● 000-911	Thailand ❬......001-999-111-11
Norway...............800-190-11	Turkey ●..........00-800-12277
Panama 00-800-001-0109	U.A. Emirates ●.........800-121
Philippines ● 105-11	U.K. 0800-89-0011
Poland ● ▲..00-800-111-1111	Venezuela 800-11-120

FOR EASY CALLING WORLDWIDE

1. Just dial the AT&T Access Number for the country you are calling from.
2. Dial the phone number you're calling.   *3.* Dial your card number?

For access numbers not listed ask any operator for **AT&T Direct®** Service.
In the U.S. call 1-800-222-0300 for **AT&T Direct** Service information.
Visit our Web site at: **www.att.com/traveler**
Bold-faced countries permit country-to-country calling outside the U.S.

●   Public phones require coin or card deposit to place call.
✛   Public phones and select hotels.
▲   May not be available from every phone/payphone.
○   Collect calling only.
▽   Includes "Ladatel" public phones; if call does not complete,
     use 001-800-462-4240.
☺   From St. Maarten or phones at Bobby's Marina, use 1-800-USA-ATT1.
❬   When calling from public phones, use phones marked Lenso.
*   AT&T Calling Card, AT&T Corporate, AT&T Universal, MasterCard®,
     Diners Club®, American Express®, or Discover® cards accepted.

When placing an international call *from* the U.S., dial 1-800-CALL ATT.
WW   © 6/00 AT&T

Israel 1-800-94-94-949	Portugal ▲.........800-800-128
Italy ●. 172-1011	Saudi Arabia ▲ 1-800-10
Jamaica ● 1-800-USA-ATT1	Singapore 800-0111-111
Japan ● ▲ 005-39-111	South Africa 0800-99-0123
Korea, Republic ● ...0072-911	Spain 900-99-00-11
Mexico ▽ ● ..01-800-288-2872	Sweden.............020-799-111
Netherlands ● ..0800-022-9111	Switzerland● 0800-89-0011
Neth.Ant. ▲☺001-800-USA-ATT1	Taiwan............0080-10288-0
New Zealand ● 000-911	Thailand ❬......001-999-111-11
Norway...............800-190-11	Turkey ●..........00-800-12277
Panama 00-800-001-0109	U.A. Emirates ●.........800-121
Philippines ● 105-11	U.K. 0800-89-0011
Poland ● ▲..00-800-111-1111	Venezuela 800-11-120

FOR EASY CALLING WORLDWIDE

1. Just dial the AT&T Access Number for the country you are calling from.
2. Dial the phone number you're calling.   *3.* Dial your card number?

For access numbers not listed ask any operator for **AT&T Direct®** Service.
In the U.S. call 1-800-222-0300 for **AT&T Direct** Service information.
Visit our Web site at: **www.att.com/traveler**
Bold-faced countries permit country-to-country calling outside the U.S.

●   Public phones require coin or card deposit to place call.
✛   Public phones and select hotels.
▲   May not be available from every phone/payphone.
○   Collect calling only.
▽   Includes "Ladatel" public phones; if call does not complete,
     use 001-800-462-4240.
☺   From St. Maarten or phones at Bobby's Marina, use 1-800-USA-ATT1.
❬   When calling from public phones, use phones marked Lenso.
*   AT&T Calling Card, AT&T Corporate, AT&T Universal, MasterCard®,
     Diners Club®, American Express®, or Discover® cards accepted.

When placing an international call *from* the U.S., dial 1-800-CALL ATT.
WW   © 6/00 AT&T

CONTENTS

Getting Acquainted

ESTONIA

The official title of the country is the Republic of Estonia *(Eesti Vabariik)*. The highest office in the land is that of president (in Estonian *Riigivanem*, meaning "state elder"). Lennart Meri gained office in the first elections after independence, held in September 1992. He was re-elected in September 1996 for a second term in office.

The parliament *(Riigikogu)* is the highest body in the land, and the president represents the parliament in internal and international contacts. The parliament is responsible for all national legislative matters. Parallel to this body is the Government of the Republic of Estonia, headed by a prime minister approved by the parliament. The prime minister is responsible for the day-to-day running of the country. Mart Laar was elected to the post in 1992; in 1995 he was voted out of office but in March 1999 he returned to head of a coalition government,

LATVIA

Latvia's political apparatus has seen several changes in recent years. In March 1990, the Supreme Council was established when the pro-independence Popular Front gained over two-thirds of the seats. Pro-Soviet Communists (mostly Russians) took the other seats. On 21 August 1991, the Supreme Council declared full independence. Soviet recognition soon followed.

The political landscape in Latvia was to change again almost immediately. After the June 1993 elections, the 100-member *Saeima*, or parliament, was formed, replacing the Supreme Council.

The government is the executive branch of the state in Latvia. It answers to the *Saeima* which can approve or reject the appointment of ministers, as well as government decrees and resolutions. Government personnel, from the head of state to the 12 ministers and the prime minister, are also all elected by the *Saeima*.

In June 1999, Canadian-Latvian Vaira Vīķe-Freiberga became Latvia's first female president.

LITHUANIA

Lithuania is a parliamentary democracy. The government is subordinate to parliament, the *Seimas*, which was formed after the elections in October 1992. At the same time, the country adopted a new constitution.

In the first free elections, the pro-independence communist party, the Democratic Labour Party, won a surprise victory over the centre-right Sajūdis party of Vytautas Landsbergis, who had steered the country to independence. In 1996 the conservatives were voted back into power, with Landsbergis elected as president of the *Seimas*. He decided to run for the post of Lithuanian president in 1998, but lost the elections to the American-Lithuanian Valdas Adamkus. The new president took over from DLP party leader Algirdas Brazauskas, who had headed Lithuania since February 1993.

ESTONIA

Estonia is the northernmost of the three Baltic States. To the south it shares a land border with Latvia, but for the most part its borders are denoted by water. The eastern border is with Russia, much of it running through the 1,350 sq. mile (3,500 sq. km) Lake Peipsi. To the west is the Baltic Sea, which becomes the Gulf of Finland as it laps the northern coastline. Estonia is the smallest of the Baltic states and covers around 17,375 sq. miles (45,227 sq. km). It is still, however, larger than Denmark, The Netherlands or Switzerland. The country is pocked with lakes just as the surrounding coastline is dotted with more than a thousand islands. The landscape is remarkably flat and over 40 percent of the country is covered with dense forest.

Estonia has a population of 1,439,00 with almost a third (408,330) living in and around Tallinn. Other major settlements include Tartu (pop. 101,740), Narva (pop. 73,295), Kohtla-Järva (pop. 65,570) and Pärnu (pop. 50,970),

Ethnically the composition of Estonia is approximately 65 percent Estonian, 28 percent Russian, with the remainder composed of other ex-Soviet nationalities such as Ukrainians and Belarusians. The composition of the populace in any particular region varies greatly. In the industrial towns of north-eastern Estonia, Russians account for some 95 percent of the population, while in rural areas Estonians form over 90 percent of the population.

LATVIA

The Republic of Latvia, the middle of the three states, lies on the eastern coast of the Baltic Sea, less than an hour's flight from Stockholm or Helsinki. It is bounded by Estonia to the north, Lithuania to the south and Russia and Belarus to the east. The territory covers 24,950 sq. miles (64,589 sq. km). The average north-south distance is 130 miles (210 km) and the greatest east-west distance in a straight line is 255 miles (410 km). The 640-mile (1,030-km) River Daugava enters the Baltic Sea in Riga Bay and the dune-backed coast runs for more than 310 miles

(500 km). The country is generally flat and forested, with uplands in the northwest and in the east, where most of the lakes lie. The highest point in Latvia is Galzinkalns, which reaches just 1,025 ft (312 metres).

The population of Latvia is 2,387,470, of whom 769,500 live in Riga. Latvia's second city is Daugavpils (pop. 115,590), followed by Liepāja (pop. 89,515), Jelgava (pop. 63,915), Jūrmala (pop. 55,570) and Ventspils (pop. 44,050). Latvians make up 58 percent of the population, while Russians account for 30 percent of the total. Belarusians number 4 percent and Ukrainians form 3 percent of the population. Latvians are a minority in the country's larger cities, but a majority in the smaller towns and countryside.

LITHUANIA

Lithuania is the largest of the three Baltic countries, covering 25,175 sq. miles (65,300 sq. km), twice the size of Belgium. It borders Latvia in the north, Belarus in the east and south and Poland and the Russian enclave of Kaliningrad in the southwest. Its claim to fame is that it is the centre of Europe: the dead centre of the continent lies near Bernotai, 15 miles (25 km) north of Vilnius. The countryside is slightly more undulating than its northern neighbours and it is covered with rivers and lakes, 2,833 of which exceed an acre. It has the shortest coastline of the three states, covering 60 miles (99 km), much of which is taken up by the extraordinary sand dunes of Neringa Spit, where the 582-mile (937-km) River Nemunas reaches the sea via a large lagoon.

Lithuania has a population of 3,699,500. Vilnius, the capital, is the biggest city with 579,000 inhabitants, followed by Kaunas (pop. 415,800), Klaipėda (pop. 202,000), Šiauliai (pop. 148,000) and Panevėžys (pop. 129,000). Lithuanians make up the majority of the population: just over 81 percent of the total. The second largest ethnic group is Russian (8 percent) followed by Poles (7 percent), who mainly inhabit the southeastern part of the country.

Climate & Clothing

June is by far the best time to visit the Baltic states. During this month the days are longest with the most hours of sun. Rain often comes in July and it may increase as the summer progresses. In June the temperature is usually mild: the last of spring's icy spells having ended in May in Estonia and earlier in Lithuania. July is the hottest month, when mid-summer temperatures can reach up to 86°F (30°C). The average for the month is a pleasant 63°F (17°C).

In winter, temperatures as low as -22°F (-30°C) have been recorded in Estonia and -4°F (-20°C) in Lithuania. In recent years winter temperatures have tended to be milder, seldom falling below around the 23°F (-5°C) mark, and temperatures inland are generally lower than near the coast. Despite this, winters can often seem extremely cold because of the piercing coastal winds.

Snow is most prolonged in Estonia where it can fall from January through to March. In recent years, however, the average fall has been decreasing and there is often no lasting snow cover.

The biggest drawback for visitors in winter is generally not the cold or the snow but the lack of sunlight. From early November through until late March darkness never seems to completely lift, and the six or seven hours of daylight are often marred by overcast, misty conditions.

What to wear

Although people tend to dress up for concerts, the theatre and official business, the dress code is otherwise fairly informal. When packing, bear in mind how cold the winter climate can be. From November to April minimum requirements are a heavy woollen

Language

Each of the three countries has its own official language – Estonian, Latvian and Lithuanian – and each of these uses the Latin alphabet. Estonian is based on the Finno-Ugric family of languages, while Latvian and Lithuanian are the last remaining dialects of the Baltic family of Indo-European languages, which Estonians cannot understand. A Latvian and a Lithuanian can usually at least get the gist of what each other is trying to say.

Although Russian is common to all three countries, it is not now being taught as a first language and many Balts prefer not to speak it out of national pride. However, large populations of Russians, particularly in Latvia and Estonia, keep the language alive here. Many Russians work in the service industries in Latvia and Estonia, and a lot of the road signs are in Russian. In theory every Balt between the ages of 15 and 45 should be able to speak Russian, as under Soviet occupation the language was a compulsory part of schooling. In practice, however, few Balts choose to speak Russian and, as a visitor, if you do speak some Russian yourself it is usually tactful to try to converse in your own language first. Estonians are often multilingual, and many people speak English as well as Finnish. In Latvia, English has become the language of choice for students, followed by German and French. In Lithuania English is generally more commonly understood than German.

A more comprehensive guide to the languages, plus some useful words and phrases, can be found on page 423.

jumper, thermal underwear, leggings and something thick-soled and waterproof on your feet. From January to March it is highly advisable to wear gloves and a hat and scarf.

In summer lightweight garments and even shorts and T-shirts are adequate. Evenings can turn chilly, so bring a sweater and jacket to keep you warm if you go out at this time. It is also advisable to pack waterproof clothing and an umbrella, if you have room. Sensible, comfortable footwear is highly recommended as the cities' cobbled streets are uncomfortable in thin-soled shoes and treacherous in high-heels.

Religion

ESTONIA

The state church is the Estonian Evangelical Lutheran Church, which has held sway since the Reformation in the 16th century. The Orthodox and Baptist churches also draw large congregations, mainly from the Russian community. Estonians have never been a particularly religious people. However, since independence there has been a renewed interest in the church and attendances have risen. The principal churches open for services in Tallinn are:
St John's Church (Jaani Kirik), Vabaduse väljak 1 (Lutheran).
Church of the Holy Ghost (Pühavaimu kirik), Pühavaimu 2 (Lutheran). Services in English every Sunday at 3pm.
Dome Church/St Mary's Church (Toomkirik), Toom-Kooli 6 (Lutheran).
St Charles's Church (Kaarli kirik), Toompea 10 (Lutheran).

Time Zones

All three Baltic states have abolished daylight savings time, so from November to the end of March they are two hours ahead of GMT but only one hour ahead of this for the rest of the year.

Alexander Nevski Cathedral, Lossi plats 10, Toompea (Russian Orthodox).
St Olaf's Church (Oleviste kirik), Lai 50, (Evangelist-Baptist).
Church of St Peter and Paul, Vene 18 (Catholic).
Church of the 7th Day Adventists, Mere pst.
Jewish synagogue, Lastaia 9.

LATVIA

Prior to World War II, 55 percent of Latvia's population was Lutheran and 24 percent was Catholic (concentrated in Latgale, the eastern region). The rest of the people were Russian Orthodox, Baptist or Jewish.

Although there was something of a religious revival in 1988, this seems to have abated in recent years. Many of the younger generation are agnostic and they have generally become more concerned with making ends meet than going to church. Minority religious groups such as the Hare Krishnas and the Moonies are more prominent nowadays than in the past in all three states.

The principal churches in Riga are listed below:
St Saviour's Church, Anglikānu 2a (Anglican). An English service takes place every Sunday at 10am.
Dome Cathedral, (Doma baznīca), Doma laukums 1 (Lutheran).
St Peter's Church, (Peterbaznīca), Skārņu 19 (Lutheran).
St John's Church, Jāņa 7 (Lutheran)
Old St Gertrūde's Church, Ģertrūdes 8 (Lutheran).
Church of Jesus, Odessas 18 (Lutheran).
St Jacob's Cathedral, Klostera 2 (Catholic).
Orthodox Cathedral, Kr. Barona 126. (Orthodox).
St Alexander Nevsky Church, Brīvības 56 (Orthodox).
Orthodox Cathedral, Brīvības bulv. 23. (Orthodox).
Grebenschikov's Church, Krasta 73 (Russian Old Believers).
Jewish Synagogue, Peitavas 6–8.

LITHUANIA

Predominantly Catholic, Lithuania could be described as the most religious of the three countries – the flame of religion having been kept alive throughout the communist era by the church in Rome. The majority of the country's churches were converted for secular use during the communist years but since February 1989 most have been re-consecrated and a lot of money has been poured into churches, monasteries and seminaries to re-establish Vilnius in particular as a major Catholic centre in Europe. These are the principal churches in the city:
Cathedral, Arkikatedros aikšte 23 (Catholic).
Gates of Dawn, Aušros Vartų 12 (Catholic shrine).
Bernardine Church, Maironio 8 (Catholic).
Church of the Holy Spirit, Dominikonų 8 (Catholic).
Orthodox Church of the Holy Spirit, Aušros Vartų 10. (Catholic).
St Anne's Church, Maironio 8. (Catholic).
St Casimir's Church, Didžioji 34 (Catholic).
St Johns' Church, Šv. Jono 12 (Catholic).
St Michael's Church, Šv. Mykolo 9 (Catholic).
St Nicholas Church, Šv. Mikalojaus 4 (Catholic).
Sts Peter & Paul's Church, Antakalnio 1 (Catholic).
Sts Philip and Jacob's Church, Lukiškiu aikšte 10 (Catholic). Sunday mass in English at 9am/1pm.
Orthodox Church of the Holy Spirit, Aušros Vartų 10 (Russian Orthodox).
Orthodox Church of Paraskovila Piatnickaya, Didžioji 2 (Russian Orthodox).
St Nicholas the Wonder Worker, Didžioji 12 (Russian Orthodox).
Evangelical Lutheran Church, Vokiečių 20. Protestant worship in English on the second and fourth Sunday of each month at noon.
Synagogue, Pylimo 39 (Jewish).

Business Hours

ESTONIA

A 9am–6pm five-day working week is standard. Lunch is normally taken around 1pm. Shops, however, usually open from 10am– 6pm without a lunch break; many close early on Saturday.

In Tallinn the Finnish Stockmann shopping mall on Liivalaia 53 (tel: 633 9500; fax: 633 9556), the Viru Shopping Centre on Viru väljak 4 and the Tallinna Kaubamaja on Gonsiori 2 are open daily 10am–8pm. The Rocca-al-Mare Kaubanduskeskus (shopping centre) on Paldiski mnt. 102, is open daily 10am–10pm.

There are several 24-hour grocery and alcohol stores in Tallinn. Try the Rema 1000 Sakala on Pärnu mnt. 36, Väravavaht on Viru 23 and Westmanni Äri on Pärnu mnt. 19

Museums and galleries generally close on Mondays (often also on Tuesdays) but they tend to stay open through the weekend. Restaurants open at around midday and close at 11pm, with last orders usually taken 30 minutes before that. If you want to eat later, hotels sometimes serve food beyond 11pm, otherwise you can opt for a pizza takeaway. If you are really desperate for sustenance, you can always visit one of the 24-hour burger kiosks that are dotted around town (Vabaduse väljak, Viru väljak, at the intersection of Liivalaia and Tartu mnt).

LATVIA

Banks are generally open from 9am–5pm Monday to Friday and most are closed on weekends. On weekdays **shops** generally open from 10am–7pm, and until 4pm on Saturdays. Food and department stores usually open between 8am–7pm. Most **offices** close at some time between 5–6pm, although on Friday people tend to leave earlier in order to make the most of the weekend. There are

Electricity

Mains electricity is 220v AC and sockets take two-pronged plugs. It is possible to buy plugs, leads, adaptors and most electrical accessories in local stores. Batteries are usually available at photographic supply shops.

countless 24-hour stores in Riga where you can find almost anything any time of day. Amongst these stores are: Abolitis on Kr. Barona 17, Avots on Čaka 22, Delikatesen on Šķūņu 7, Elida-L on Grēcinieku 10, Interpegro on Raiņa bulv. 33 or Visbija on Brīvības 68.

LITHUANIA

Lithuanians usually work from 9am–1pm and 2–6pm. Shops tend to be open between 10am–7pm with a shorter day on Saturday. Food shops and supermarkets are also open on Sunday until 10pm. Banks are open from 8am–4pm and close earlier on Friday. Museums and galleries are generally shut on Mondays and sometimes on Tuesdays – it's advisable to check this out before travelling.

Public Holidays

Public holidays are cause for great celebration in the Baltics. Each state flies the flags of the other two nations on these special days, as well as on their own flag – in Latvia the national flag must, by law, be displayed prominently on facades by the front door on public holidays.

Midsummer (St John's Day) is an important date in the calendar. Called *Jaanipäev* in Estonia and *Jāņi* in Latvia, it is a festival of pagan origins, deeply rooted in peasant culture. The date marks the end of spring labours in the fields and used to be seen as a night of omens and sorcery. One tradition that still exists to this day is that of leaping over bonfires. A successful clearance of the flames used to indicate

similar success for the year ahead. On the days leading up to this festival Tallinn is drained of people, as everyones heads for the countryside. At Jāņi in Latvia special beers and cheeses are made for the occasion and citizens sport floral wreathes.

ESTONIA

- **January** New Year's Day (1)
- **February** Independence Day (24)
- **March/April** Good Friday.
- **May** May Day (1)
- **June** Victory Day (23)
- **June** Midsummer (24)
- **December** Christmas (25/26)

LATVIA

- **January** New Year's Day (1)
- **March/April** Good Friday and Easter Monday
- **May** May Day (1)
- **June** Līgo Day (23)
- **June** Jāņi (summer solstice) (24)
- **November** Independence Day (18)
- **December** Christmas (25/26)

Memorial Days
- **March** mass deportation of Balts to Siberia in 1949 (25)
- **May** Proclamation of Independence (4)
- **May** World War II Memorial Day (9)
- **June** first mass deportation of Balts to Siberia, 1941 (14)
- **July** Jewish Genocide Day (4)
- **November** 1919 battle, during which invading German forces were repulsed from Riga (11)

LITHUANIA

- **January** New Year (1)
- **February** Restoration of Lithuanian statehood (1918) (16)
- **March** Restoration of Lithuania's statehood (11)
- **March/April** Easter
- **May** Mothers' Day (first Sunday)
- **July** Crowning of Mindaugas, Day of statehood (6)
- **November** All Saints' Day (1)
- **December** Christmas (25/26)

Planning the Trip

Visas & Passports

The three Baltic countries form a common visa zone. If you hold a visa for one of them you do not need another visa for the other two, as long as you do not leave the common visa zone.

ESTONIA

Citizens of Andorra, Australia, Austria, Belgium, Bulgaria, Cyprus, the Czech Republic, Denmark, Finland, France, Greece, Germany, Hungary, Iceland, Ireland, Italy, Japan, Korea, Latvia, Liechtenstein, Lithuania, Luxembourg, Malta, Monaco, The Netherlands, New Zealand, Norway, Poland, Portugal, San Marino, Singapore, Slovakia, Slovenia, Spain, Sweden, Switzerland, the UK, US and Vatican City need only to carry a valid passport to enter Estonia.

Citizens of Canada, Israel and South Africa need an Estonian visa, unless they already hold a valid visa for Latvia or Lithuania.

Nationals of all other countries require an invitation issued by any legal citizen or institution of Estonia and have to apply for a visa at any of the Estonian consulates or embassies (see p.386).

Visas are not issued at the border, airport or any other point of entry. Visas are issued in three forms: transit (for stays of up to three days only), single entry (usually for stays of up to 30 days) and multiple entry. Costs vary by embassy but a single entry visa is around US$10 (transit visas are cheaper; multiple entry costs about US$30). Visas can be extended at

the immigration office, at Lai 38/40 in the Old Town, Tallinn.

LATVIA

Visas are not needed for citizens of Andorra, Austria, Belgium, Croatia, the Czech Republic, Denmark, Estonia, Finland, France, Germany, Greece, Hungary, Iceland, Ireland, Italy, Japan, Liechtenstein, Lithuania, Luxembourg, Malta, Netherlands, Norway, Poland, Portugal, Slovakia, Slovenia, Spain, Sweden, Switzerland, the UK, US and Vatican City. Other nationalities may be able to obtain visas from Riga Airport and sea passenger ports, but it is safer to get them at Latvian representations abroad. A Latvian visa is also good for stays in Estonia and Lithuania.

LITHUANIA

Citizens of Andorra, Australia, Austria, Belgium, Bulgaria, Canada, Chile, Croatia, Cyprus, the Czech Republic, Denmark, Estonia, Finland, France, Germany, Greece, Hungary, Iceland, Ireland, Italy, Japan, Korea, Latvia, Liechtenstein, Luxembourg, Malta, Monaco, Netherlands, New Zealand, Norway, Poland, Portugal, San Marino, Slovakia, Slovenia, Spain, Sweden, Switzerland, the UK, US, Vatican City and Venezuela do not need a Lithuanian visa. Others nationals should buy a visa via any Lithuanian representation abroad.

Customs & Export

Individuals entering and leaving the Baltic states may carry with them most articles, personal property and other valuables in unlimited quantities. However, weapons and ammunition of any kind, drugs and psychotropic substances are not allowed. Lithuania also forbids the import of meat, dairy products, eggs and sausages and the export of more than 10kg of fresh and 5kg of dried mushrooms or berries.

The import and export of tobacco

and alcohol is limited in all three countries to 1 litre of spirits, 2 litres of wine, 3 litres of beer and 200 cigarettes or 20 cigars or 250g of tobacco. Estonia's alcohol allowances are slightly higher. There are no currency restrictions but Lithuania forbids the export of cash exceeding five hundred thousand Litas (around US$125,000), while Estonian customs officials will start to ask questions if you take out more than 200,000 Estonian krooni (US$13,000) in cash.

In all three countries works of art made before 1945 require a special export licence obtainable from antiques shops or from customs. Contact:

Estonian Customs, Lõkke 5, Tallinn. Tel: 696 7435/696 7436/696 7722; fax: 696 7727; info@customs.ee; www.customs.ee.
Latvian Customs Department, Riga, Citadeles 1. Tel: 732 1960.
Lithuanian Customs Department, Vilnius, A. Jakšto 1/25. Tel: 613 027/226 415; fax: 224 948; info@cust.lt; www.cust.lt.

Currency & Exchange

Now that currency restrictions have been removed in all three states, there is no need to carry large amounts of cash when travelling through the Baltics. There are now numerous automatic teller machines (ATMs) throughout Estonia, Latvia and Lithuania, which usually accept at least Visa cards and Mastercards/Eurocards. Most hotels, restaurants and shops will gladly accept payment by credit card. Travellers' cheques can only be cashed in banks and some service bureaux of major hotels.

ESTONIA

The official currency of Estonia is the Estonian *kroon* (pronounced "krone"; abbreviated to EEK; plural: *krooni*). Notes are printed in denominations of 1, 2, 5, 10, 25, 50, 100 and 500 *krooni*. Coins are minted at the values of 5, 10, 20 and 50 sents and 1 and 5 *krooni*, with one hundred sents to the *kroon*. Since its introduction in June 1992 the *kroon* has been stable at a fixed rate of 15.65EEK to 1 Euro. US$1 is equivalent to around 16 *krooni*. All transactions must be made in *krooni*. Trading in any other currency (including the Russian rouble and the US dollar) is illegal.

Exchange points exist at the harbour, the airport, all major hotels, the central post office, department stores and in numerous other locations. Exchange rates are set by the Bank of Estonia and are posted daily.

Credit cards are widely accepted in Estonia and can be used at most hotels, restaurants and shops.

LATVIA

In 1993 the *Lats* (plural *lati*) superseded the Latvian rouble, an intermediate currency which replaced the Russian rouble. It has become one of the most stable currencies in the world at 0.57Ls to 1 Euro and 0.60 to US$1. The *Lats* is made up of 100 *santīms*. Banknotes are in denominations of 5, 10, 20, 50, 100 and 500 *Lats*. There are 1, 2, 5, 10, 50 santimi and 1 and 2 *Lats* coins. Finding an exchange point in Latvia should not be a problem. Opening hours between Monday and Saturday are 10am–6pm. If exchanging large amounts of money, it is worthwhile shopping around, because the rates vary slightly from place to place and from day to day. Hotels give lower rates, so it is best not to change your currency there unless you really have to.

Credit cards are widely accepted in most hotels, restaurants and shops and there are ATMs all over the country.

LITHUANIA

Lithuania's national currency is the *Litas*, and bank notes come in 1, 2, 5, 10, 25, 50 and 100 denominations. *Litas* are the only legal tender and transactions in any

other currency is illegal. Currency can be changed in banks – changing money on the street is illegal.

Credit cards are accepted in most hotels and restaurants and there are ATMs in the major towns.

Getting There

GENERAL INFORMATION

The three Baltic states offer a variety of entry points by land sea and air. None of the capitals is far from the others, and it is easy to travel from one to another. As more major airlines add the Baltic states to their itineraries, flights into the three countries are becoming cheaper and increasing accessible.

The long lines at the Polish-Lithuanian border are a thing of the past and the border crossing is swift and smooth. Inner-Baltic customs and border controls have also been harmonised and are usually a straightforward affair.

Anyone contemplating travelling to the Baltic states through Russia, including the enclave of Kaliningrad in the south, is advised to apply for a visa three months in advance. Note that if you arrive via Belarus by car or train you will be charged around US$30–50 for the Belarusian transit visa.

TOUR OPERATORS

Tour operators offer a relatively stress-free alternative to independent travel and can offer help getting to places where language may be a problem. The following agents all have experience in arranging travel to the Baltics:

Australia
Well-Connected Travel, 89 Ferguson Street, Forestville, NSW 2087. Tel: 61-2 9975 2355; fax: 61-2 9451 6446.
info@wctravel.com.au
www.wctravel.com.au

Canada
Goliger's Travel, 5650 Yonge Street, Retail Concourse North

York, Ontario M2M 4G3. Tel: 416 221 3113, toll free 1-888-226-3628; fax: 416 221-4885.
oravtrav@netcom.ca
www.baltic-design-tours.on.ca
Intra Travel, Woodside Square Mall, 1571 Sandhurst Circle, Scarborough, Ontario.
Tel: 416 298 2160/1-800-263-2721; fax: 416 298-8182.
woodside@intra.com

Denmark
Fremad Rejser, Vesterbrogade 43, Copenhagen. Tel: 45-31 220 404; fax: 45-31 222 277.

Finland
Tallink, 00130 Helsinki, Eteläranta 14. Tel: 358-9 228 311, fax: 358-9 649 808. tallink@tallink.fi

Germany
Greif Reisen Manthey, Universitätsstr. 2, D-58455 Witten. Tel: 49-2302 24044, fax: 49-2302 25050.
Hein Reisen, Zwergerstr. 1, D-85579 Neubiberg/Munich. Tel: 49-89 637 39 84, fax: 49-89 679 28 12.
www.heinreisen.de
Ost Reise Service Fachreisebüro für Ost-Touristik, Artur Landeckstr. 139, D-33647 Bielefeld.
Tel: 0521/417 3333.
Rautenberg Reisen, Blinke 8, Postfach 1909, D-26769 Leer. Tel: 49-491 92 97 03, fax: 49-491 92 97 07.
reisen@rautenberg-druck.de
www.rautenberg-druck.de
Schnieder Reisen, Schillerstr. 43, D-22767 Hamburg. Tel: 49-40 380 2060/380 20671; fax: 49-40 388 965/380 20688.
info@schniederreisen.de
www.schniederreisen.de

UK
ACE Study Tours, Babraham, Cambridgeshire CB2 4AP.
Tel: 01223 835 055; fax: 01223 837 394.
ace@study-tours.org
www.study-tours.org
Art trips and general-interest tours.
Explore Worldwide, 1 Frederick Street, Aldershot, Hants GU11 1LQ.

Tel: 01252 319 448;
fax: 01252 760 001
info@explore.co.uk
www.explore.co.uk
General-interest tours.
Interchange, 27 Stafford Road,
Croydon, Surrey CRO 4NG.
Tel: 020 8681 3612; fax: 020
8760 0031.
interchange@interchange.uk.com
www.interchange.uk.com
Hotel bookings in the Baltics and
home-stays in Russia.
Martin Randall Travel,
10 Barley Mow Passage, London
W4 4PH. Tel: 020 8742 3355,
fax: 020 8742 7766.
info@martinrandall.co.uk
www.martinrandall.co.uk
Art and architecture group tours.
Regent Holidays, 15 John Street,
Bristol BS1 2HR. Tel: 0117 921
1711; fax: 0117 925 4866.
regent@regent-holidays.co.uk
www.regent-holidays.co.uk
Cheap flights, individual hotel
bookings and general-interest tours.

US
Union Tours, 245 Fifth Avenue, New
York, NY 10016. Tel: 212 683
9500; fax: 212 683 9511.
travel@uniontours.com
www.uniontours.com
Baltic specialists of long standing,
Union Tours offers both group tours
and individual itineraries.
Vytis Tours, 40–42 235th Street,
Douglaston, NY 11363. Tel: 718
423 6161, toll free 1-800 77-
VYTIS; fax: 718 423 3979
vyttours@earthlink.net
www.vytistours.com
American Travel Service, 9439
South Kedzie Ave., Evergreen Park,
Chicago, IL60805-2325. Tel: 708
422 3000; fax: 708 422 3163.
atsvl@worldnet.att.net
www.americantravelservice.com
Tours and individual itineraries.
ITS Tours and Travel, College
Station, Texas TX77840. Tel: 409
764 9400; fax: 409 693 9673.
its-tour@myriad.net
www.sightseeing.com
Tours and individual itineraries.
Scantours, 3439 Wade Str., Los
Angeles, CA90066-1533.
Tel: 310 636 4656, toll free 1-800

223-7226; fax: 310 390-0493.
info@scantours.com
www.scantours.com
Exclusive chauffeured tours.

Getting to Estonia

BY AIR

Estonia's international airport
Lennujaam is on the outskirts of
Tallinn by the shores of Lake
Ülemiste. It was built during the
boom that came with the 1980
Moscow Olympics, when Tallinn was
the venue for the yachting events.
The terminal has been renovated
and offers standard airport facilities
including car hire, post office, cash
exchange and an information desk.
Three international carriers, **Finnair**,
LOT and **SAS**, along with the state
airline, **Estonian Air**, currently fly
out of Tallinn. It is possible to get
discounted airfares to Tallinn, so
check with a travel agency before
booking any flight. Tallinn Airport
has direct flights to 14 major
European cities: Copenhagen,
Frankfurt, Hamburg, Helsinki, Kyiv,
London, Minsk, Moscow, Riga,
Stockholm, St. Petersburg, Vienna,
Vilnius and Warsaw.
  Some airlines such as Lufthansa
have cancelled scheduled flights to
Tallinn and fly into nearby Helsinki
instead, from where you can either
take a 20-minute helicopter flight to
Tallinn harbour or one of the
frequent flights to Tallinn airport.

From the Airport
A taxi ride into the old town will cost
around 50EEK. If your luggage isn't
too cumbersome, it works out
cheaper to take the bus. City bus
No 2 runs every 20 minutes to the
Viru hotel for 15EEK. It is a 10-
minute ride down into the Old Town.
Tickets can be bought on the bus.
  Carrier contacts in Tallinn are:
Estonian Air to Copenhagen,
Frankfurt, Hamburg, Kyiv, London-
Gatwick, Minsk, Moscow, Riga,
Stockholm and Vilnius, Vabaduse
väljak 10.
Tel: 631 3302; fax: 631 2740.
ov@estonian-air.ee
www.estonian-air.ee

Finnair to Helsinki, Roosikrantsi 2.
Tel: 611 0950; fax: 611 0945.
finnair@finnair.ee; www.finnair.ee
LOT to Warsaw, Lembitu 14.
Tel: 646 6051/646 6052;
fax: 645 4298. www.lot.com
SAS to Stockholm, Rävala 2.
Tel: 627 9399; fax: 627 9390.
www.sas.se
ELK Airways, Airport departure hall.
Tel: 605 8199. Regular flights to
Visby Sweden via Kärdla on Hiiumaa
and to Adler Russia.

BY SEA

A flotilla of all shapes and sizes
eases in and out of the harbour at
Tallinn, ferrying passengers by
various routes across the Baltic.
From Helsinki passage can be
taken at almost any hour of the day.
There are several hydrofoils making
early morning crossings with a
journey time of between one and
two hours depending on the
particular craft and the weather.
  The *Tallink Express* and *Tallink
AutoExpress*, owned by Tallink, each
make three crossings a day from
the Finnish capital. The Nordic Jet
Lines makes the 100-mile (160-km)
round trip six times a day in little
over one hour, while the Lindaline
hydrofoil has the same crossing
time and departs every two hours.
Viking Line operates the *M/S Viking
Express*, a large jet catamaran
which makes the round trip three
times a day. Each crossing takes
approximately 1½ hours each way.
  Four larger ships – the *M/S Vana
Tallinn*, *George Ots*, *Meloodia* and
Fantaasia, all owned by Tallink –
take a more leisurely 3½ hours to
cross each day; these offer
restaurants, bars, videos and
cabins on board to help pass the
time. Estline operates the *M/S
Regina Baltica* and the *M/S Baltic
Kristina*, which sail daily from
Stockholm to Tallinn. These two
boats have replaced the *M/S
Estonia*, which sank in 1994. Silja
Line's *Finnjet* sails three times a
week from Rostock Germany to
Tallinn and further to Helsinki. If you
are planning to sail from Sweden

then you may want to consider sailing to Helsinki and picking up the ferry from there as a cheaper alternative. Two lines, Silja and the Viking line, operate the Stockholm-Helsinki route. Tickets bought in Finland are subject to a travel tax of 30 Finnish marks, so it is wise to book in Tallinn.

From the harbour
The harbour *(sadam)* is a 15-minute walk from the Old Town. On trams 1 or 2 the Old Town is the next stop after Viru väljak, or from the opposite direction, two stops from the railway station.

Below is a list of the companies running services to and from the three Baltic states:

Estline, Stockholm, Frihamn, Magazini 2, Tallinnterminalen. Tel: 46-8 667 0001; fax: 46-8 666 6052; passenger@estline.se; www.estline.com. Tallinn, Terminal D. Tel: 631 8888; fax: 631 3633. Head office at Aia 5a. Tel: 644 8348; estline@estline.ee; www.estline.ee. Overnight crossings from Stockholm to Tallinn.

Lindaline, Helsinki, Makasiiniterminaali Eteläsatama. Tel: 358-9 668 9700; fax: 358-9 668 970 70; sales@lindaline.fi; www.lindaline.fi. Tallinn, Linnahall Terminal, Mere pst. 20. Tel: 641 2412; fax: 641 2270; www.lindaline.ee.

Nordic Jet Lines, Helsinki, Kanavaterminaali K5. Tel: 358-9 681 770; fax: 358-9 681 77 111; booking@njl.fi; www.njl.fi. Tallinn, Terminal C. Tel: 613 7000; fax: 613 7222; njl@njl.ee; booking@njl.ee; www.njl.ee.

Silja Line, Helsinki, Mannerheimintie 2. Tel: 358-9 2037 4552/9180 4510; fax: 358-9 180 4279. Lübeck Germany, Zeißstr. 6. Tel: 49-451 58 99-222; fax: 49-451 58 99-243; info@siljaline.de; www.siljaline.de. Tallinn, Terminal D, Lootsi 13. Tel: 611 6663; fax: 631 8264; terminal@silja.ee; Stockmann department store: tel: 611 6661; fax: 626 1237; booking@silja.ee; www.silja.com. Silja sails between Tallinn and Rostock in Germany.

Tallink, Helsinki, Eteläranta 14. Tel: 358-9 228 311; fax: 358-9 649 808; tallink@tallink.fi. Tallinn, Pärnu 12. Tel: 640 3641; fax: 640 3545. Booking centre: tel: 640 9808; fax: 640 9815. Terminal A. Tel: 631 8217; fax: 631 8246, Terminal D. Tel: 631 8320; fax: 631 8325; info@hansatee.ee; www.tallink.ee. Numerous daily services on express boats and larger ferries.

Viking Line, Helsinki, Mannerheimintie 14. Tel: 358-9 12 351; fax: 358-9 647 075; vlres@vikingline.fi; www.vikingline.fi. Tallinn, Ahtri 12. Tel: 611 6640. Sales agents: Estravel, Liivalaia 33. Tel: 626 6300; fax: 631 5871. Estravel, Suur-Karja 15. Tel: 626 6626; fax: 626 6262; sales@estravel.ee. Viking lines ply between Helsinki and Stockholm.

Estonia by Rail

Tallinn's train station *(baltijaam)* is poorly served by international trains. Due to lack of demand the Baltic Express, linking Tallinn to Warsaw, has been suspended. There is a cumbersome 8-hour service from Tallinn to Riga with a change of trains in the border towns of Valga and Valka. Tallinn has one overnight train to and from St. Petersburg and there are two daily return services to Moscow. Contact: **Estonian Railways**, Tallinn Train Station. Tel: 615 6851. Head office: Pikk 36. Tel: 615 8610; fax: 615 8710; info@evr.ee; www.evr.ee.

BY ROAD

Entering by car one gets a sense of just how seriously Estonia takes the idea of being seen to be a separate country. Elsewhere in Europe borders are coming down but in the Baltics they are being enforced with a vengeance. Coming from Latvia the crossing is efficient, but crossing the main Russian-Estonian border at Narva can be time-consuming because most vehicles are searched by border guards.

By Bus
Eurolines travels six times per week to Berlin, via Riga, Kaunas and further to Stuttgart twice weekly, Cologne thrice weekly and Munich once a week. The company also has services to Oslo twice weekly, Riga four times a day, Vilnius twice a day, St. Petersburg four times a day and Kaliningrad once a day via Riga and Šiauliai.
Eurolines, Lastekodu 46. Tel: 601 0700; fax: 601 0701; mreis@online.ee; www.eurolines.ee.

Getting to Latvia

BY AIR

Riga International Airport has frequent direct flights to 15 major European cities. These are Budapest, Copenhagen, Frankfurt, Helsinki, Kyiv, London, Moscow, Prague, Stockholm, Tallinn, Tel-Aviv, Vienna, Vilnius, Warsaw and Zurich. Travellers arriving from other countries can transfer to the above European cities and then pick up a flight to Riga.

Riga airport has an information booth on the first floor. Tel: 720 7009/722 3305; office@riga-airport.com; www.riga-airport.com. The airport offers various cafés, bars, newsstands and souvenir kiosks. Money can be exchanged from 6am–10pm on the ground floor just after passing through customs, and baggage can be stored 24 hours a day on the ground floor. Phone calls can be made from any public phone. Public phones require a chip card, which can be bought at any of the airport's kiosks and in some hotels.

From the airport
Riga airport is a 30-minute ride from the centre of the city on bus No. 22, which leaves every half hour from the opposite side of the parking lot. Tickets can be bought from the driver for 0.20Ls. The official taxis in the taxi rank in front of the arrival terminal will charge 2Ls for ordering, 0.40Ls per bag and 0.30Ls per kilometre. A ride to town should not cost you more than

US$15. Most tour operators can
book transfers to your hotel for you.
Ask before you arrive in Latvia.

Airlines serving the Baltics:
Aeroflot to Moscow, Riga Airport.
Tel: 720 7472. Ģertrūdes 6.
Tel: 727 8774/727 5438.
Aerosweet to Kyiv, Riga Airport.
Tel: 720 7502.
AirBaltic Latvian National Carrier to
Budapest, Copenhagen, Frankfurt,
Helsinki, Stockholm, Tallinn, Vilnius,
Warsaw, Riga Airport. Tel: 720
7401; fax: 720 7505; airbaltic@
mail.bkc.lv; www.airbaltic.com. Kaļķu
15. Tel: 720 7777; fax: 722 4282.
Austrian Airlines to Vienna, Kaļķu
8. Tel: 708 5070; fax: 782 0020.
British Airways to London-Gatwick,
Torņa 4/IIIa. Tel: 732 6737; fax:
732 6747.
ČSA to Prague, Riga Airport.
Tel: 720 7636/720 7936; fax: 720
7337; csatomas@apollo.lv.
Estonian Air to Tallinn, Riga Airport.
Tel: 720 7458; www.estonian-air.ee.
Finnair to Helsinki, Riga Airport. Tel:
720 7010/720 7360;
www.finnair.lv. Kr. Barona 36.
Tel: 724 3008; fax: 724 3010.
Latpass to Tel-Aviv, Pils laukums 2.
Tel: 722 1818; fax: 722 6738.
LOT to Warsaw, Maza Pils 5.
Tel: 722 7234/722 7263/724
2870; fax: 724 2869; www.lot.com.
Lufthansa to Frankfurt. Riga Airport.
Tel: 720 7183/720 7381; fax: 720
7026; www.lufthansa.com.

Latvia by Rail

Since the Baltic Express train
from Warsaw was cancelled,
there has only been one daily
overnight train from Vilnius to
Riga. The latter is well connected
with the East with two daily
services to Moscow, a daily
service to St. Petersburg and
some trains to Minsk in Belarus
and Lviv in Ukraine. For Riga
Central Railway Station, tel: 583
3095/583 3134.
Latvian Railways, Gogoļa 3.
Tel: 583 4940/583 4208;
fax: 782 0231/722 9556;
info@ldz.lv; www.ldz.lv.

SAS to Copenhagen, Stockholm,
Riga Airport. Tel: 720 7055; fax:
720 7505. Kaļķu 15. Tel: 721
6139; fax: 722 4282; www.sas.se.
Transeast Airlines to Billund,
Jönköping, Riga Airport. Tel: 720
7771; fax: 720 7772.

BY SEA

Ferry services to and from Riga
have been cut drastically in recent
years and at the time of writing
there was no ferry service to and
from Riga's harbour. Check before
travelling as this may change.
Scandlines operates two ferries
between the Latvian port city
Liepāja and Rostock (Germany) and
Karlshamn (Sweden). There is a
sailing between Rostock-Liepāja-
Rostock twice a week, which takes
25 hours in total.
Scandlines Rostock, Am Warnowkai
8. Tel: 49-381 673 1217; fax: 49-
381 673 1213; info@scandlines.de;
www.scandlines.de.
Liepāja-Karlshamn-Liepāja. Three
times per week; duration: 16hrs.
Scandlines Karlshamn.
Tel: 46-45 419 080;
kundservice@scandlines.se;
www.scandlines.se.
In Liepāja, telephone Scandlines on
342 7214.

BY ROAD

Customs posts on the borders with
Estonia and Lithuania should
present no problems to visitors,
and the roads are generally good.
High-grade petrol is easily available
outside Riga. Roadside hotels and
rest stops are slowly appearing
along the Via Baltica, the main road
linking the three capitals. You can
get good road maps in most petrol
stations. The speed limit on
highways is 55mph (90kph) and
37mph (60kph) in residential areas.
Headlights must be turned on all
the time.

By Bus

Riga is well served by **Eurolines**
buses with a daily coach service to

Berlin, travelling further to Stuttgart
twice weekly, Cologne twice weekly,
Hamburg and Bremen twice weekly
and Munich once a week. The
Latvian-run Ecolines buses run daily
services to Germany, Brussels and
Paris. The local bus company has a
daily service to Warsaw. There are
numerous daily services to and
from Lithuania, Estonia, Moscow,
Minsk and St. Petersburg. Most
overnight vehicles are equipped to a
high standard, with toilet facilities.
Eurolines/Baltijas Autobusu
Līnijas, Riga Bus Station, Prāgas 1.
Tel: 721 4080; fax: 750 3134;
agency@eurolines.lv;
bal@eurolines.lv; www.eurolines.lv.

Getting to Lithuania

BY AIR

There are frequent direct flights to
14 major European cities from
Vilnius: Amsterdam, Berlin,
Copenhagen, Frankfurt, Helsinki,
Kyiv, London, Moscow, Paris, Riga,
Stockholm, Tallinn, Vienna and
Warsaw. Air Lithuania is based in
Kaunas and flies from Kaunas via
Palanga on the coast to Billund
Sweden, Cologne, Hamburg,
Kristianstad and Oslo. The following
airlines serve the Lithuanian capital:
Aeroflot to Moscow, Tauro 8/30.
Tel: 621 834. Vilnius Airport. Tel:
260 357.
AirBaltic to Riga, Vilnius Airport.
Tel: 233 345; fax: 306 140;
www.airbaltic.com.
Austrian Airlines to Vienna, Vilnius
Airport. Tel: 226 063.
Estonian Air to Tallinn, Vilnius Airport.
Tel: 739 022; www.estonian-air.ee.
Finnair to Helsinki, Rūdninkų 18/2.
Tel: 619 339. Finnair Vilnius Airport.
Tel: 330 810; www.finnair.com.
Lithuanian Airlines, Ukmergės 12.
Tel: 752 585/752 588; fax: 724
852; info@lal.lt, www.lal.lt. Vilnius
Airport. Tel: 233 345.
LOT to Warsaw, Hotel Skrydis, room
104, Rodūnės kelias 2. Tel: 739
020; fax: 739 019; lotvno@lot.com;
www.lot.com.
Lufthansa to Frankfurt, Vilnius
Airport. Tel: 262 222/306 031;
www.lufthansa.com.

SAS to Stockholm, Vilnius Airport. Tel: 395 500; fax: 395 501; www.sas.se.
Vilnius airport (Oro uostas), Rodūnės kelias 2. Tel: 306 666/752 600; www.vilnius-airport.lt. This airport is 3 miles (5km) south of the city. Bus No. 2 from Lukiškiu aikšte or No. 1 from the train station run every half hour. A taxi ride will cost abou US$4 into town – less when you order a taxi to the airport.

Kaunas-based **Air Lithuania** operates international flights from Kaunas to Billund (Denmark), Cologne and Hamburg (Germany), Kristianstad (Sweden) and Oslo (Norway) via Palanga. For information contact: Kaunas: Šv. Gertrūdos 7. Tel: 7-229 706/228 176; fax: 7-228 504; hdoffice@airlithuania.lt; www.airlithuania.lt. Kaunas Airport. Tel/fax: 7-399 401, Klaipėda, Taikos pr. 28. Tel: 6-310 311/310 487; fax: 6-310 488. Palanga Airport: Liepojos 1. Tel/fax: 36-52 234. Vilnius: Švitrigailos 26/40-18. Tel: 231 322; fax: 231 566. Kaunas International Airport Karmelava. Tel: 7-399 374/399 307; fax: 7-399 434; oro.uostas@kaunas.omnitel.net; www.ftz.lt/Airport. Palanga Airport, Liepojos 1. Tel/fax: 36-52 020.

BY SEA

Several ferry lines link the Lithuanian port of Klaipėda to Kiel and Sassnitz/Mukran Germany, Åhus Sweden and Åbenrå and Århus Denmark.

The journey from Kiel-Klaipėda-Kiel takes 31 hours. The M/S *Vilnius*, *Kaunas* and *Greifswald* run every day and are operated by the Lithuanian Shipping company.

Tickets in Germany can be ordered from Schnieder Reisen, Schillerstr. 43, D-22767 Hamburg. Tel: 49-40 380 2060/380 20671; fax: 49-40 388 965/380 20688; info@schniederreisen.de; www.schniederreisen.de.

M/S *Petersburg* to Sassnitz/Mukran in Germany departs three

Lithuania By Rail

Direct rail links from Warsaw to Vilnius only go through Belarus, and Belarusian border guards require a transit visa, costing anywhere between US$30–50, to cross their country. It may be cheaper, though not easier, to obtain a visa before travelling. The European standard railway line from Šeštokai (Lithuania) to Suwałki (Poland) has direct daily connections from Vilnius to Warsaw with a change of trains in the border town of Šeštokai.

times a week. In Germany contact **Scandlines**, Fährhafen Sassnitz Mukran. Tel: 49-38392 64 420/49-1805 722 635 4637; fax: 49-38392 64 429, info@scandlines.de; www.scandlines.de.

The sailing between Stockholm-Klaipėda-Stockholm is run by Krantas Shipping and takes 17½ hours. The M/S *Palanga* runs three times per week.

Taking the boat from Åbenrå-Århus-Klaipėda-Åbenrå-Århus takes 32 hours. The ferry leaves twice a week to Åbenrå and continues to Århus in northern Denmark. For information, contact **Scandlines Åbenrå**. Tel: 45-74 620 374 or Scandlines Copenhagen, Havnegade 44. Tel: 45-33 151 515/128 088; fax: 45-33 151 020/933 310; scandlines@scandlines.dk; www.scandlines.dk.

In Lithuania contact **Scandlines**, Hotel Klaipėda, N. Sodo 1-111. Tel: 6-310 561; www.scandlines.lt.
Krantas Shipping, Klaipėda, Lietuvininku 5. Tel: 6-395 111; fax: 6-395 222; travel@krantas.lt. Also at the ferry terminal, Perkėlos 10. Tel: 6-395 050; fax: 6-395 052; passenger@krantas.lt.
Vilnius, Pylimo 4. Tel: 227 913/227 084; fax: 629 120; vilnius@krantas.lt. Kaunas, Kanto 22. Tel: 7-337 258/337 259; fax: 7-226 793; kaunas@krantas.lt, www.krantas.lt.

BY ROAD

The entry into Lithuania by car is usually a straightforward affair. The long queues at the Lithuanian-Polish border crossing of Lazdijai/ Ogrodnicki are a thing of the past. Today, you can whisk through in around 15 minutes. The second border crossing at Kalvarija is reserved for lorries.

By Bus

Vilnius has numerous daily services to Poland. There are four buses a day to Warsaw, one daily bus to Gdaøsk one and one to Białystok . There are also daily Eurolines buses linking the Lithuanian capital with Berlin daily and further destinations in Germany and Western Europe. The trip to London, for example, takes about a day. Most Eurolines buses from Riga and Tallinn, however, only stop in Kaunas. Buses between Vilnius and Kaunas take 2 hours and run every half hour. There is also a weekly bus from Klaipėda via Vilnius to Erfurt in Germany and a twice-weekly bus from Kaunas, via Vilnius and Polock Belarus to St. Petersburg.
Eurolines, Vilnius Bus Station, Sodu 22. Tel: 251 377; fax: 251 376; info@eurolines.lt; www.eurolines.lv. Kautra, Kaunas Bus Station, Vytauto pr. 24. Tel: 7-201 963; fax: 7-322 222.

Practical Tips

ESTONIA

Estonia has good international postal links. Letters generally take about five days to reach Europe and around seven days to arrive in the US. Stamps can be bought at post offices or hotels, which are also the best places to post your letters.

Tallinn Central Post Office: Narva mnt. 1 (opposite the Hotel Viru). Tel: 625 7300/661 6616; fax: 661 6047; tallpost@infonet.ee. Open weekdays 8am–8pm, Saturday 8am–6pm. If you wish to send letters by registered post, head for counter No. 21, which is labelled *tahetud*. EMS courier services also have a counter here.

DHL, Jõe 9. Tel: 626 1084.

Federal Express, Tulika põik 4. Tel/fax: 625 8727; tel: 509 0966.

TNT Worldwide, Kesk-Sõjamäe 10a. Tel: 627 1900; fax: 627 1901; tnt@online.ee.

UPS, Suve 5. Tel: 641 9090; fax: 646 6179; ups@online.ee.

Tartu Post Office: Lai 29.

Pärnu Post Office: Akadeemia 7. Tel: 044-71 101; fax: 044-72 102.

LATVIA

Letters to and from Europe take anywhere between two days and a week to reach their destination. The postal index system begins with LV – followed by four digits.

Riga Central Post Office, Brīvības 19. Tel: 701 8738. Open 24hrs.

Express mail: Stacijas laukums 1 (near the central railway station). Tel: 701 8804. Open weekdays 8am–7pm, Saturday 8am–4pm, Sunday 10am–4pm.

DHL, Brīvības 55. Tel: 701 3292/701 3293/701 3294, toll free: 800 0345; fax: 701 3297/ 701 3298.

FedEx, Pumpura 5-1a. Tel: 732 6067; tel/fax: 732 6023.

TNT, Express Worldwide, Rēzeknes 1. Tel: 713 8432.

UPS, 13. Janvara 33. Tel: 721 2185/722 2247.

Kuldīga Post Office: Liepājas 34.

Sigulda Post Office: Pils 2.

LITHUANIA

Letters and postcards sent to Western Europe take from two to seven days to arrive at their destination. Mail directed elsewhere will generally take a few days longer. Express letters can be sent from the post office. Federal Express, DHL and TNT have offices in Vilnius, Kaunas and Klaipėda.

Vilnius Central Post Office, Gedimino pr. 7. Tel: 616 759. Open weekdays 7am–7pm, Saturday 9am–4pm.

Old Town Post Office, Vilnius 33. Tel: 619 960. Open weekdays 8am–1pm, 2–7pm, Saturday 8–11am, noon–3pm.

DHL, Dariaus ir Girėno 40. Tel: 267 722; vnotrc@vo-co.lt.dhl.com.

Express Mail Service, Vokiečių 7. Tel: 618 024.

FedEx, Dariaus ir Girėno 40. Tel: 306 795.

TNT, Express Worldwide, Dariaus ir Girėno 42. Tel: 397 555.

UPS, Vasario 16-osios 2a. Tel: 226 111.

Kaunas Central Post Office: Laisvės al. 102. Tel: 7-324 286; fax: 7-324 341.

Klaipėda Central Post Office: Liepų 16. Tel: 6-215 378.

Nida Post Office,Taikos pr. 13. Tel: 59-52 647.

If there is one indicator of the massive changes in the Baltics since independence was declared, it is the phone system. In the space of a few years the old Soviet system was dumped and new digital exchanges now allow direct dial to any country on the globe from almost any phone in the Baltic states. Latvia will become entirely digitalised by 2005. Mobile phones are all the rage and the operators are gearing up for the new WAP generation.

ESTONIA

All public phones in Estonia are card operated. Colourful chip-cards can be bought from post offices, kiosks and hotels for 30, 50 or 100 *krooni*. You can call abroad from any phone in Estonia.

In Tallinn most telephone numbers are now digital and have seven digits starting with 6, while analogue numbers only have six digits. In smaller towns analogue numbers only have five digits. If you are calling within Estonia, dial the area code starting with 0, followed by the subscriber's number.

From abroad
The code for Estonia is 372, followed by the area code without the initial zero. When calling a seven-digit digital number in Tallinn you do not have to dial the city code.

You can dial overseas almost everywhere direct from any phone. To make an international phone call, dial 00 followed by the country code, the area code and the subscriber's number.

For countries that you cannot dial direct, call the operator on 115/116. Calls cost around US$1 per minute to Europe and twice that to the US.

Haapsalu 047, Harjumaa 02, Hiiumaa 046, Jõgeva 077, Jõhvi, Kohtla-Järve 033, Narva 035, Paide 038, Pärnu 044, Põlva 079, Rakvere 032, Rapla 048, Saaremaa 045, Sillamäe 039, Tartu 07, Valga 076, Viljandi 043, Võru 078.

Tallinn's city code is 02 if you are dialling a digital number and 022 for an analogue subscriber.

Calls to mobile phones

Almost every third Estonian is a proud owner of a mobile telephone. Estonian portable phone numbers start with 050, 051, 052, 053, 055, 056 or 057. To call a mobile phone dial the subscriber's number starting with 0. From abroad dial Estonia's country code (372), followed by the subscriber's mobile phone number, dropping the 0.

Fax and telegrams

Faxes and telegrams can be sent from Tallinn's central post office. Faxes can also be sent from the service bureaux at the Palace, Viru and Olümpia hotels.

LATVIA

Almost all public phones are card-operated, with the odd coin-operated phones still in use in train stations and at the airport. Telephone cards worth 2, 3 or 5 Lats can be bought from post offices, most shops and kiosks. Some card phones can also be used with your credit card and all of them accept incoming calls.

Most telephones in Riga are now digital, with seven digits numbers; analogue phones in Riga have six-digit numbers. At present most numbers elsewhere in the country have only five digits, although this may soon change, as plans are afoot to digitalise the entire country. Area codes will be tagged onto the existing five-digit numbers to form seven-digit numbers; area codes will then no longer be used. This change has already taken place in Kuldīga and Liepāja.

Calling within Latvia

When using a digital phone or public phone simply dial the area code and the number. From an analogue phone, dial 1, wait for the dial tone, then input the area code and the subscriber's number.

Dialling from abroad

The code for Latvia is 371, followed by the area or city code plus 2 for Riga's analogue subscribers. When

Latvian Area Codes

Aizkraukle 51, Alūksne 43, Balvi 45, Bauska 39, Cēsis 41, Daugavpils 54, Dobele 37, Gulbene 44, Jēkabpils 52, Jelgava 30, Krāslava 56, Limbaži 40, Ludza 57, Madona 48, Ogre 50, Preiļi 53, Rēzekne 46, Rīga 2, Saldus 38, Talsi 32, Tukums 31, Valka 47, Valmiera 42, Ventspils 36.

calling a seven-digit digital phone number in Latvia you do not need to dial the city code. You can make overseas calls from any phone. To make an international phone call, dial 00 followed by the country code, the area code and the subscriber's number.

For countries that you cannot dial direct, call the operator on 115. Calls cost around US$1 per minute to Europe and the US.

Calls to mobile phones

Mobile phones have seven digits starting with 9. Digital rules apply *(see above)*. From abroad, dial Latvia's country code (371), followed by the subscriber's mobile phone number.

Fax and telegrams

Faxes and telegrams can be sent from the central post office in Riga. Faxes can also be sent from the service bureaux of the major hotels but this works out considerably more expensive than sending them from the post office.

LITHUANIA

All public phones in Lithuania are card operated. The square-shaped phones accept chip cards, while the older phones use old-style magnetic cards. Both types of cards can be bought from post offices and kiosks. You can call abroad from any public phone in Lithuania. Calls within Lithuania: dial 8, wait for the dial tone, follow this by dialling 2, the city code, and then the subscriber's number.

Area codes from abroad

When phoning abroad, dial the code for Lithuania 370, followed by the area code.

Overseas calls

You can dial almost everywhere direct from any phone in Lithuania. To make an international phone call dial 8, wait for a constant tone, then dial 10, followed by the country code, the area code and the person's number.

For countries you cannot dial direct, call the operator on 8-193 or 8-194. Calls are roughly a dollar per minute to Europe and US$1.50 to the US.

Calls to mobile phones

Mobile phones are extremely popular in Lithuania. They have special access codes, which are: 85, 86, 87, 89, 90, 98 and 99. To call a portable phone, dial 8, wait for the dial tone, then input 2, the access code and the subscriber's number. From abroad, dial Lithuania's country code (370), followed by the subscriber's mobile phone access code and number.

Lithuanian Area Codes

Alytus 35, Birštonas 10, Biržai 20, Druskininkai 33, Ignalina 29, Kaunas 7, Klaipėda 6, Lazdijai 68, Marijampole 43, Mažeikiai 93, Molėtai 30, Neringa Nida 59, Palanga 36, Panevėžys 5, Šiauliai 1, Trakai 38, Varėna 60, Vilnius 2, Zarasai 70.

Fax and telegrams

Faxes and telegrams can be sent from the central post office in Vilnius. Faxes can also be sent from major hotels or the Telegrafo Centras, Universiteto 14/2. Tel: 626 649; fax: 223 451. Service available 24 hours.

The Internet

The Baltic countries have embraced the Internet and embarked on a "tiger leap", as the Estonian governmental programme is dubbed. Most hotels have email addresses and accept reservations via their internet websites.

The following is a list of public internet access points and internet cafes, which generally charge about US$2–3 per hour of surfing time:

Tallinn

@5, Gonsiori 2 (5th floor of the Tallinna Kaubamaja).
Baltic Computer Systems, Narva mnt.7. Tel: 699 8171.
Central Library, Estonia pst. 8. Tel: 644 1286. Free Internet access.
Estonian National Library, Tõnismägi 2, 7th floor. Tel: 630 7381.
Enter, Tartu mnt.1. Tel: 626 7367.
Tallinn Airport, Lennujaama 2. Tel: 605 8888. Free Internet access.

Pärnu

Asum II, Rüütli 41. Tel: 04459 670; asum.parnu@neti.ee.
Pärnu Art Centre, Esplanaadi 10. Tel: 044-30 772; fax: 04430 774; aip@chaplin.ee.

Internet Resources

The best Baltic-related Internet resources are: www.ee (search the Estonian-wide web); www.lv (search the Latvian web); www.all.lv (all Latvian links); www.on.lt (Lithuanian links); www.inyourpocket.com (the entire contents of the print guides are available online; information on events is updated monthly).

Tartu

Virtuaal, Pikk 40. Tel/fax: 07402 509.

Riga

Try any of the internet cafés and clubs in the Latvian capital. The following is just a selection:
C & I Internet Club, Merķeļa 11-308. Tel/fax: 721 2040; club@icc-info.lv.
Internet Cafe, Jēkaba 20. Tel: 732 3361; info@binet.lv; www.binet.lv. There is also a cafe in the same chain at Elizabetes 75. Tel: 728 2876.
Internet Klub, Kaļķu 10. Tel: 750

3595; goblin@navigators.lv.
Svenix, Kr. Barona 16/18, svenix@omcentrs.lv.

Vilnius

Interneto Kavinė, Gedimino pr. 4. Tel: 221 481; admin@teatras.lt; www.ic.lt.
Martynas Mažvydas Lithuanian National Library, Gedimino pr. 51. Tel: 617 028; fax: 627 129; biblio@lnb.lrs.lt.
Netcafe, Antakalnio 36. Tel: 709 833; info@netcafe.lt; www.netcafe.lt.
Penki Kontinentai, Stulginskio 5. Tel: 221 482; fax: 226 115; info@5ci.lt; www.5ci.lt.
Ralinga Internet Centre, Pylimo 20. Tel/fax: 611 966; info@ralinga.lt; www.ralinga.lt.
VOO2, Ašmenos 8. Tel: 791 866; ianplinka@post.5ci.lt; www.voo2.lt.

Kaunas

Kavinė Internetas, Daukšos 12. Tel: 7-225 364; www.cafenet.ot.lt.

Nida

Interneto kavinė, Nida Cultural House Agila, Taikos 5, nida@ic.lt.

The Media

Newspapers & magazines

The Baltic Times is the only pan-Baltic English-language newspaper covering all three states. Printed in Riga, the 16-page weekly is a merger of the *Baltic Independent* and the *Baltic Observer*. Its editorial team, which has offices in each city, provides thorough coverage of current political, economic and cultural events in all three states. The paper is sold in kiosks for US$1 but you can find it for free in major hotels around the Baltics. *The Baltic Times*, Riga, Šķūņu 16. Tel: 722 9978; fax: 722 6041; editorial@baltictimes.com; www.baltictimes.com.

ESTONIA

Tallinn's *City Paper* is a quarterly colour publication with news features and useful city listings

covering all three capital cities. The 112-page, A4 glossy magazine is available for the equivalent of US$2 from kiosks in the three capitals. Alternatively, contact *City Paper* at Pärnu mnt. 67a. Tel: 646 1102; fax: 646 1103; citypaper@balticsww.com; www.balticsworldwide.com.

Tallinn In Your Pocket is a handy city guide, published five times per year with an updated calendar of events, full reviews about Tallinn's ever-changing restaurants, cafes and bars, and a selection of tourist sites. The In Your Pocket team also publishes a yearly *Pärnu In Your Pocket*. The A5 guides are on sale in most kiosks, newsstands and hotels for US$1 or can be ordered from their office, Vana-Viru 4. Tel: 631 3350; fax: 644 6470; tallinn@inyourpocket.com; www.inyourpocket.com.

Tallinn This Week is a tourist brochure available for free in the some of the major hotels. A wide selection of foreign newspapers and journals are carried by some of the larger hotels.

Radio

There are 18 radio stations on Tallinn's FM band. The state-owned Vikerraadio airs the BBC World Service every day between noon and 5pm on 103.5FM. Vikerraadio also broadcasts local news in English daily at 6pm and 10pm.

LATVIA

Newspapers & magazines

For current events check the weekly *Baltic Times* or get *Riga In Your Pocket*, which is published every two months. Available from kiosks and hotels for US$1 or from Pils laukums 4-112. Tel: 722 0580; fax: 722 3416; riga@inyourpocket.com; www.inyourpocket.com.

Alternatively, pick up the free *Riga This Week* tourist brochure, available in most big hotels. *The International Herald Tribune*, *The Financial Times*, *The Times* and the *New York Times* are also on sale in the main hotels.

Radio

There are 13 FM radio stations on in the capital, notably Radio Latvia Latvijas Radio, which has three channels including Klasiska radio, a classical radio station on 103.7FM. The BBC World Service can be picked up 24 hours a day on 100.5FM. Of the private music & news radios SWH on 105.2FM is well worth a listen.

LITHUANIA

Newspapers & magazines

The English-language city guide *Vilnius In Your Pocket* is published every two months and provides thorough information about tourist attractions, things to do in town, complete opera and theatre listings and helpful restaurant reviews. It is available in most kiosks and hotels for US$1.

The yearly *Klaipėda In Your Pocket* and *Kaunas In Your Pocket* can be bought in most kiosks or directly from the publisher at Vokiečių 10-15. Tel: 222 976; fax: 222 982; vilnius@inyourpocket.com; www.inyourpocket.com.

Radio

You can pick up 15 different FM radio stations in Vilnius. For news in English tune to the BBC World Service on 100.1 FM, VOA Europe on 105.6 FM or the French Radio France Internationale on 98.3 FM.

Emergencies

Crime

Economic hardship and chronically understaffed and ill-equipped police forces have contributed to a sharp increase in crime in recent years. However, violent crime tends to be gangland related and assaults on foreigners are rare. Unfortunately, theft is very common – anything that you are not physically attached to is liable to walk, so be extremely watchful. This applies equally to valuables left in hotel rooms – even in top hotels. Don't tempt the staff by leaving things out on view. Further good advice to visitors is to

Emergencies

Police: Dial **02** in Lithuania and Latvia and **110** in Estonia no coins needed.
Ambulance: Dial **03** in Lithuania and Latvia and **112** in Estonia.

remain sober; nothing could present a more appealing target than an inebriated tourist staggering through dimly lit streets.

Medical Services

There are no real problems with medical care, and most Western medicines are available in all three states. If you feel unwell, your best first stop is a pharmacy or drugstore, where you can often find most of what you might need to cure common, temporary ailments. Many pharmacies carry everything from Pepto Bismol, Advil and antibiotics to such goods as Visine, condoms and Slim Fast.

If over-the-counter medicines do not do the trick, it is advisable to seek help from a qualified doctor. Unfortunately there are some people who prey on foreigners' gullibility and are out to make a quick buck. When seeking assistance at an outpatient or emergency clinic, keep in mind the following points:
• Emergency medical care is not free of charge in all three states.
• Prices for simple medical procedures are fixed in Lithuania. In Estonia and Latvia they may vary,

depending on the complexity of the procedure and, in the case of foreigners, the agreements between the two countries involved. To date only Latvia and Poland have signed up for mutual health care.

While health-care systems are undergoing crises due to budget cuts, foreigners are generally well-treated. Doctors and nurses are grossly underpaid but still try to provide an adequate service. If you want to, you can show your appreciation by giving a gift after you have been treated. Hospitals are usually spartan, but sanitary.

ESTONIA (TALLINN)

Sütiste 10, Tallinn Central Hospital, Ravi 18. Tel: 620 70 10. Open 24 hours.

Pharmacies

Koduapteek, Aia 7, in the Kaubahall department store. Tel: 430 220/641 8009; fax: 641 9137.
Tallinna Linnaapteek, Pärnu mnt. 10. Tel: 644 2262.
Tervis Keskus, Suur-Karja 4. Tel: 644 4803; fax: 631 3232.
Vanaturu Apteek, Vene 1. Tel: 644 6452; fax: 644 6604.
Tõnismäe Apteek, Tõnismägi 5. Tel: 442 282; fax: 449 117.

Dentists

Baltic Medical Partners, Tartu mnt. 32. Tel: 601 0550; fax: 601 0549.
Kaarli Hambapolikliinik, Toompuiestee 4. Tel: 611 9119.

Health

Unless you have a specific health problem you are generally just as safe in the Baltic states as anywhere in Western Europe. The water in some places may taste funny but is perfectly fine. In Riga, however, drinking un-boiled water can be risky.

If, however, you are particularly susceptible to upset stomachs, suffer from migraines or similar complaints then it's advisable to take any medication you might

require with you on holiday. If you are here during the summer pack, something for mosquito bites.

There are no compulsory vaccinations for these states, but it's wise to have a Hepatitis A injection. Anyone camping or spending time in the countryside should consider having a vaccination for tick-borne encephalitis. This treatment requires a course of injections, spread over a few weeks.

Kentmanni hambaravi, Kentmanni
11a. Tel: 644 0186/645 4264.

LATVIA (RIGA)

Pharmacies
Grindex, Audeju 20. Tel: 721 3340.
Lauvas aptieka, Kaļķu 20.
Tel: 722 6519.
Marijas aptieka, Audeju 16 (in the
Centrs shopping centre).
Meness aptieka, Elizabetes 91/93.
Tel: 750 2230. Another outlet on
Brīvības 121. Tel: 7377 889. Open
24 hours. Also on Raiņa bulv. 17.
Tel: 722 4170.
Rīgas centra aptieka, Brīvības 38.
Tel: 728 9761.
Torņa aptieka, Torņa 4 IIIC-1.
Tel: 722 7494.
Zala aptieka, Vagncra 15.
Tel: 721 6885.

All-Night Pharmacies
Krastmalas aptieka, Novembra
krastmala 29. Tel: 722 3065.
Rudens aptieka, Ģertrūdes 105/1.
Tel: 724 4322.

Emergency Medical Care
ARS, Skolas 5. Tel: 720 1001/720
1007 or 1003/1005 (emergencies).
Baltija Orthopedic Clinic, Duntes
12/22. Tel/fax: 739 2563. Open
24 hours.
Children's Hospital, Vienības gatve
45. Tel: 762 2997. Open 24 hours.
Diplomatic Service Medical Centre,
Elizabetes 57. Tel: 728 2534; fax:
728 9413; dsa@com.var.lv.
Gailezera hospital, Hipokrata 2.
Tel: 536 660.
Latvian–American Eye Centre,
Tallinas 93. Tel: 272 257.
P. Stradins Hospital, Pilsoņu 13.
Tel: 761 1201.
Hospital No. 7 Eye Care,
P. Dauges 2. Tel: 753 6339.
Psychiatric Hospital, Tvaika 2.
Tel: 739 2463.
Baltic Railway Children's Hospital,
Lielvārdes 68. Tel: 757 6255.

Sexually Transmitted Diseases
AIDS Centre, Krijanu iela.
Tel: 737 2275.
AIDS hotline, Tel: 522 222.
Association for Family Planning &

Dentists
A+S Health Centre, Lačplēša 60.
Tel: 728 9516.
**Diplomatic Service Medical
Centre**, Elizabetes 57.
Tel: 722 9942; fax: 728 9413;
dsa@com.var.lv.
Dr. Butkevica, Dzirnavu 45/47.
Tel: 724 2470; fax: 724 2471.
Dr. Müller, Lačplēša 59.
Tel: 724 3024.
Also at Kr. Valdemāra 57/59.
Elladent, Vilandes 18.
Tel: 733 3145/733 3004.
Sandent, Blaumana.
Tel: 728 0371.

Sexual Health, Kaniera 10a. Tel:
255 414/253 869; fax: 713 5277.
Centre for Sexual Diseases,
Briāna 2. Tel: 272 198.

Accidents
Hospital No. 1, Bruņinieku 8.
Tel: 729 6734.
Gimnastikas 1, Tel: 762 2168.

LITHUANIA (VILNIUS)

Pharmacies
Gedimino Vaistinė, Gedimino pr.
27. Tel: 624 930/610 135.
Gulbė, Didžioji 39. Tel: 629 717.
Lukiškiu Vaistinė, Vasarios 16-
osios 2. Tel: 619 839.
Naugarduko Vaistinė, Naugarduko
15/28. Tel: 232 833.
Operos Vaistinė, Vienuolio 6-21.
Tel: 226 116/226 184.
Prancuzu Vaistinė, Pylimo 8/2-30.
Tel: 227 094.
Prie Hales, Pylimo 61.
Tel: 222 362.
Senamiesčio Vaistinė, Vilniaus 22.
Tel: 618 387.
Šv. Kristoforo Vaistinė, Gedimino
pr. 56. Tel: 312 168.
Universiteto Vaistinė, Universiteto
2. Tel: 221 219.
Vokiečių Vaistinė German pharmacy,
Didžioji 13. Tel: 224 232.

Hospitals
Antakalnis Hospital, Antakalnio
124. Tel: 746 041.
Baltic–American Medical &

Surgical Clinic, Antakalnio 124.
Tel: 342 020; fax: 767 942;
bak@takas.lt; www.baclinic.com.
Emergency Hospital, Šiltnamiu 29.
Tel: 269 069/269 140.
Health Centre Sanvita, Šeimyniškių
21. Tel: 750 036.
Red Cross Hospital, Žygimantų 6.
Tel: 616 258.
Santariškių Hospital, Santariškių 2.
Tel: 779 912.
SBT Private Clinic, Šeškinės 24.
Tel: 468 583, Polyclinic No. 10.
English spoken.
Vilnius Clinic No. 6, Antakalnio 57.
Tel: 744 519.
Diagnostikos Poliklinika, Didžioji
30. Tel: 622 570/617 639.
Širdies Chirurgijos Centras,
Laisvės pr. 64a. Tel: 305 348.
Medical Diagnostic Centre, Grybo
32/10. Tel: 709 120;
mdc@mdc.elnet.lt.
Šeimos Medicinos Centras,
Pylimo 9. Tel: 623 653/611 378.
Trauma Department, St Jacob
Hospital, Lukiškiu aikšte 10.
Tel: 624 483.

Dentists
Dentamed, Tilto 1/2. Tel: 227 582.
Dr. Sidaravicius Dental Clinic,
Klaipėdos 2/14-3. Tel: 629 760.
Stoma, Sausio 13-osios 31.
Tel: 458 474/98-84 064.
Stomatologijos Klinika, Universiteto
2. Tel: 312 952.

Sexually Transmitted diseases
Lithuanian AIDS Centre, Kairiųksčio
2. Tel: 720 465/720 333.

Tourist Information Centres

ESTONIA

Estonian Tourism Board, Mündi 2,
EE10146 Tallinn. Tel: 699 0420;
fax: 699 0432; etb@tourism.ee;
info@tourism.ee; www.tourism.ee.
**South-Estonian Bureau of the
Estonian Tourism Board**, Tartu,
Raekoja plats 9. Tel/fax: 07441
756; info@south.tourism.ee.

Tallinn
Tallinn, Raekoja plats 10. Tel: 645
7777; fax: 645 7778; turismiinfo@

tallinn.ee; www.tallinn.ee. Open weekdays 9am–6pm, weekends 10am–4pm. In winter closed Sunday.

Elsewhere in Estonia

Haapsalu, Raudtee 2. Tel: 04733 248; info@haapsalu.tourism.ee; www.haapsalu.ee.
Harjumaa, Jõelähtme. Tel/fax: 603 3097; Margit.Partel@mail.ee.
Hiiumaa, Hiiu tn 1. Tel: 04622 232; fax: 046 22 234/051 82 233; info@hiiumaa.tourism.ee; www.hiiumaa.ee.
Jõhvi, Rakvere 13a. Tel/fax: 0330 568; info@johvi.tourism.ee.
Kuresaare, Tallinna 2. Tel/fax: 04533 120; info@oesel.tourism.ee.
Narva, Puškini 13. Tel: 03560 184; fax: 03560 186; info@narva.tourism.ee.
Otepää, Lipuväljak 13. Tel: 07655 364; fax: 07661 246; otturinf@estpak.ee.
Paide, Pärnu 6. Tel/fax: 03850 400; info@paide.tourism.ee.
Palamuse, Tel: 07768 520; fax: 077 68 521; ipunkt@jogevamv.ee.
Pärnu, Rüütli 16. Tel: 04473 000; fax: 04473 001; info@parnu. tourism.ee; www.parnu.ee.
Põlva, Kesk 16. Tel/fax: 07994 089; info@polva.tourism.ee.
Rakvere, Laada 14. Tel/fax: 03242 734; info@rakvere.tourism.ee.
Rapla, Tallinna 14.
Tel: 04857 349; fax: 04855 672; Helika.Riipulk@mail.ee.
Tartu, Raekoja plats 14. Tel/fax: 07432 141; info@tartu. tourism.ee; www.tartu.ee.
Valga, Kesk 11. Tel/fax: 07661 699; info@valga.tourism.ee.
Viljandi, Tallinna 2b. Tel/fax: 04333 755; info@viljandi.tourism.ee.
Võru, Tartu mnt 31. Tel/fax: 07821 881; info@werro.tourism.ee.

LATVIA

Latvian Tourism Board, Riga, Pils laukums 4, LV-1050 Riga. Tel/fax: 722 9945; ltboard@latnet.lv; www.latviatravel.com.

Riga

Riga International Airport.
Tel: 720 7800; fax: 720 7100;

tourinfo@lgs.lv; www.riga800.lv. Open weekdays 10am–6pm. There are plans to open a tourist office in the Blackheads' House.
Tel: 722 1731; fax: 722 7680; tourinfo@latnet.lv; www.riga800.lv.
Riga In Your Pocket, Pils laukums 4-112. Tel: 722 0580; fax: 722 3416; riga@inyourpocket.com.

Elsewhere in Latvia

Aizkraukle, Lačplēša 1.
Tel: 5122 371.
Aizpute, Skolas 1. Tel: 344 8956; fax: 344 8956.
Alūksne, Darza 8a. Tel: 43-22 804; fax: 43-22 804.
Balvi, Berzpils 1a. Tel: 4522 083; fax: 789 45 30; armands@apollo.lv.
Bauska, Ratslaukums 1.
Tel: 3923 797; fax: 3923 797.
Cēsis, Pils 9.
Tel: 4121 815; fax: 4121 815; www.cesis.lv.
Daugavpils, Rigas 50/52.
Tel: 5429 712; fax: 5428 285.
Dobele, Brīvības 7. Tel: 3725 474; fax: 3722 237. Also on Skolas 23. Tel/fax: 3723 932.
Ergli, Rigas 5, Madona district.
Tel: 4871 430; fax: 4871 145; azarins@lanet.lv.
Gulbene, Rigas 12. Tel/fax: 4423 558; ingak@gulbgymn.edu.lv.
Jaunkalsnava, Vesetas 6, Madona district. Tel: 4837 622; fax: 4823 845.
Jelgava, L6. Tel: 3023 874; fax: 3021 891.
Jēkabpils, Vecpilsetas laukums 3.
Tel: 5233 822; fax: 5232 723.
Jurkalne, Krasti, Venstpils district.
Tel: 3697 131; fax: 3697 131.
Jūrmala Spa and Tourism Info Centre, Jomas 42. Tel: 776 4276/776 2167; fax: 776 4672; jurmalainfo@mail.bkc.lv; www.jurmala.lv.
Koknese, Blaumaņa 3, Aizkraukle district, LV-5113. Tel: 927 5412; fax: 5161 298; pp@koknese.apollo.lv.
Krāslava, Skolas 7. Tel: 5623 073; fax: 5622 238; iveta@kraslava.apollo.lv.
Kuldīga, Pilsetas laukums 5. Tel/fax: 332 2259; inga@kuldiga.parks.lv.
Liepāja Southern Kurzeme Tourist information, L11. Tel/fax: 348 0808; ltib@apollo.lv.

Limbaži, Burtnieku 5.
Tel: 4023 108; fax: 4021 894.
Ludza, Baznicas 42-11.
Tel: 5723 922; fax: 5723 922.
Madona, Rigas 1a. Tel: 4822 823; fax: 4822 033. Also on Saieta laukums 1. Tel: 4823 125; fax: 4822 230; madinfo@madona.lv.
Nigrande, Ventas 2. Tel: 3874 803; fax: 3874 847.
Pavilosta, Dzintaru 1. Tel: 349 8276.
Preiļi, Tirgus laukums 1. Tel: 5322 041; fax: 5322 041; tic@axel.lv.
Rēzekne, Atbrivosanas 93.
Tel: 4623 213; fax: 4622 338.
Rucava, Liepāja district.
Tel: 349 4766; fax: 348 6388; rpp@ant.lv.
Rujiena, Rigas 12, Valmiera district.
Tel: 4263 767; fax: 4263 767.
Salacgriva, Sila 2, Limbaži district.
Tel: 4041 254; fax: 4071 327; saltic@taka.lv.
Saldus, Striku 3. Tel: 3822 056; fax: 3823 889.
Saulkrasti, Raiņa 8. Tel: 2952 963/951 250; fax: 2951 150.
Sigulda, Pils 4a. Tel: 2971 335; fax: 2971 335; sigulda@rrp.lv, www.zl.lv/new1.
Smiltene, Darza 3. Tel: 4773 547; fax: 4773 547.
Talsi, Kareivju 16. Tel/fax: 3224 165.
Tukums, Pils 3. Tel: 3124 451; fax: 3122 237; tuktic@tukums.parks.lv.
Valmiera, Lačplēša 2.
Tel: 4233 660; fax: 4233 660; anita@vta.apollo.lv.
Ventspils, Annas 13. Tel: 3624 777; fax: 3624 777.
Vergale, Dikenieki, Liepāja district.
Tel: 349 5435.
Viesite, Smilšu 2. Tel: 5245 170; fax: 5245 179.

LITHUANIA

Lithuanian State Department of Tourism, Vilniaus 4/35.
Tel: 227 466/622 610; fax: 226 819; tb@tourism.lt, www.tourism.lt.

Vilnius

Vilnius Tourist Information Centre, Pilies 42. Tel: 626 470; Tel/fax: 620 762; turizm.info@vilnius.sav.lt; www.vilnius.lt/tourism. Open weekdays 9am–7pm, Saturday noon–6pm. There is also a smaller branch of the tourist office on Vilniaus 22. Tel: 629 660; fax: 628 169. Open weekdays 9am–6pm. The publishing group *Vilnius In Your Pocket* operates a very helpful Tourist Information Centre at Vilnius Airport. Tel: 99-99 721. Open weekdays 9am–5pm, Saturday 9am–3pm.

Kaunas
Kaunas, Kaunas region Tourist Information Centre, Mickevičiaus 36/Laisvės al. 40. Tel/fax: 7423 678; turizmas@takas.lt.
Kaunas, "Musu odiseja" Tourist Information Centre, M. K. Čiurlionio 15. Tel: 7220 426; fax: 7204 786; ja@kaunas.omnitel.net.

Klaipėda and the Coast
Klaipėda tourist information centre, Tomo 2. Tel: 6412 185; fax: 6255 124; tourinfo@klaipeda. omnitel.net; kltic@takas.lt. Open weekdays 8.30am–5.30pm, Saturday 9am–1pm.
Kretinga, Rotušės aikšte 3. Tel: 5851 341; itc@kretinga.omnitel.net.
Nida Tourist Information Centre, Taikos 4. Tel: 5952 345; fax: 5952 344. Open daily 9am–7pm.
Palanga Tourist Information Centre, Kretingos 1.Tel: 3648 811; fax: 3648 461; palturas@is.lt. Open daily 8am–8pm.

Elsewhere in Lithuania
Alytus, Rotušės aikšte 14a. Tel: 3535 404; fax: 3538 565; tour.info@alytus.omnitel.net; www2.omnitel.net/alytur/en/intro
Anykščiai, Gegužes 1. Tel/fax: 5159 177; anyksciai.turizmas@is.lt; anyr@sav.lt.
Biržai, Vytauto 27. Tel/fax: 2033 496; tic.birzai@post.omnitel.net; www.tourism.lt/region/panevez/ birzai
Druskininkai, Gardino 1. Tel/fax: 3351 777; druskininkutib@post. omnitel.net; www.druskonis.lt/ info/introduc.htm.
Ignalina, Laisvés aikšte 70. Tel: 2952 597; fax: 2953 148; tic@ignalina.lt.

Jurbarkas, Dariaus ir Girėno 94. Tel/fax: 4851 204; tour.info.c@jurbarkas.omnitel.net.
Rumšiškes, S. Nėries 4-6. Tel/fax: 5647 569; turinfo@takas.lt.
Lazdijai, Vilniaus 1. Tel/fax: 6851 160.
Molėtai, Inturkes 4. Tel: 98-43 008; Tel/fax: 30-51 187.
Šiauliai, Vilniaus 213. Tel: 1-523 110; fax: 1-523 111; tourism.info@Šiauliai.lt; www.Šiauliai.sav.lt/tourism/index.htm
Trakai, Vytauto 69. Tel/fax: 38-51 934; trakaitic@is.lt; tic@is.lt; www.tourism.lt/region/vilnius/ trakai.htm.
Utena, Utenio 5. Tel/fax: 39 54 346; turizmas@utena.omnitel.net; www2.omnitel.net/utena_tic/english
Zarasai, Šelių aikšte 22. Tel/fax: 70-51 230; fax: 70-51 240; zarasai@lsa.lt.

Embassies & Consulates

ESTONIA

Embassies & Consulates Abroad
Australia, Honorary Consulate, 86 Louisa Road, Birchgrove, NSW, 2041. Tel: 61 2 9810 7468, 91 50 80 34; fax: 61 2 9818 1779; eestikon@ozemail.com.au.
Austria, Wohllebengasse 9/13, Wien 1040. Tel: 43 1 503 7761; fax: 43 1 503 7762; Embassy.Vienna@mfa.ee.
Belarus, Doroshevicha 6a, Minsk. Tel: 375 172 34 59 65; fax: 375 172 10 12 60; esindus@minsk.vm.ee.
Belgium, av. Isidore Gerard 1, B-1160 Brussels-Auderghem. Tel: 32 2 779 07 55; fax: 32 2 770 71 93; Embassy.Bruemb@mfa.ee; www.estemb.be.
Canada, Honorary Consulate General, 2902-958 Broadview Avenue, Toronto, Ontario M4K 2R6. Tel: 1 416 461 07 64; fax: 1 416 461 03 53; estconsu@inforamp.net.
Czech Republic, Na Kampe 1, 118 00 Praha 1. Tel: 420 2 57 53 05 12; fax: 420 2 57 53 05 13; sekretar@estemb.cz.

Denmark, Aurehøjvej 19, DK-2900 Hellerup-København. Tel: 45 39 46 30 70; fax: 45 39 46 30 76; Embassy.Copenhagen@mfa.ee.
Finland, Embassy, Itäinen Puistotie 10, 00140 Helsinki. Tel: 358 9 622 02 60; fax: 358 9 622 02 610. www.estemb.fi.
Consular Department, Kalliolinnantie 18, 00140 Helsinki. Tel: 358 9 622 02 88; fax: 358 9 622 02 850.
France, 46, rue Pierre Charron, 75008 Paris. Tel: 33 1 5662 22 00; fax: 33 1 4952 05 65; Embassy.Paris@mfa.ee.
Germany, Kurfürstendamm 56, 10707 Berlin. Tel: 49 30 32 70 53 55; fax: 49 30 32 70 72 63; Embassy.Berlin@mfa.ee.
Greece, Patriarchou Ioakeim 48, GR-106 76 Athens. Tel: 30 1 722 98 03; fax: 30 1 722 98 04; estemb@mail.otenet.gr.
Hungary, Budapest VI, Lendvay u. 12 fszt. 3. Honorary Consulate, 1113 Budapest, Bocskai út 34/B VII. I.. Tel/fax: 36 1 361 2425; bereczki@isis.elte.hu.
Iceland, Granaskjol 27, 107 Reykjavik. Tel: 354 511 11 11; fax: 354 511 11 12.
Ireland, Merlyn Park 24, Ballsbridge, Dublin 4. Tel: 353 1 269 15 52; fax: 353-1 260 51 19; asjur@gofree.indigo.ie.
Israel, Honorary Consulate, 6 Hadassah Street, Tel Aviv. Tel: 972 3 523 16 58; mobile: 972 3 254 306044; fax: 972 3 527 93 80; shekel@netvision.net.il.
Italy, Viale Liegi 28, int.5, 00198 Roma. Tel: 39 06 844 07 51; fax: 39 06 844 07 51 19; saatkond@rooma.vm.ee.
Japan, 3 F. Akasaka Royal Office Bldg., 6-9-17 Akasaka, Minato-Ku, Tokyo 107. Tel: 81 3 554 57 171; fax: 81 3 554 57 172; Embassy.Tokyo@mfa.ee.
Latvia, Skolas 13, Riga LV 1010. Tel: 371 781 2020/ 722 6845/781 2026; fax: 371 781 2029; Embassy.Riga@mfa.ee.
Lithuania, Mickevičiaus 4a, LT-2004, Vilnius. Tel: 370 2 220 486/757 970; fax: 370 2 220 461; Embassy.Vilnius@mfa.ee.

Foreign Embassies & Consulates in Estonia

TALLINN

Australian Consulate, Kopli 25. Tel: 650 9308; fax: 667 8444; mati@standard.ee.

Austrian Embassy, Vambola 6. Tel: 627 8740/627 8745; fax: 631 4365; austroemb@teleport.ee.

Belarusian Consulate, Magdaleena 3. Tel/fax: 655 8001.

Canadian Embassy, Toom-Kooli 13. Tel: 627 3311; fax: 627 3312; canembt@zzz.ee.

Chinese Embassy, Narva 98. Tel: 641 9041; fax: 641 9044; chinaemb@online.ee.

Danish Embassy, Wismari 5. Tel: 630 6400; fax: 630 6422; dan.emb@online.ee.

Finnish Embassy, Kohtu 4. Tel: 610 3200; fax: 610 3283; www.finemb.ee.

Finnish Consulate: Pikk jalg 14. Tel: 610 3300; fax: 610 3235.

French Embassy, Toom-Kuninga 20. Tel: 631 1492; fax: 452 436; info@ambfrance.ee.

German Embassy, Toom-Kuninga 11. Tel: 627 5300; fax: 627 5304; saksasaa@online.ee.

Hungarian Honorary Consulate, Estonia pst. 3/5. Tel: 631 3791; fax: 631 3796; huembtal@mfa.neti.ee.

Icelandic Consulate, Tõnismägi 3a. Tel: 640 8711; fax: 640 8713; joja@online.ee.

Italian Embassy, Müürivahe 3. Tel: 625 6444; fax: 631 1370; italemb@online.ee.

Japanese Embassy, Harju 6. Tel: 631 0531; fax: 631 0533.

Korean Honorary Consulate, Hospidali 4. Tel: 631 3781; fax: 631 3780; woodex@online.ee.

Latvian Embassy, Tõnismägi 10. Tel: 646 1313/646 1310; fax: 631 1366; gints@latvia.ee.

Lithuanian Embassy, Uus 15. Tel: 631 4030/641 2014/631 4053; fax: 641 2013; amber@anet.ee.

Norwegian Embassy, Harju 6. Tel: 627 1000; fax: 627 1001; noramb@uninet.ee.

Polish Embassy, Pärnu 8. Tel: 631 4088/644 0609; fax: 644 5221; ambrptal@netexpress.ee.

Russian Embassy, Pikk 19. Tel: 646 4169/646 4166; fax: 646 4178.

Swedish Embassy, Pikk 28. Tel: 640 5600; fax: 640 5695; swedemb@estpak.ee.

Swiss Honorary Consulate, Roosikrantsi 11. Tel: 601 5815; fax: 601 5816.

Ukraine Embassy, Lahe 6. Tel: 631 1555/644 2355; fax: 631 1556; embukr@eol.ee.

UK Embassy, Wismari 6. Tel: 667 4700; fax: 667 4756.

US Embassy, Kentmanni 20. Tel: 631 2021/646 6521; fax: 631 2025.

TARTU

Finnish Consulate, Veski 35. Tel: 07 421 907; fax: 07 421 956; tartu@finemb.ee.

Hungarian Honorary Consulate, Ülikooli 18. Tel: 07 375 221; fax: 07 375 222; kunnap@dul.ut.ee.

NARVA

Russian Consulate, Vilde 8. Tel: 035 31367; fax: 035 60654.

Norway, Parkveien 51a, 0244 Oslo. Tel: 47 22 54 00 70; fax: 47 22 54 00 71; sekretar@oslo.mfa.ee.

Poland, Karwinska 1, 02 639 Warszawa. Tel: 48 22 646 4480, 48 22 646 4484; fax: 48 22 646 4481; Embassy.Varssavi@mfa.ee; www.estemb.pl.

Portugal, Rua Camilo Castelo Branco 34-4, 1050-045 Lisboa. Tel: 351 21 319 41 50; fax: 351 21 319 41 55; Embassy.Lisbon@mfa.ee.

Russia, Malo Kislovski 5, 103 009 Moscow. Tel: 7 095 290 50 13/737 36 40; fax: 7 095 737 36 46; Embassy.Moskva@mfa.ee; Consular Department. Tel: 7 095 737 36 48; fax: 7 095 291 10 73; Consulate.Moskva@mfa.ee. Consulate General in St. Petersburg, Bolšaja Monetnaja 14, St. Petersburg. Tel: 7 812 238 18 04; fax: 7 812 325 42 46;

Consulate.Peterburg@mfa.ee. Consulate General in Pskov, Narodnaja 25, Pskov. Tel: 7 8112 445 939; fax: 7 8112 156 864; redpap@ellink.ru.

Spain, Calle Claudio Coello 91, 1D Madrid 28006. Tel: 34 91 426 16 71; fax: 34 91 426 16 72; Embassy.Madrid@mfa.ee.

Sweden, Tyrgatan 3, Box 26076, 10041 Stockholm. Tel: 46 8 5451 22 80; fax: 46 8 5451 22 99; Consular Dept. Tel: 46 8 5451 22 82; fax: 46 8 5451 22 98; info@estemb.se; www.estemb.se.

Switzerland, Honorary Consulate, Bergstrasse 52, CH-8712 Stäfa. Tel: 411 926 19 60; fax: 411 926 48 78.

Netherlands, Parkstraat 15 2514 JD, Den Haag. Tel: 31 70 34 56 252; fax: 31 70 42 79 243; Andrus.Normet@planet.nl.

Ukraine, Volodymyrska 61/11-37, Kiyv, 252033. Tel: 380 44 224 83 61; fax: 380 44 234 14 03; Embassy.Kiev@mfa.ee, Consular Department, Reitarska st. 20/24, Kyiv 252034. Tel: 380 44 229 56 68; fax: 380 44 464 0872; Consulate.Kiev@mfa.ee.

UK, 16 Hyde Park Gate, London SW7 5DG. Tel: 44 20 7589 3428, fax. 44 20 7589 3430; Embassy.London@mfa.ee; www.estonia.gov.uk.

US, 2131 Massachusetts Avenue, NW, Washington, D.C., 20008. Tel: 1 202 588 0101; fax: 1 202 588 0108; Emb.Washington@mfa.ee; www.estemb.org. Consulate General New York, 600 Third Avenue, 26th Floor, New York, N.Y. 10016-2001. Tel: 1 212 883 06 36, Consular Department. Tel: 1-212 883 06 36; fax: 1 212 883 06 48.

LATVIA

Embassies & Consulates Abroad

Austria, Währinger Str. 3/8, A-1090 Vienna. Tel: 43 1 403 31 12/403 31 12/13; fax: 43 1 403 31 12; lettbot@netway.at.

Belarus, 6a Doroshevica Str., Minsk 220013. Tel: 375 17 2 849 393/ 847 277/2 847 288/2 847 475; fax: 375 17 2 847 334; daile@belsonet.net. Consulate in Vitebsk, 27a B. Hmelnickogo Str., 210015 Vitebsk. Tel: 8 0212 365 854/7 0176 763 937/8 0212 372 143; fax: 8 0212 370 140; armands@mfa.gov.lv, www.mfa.gov.lv/lrkv.

Belgium, 158 ave. Molière, 1050 Brussels. Tel: 32 2 344 16 82/344 04 58; fax: 32 2 344 74 78; lvembassybenclux@arcadis.be.

Canada, 280 Albert Street, Suite 300, Ottawa, Ontario, K1P 5G8. Tel: 1 613 238 60 14/613 238 68 68; fax: 1 613 238 70 44; latvia-embassy@magmacom.com; www2.magmacom.com/~latemb.

China, 3-2-21 San Li Tun Diplomatic Compound, Beijing 100600. Tel: 86 10 653 201 06; fax: 86 10 653 201 07; kina@public.bta.net.cn.

Czech Republic, 3 Hradeshinska Str., P.O. Box 54, 10100 Prague. Tel: 420 2 242 524 54/242 506 54/242 545 87; fax: 420 2 242 550 99; zibens@lrvpraga.anet.cz.

Denmark, 17 Rosbaeksvej Str., 2100 Copenhagen. Tel: 45 39 276 000/168; fax: 45 39 276 173; latemb@latemb.dk.

Estonia, Tõnismägi 10, Tallinn EE 0001. Tel: 372 646 1313/646 1310; fax: 372 631 1366; gints@latvia.ee.

Finland, 10 Armfeltintie, 00150 Helsinki. Tel: 358 9 476 472 44/476 472 33; fax: 358 9 476 472 88; latemb.fin@latemb.inet.fi.

France, 6, Villa Said, 75116 Paris. Tel: 33 1 53 64 58 10; fax: 33 1 53 64 58 19; ambleton@wanadoo.fr.

Germany, Reinerzstr. 40/41, 14193 Berlin. Tel: 49 30 82 60 02 22/11; fax: 49 30 82 60 02 33/82 60 02 44; latembger@mfa.gov.lv. Mission in Bonn: Adenaueralle 100, 53113 Bonn. Tel: 49 228 26 42 42; fax: 49 228 26 58 40.

Greece, 9 Irodotou Str., Kolonaki, 10674 Athens. Tel: 30 1 729 44 83; fax: 30 1 729 44 79; latvia@otenet.gr.

Israel, 52 Pinkas Str., Apt. 51, Tel Aviv 62261. Tel: 972 3 546 24 38/544 41 45; fax: 972 3 544 43 72; latvembi@netvision.net.il.

Italy, Viale Liegi, 42, 00198 Rome. Tel: 39 6 884 12 29/884 12 27/ 884 12 37; fax: 39 6 884 12 39/ 884 12 37; embrom@micanet.it.

Lithuania, Čiurlionio 76, LT-2009 Vilnius. Tel: 370 2 231 260/232 125/231 140/231 240/231 220; fax: 370 2 231 130; lietuva@latvia.balt.net; http://latvia.balt.net.

Norway, Bygdøy Allé 76, Post Box 3163 Elisenberg, 0268 Oslo. Tel: 47 22 542 280/22 542 281; fax: 47 22 546 426; latve@sensewave.com; www.mfa.gov.lv/lrvno/.

Poland, 15–19 Tadeusza Rejtana, 02516 Warsaw. Tel: 48 22 848 19 47/22 848 98 05 48 22 849 57 06; fax: 48 22 848 02 01; amlotew1@warman.com.pl.

Portugal, Avenida Miguel Bombarda 36, 5C, 1050-165 Lisbon. Tel: 351 217 815 120; fax: 351 217 963 242; np95im@mail.telepac.pt.

Russia, 3 Chapligina Str., 103062 Moscow. Tel: 7 095 925 27 07/ 925 27 03/924 88 86/923 87 72; fax: 7 095 923 92 95/923 72 25; latemb@co.ru; latembru@mfa.gov.lv. Consulate General in St. Petersburg, Vasilevskij ostrov, 10 linija, 11, St. Petersburg. Tel: 7 812 327 60 53/54/55; fax: 7 812 327 60 52; gclatspb@mail.wplus.net. Consulate in Pskov, Narodnaja 25, 180600 Pskov. Tel: 7 811 2 465 563/811 2 466 586; fax: 7 811 2 461 289; konsul@latvia.psc.ru; konsulate@latvia.psc.ru.

Spain, c/Diego de León 36-4°, 28006 Madrid. Tel: 34 91 563 17 45; fax: 34 91 411 04 18; letspan@lite.eunet.es.

Sweden, Odengatan 5, Box 19167, 104 32 Stockholm. Tel: 46 8 700 63 00; fax: 46 8 140 151/8 144 103;

lettlands.ambassad@swipnet.se; www.lettland.nu/ambassad.

The Netherlands, Balistrat 88, 2585 XX's-Gravenhage. Tel: 31 70 306 39 34; fax: 31 70 306 28 58; amb.letland@cornnet.nl.

Ukraine, 4/6 Desiatinna Str., 252025 Kyiv. Tel: 38 044 462 07 08/044 462 07 19/044 229 38 80; fax: 38 044 229 27 45/044 462 07 19; cha.kiev@mfa.gov.lv.

United Kingdom, 45 Nottingham Place, London W1M 3FE. Tel: 44 20 7312 0040; fax: 44 20 7312 0042; embassy@embassyoflatvia.co.uk.

US, 4325 Seventeenth Str., N.W. Washington, D.C. 20011. Tel: 1 202 726 82 13/202 726 82 14; fax: 1 202 726 67 85; latvia@ambergateway.com; www.latvia-usa.org.

Uzbekistan, 6 Murtozajeva Str., Tashkent. Tel: 37 12 349 213 998/349 213/342 489; fax: 737 1 120 70 36 998 71 120 70 36; latvemb@bcc.com.uz.

LITHUANIA

Embassies & Consulates Abroad

Austria, Löwengasse 47/4, 1030 Vienna. Tel: 43 1 718 5467/664 451 00 73; fax: 43 1 718 5469; chancery@mail.austria.eu.net.

Belarus, Varvasheni 17, 220029 Minsk. Tel: 375 17 2347 200/ 2347 784/2893 472/2893 473; fax: 375 17 2893 471; ambasada@belsonet.net.

Belgium, rue Maurice Lietart 48, 1150 Bruxelles. Tel: 32 2 772 27 50; fax: 32 2 772 17 01; arvydas. daunoravicius@pophost.eunet.be.

Canada, 130 Albert Str., Suite 204, Ottawa, Ontario K1P 5G4. Tel: 1 613 567 54 58; fax: 1 613 567 53 15; litemb@storm.ca.

China, E 18, King's Garden Villa, No.18 Xiaoyun Road, Chaoyang District, 100600 Beijing. Tel/fax: 86 10 64 68 1150; emlituan@public3.bta.net.cn.

Czech Republic, Pod Klikovkou 1916/2, 15000 Praha 5, Smichov. Tel: 42 02 572 101 22/3; fax: 42 02 572 101 24; ltembcz@mbox.vol.cz; www.ltembassycz.urm.lt.

Foreign Embassies & Consulates in Latvia

RIGA

Australian Consulate,
Raiņa bulv. 3.
Tel: 722 2383; fax: 722 2314;
australian.consulate.riga@latnet.lv.

Austrian Embassy,
Basteja bulv. 14.
Tel: 721 6121; fax: 721 4401;
austrian.embassy@mailbox.riga.lv.

Austrian Consulate,
Ģertrūdes 19/21-12a.
Tel: 733 4231; fax: 782 0364.

Belarusian Embassy,
Jēzusbaznīcas 12.
Tel: 732 3411/732 2550,
fax: 732 2891.

Canadian Embassy,
Doma laukums 4.
Tel: 722 6315; fax: 783 0140;
canembr@bkc.lv.

Chinese Embassy,
Ganību dambis 5.
Tel: 735 7023; fax: 735 7025.

Czech Republic Embassy,
Elizabetes 29.
Tel: 721 7814/ 728 7306,
fax: 721 7821.

Danish Embassy,
Pils 11.
Tel: 722 6210; fax: 782 0234;
ambdk@amdkriga.org.lv.

Dutch Embassy,
Torņa 4-la.
Tel: 732 6147; fax: 732 6151;
nlgovrig@mailbox.riga.lv.

Estonian Embassy,
Skolas 13.
Tel: 781 2020/722 6845/781
2026; fax: 781 2029;
Embassy.Riga@mfa.ee.

Finnish Embassy,
Kalpaka bulv. 1.
Tel: 733 2005/733 35 96;
fax: 733 3597.

French Embassy,
Raiņa bulv. 9.
Tel: 721 3972; fax: 782 0131;
philippe.merlin@diplomatic.fr.

German Embassy,
Raiņa bulv. 13.
Tel: 722 9096/722 9764;
fax: 782 0223/782 0224.

Hungarian Honorary Consulate,
Aspazijas bulv. 22. Tel: 704
4231/722 2802; fax: 721
6287; telga@mailbox.riga.lv.

Icelandic Consulate General,
Kr. Valdemāra 21.
Tel: 703 5383; fax: 703 5252;
ineta@nordicindustries.lv.

Irish Honorary Consulate,
Brīvības 54.
Tel: 702 5222/702 5259;
fax: 702 5260;
gorlovskaja@rietumu.lv.

Israeli Embassy,
Elizabetes 2.
Tel: 732 0980; fax: 783 0170.

Italian Embassy, Teātra 9.
Tel: 721 6069; fax: 721 6084;
ambitalia.riga@apollo.lv.

Japanese Embassy,
Kr. Valdemāra 21.
Tel: 781 2001/2; fax: 781 2004.

Korean Honorary Consulate,
Teātra 9.
Tel: 721 3243; fax: 722 9069.

Lithuanian Embassy,
Rūpniecības 24. Tel: 732
1519/732 0948/732 0919; fax:
732 1589; lithemb@ltemb.vip.lv.

Norwegian Embassy,
Zirgu 14. Tel: 721 6744/721
6746; fax: 781 41 08.

Polish Embassy,
Elizabetes 2a.
Tel: 732 1617/732 2233;
fax: 733 8196; ambpol@apollo.lv.

Russian Embassy,
Antonijas 2. Tel: 721 2579/721
0123; fax: 783 0209.

Swedish Embassy,
Pumpura 8. Tel: 733 8770; fax:
782 8031; ambassaden.riga@
foreign.ministry.se

Swiss Embassy,
Elizabetes 2.
Tel: 733 8351; fax: 733 8354;
swissemriga@apollo.lv.

Ukrainian Embassy,
Kalpaka bulv. 3. Tel: 724 3082/
733 2956; fax: 732 5583.

UK Embassy,
Alunāna 5.
Tel: 733 8126; fax: 733 8132;
british.embassy@apollo.lv.

US Embassy,
Raiņa bulv. 7. Tel: 721 0005;
fax: 782 0047.

Uzbekistan Embassy, Elizabetes
11-11. Tel: 732 2424/732
2346; fax: 732 2306.

Denmark, Bernstorffsvej 214, DK-
2920 Charlottelund, Copenhagen.
Tel: 45 39 636 207; fax: 45 39
636 532; lrambdan@inet.uni2.dk;
www.inet.uni2.dk/home/ltembassydk.

Estonia, Uus tn. 15, Tallinn EE
0100. Tel: 372 631 40 30/641 20
14/631 40 53; fax: 372 641 20
13; amber@anet.ee.

Finland, Rauhankatu 13a, 00170
Helsinki. Tel: 358 9 608 210/278
10 05; fax: 358 9 608 220;
embassy@liettua.pp.fi;
www.liett.pp.fi.

France, 14 bd. Montmartre, 75009
Paris. Tel: 33 1 48 01 00 33;
fax: 33 1 48 01 03 31;
amb.lituanie@wanadoo.fr.

Germany, Katharinenstrasse 9,
10711 Berlin.
Tel: 49 30 890 6810;
fax: 49 30 890 681 15;
botschaftlitauen@ t-online.de;
www.botschaft.lt.

Greece, 49, Vasilissis Sofias Ave.
GR – 106 76 Athens.
Tel: 30 1 72 94 356;
fax: 30 1 72 94 347;
lietamb@otenet.gr.

Israel, Top Tower 14th floor,
Dizengoff 50, Suite 1404, Tel Aviv
64332. Tel: 972 3 528 85 14;
fax: 972 3 525 7265;
lrambizr@netvision.net.il.

Italy, Viale di Villa Grazioli 9,
00198 Rome. Tel: 39 06 855 90
52/854 04 82; fax: 39 06 855 90
53; ltemb@tin.it.

Japan, 401 Pure City Roppongi,
7-11-12 Roppongi, Minato-ku,
Tokyo 106-0032. Tel: 81 3 5414
3433; fax: 81 3 5414 3434;
lithemb@gol.com.

Kazakhstan, Gornij Gigant,
Iskenderovo 15, 480099 Almaty.
Tel: 32 72 65 61 23; fax: 32 72 65
14 60; ambasadorius@kaznet.kz;
konsulas@kaznet.kz.

Latvia, Rūpniecības 24, LV-1010
Riga. Tel: 371 732 1519; fax: 371
732 1589; lithemb@ltemb.vip.lv.

Norway, Gimle Terrasse 6, 0244
Oslo. Tel: 47 225 581 50; fax: 47
225 567 30; litauens@online.no.

Poland, Al. Jana Chrystiana Szucha
5, 00-580 Warszawa.
Tel: 48 22 625 33 68;
fax: 48 22 625 34 40;
litwa_amb@waw.pdi.net.

Portugal, Av. 5 de Outubro, 81–1 Esq., Apartado 14160, 1064-002 Lisboa Codex.
Tel: 351 21 799 01 10;
fax: 351 21 799 63 63;
emb.lituania@mail.telepac.pt.
Russia, Borisoglebskij per. 10, 121069 Maskva.
Tel: 7 095 291 16 98;
fax: 7 095 202 35 16;
unic13@glasnet.ru
Spain, C.Fortuny 19, 28010 Madrid. Tel: 34 91 310 20 75; fax: 34 91 310 40 18.
Sweden, Strandvagen 53, 115 23

Stockholm. Tel: 46 8 667 54 55;
fax: 46 8 667 54 56;
litemb.sweden@urm.lt.
Ukraine, 22 Gorkoho str., 252005 Kyiv. Tel: 380 44 227 10 42;
Tel/fax: 380 44 227 45 85/227 43 72; regis@ambaliet.carrier.kiev.ua.
UK, 84 Gloucester Place, London W1H 3HN.
Tel: 44 20 7486 64 01;
fax: 44 20 7486 64 03;
Iralon@globalnet.co.uk;
www.users.globalnet.co.uk.
US, 2622 16th Str., N.W., Washington, D.C., 20009.

Tel: 1 202 234 5860;
fax: 1 202 328 0466;
admin@ltembassyus.org;
www.ltembassyus.org.
Vatican, Piazza Farnese 44, 00186 Rome.
Tel: 39 6 686 78 55; fax: 39 6 686 57 86; lit.vat@flashnet.it.
Venezuela, Centro Plaza, Torre A, nivel 9, Av. Fco. De Miranda, Caracas 1062, P.O. Box. Apartado Postal 62818 Chacao, Caracas 1060. Tel: 58 2 286 26 49;
fax: 58 2 286 12 68;
Irambven@sa.omnes.net.

Foreign Embassies & Consulates in Lithuania

VILNIUS
Australian Consulate,
Karmelitų 4-12.
Tel/fax: 223 369;
Aust.Con.vilnius@post.omnitel.net.
Austrian Embassy,
Gaono 6.
Tel: 791 347;
fax: 791 363.
Belarusian Embassy,
Mindaugo 41.
Tel: 251 666;
fax: 251 662.
Belarusian Consulate,
Muitinės 41.
Tel: 330 626.
Belgian Embassy,
Jogailos 8.
Tel: 226 769/226 796;
fax: 226 444.
Canadian Embassy,
Gedimino pr. 64.
Tel: 220 853;
fax: 220 884.
Chinese Embassy,
Algirdo 36.
Tel: 262 861;
fax: 262 682.
Czech Republican Embassy,
Juozapavičiaus 11.
Tel: 721 931;
fax: 724 843;
vilnius@embassy.mzv.cz.
Danish Embassy,
Kosciuškos 36.
Tel: 253 434;
fax: 312 300;
dkemb@taide.lt;
www.denmark.lt.

Estonian Consulate,
Mickevičiaus 4a.
Tel: 220 486/ 757 970;
fax: 220 461.
Estonian Embassy
Vilnius@mfa.ee.
Finnish Embassy,
Klaipėdos 6.
Tel: 221 621/222 775;
fax: 222 463;
finemb.vilnius@post.omnitel.net
; www.finland.lt.
French Embassy,
Didžioji 1.
Tel: 222 979;
fax: 223 530.
German Embassy,
Sierakausko 24/8.
Tel: 650 272/231 814;
fax: 231 812/231 813.
Italian Embassy,
Tauro 12.
Tel: 220 620; fax: 220 405;
ambitvilnius@post.omnitel.net.
Japanese Embassy,
Čiurlionio 82b.
Tel: 310 462/310 463;
fax: 310 461.
Kazakhstan Embassy,
Akmenų 7.
Tel: 222 123;
fax: 313 580.
Kazakhstan Consulate,
Turniškių 2-3.
Tel: 313 070.
Latvian Embassy,
Čiurlionio 76.
Tel: 231 260/232 125/231 140/231 240/231 220;
fax: 231 130;

lietuva@latvia.balt.net;
http://latvia.balt.net.
Norwegian Embassy,
Poškos 59.
Tel: 726 926;
fax: 726 964.
Polish Embassy,
Smėlio 20a.
Tel: 709 001;
fax: 709 007.
Romanian Embassy,
Turniškių 41.
Tel: 779 840.
Russian Embassy,
Latvių 53/54.
Tel: 721 763/723 893;
fax: 723 877/723 375.
Spanish Embassy,
Stiklių 14/1.
Tel: 223 763.
Swedish Embassy,
Didžioji 16.
Tel: 685 010;
fax: 685 030.
UK Embassy,
Antakalnio 2.
Tel: 222 070/227 071;
fax: 727 579;
www.britain.lt.
Ukrainian Embassy,
Teatro 4.
Tel: 221 536;
fax: 220 475.
Ukrainian Consulate,
Justiniškių 64.
Tel: 705 115.
US Embassy,
Akmenų 6.
Tel: 223 031;
fax: 312 819.

Getting Around

BY AIR

The private Estonian Aviation Company ELK Airways flies twice a week to Kärdla on Hiiumaa.
ELK Airways: Tallinn Airport. Tel: 605 8199. There are no flights to Saaremaa.

BY RAIL

Lines radiate out from Tallinn railway station *(Balti jaam)*, connecting the capital to Estonia's major towns. Though the service is frequent, it is slow. Information on trains is presented clearly on boards at the stations.

Trains to Moscow and St. Petersburg travel overnight, departing from Tallinn in the late afternoon. The service is particularly good. Beds can be booked in four-berth coupés or – for more privacy – luxurious but more expensive two-bed coupés. The attendant gives a wake-up call around 8am shortly before the train arrives, and a pillow and sheets can be provided for a small charge. Hot water is permanently kept on the boil for use by passengers.

BY BUS

For journeys within Estonia it's often better to travel by bus than by train – buses depart more often, travel faster and are generally much more comfortable than trains. The only drawback is that the buses have no luggage compartments or overhead racks inside. The only place to put large bags on the bus is behind the rear seats and this space is usually at a premium. Another possible problem is that many of the buses do not make any stops en route and they are not equipped with toilets.

Most of the buses leave from the main bus station but check this when booking because there may be other departure points.

Tickets can be booked at stations or in Tallinn from the office at Pärnu mnt. 24, just behind the Palace hotel. Try to avoid travelling at weekends during the summer.

Distance Guide

The following is a list of distances from Tallinn to other major towns in Estonia. The times given indicate how long it typically takes to make these journeys by bus.
Tallinn-Pärnu
80 miles/128 km   (2½ hours)
Tallinn-Tartu
116 miles/187 km   (3 hours)
Tallinn-Narva
132 miles/212 km   (5 hours)
Tallinn-Kuressaare
138 miles/222 km   (4 hours)
Tallinn-Riga
190 miles/307 km   (5½ hours)
Tallinn-Vilnius
377 miles/607 km   (10 hours)

BY CAR

Having a car at your disposal is by far the best way to see Estonia. One of the rare benefits of the Soviet occupation is that there are now excellent roads connecting Tallinn's urban centres. However, roads are becoming increasingly congested as more and more people become car owners. The real pleasure is in taking off from the main routes and following the minor roads as they wind between walls of towering dense forest. There are numerous service stations along the main roads, where you can easily obtain petrol. The speed limit on open roads is 55 mph (90 kph). In built-up areas this decreases to 37 mph (60 kph). Headlights have to be switched on at all times and it is compulsory to wear seat belts in the front of a car. Parking is rarely a problem but it should be noted that cars are not admitted into the Old Town of Tallinn without a permit. When driving in Tallinn beware of trams – they run along the centre of the road, and all traffic has to stop for them, when they stop to let passengers off.

Car Rental

Most major international car-rental agencies have set up shop in Tallinn's airport, offering everything from one-way rentals within the Baltics and to Belarus to weekend deals and special discounts for long-term rental. Almost all car-rental agencies accept credit cards.

Drivers must have a valid licence and passport and are generally required to be over 22 years of age. Prices for a self-drive car start at around US$50 a day and include unlimited mileage.
Avis, Tallinn Airport. Tel: 605 8222; fax: 605 8220. Olümpia Hotel, Liivalaia 33. Tel: 631 5930; fax: 631 5931; tll@avis.ee; avisres@avis.ee; www.avis.ee.
Balti Autoliising, Liivalaia 12. Tel: 613 1830; fax: 613 1831; info@autoliising.ee; www.autoliising.ee. Tallinn Airport. Tel: 605 8148; fax: 605 8142; rent@autoliising.ee.
Budget, Harju 13. Tel: 696 9159/696 9158/0 51 15 780; fax: 696 9157. Tallinn Airport. Tel: 605 8600; fax: 605 8599; info@budget.ee; www.budget.ee.
Europcar, Tallinn Airport. Tel: 605 8031; fax: 605 8151; www.europcar.ee. Central Hotel, Narva 7c. Tel: 633 9911; fax: 633 9926. Toompuiestee 27. Tel: 627 1777; fax: 627 1770.
Hertz, Tallinn Airport. Tel: 605 8923; fax: 605 8953; hertz@online.ee.
National, Tallinn Airport. Tel: 605 8071; fax: 605 8079; arental@online.ee.
Toyota Rent a Car, Tallinn Airport. Tel: 605 8059/0 56 495 295, fax: 605 8060; fin.auto@online.ee.

Tulika Rent, Tulika 33a.
Tel: 612 0012/0 50 90 717;
fax: 612 0013; tulika@online.ee.

ORGANISED TOURS

A number of travel agencies offer
daily sightseeing trips around Tallinn
and excursions to other places of
interest. Most take care of flight and
ferry bookings and car hire and can
also organise trips to neighbouring
states and St. Petersburg on request.

Tallinn
Baltic Tours, Pikk tänav 31.
Tel: 630 0400; fax: 630 0411;
baltic.tours@bt.ee.
CDS Reisid, Jaama tänav 2.
Tel: 644 5262; fax: 631 3666;
cdsr@online.ee.
Estonian Holidays, Pärnu mnt. 12.
Tel: 631 4106; fax: 631 4109;
holidays@holidays.ee.
Estravel American Express Centre,
Suur-Karja 15. Tel: 626 6266;
fax: 626 6262; sales@estravel.ee.
Mainedd, Raekoja plats 18. Tel/fax:
644 4744; mainedd@datanet.ee.
Neiris, Vana-Posti 2. Tel: 627 0627;
fax: 627 0630; neiris@neiris.ee.
Reisiekspert, Roosikrantsi 17.
Tel: 610 8600; fax: 631 3083;
reisiekspert@reisiekspert.ee.
Wris Tours, Toompuiestee 17a.
Tel: 631 2057; fax: 641 8016.
Travel House, Niguliste 2 – 33.
Tel: 631 3119; fax: 631 3123;
info@travelhouse.ee.

CITY TRANSPORT

Travel in Tallin is generally painless,
although roads can be crowded at
times. The public transport is good
with a system of trams, buses and
trolley buses covering.

Trams
There are four main tram routes,
numbered 1, 2, 3 and 4. They run
east-west across the centre of the
city. Trams 1 and 2 originate in the
district of Kopli and terminate at
Kadriorg and Ülemiste respectively.
Trams 3 and 4 originate at Tondi
and also terminate at Kadriorg and

Ülemiste. Trams 1 and 2 stop at
the railway station and pass close
to the harbour. Trams 2 and 4 serve
the main bus terminus.

Trolleybuses:
These are the vehicles with
grasshopper antenna. They run
beneath their electrified cables from
either the train station or
department store out to the
residential districts of Mustamäe
and Olismäe.

Buses
Buses cover all of the above routes
plus many more. Bus No. 2, which
you can catch at Viru väljak, just in
front of the Viru hotel, is the bus to
take for the airport.

Tickets:
Tickets *(talong)* can be purchased
from kiosks around town or from
drivers for US$1. One ticket is used
each time you travel. The ticket
must be punched using the small
machines affixed in the interiors of
the vehicles. The system relies on
honesty, though authorities do
occasionally patrol to check on
passengers' tickets and fines are
levied on those travelling unlawfully.
An unlimited monthly travel card
(kuupilet) is also available.

Maps
Tallinn In Your Pocket has useful
city maps in its centre spread.
*Tallinn: City Plan with Public
Transport* is an invaluable map
providing clear and up-to-date
information, marking all the tram,
bus and trolleybus routes. Both are
on sale at bookshops and kiosks.

Elsewhere in Estonia
There are no trams or trolleybuses
in towns outside of Tallinn, just
buses. All buses operate similar
ticketing systems, with non-
transferable tickets only. In rural
areas tickets can only bought from
the driver.

Taxis
There are only around ten taxi firms
in Tallinn; all of these offer a 24-
hour service and taxis can be

ordered to collect. It is advisable to
order a taxi over the phone or
through a reception desk. Taxis
charge between 4 and 6EEK/km.
Edu. Tel: 657 5555/655 8121.
Esra. Tel: 642 5425.
Kroonitakso. Tel: 605 1111.
Linnatakso. Tel: 644 2442.
Radiotakso. Tel: 644 6000.
Tulika. Tel: 612 0000.

Latvia

BY AIR

There are no regular internal flights
within Latvia. However, if you are in
a hurry and money is no object, you
can charter a business jet from
V.I.P. Aviation, Kr. Barona 20/22.
Tel: 701 0068; fax: 701 0069. A
one-flight hour will cost you
US$2,400.

BY TRAIN

Travel by train here is cheap by
Western standards and the seating
offered is still fairly comfortable.
However, opting for the train does
mean spending longer getting from
A to B than if you travel by bus.
Even express trains stop in the
larger urban centres along the route
between the Baltic capitals, so
keep that in mind if you are in a
hurry. Riga to Ventspils, for
example, a distance of 125 miles
(202 km) will take between three
and four hours by train.
  Trains travelling within Latvia
have no toilets but those travelling
abroad are fully equipped in this
respect. You can reserve a place in
a coupé, which has four beds per
car, or you can opt for a *platskarte*
– a whole carriage that is set up
with beds, rather like a dormitory.
  Electric commuter trains are fast
and convenient and they provide an
easy way to reach Jūrmala: in Riga
tickets can be bought minutes
before departure at the central train
station. Head for the section
closest to the big clock in the
square. The other section is for
longer-distance travel. Tel: 583
2134 for train information.

BY BUS

Travel by bus is inexpensive by Western standards, fairly comfortable and generally quicker than travel by train, especially if you're travelling by express bus. The lack of toilet facilities is only a minor inconvenience, since facilities can normally be used in bus stations en route.

Mini-buses for destinations around Riga stop at the Riga bus station at Prāgas iela, tel: 900 0009; these vehicles are faster but more expensive than bigger buses. Another mini-bus terminal is located just a short walk across the street from Riga Central Railway Station.

BY CAR

Except for a small stretch between Riga and Jūrmala and another one between Riga and Jelgava, there are no multi-lane superhighways running through Latvia. However, the road network is generally adequate for car and bus travel. The country's 30 major urban centres are all connected by two-lane paved roads, which for the most part are in good repair; however, watch out for potholes and construction work taking place in the neighbourhood – more often than not, these are poorly signposted. The streets in the main cities, particularly Riga, are not always in good condition, and cobblestones in older sectors will punish your shock absorbers.

Maximum speed in urban areas is 37mph (60kph). Outside cities/villages the limit is 55mph (90kph) and 60mph (100kph) on motorways and where indicated by a road sign. Seat belts must always be worn in the front seat and headlights have to be switched on at all times.

You must not consume any alcohol just before or while you are driving, as this can result in the loss of your licence or criminal proceedings being initiated.

There are good road-connections from Riga to all parts of the country. Neste, Statoil, Shell and Texaco service stations can be found all over Latvia selling diesel, high-grade and unleaded petrol. Prices can vary between petrol stations, so it is worth asking around for the best deals.

Car Rental

Almost all car-rental agencies accept credit cards and offer weekend deals and special discounts for long-term rental. The major international agencies offer one-way rental within the Baltics.
Avis, Riga Airport. Tel: 720 7353. Aspazijas bulv. 32. Tel: 722 5876; fax: 784 0221; avis@avis.lv; www.avis.com.
Baltijas Autolīzings, Antonijas 22. Tel: 733 4480/733 6110; fax: 733 4867, info@carlease.lv; www.carlease.lv. Riga Airport. Tel: 720 7121/927 3132; car.rent@carlease.lv.
Budget, Riga Airport. Tel: 720 7327/926 3350; fax: 720 7627; budget.lv@defli.lv.
Europcar, Riga Airport. Tel: 720 7825/922 2637. Basteja bulv. 10. Tel: 722 2637/721 2652; fax: 782 0360; europcar@mail.eunet.lv.
Hertz, Riga Airport. Tel: 720 7980; fax: 720 7981; mail@hertz.apollo.lv. Krasta 54. Tel: 709 6560; fax: 709 6561.
National Car Rental, Riga Airport. Tel: 720 7710/924 0735; fax: 720 7709. Aspazijas bulv. 24. Tel/fax: 722 5619.

By Taxi

Taxis are available in every urban centre in Latvia. They can be ordered by telephone and this is often cheaper than if you hail one in the street. There are five taxi companies in Riga, which are recognisable by their official yellow plates. Do not get in any vehicle without this branding. At the time of writing the official tarriff was 0.30Ls/km during the day and 0.40Ls/km at night. Be sure to check that the meter is turned on before you step in.
Bona-M. Tel: 800 5050.
Rīga Taxi. Tel: 800 1010.
Rīgas Taksometru Parks. Tel: 733 4040.

Taxis. Tel: 733 0000/707 7077/733 4041.

As is the case elsewhere in Eastern Europe, many taxi drivers in Latvia believe that all foreigners are wealthy, so be prepared to pay through the nose at typical tourist pickups such as the airport, bus depot, train station and main hotels.

Hitchhiking

In the countryside it is normal to make local journeys by hitchhiking. Note that hikers always pay for their share of the petrol.

ORGANISED TOURS

A number of operators run excursions to the best-known sites and destinations in the country. Many of these tours can be booked through the major hotels.
Balta, Basteja bulv. 10. Tel: 721 6444; fax: 724 3100; balta2@apollo.lv.
Baltic Travel Group, Vecpilsetas 3/2. Tel/fax: 722 8337; btgroup@delfi.lv.
Express Travel, Elizabetes 69. Tel: 728 0840; fax: 731 0067; extravel@parks.lv.
Impro, Torņa 4, III-C. Tel: 732 3099; fax: 732 3360; www.impro.lv.
Latvia Tours, Kaļķu 8. Tel: 708 5001; fax: 782 0020; lt@latviatours.lv; www.latviatours.lv.

Nature Tours

Latvia is famous for its rich nature and fauna and its great outdoors. The following two addresses are for travel agents, who arrange tailor-made nature/ outdoor packages.
Eastbird. Tel: 736 8083; eastbird@latnet.lv. Small firm running birdwatching tours.
Makars Tourism Agency, Sigulda, Peldu 1. Tel: 924 49 48/2-973 724; fax: 797 01 64; makers@junik.lv. For boat tours, canoeing and rafting as well as bike and horse-riding tours.

Rigas turisma agentura, Aspazijas bulv. 28. Tel: 722 0368; fax: 722 2398; rta@parks.lv.
TAS Travel Agency, Raiņa bulv. 21. Tel: 722 2901; fax: 782 0285. Also on Kaļķu 20. Tel: 721 6216; fax: 782 0285; tas@latnet.lv.
TP Travel/American Tours, Brīvības 68-2. Tel: 731 0310; fax: 731 0778; tpriga@latnet.lv.
Via Hansa Tours, Vagnera 3. Tel: 722 7232; fax: 782 0294; riga@viahansa.com; www.viahansa.com.
Via Riga, Kuģu 24 inside the Radisson-SAS hotel. Tel: 706 1171; fax: 706 1172; vr@viariga.lv; vr2@viariga.lv; www.viariga.lv. Also on Kr. Barona 7/9. Tel: 728 5901; fax: 782 8199.

Latvian Waterways

River-borne traffic has for many years been a common feature on the Daugava and Lielupe Rivers, though a fall in tourism and an increase in fuel prices have reduced the number of services available. You can still catch the *M/S Modus* from Old Riga to Lielupe, tel: 910 1289.

CITY TRANSPORT

Riga is criss-crossed by eight tram lines, 23 trolleybus lines and 39 bus routes operating between 5.30am–midnight. Tickets are sold solely from the conductor on buses, trolleybuses and trams. Tickets are valid for one trip only and another ticket is needed if you switch vehicles. Children under seven travel free. Monthly passes are also available.

Lithuania

BY AIR

There are no internal flights from Vilnius to Kaunas or Palanga, the seaside resort near Klaipėda. However Kaunas-based Air Lithuania operates international flights from Kaunas to Cologne and Hamburg (Germany), Billund (Denmark), Kristianstad (Sweden) and Oslo (Norway) via Palanga.
Air Lithuania, Šv. Gertrūdos 7. Tel: 7229 706/228 176; fax: 7228 504; hdoffice@airlithuania.lt; www.airlithuania.lt. Kaunas airport. Tel/fax: 7399 401. Klaipėda: Janonio 5/1. Tel: 6210 665. Palanga airport: Liepojos 1. Tel: 36 52020.

BY RAIL

Frequent trains link Vilnius to Kaunas in 2 hours, to Klaipėda in 10 hours and to many other cities in Lithuania. Similar conditions of travel apply in Lithuania as in Estonia and Latvia.
Vilnius Train Station, Geležinkelio 16. Tel: 330 088/330 087/330 086. Last-minute tickets for same-day travel and for domestic destinations have to be bought at the station.
Druskininkai Train Station, Gardino 3. Tel: 33-53 443.
Kaunas Train Station, Čiurlionio 16. Tel: 7-221 093/292 260.
Klaipėda Train Station, Priestoties 7. Tel: 6-313 676.

BY BUS

Travelling by bus is quite popular in Lithuania, since trains do not serve every town and village. Travel by bus is the cheapest way to get around but a long ride can be quite uncomfortable.
Vilnius Bus Station: Sodū 22 (next to the Railway Station). Tel: 262 482/262 483. Advance Booking: Tel: 262 977. International Booking: Tel: 335 277.

BY CAR

Lithuania's roads and highways are comparatively well kept. The highway from Vilnius to Klaipòda and the M12 from the Polish border via Kaunas to Panevòĩys are both quite good. On secondary roads and in towns watch out for treacherous potholes and open sewers. Avoid driving at night and watch out for unexpected debris on the road. Drinking and driving is strictly forbidden – if caught, you risk a hefty fine and the Lithuanian police may take you straight to the police station for a blood test. The speed limit is 37mph (60kph) in cities, 55mph (90kph) on the open roads and 80mph (130kph) on Lithuania's highways.
As in Estonia, Neste, Statoil and Shell operate service stations across Lithuania. They all sell diesel, high-grade and unleaded petrol.

Hitchhiking
Hitching a ride is quite common in Lithuania. It is normal practice for passengers to pay for their share of the petrol.

Car Rental
Almost all rental agencies accept payment by credit card; most offer weekend deals and discounts for long-term rental. Major international agencies also usually offer one-way rental within the Baltics.
Avis, Darius ir Girėno 32a. Tel: 306 820/98-44 831; fax: 306 821; reservations@avis.lt; www.avis.lt. Vilnius Airport. Tel/fax: 262 229.
Baltijos Autolizingas, Švitrigailos 11c. Tel: 339 632/339 628; fax: 338 918; info@autolizingas.lt; rent@autolizingas.lt; www.autolizingas.lt.
Budget, Vilnius Airport. Tel: 306 708/306 560, fax: 306 709; budget@budget.lt; www.budget.lt. Also at: Klaipėda, Naujojo Sodo 1-223. Tel: 6394 473; fax: 6394 473; klaipeda@budget.lt.
Europcar, tuokos-Guceviciaus 9-1. Tel: 222 739; fax: 220 439; city@europcar.lt. Vilnius Airport, Rodūnės kelias 2. Tel: 263 442.
Hertz, Ukmergės 2. Tel: 726 940/292 247; fax: 726 970; hertz@auste.elnet.lt. Vilnius Airport. Tel/fax: 260 394. Klaipėda: Naujoji sodo 1. Tel: 6-310 737.
Litinterp, Bernardinų 7-2. Tel: 223 850; fax: 223 559; vilnius@litinterp.lt, www.litinterp.lt.

Rimas. Tel/fax: 776 213;
rimas.cars@is.lt.

Taxis

The majority of taxi drivers in Vilnius are honest and they will charge you approximately 1Lt per kilometer. Avoid taxis without meters and make sure that the meter is turned on when you get in. At Vilnius airport you can take any of the official taxis waiting in front of the arrival hall.
Baltas taksi. Tel: 220 909/251 100.
Denvila. Tel: 444 444/448 182.
Fiakras. Tel: 705 705/705 706.
Kabrioletas. Tel: 232 332/
332 233/233 223.
Martono taksi. Tel: 400 040.
Romerta. Tel: 757 575/757 228.
Taksomotoras. Tel: 268 888/268 405.
Užovėja jums. Tel: 616 161.
Vilniaus Taksi. Tel: 006/228 888.
Vintela. Tel: 414 141/414 244.

CITY TRANSPORT

Lithuania has a good public transport system. In Vilnius around 50 bus lines and 20 trolley-bus lines criss-cross the capital. Tickets can be bought in most kiosks (*spaudos kioskas*) and they must be punched in the validation machines found on buses.

ORGANISED TOURS

Baltic Tours, Tumo-Vaižganto 9.
Tel: 227 979/313 311;
fax: 226 767;
baltic.tours@post.omnitel.net.
Baltic Travel Service,
Subačiaus 2. Tel: 220 220;
baltic.travel.service@post.omnitel.net.
Gedimino pr. 21. Tel: 626 111.
Ukmergės 12. Tel: 726 777.
Gedimino Tours, Basanavičiaus 16.
Tel: 224 738;
ged.turas@tdd.lt.
GT International, Gedimino pr. 37.
Tel: 223 147;
fax: 223 149;
gtinternational@post.omnitel.net.
Lithuanian Holidays, Aušros Vartų
17-9. Tel/fax: 312 872;
lt.holidays@post.omnitel.net.

Lithuanian Waterways

During the summer you can catch a hydrofoil down the Nemunas River from Kaunas to Nida on the Neringa Spit. The speedy passenger boat leaves daily from the Prieplauka, Raudondvario plentas 107. Tel: 7261 348. Neringa ticket office: Naglių 16. Tel: 59 52 333. Two ferries link Klaipėda with the Neringa Spit. The boats leave every half hour and the crossing takes 10 minutes. For more information tel: 6311 157/345 780.

Lithuanian Tours, Šeimyniškių 18.
Tel: 724 156; fax: 721 815,
contact@LithuanianTours.com.
Liturimex, Basanavičiaus 11/1.
Tel: 226 063/791 416;
fax: 791 417;
center@liturimex.lt;
www.liturimex.lt.
Mondus, Pamenkalnio 5.
Tel: 224 444;
mondus@taide.lt;
www.mondus.lt.
Piligrimas, Dominikonų 4.
Tel: 611 800.
Tel/fax: 615 558.
Vilnius tours and trips to Trakai.
Svebas, Tumo-Vaižganto 9/1.
Tel: 226 620; fax: 226 551;
svebas@post.omnitel.net;
www.svebas.lt.
West Express, Stulginskio 5.
Tel: 222 500;
wexpres@post.5ci.lt.
WrisLit, Rūdninkų 18/2.
Tel: 222 081;
fax: 222 098;
wrislit@wrislit.lt; www.wrislit.lt.

Where to Stay

Since the early 1990s international groups have opened world-class hotels in the Baltics, with smart room furnishings and new amenities such as service bureaux, satellite TV, ISDN lines and internet hook-ups. Many hotel restaurants have also been transformed. In top-class hotels most rooms are non-smoking and fully equipped to cater for disabled travellers.

Numerous smaller luxury hotels have opened in old town houses, which often rival their western counterparts in terms of quality, service and price. Country hotels tend to be more basic. If you are on a tight budget you should consider bed-and-breakfast or home-stay accommodation. Most hotels take credit cards unless otherwise noted.

Price Guide: Estonia

Almost all hotels in Estonia boast a sauna and small pool. The star-ratings beside the hotels are those of the researcher and are not official. Price ratings, which are given as a guide only, reflect the price of a double room for one night:
SSSS = over 2,500EEK
SSS = 1500–2,500EEK
$$ = 600–1500EEK
$ = below 600EEK

Hotels in Estonia

TALLINN

Park Consul Schlössle ☆☆☆☆☆
Pühavaimu 13-15
Tel: 699 7700
Fax: 699 7777
schlossle@consul-hotels.com
www.consul-hotels.com

Estonia's only five-star hotel is set in a yellow 15th-century merchant's house in the heart of Tallinn's old town. It is expensive but worth it. The 27 rooms in this historical gem offer all the modern conveniences a traveller needs. The vaulted cellar is home to the top-class Stenhus restaurant. The hotel is often booked for months at a time and it is recommended to reserve in advance. **$$$$**

St. Petersbourg Hotel ✩✩✩✩✩
Rataskaevu 7
Tel: 628 6500
Fax: 628 6565
stpetersbourg@consul-hotels.com
www.consul-hotels.com
This former government hotel is also run by the Consul group and is no less luxurious than the Park Consul Schlössle. Although it does not boast five official stars, its 27 rooms are furnished with the latest amenities and are worth the expense. **$$$**

Grand Hotel Mercure Tallinn
✩✩✩✩
Toompuiestee 27
Tel: 667 7000
Fax: 667 7001
mercure@online.ee
Well situated at the foot of Toompea and close to the railway station, this hotel was completely renovated by the French Accor hotel group and now ranks among the best in town. Its restaurants have a definite French touch. **$$$**

Scandic Hotel Palace ✩✩✩✩
Vabaduse väljak 3
Tel: 640 7300
Fax: 640 7299

palace@scandic-hotels.ee
www.scandic-hotels.com
After independence in 1991, the Palace was home temporarily to at least three Western embassies. Run by the Scandic hotel group, the Palace remains one of the the city's top establishments. The Leonardo is a high-class restaurant, and there is a more modest pizzeria on site as well. **$$$$**

Scandic Hotel St Barbara ✩✩✩✩
Roosikrantsi 2a
Tel: 631 3991
Fax: 631 3992
st.barbara@scandic-hotels.ee
st_barbara.res@scandic-hotels.com
www.scandic-hotels.com
The least expensive of the Scandic Hotels is just around the corner from the Palace Hotel and a block away from central Vabaduse square. The hotel is in a luxurious limestone building but it lacks a restaurant. **$$$**

Metropol ✩✩✩✩
Mere pst. 8b
Tel: 667 4555/667 4500
Fax: 667 4600
hotell@metropol.ee
booking@metropol.ee
www.metropol.ee
This 144-room luxury-hotel complex was built in late 1999. It is located just a stone's throw from the harbour and the old town. Book the rooms with private saunas if you can. **$$**

Olümpia ✩✩✩✩
Liivalaia 33
Tel: 631 5333/631 5555
Fax: 631 5675
hotel@olympia.ee
www.olympia.ee
A lot of money has been spent on Tallinn's second hotel tower and it shows. The interior may be a rather garish mix of Euro-kitsch but it is very smart and clean. The Elysée restaurant, brasserie, 24-hour coffee shop and Bonnie & Clyde nightclub are all well worth a visit. **$$$$**

Park Hotel & Casino ✩✩✩✩
Kreutzwaldi 23
Tel: 630 5305
Fax: 630 5315
hotel@parkhotel.ee
www.parkhotel.ee

The main attraction of the Park, which is situated slightly out of the main town centre, is its swanky casino. **$$**

Ilmarine Residence ✩✩✩
Põhja pst. 23
Tel: 614 0900
Fax: 614 0901
ilmarine@domina.ee
ilmarine@ilmarine.ee
www.ilmarine.com
An Italian hotel group has tastefully converted this characterful old warehouse set in the harbour area between the port and the old town. The 43 split-level rooms are modern and comfy with the very latest amenities. **$$$**

Viru ✩✩✩
Viru väljak 4
Tel: 630 1390/630 1381
Fax: 630 1303
reservation@viru.ee
www.viru.ee
Possibly Tallinn's most infamous landmark, this old hotel has now shed its Soviet trappings. The views of the old town are wonderful and they make dining in the 22nd floor restaurant a pleasure. The Viru possesses two other restaurants as well as a ground-floor café and a couple of bars. Amenities include a conference centre, beautician, hairdressers, fitness centre, florist, gift shop and news kiosk. **$$$**

Peoleo ✩✩
Pärnu mnt. 555
Laagri
Tel: 650 3965
Fax: 650 3900
hotel@peoleo.ee
An American-run, 52-room travel lodge on the road to Pärnu and a 15-minute drive into town. **$$**

Pirita ✩✩
Regati pst 1
Pirita
Tel: 639 8822/639 8600
Fax: 639 8821
pirita@top.ee
Built for the 1980 Olympic yachting events, the former Sport hotel is attractively located in a forested coastal strip. It is 3 miles (5 km) from the town centre but the adjacent beach, marina and forest walks offer more than adequate compensation. **$$**

Eeslitall
Dunkri 4
Tel: 631 3755
Fax: 631 3210
donkeys@eeslitall.ee
www.eeslitall.ee
The Donkeys' Stable has 9 rooms and offers the best budget accommodation in town. It is situated just metres away from the main square. Showers are shared and credit cards are not accepted. Reservations are recommended. **$**

Rotermann
Mere pst. 6a
Tel: 613 7900
Fax: 613 7999
rothotel@infonet.ee
The newer and more expensive of the two Rotermanni establishments opposite each other. **$$**

Rotermanni Viiking ✫✫✫
Mere pst. 6a
Tel: 660 1934
Fax: 613 7901
viiking@anet.ee
www.vikinghotel.ee
This establishment looks like a warehouse from the outside. On the inside the rooms are comfortable and simple. **$$**

Bed & Breakfast

Rasastra
Mere pst. 4
Tel/fax: 641 2291
rasastra@online.ee
Organises homestays throughout the whole of Estonia.

Hostels

Hotell Vana Tom
Väike-Karja 1
Tel/fax: 631 3252
Formerly known as "The Barn", this hostel is the backpacker's favourite, located in the old town below a striptease joint. Shared showers, no cards accepted. **$**

Estonian Youth Hostel Association

Eesti Puhkemajad
Tatari 39-310
Tel: 646 1455/646 1457
Fax: 646 1595
puhkemajad@online.ee
eyha@online.ee
www.eyha.jg.ee
Part of the international youth hostel network, the Estonian Youth

Hostel Association operates four hostels in Tallinn (Merevaik, Mahtra, Vikerlase and Gabriel), one in Tartu, one in Taevaskoja (southeast Estonia), one in Kuressaare (Saaremaa) and one in Narva-Jõesuu (northeast Estonia). All hostels have cooking facilities and supply sheets. They cost between 100–160EEK for a place in a two- to four-bed room. You do not have to be a member of a youth hostelling association to stay here.

HAAPSALU

Promenaadi ✫✫✫
Sadama 22
Tel: 047 37 250
Fax: 047 37 250
promenad@estpak.ee
www.promenaadi.ee
Hotel on the waterfront.

NARVA

Elektra ✫✫✫
Kerese 11
Tel/fax: 035 66 651
Six-room luxury guesthouse on the premises of the Narva electricity company. **$$**

Vanalinn ✫
Koidula 6
Tel: 035 22 486
Fax: 035 24 120
This is the best hotel Narva has to offer. Located in a quaint medieval building overlooking the friendship bridge. Basic but clean. **$$**

PARNU

Ammende Villa ✫✫✫✫
Mere pst. 7.
Tel: 044 73 888
Fax: 044 73 887
ammende@transcom.ee
This, Pärnu's top hotel, opened in 2000 in an historic 1905 Art Nouveau villa. **$$**

Rannahotell ✫✫✫✫
Ranna pst. 5
Tel: 044 38 950/42 955
Fax: 044 38 318
rannahotell@scandic-hotels.com

www.scandic-hotels.com
Opened in summer 1994 by the Scandic hotel group after extensive renovation, this beautiful and stylish hotel built in 1937 sits right on the beach. **$$**

Strand ✫✫✫
A. H. Tammsaare pst. 27d
Tel: 044 39 333
Fax: 044 39 211
strand@estpak.ee
www.strand.ee
The hotel and conference centre, built in 1988, is named after its location right on the beach. **$$**

Bristol ✫✫✫
Rüütli 45
Tel: 044 31 450
Fax: 044 43 415
bristol@hot.ee
Sister hotel of the Victoria, housed in a red-brick building. **$$**

Victoria ✫✫✫
Kuninga 25
Tel: 044 43 412
Fax: 044 43 415
victoria@hot.ee
Very attractive *belle-epoque* hotel with 23 well-appointed rooms. **$$**

Best Western Hotel Pärnu ✫✫
Rüütli 44
Tel: 044 78 911
Fax: 044 78 905
hotparnu@www.ee
www.ee/hotparnu
The centrally located hotel block has been extensively refurbished and is now proudly affiliated to the Best Western hotel chain. **$$**

Emmi ✫✫
Laine 2
Tel: 044 76 444
Fax: 044 76 445
This hotel lies 1 mile (2 km) out of the town centre, beside the sea. Mudbath treatments available. **$$**

TARTU

Barclay ✫✫✫✫
Ülikooli 8
Tel: 07 447 100
fax: 07 447 101
barclay@estpak.ee
Set in what was once the local headquarters of the Soviet Army, the reconstructed Barclay hotel exudes early 19th-century elegance.

Price Guide: Estonia

Almost all hotels in Estonia boast a sauna and small pool. The star-ratings beside the hotels are those of the researcher and are not official. Price ratings, which are given as a guide only, reflect the price of a double room for one night:

SSSS = over 2,500EEK
SSS = 1500–2,500EEK
$$ = 600–1500EEK
$ = below 600EEK

Ask for the Dzhokhar Dudayev room, which was named after the first president of Chechnya who was stationed here from 1987–1991 while serving as an officer in the Soviet army. **$$$**

Draakon ☆☆☆☆
Raekoja plats 2
Tel: 07 442 045
Fax: 07 434 540
tonyas@solo.delfi.ee
The newest addition to the Tartu hotel scene, the "Dragon" is set right next to the Town hall and boasts 35 rooms. **$$**

Pallas ☆☆☆☆
Riia 4
Tel: 07 301 200
Fax: 07 301 201
pallas@kodu.ee
This hotel is set on top of a business centre overlooking the city. It is named after Estonia's first School of Fine Arts, which stood on the same spot until it was bombed and destroyed in 1944. The hotel has 43 rooms and the luxurious suites are wonderfully decorated according to the designs of Estonian 20th-century painters, all of whom were students of the Pallas Art School. **$$$**

Park ☆☆
Vallikraavi 23
Tel: 07 427 000
Fax: 07 434 382
Park is in a fine location on wooded slopes and offers a bar, café and sauna. **$$**

Kantri ☆☆
Riia 195
Tel: 07 383 044
Fax: 07 477 213

jantri@server.ee
As its name (meaning "country") implies, this is a rustic hotel, set on the outskirts of Tartu on the road to Riga. **$$**

Tartu Hostel ☆
Soola 3
Tel: 07 432 091
Fax: 07 433 041
tarhotel@server.ee
Situated next to the bus station, just behind McDonalds, this friendly hostel is the cheapest place to stay in Tartu. You can obtain a reduction on the price by presenting an international youth hostel card. **$**

VILJANDI

Centrum
Tallinna 24
Tel: 043 51 100/125
Fax: 043 51 101
centrum@matti.ee
www.centrum.ee
A three-star hotel located – true to its name – in the centre of Viljandi.

Kivi farm
Viljandi maakond
Ramsi
Tel: 043 91 457
kivitalu@hot.ee
www.hot.ee/kivitalu
You will receive a very warm welcome in this charming farm situated 3 miles (5 km) from Viljandi in the village of Ramsi. Kivi comprises a self-contained building of six bedrooms, lounge, dining room, shower and sauna. **$**

Sammuli
Männimäe tee 28
Tel: 050 49 716
Large lodge on the shores of Lake Viljandi, 4 miles (6 km) out of town. Rooms are basic with shared bathrooms but comfortable; those with balconies overlook the lake. **$**

OTEPAA

Karupesa
Tehvandi 1a
Tel: 076 61 500
Fax: 076 61 601
karupesa@scandic-hotels.ee
www.scandic-hotels.com

Part of the Scandic hotel group, this is the best place to stay in Estonia's winter resort.

Motels & Camping
Pesa ☆☆☆
Uus 5
Põlva (a small town 26 miles/ 42 km from Tartu)
Tel: 079 98 530
Fax: 079 98 531
kagureis@kagureis.ee
www.kagureis.ee
All 32 rooms have telephones, satellite TV and shower. This hotel organises hunting expeditions. **$$**

Hotels in Latvia

Riga has countless expensive luxury hotels. Medium-range hotels are scarce and usually need to be booked months in advance. When travelling throughout the country, you will find the majority of towns have at least one hotel. Facilities are usually basic but acceptable.

Private bed-and-breakfast accommodation is becoming increasingly popular and usually costs around half the price of a hotel room. Farmhouse and cottage accommodation can be arranged through Lauku ceļotājs (Country Traveller), Kuģu 11. Tel: 761 7600/761 7024; fax: 783 0041.

Price Guide: Latvia

The star ratings beside hotel names are those of the researcher and not official ones. The ranges given, which are intended as a guide only, are for a double room for one night:

SSSS = over 100Ls
SSS = 50–100Ls
$$ = 30–50Ls
$ = below 30Ls

RIGA

Eurolink ☆☆☆☆
Third floor
Riga Azpāzijas bulv. 22
Tel: 722 0531
Fax: 721 6300
eurolink@brovi.lv

The Eurolink is managed by the same Swedish group as Metropole team but is slightly cheaper. **$$$**

Grand Palace Hotel ☆☆☆☆☆
Pils 12
Tel: 704 4000
Fax: 704 4001
hotel@grandpalace.lv
grandpalace@consul-hotels.com
www.consul-hotels.com
Riga's most luxurious hotel, based in the heart of the old town. **$$$$**

Hotel de Rome ☆☆☆☆
Kaļķu 28
Tel: 708 7600
Fax: 708 7606
reservation@derome.lv
www.derome.lv
One of the smartest places to stay in Latvia, this hotel is centrally located on the edge of the old town facing the Freedom monument. Treat yourself to a nibble in the Otto Schwarz restaurant if your budget stretches to it. **$$$$**

Karavella ☆☆☆
Katrinas dambis 27
Tel: 732 3130
Fax: 783 0187
hotel@karavella.lv
www.karavella.lv
Although this hotel is located slightly out of town, on the way to the harbour, rooms are very reasonably priced. **$$**

Konventa Sēta ☆☆☆☆☆
Kalēju 9/11
Tel: 708 7501
Fax: 708 7515
reservation@konventa.lv
www.derome.lv
Housed in a medieval convent in the heart of town, the "Convent Courtyard" *(Konventhof)* is run by the same team as the Hotel de Rome and is definitely one of the best hotels in the Baltics. **$$$**

Metropole ☆☆☆☆
Aspazijas bulv. 36–38
Tel: 722 5411
Fax: 721 6140
metropole@brovi.lv
www.eunet.lv/metropole
A Swedish-run top-quality hotel on the edge of the old town. **$$$$**

Park Hotel Rīdzene ☆☆☆☆
Reimersa 1
Tel: 732 4433
Fax: 728 2100
park.hotel@ridzene.lv
www.parkhotelridzene.com
This former Communist Party hotel, which is in a lovely setting in the garden ring behind the US embassy, was entirely renovated in 1999. It has everything you'd expect from a world-class hotel. **$$$**

Radisson-SAS Daugava ☆☆☆☆
Kuģu 24
Tel: 706 1111
Fax: 706 1100
radisson@com.latnet.lv
www.radissonsas-riga.lv
The Radisson boasts 361 rooms and offers the Radisson comfort and service with the price tag to match. Its major drawback, the location on the southern bank of the Daugava River, is tempered by the beautiful views it offers of Riga's skyline. **$$$**

Radi un Draugi ☆☆☆☆
Mārstaļu 1/3
Tel: 722 0372
Fax: 724 2239
This British-Latvian joint venture has been booked up ever since it opened and with good reason: it offers moderately priced accommodation in the heart of the old town. Reservations are essential. **SS**

Hostels

Riga Technical University Dormitory
Kaļķu 1
Tel: 708 9395
Reservations are essential in this student dormitory in the heart of town. **S**

Studentu Kopmitne (Student Dormitories)
Basteja bulv. 10
Tel: 721 6221
More centrally located student dormitories. Note that there is a curfew at midnight. **S**

Placis
Laimdotas 2a
Tel: 755 1824/755 1271
This hostel, which is situated out of the centre of town, is affiliated to the International Youth Hostel Association, so you should get a discount if have one of their membership cards. To get here, take trolleybus No. 4 as far as the Teika stop.**S**

JURMALA

The seaside resort of Jūrmala can be easily reached by electric commuter train from Riga in less than half an hour. It has white, sandy beaches and hotels and sanatoriums for recuperation.

Majori
Jomas 29
Tel: 776 1380/776 1390
fax: 776 1394
Probably Jūrmala's best hotel set in an old 19th-century building.

Rīgas Līcis
Dubultu pr. 51
Tel: 776 1180
fax: 776 1166
rigaslicis@rigaslicis.lv
www.rigaslicis.lv
An historic spa hotel, with some 77 rooms and a miniture golf course.

BAUSKA

Bauska
Slimnicas 7
Tel: 39 24 705
Facilities here include a bar, café and televisions in some rooms. **$**

Brencis Motel
On the M12 just north of Bauska, 22 miles (38 km) from Riga.
Tel: 39 28 033
Unusual and welcome motel accommodation in rural settings.

KULDIGA

Jāṇa Nams
Liepājas 36
Tel: 332 3456
Fax: 332 3785
Quaint and small two-storey hotel with a sauna in the centre of town.

LIEPAJA

Amrita ☆☆☆☆
Rīgas 7/9
Tel: 348 0888/340 3434
Fax: 348 0444
info@amrita.lv
www.amrita.lv
The only four star hotel outside of

Riga. The 83-room hotel is the best address in Liepāja. **$$$**

Fēja
Kurzemes pr. 9
Tel: 342 2688
Fax: 348 1447
A quaint hotel with eight rooms. **$$**

Līva
L11
Tel: 342 0102
Fax: 348 0259
This big hotel block in Liepāja has seen better days. **$**

SIGULDA

Senleja
Turaidas 4
Tel: 2 972 162
Fax: 790 1611
This is a charming hotel in the Gauja valley, just a short walk from the local caves. **$**

Sigulda
Pils 6
Tel: 2 972 263
Fax: 724 5165
hotelsigulda@lis.lv
A small modern hotel in a red-brick building in the centre of town.

Camping
Camping grounds usually have no water and only one poorly lit toilet. You are not expected to arrive and pitch your own tent but to use cabins already on site. As in most countries the camping grounds are often attractively situated by lakes and rivers, in the middle of forests or by the sea. The major campsites are on the Jūrmala coast and in Saulkrasti on the road to Tallinn.

Price Guide: Latvia

The star ratings beside each hotel's name are the researcher's and not official ratings. The ranges given, which are intended as a guide only, are for a double room for one night:
$$$$ = over 100Ls
$$$ = 50–100Ls
$$ = 30–50Ls
$ = below 30Ls

Hotels in Lithuania

Vilnius has numerous luxury hotels, many of which are hidden in ancient courtyards in the old town.

VILNIUS

Mabre Residence Hotel ☆☆☆☆
Maironio 13
Tel: 222 087/222 195
Fax: 222 240
mabre@is.lt
www.is.lt/mabre
One of Vilnius's most exclusive hotels, situated in a former Russian-orthodox monastery. Highly recommended. **$$$**

Radisson SAS Astorija Hotel
☆☆☆☆
Didžioji 35/2
Tel: 220 110
Fax: 221 762
var@vnozh.rdsas.com
www.radissonsas.lt
The Radisson hotel chain has taken over this beautiful early 20th-century building in the heart of the old town and transformed it into Vilnius's top business hotel. The hotel has 120 rooms, of which 70 are equipped for business travellers. **$$$$**

Shakespeare ☆☆☆☆
Bernardinų 8/8
Tel: 314 521
Fax: 314 522
info@shakespeare.lt
www.shakespeare.lt
The best hotel in Vilnius, this establishment opened in late 1999. Under English management all the rooms are named after literary figures and conjure up a flavour of 17th-century England. All 33 rooms are overlooking either St. Anne's church or Gediminas castle. **$$$**

Stikliai ☆☆☆☆
Gaono 7
Tel: 627 971
Fax: 223 870
stikliai@mail.iti.lt
www.iti.lt/stikliai
This eternally popular hotel was the first luxury establishment to open in Vilnius' old town. Based in a 17th-century building, it has 29 rooms and an outstanding brasserie and restaurant. **$$$$**

Šarūnas ☆☆☆☆
Raitininkų 4
Tel: 723 888/724 888
Fax: 724 355/722 325
info@hotelsarunas.lt
www.hotelsarunas.lt
Built by Lithuanian basketball star Šarūnas Marčiulionis, this hotel, which is outside the town centre, has sneakers and T-shirts of famous NBA players dangling from the ceiling of the bar. It has a fine restaurant and several conference rooms. **$$$**

V & G Hotel Club
Pilies 10
Tel: 312 206
Fax: 312 207
info@hotelclub.lt
www.hotelclub.lt
This 13-room hotel in the centre of town has sadly gone overboard in decoration, service and price. **$$$**

Mano Liza Guest House ☆☆☆
Ligoninės 5
Tel: 222 225/222 545
Fax: 222 608
hotel@aaa.lt
www.aaa.lt
This small, eight-room hotel is an insider's tip for those who are looking for quality and intimacy in the quiet back streets of Vilnius's old town. **$$**

Grybas House ☆☆☆
Aušros Vartų 3a
Tel: 608 420/221 854
Fax: 222 416
grybashouse@taide.lt
This, arguably Vilnius's most charming hotel, has only eight rooms hidden in a courtyard and is run by a friendly English-speaking couple. **$$$**

Narutis ☆☆☆
Pilies 24
Tel: 222 894/610 981
Fax: 622 882
laima@narutis.lt
www.tdd.lt/narutis
The Narutis is a charming hotel in a 16th-century townhouse on Pilies Street right in the heart of the old town. Some of the 30 rooms have retained 19th-century frescoes. Rooms overlooking the pedestrianised street offer very good views of St. John's church. **$$**

Naujasis Vilnius ✫✫✫
Ukmergės 14
Tel: 726 756/739 595
Fax: 723 161
hotelnv@is.lt
www.is.lt/LTF/Nvhome.htm
This ugly hotel block, located next to the Lietuva hotel across the river from Vilnius's old town, is home to 102 entirely renovated rooms. **$$**

Neringa ✫✫✫
Gedimino pr. 23
Tel: 610 516
Tel/fax: 614 160
neringa@tdd.lt
www.tdd.lt/neringa
Centrally located, the Neringa is one of the best bets in Vilnius for price-conscious travellers. The restaurant has an original 1960s' interior. **$$$**

Lietuva ✫✫
Ukmergės 20
Tel: 726 090/726 092
Fax: 722 130
lietuva@aiva.lt
www.aiva.lt/Lietuva
Some things never change such as the 23-storey, 316-room former Intourist flagship hotel, the Lietuva. It still offers many services but is in need of some renovation. **$$**

Price Guide: Lithuania

The star ratings beside each hotel's name are those of the researcher, rather than official ratings. The ranges given, which are intended as a guide only, are for a double room for one night:
$$$$ = over 600Lt
$$$ = 400–600Lt
$$ = 200–400Lt
$ = below 200Lt

Bed & Breakfast
Litinterp
Bernardinų 7/2
Tel: 223 850/223 291/99 14 680
Fax: 223 559
vilnius@litinterp.lt
www.litinterp.lt
The best bed-and-breakfast agency in the Baltics. Home-stays with families from Vilnius to Trakai. The helpful staff also have offices in Kaunas and Klaipėda. **$**

Hostels
Filaretai
Filaretų 17
Tel: 254 627
fax: 220 149
filaretai@post.omnitel.net
http://filaretai.8m.com
Vilnius's first Youth Hostel is located quite a distance out of town. Take bus No. 34 from the station to the Filaretų stop. **$**

Old Town Hostel
Aušros Vartų 20-15a
Tel: 625 357
fax: 220 305
lyh@jnakv.vno.soros.lt
This is Vilnius's most central Youth Hostel, situated right in the old town. To get here, just follow the signs to "LJNN Travellers' Infocentre". **$**

OUTSIDE VILNIUS

Le Méridien-Villon ✫✫✫
12 miles (19 km) north of Vilnius on the M12 to Riga
Tel: 739 600/739 700
Fax: 651 385
lemeridienvillon@post.omnitel.net
www.hotelvillon.lt
This is a country club offering the full works. Facilities include 134 rooms, a swimming pool, tennis courts, boating and fishing. Located 30 miles (19km) out of the town centre. **$$$$**

TRAKAI

Traku ✫✫
Ežero 7
Tel/fax: 38 55 505/55 503
hotel.traku@takas.lt
http://members.hotels.lt/traku
Traku's best hotel is set on the shores of Lake Totoriškės. **$**

DRUSKININKAI

Druskininkai
Kudirkos 43
Tel: 33 52 566
Fax: 33 52 217
Only the three suites have private showers, telephone and TV. **$/$$**

KAUNAS

Santakos ✫✫✫✫
Gruodžio 21
Tel: 7 302 702
Fax: 7 302 700
office@santaka.lt
www.santaka.lt
Lithuania's only Best Western hotel is set in an old red-brick warehouse in a side street. The 40 rooms are refurbished and comfortable. **$$$**

Minotel ✫✫✫
Kuzmos 8
Tel: 7 203 759/229 981
Fax: 7 220 355
minotel@kaunas.omnitel.net
www.travel.lt/minotel
This cosy three-storey hotel is located in the heart of town. **$$$**

Kaunas ✫✫✫
Laisvės al. 79
Tel: 7 323 110
Fax: 7 323 301
hotel.kaunas@takas.lt
www.kaunashotel.lt
Set in the middle of pedestrianised Laisvės al., this hotel opened in 1999. The top-floor rooms offer excellent views of the street and the management has assured us do that passers-by cannot see in. **$$**

Perkūno Namai ✫✫✫
Perkūno al. 61
Tel: 7 320 230
Fax: 7 323 678
hotel@perkuno-namai.lt
www.perkuno-namai.lt
Out of the centre next to a wooded park but worth the hike. **$$$**

Takioji Neris ✫✫
Donelaičio 27
Tel: 7 204 224
Fax: 7 205 289
takneris@takas.lt
www.travel.lt/neris/
A seven-storey hotel block in the centre of town. Most of the 178 rooms have been completely renovated. A favourite with tour groups and businessmen. **$$**

Lietuva ✫
Daukanto 21
Tel: 7 225 992
Fax: 7 206 269
metropol@takas.lt
Little has changed here since Soviet times. Service remains friendly. **$**

Bed & Breakfast
B&B Litinterp
Kumelių 15-4
Tel/fax: 7 228 718
kaunas@litinterp.lt
www.litinterp.lt
Offers rooms in the city centre and the old town. **$**

KLAIPEDA & THE COAST

Fortuna ☆☆☆
Poilsio 64
Tel: 6 348 028
Fax: 6 360 174
A small family-run guest-house situated out of the centre of town. Eight rooms. **$**
Godunas ☆☆☆
Janonio 11
Tel: 6 310 901
Fax: 6 310 900
godunas@klaipeda.omnitel.net
Set right off the main street, this hotel offers particularly good value for money. **$**
Prūsija ☆☆☆
Šimkaus 6
Tel: 6 412 081
A centrally located, calm and cosy family-run hotel with just eight rooms and two suites. **$$**
Klaipėda ☆☆
Naujoji sodo 1
Tel: 6 394 372
Fax: 6 394 382
hotel@klaipeda.omnitel.net
www.tdd.lt/klaipeda
This red-brick monster in the centre of town is Klaipėda's main hotel and the place where most large tour groups stay. Offers 220 rooms, all equipped with mod-cons. **$$**
Astra ☆☆
Pilies 2
Tel: 6 313 449
Fax: 6 216 420
This hotel between the old town and the old castle port is uninviting from the outside but its 14 rooms are modern and nicely furnished. **$$**
Jūra ☆
Malūnininkų 3
Tel: 6 393 260
Fax: 6 393 267
Klaipėda's Soviet experience. Check it out before all 38 rooms are renovated. **$**

Bed & Breakfast
Litinterp
Šimkaus 21-4
Tel: 6 411 814
Fax: 6 411 815
klaipeda@litinterp.lt
www.litinterp.lt
Organises rooms and flats in Klaipėda, Nida and Palanga. **$**

Youth Hostel
Travellers' Guesthouse
Turgaus 3-4
Tel: 6 214 935
oldtown@takas.lt
Klaipėda's Youth Hostel serves free tea and coffee; if you reserve by e-mail, you can even get a free beer and one-day bicycle rental. **$**

NERINGA

Ažuolynas ☆☆☆
Juodkrantė
Liudo Rėzos 54
Tel: 59 53 310/318
Fax: 59 53 316
This Neringa hotel is especially popular with German tour groups. **$$**
Rasytė ☆☆☆
Lotmiškio 11
Tel: 59 52 592
The rooms in this traditional fisherman's house are spartan and basic. Reservations are nevertheless essential. **$**
Auksines Kopos ☆☆☆
Kuverto 17
Tel: 59 52 212/387
Fax: 59 52 947
The "Golden Dunes" hotel is tucked away in the woods above Nida. **$$**

Linėja ☆☆
Taikos 18
Tel: 59 52 390/52 717
Fax: 59 52 718
lineja@pajuris.lt
This is one of the better establishments in Nida. Its main claim to fame is its bowling lane. **$$**
Jūratė ☆
Pamario 3
Tel: 59 52 300
Fax: 59 51 118
Jūratė has some very basic unrenovated rooms. If possible, opt for the refurbished ones instead, as these are not much more expensive but far superior. **$**

PALANGA

Du Broliai ☆☆☆☆
Vytauto 160
Tel: 36 52 889
Tel/fax: 36 52 889
Also on Kretingos 36
Tel/fax: 36 54 028
Palanga's classiest hotel is run by two brothers. **$$**
Šachmatinė ☆☆☆☆
Basanavičiaus 45
Tel: 36 48 529/36 48 2967/
36 51 655/48 259
Tel/fax: 36 51 655
This flashy nine-room hotel is set right behind the dunes next to the beach. **$$**
Baltija ☆☆☆
Ganyklų 30
Tel: 36 48 331/332
Fax: 36 49 226
baltija@is.lt
At one time, Soviet officials used to stay in some of the 505 rooms offered by the Baltijain. Rooms are spread over three locations and the more upmarket ones include:
Auska, Vytauto 11, tel: 36 49 083 and **Žilvinas,** Kęstučio 26, tel: 36 49 146, fax: 36 49 197, zilvinas@is.lt
Mama Rosa
Jūratės 28a
Tel: 36 48 581
Tel/fax: 36 48 580
www.mamarosa.lt
Palanga's prime villa has just eight rooms. It's popular so be sure to book ahead. **$$**

SIAULIAI

Šaulys
Vasario 16-osios 40
Tel: 1 520 812/520 844
Fax: 1 520 911
saulys.hotel@takas.lt
Turnė
Rūdės 9
Tel: 1 500 150
Fax: 1 429 238
turne.hotel@takas.lt

Camping in Lithuania

It is not permitted to camp in the wild, on the coastal dunes and nature reserves near to Vilnius but this is allowed in the countryside. However, you will be pitching a tent at your own risk. A selection of official campsites is listed below.

• **Rukainiai**
Rytų Kempingas
(off the highway to Minsk)
Tel: 651 195
Located 15 miles (25 km) east of Vilnius, Rukainiai comprises small summer lodgings for three to four people, with communal showers and kitchens. Tents can be pitched on this riverside campsite with a sauna and video-café. **$**

• **Trakai**
Totoriškės
Kempingas Slėnyje
Tel: 38 51 387
There is a campsite on the northern shore of Lake Galvė around 2 miles (4 km) from Trakai on the road to Vievis. **$**

Where to Eat

Food in the Baltics

Since independence the restaurant and bar scene across the Baltic states has improved markedly, with an average of one new establishment opening every month in each of the capital cities. It is now possible to feast on French haute cuisine, sample Japanese sushi or Armenian *shashlik* and wolf down vegetarian cuisine in any of the three Baltic states. Some of the bars and clubs here are so funky that they would stand out in Paris, London or New York. Service has considerably improved and most waiting staff speak English – if they don't speak English, the menu will certainly be in either English, German, French or Russian. The best hotels have imported top international chefs, serving first-class international food.

Most restaurants accept Visa and Mastercard unless otherwise noted. As there is not enough room here to give a full list of restaurants, we have tried to recommend the most notable establishements, with the stress on local cuisine.

Eating out in Estonia

Traditionally, the Estonians have always been viewed as country people with little tradition of dining out. Tables at home have always been amply supplied with produce from the fields, forests and sea. Herring, potatoes and sour cream are basic staples, supplemented by vegetables and fruit. Townsfolk maintain summer cottages in the country with adjacent plots of land that provide food for the winter larder. Berries are boiled into jams, mushrooms are sealed in brine and various herbs and grasses are dried for use later in the year.

TALLINN

Tallinn boasts numerous top-class international restaurants and countless ethnic eating options. However, traditional Estonian restaurants are scarce, perhaps because of the slightly bland local cuisine. All the luxury hotels have their own restaurants, though these are often very expensive.

Restaurants

ESTONIAN FOOD

The most common dishes in Tallinn seem to be *beseljanka* (thick soup) and *schnitzel*, but neither of these are originally Estonian cuisine. True Estonian favourites are *sült* (jellied meat), *mulgikapsas* (fatty sauerkraut), rollmops (herring rolls) and *kama* (a mixture of ground cereals). Believe it or not, Chinese food is easier to find in Tallinn than traditional Estonian fare.

Tallinna Eesti Maja
Lauteri 1
Tel: 645 5252/699 2100
Fax: 699 2101
Open daily 11am–11pm
Tallinn's Estonian House is the place to try real Estonian food: try *sült*, *mulgikapsas* and *kama*. Eating here is an experience that should not be missed. **$$**
Vanaema Juures
Rataskaevu 10/12
Tel: 626 9080
Fax: 626 9099

Price Guide: Estonia

These ranges are for a starter, main dish and dessert for one person and should be taken as a guide only:
$$$$ = above 300EEK
$$$ = 100–300EEK
$$ = 50–100EEK
$ = below 50EEK per head.
Drinks will double the bill.

Price Guide: Estonia

These ranges are for a starter, main dish and dessert for one person and should be taken as a guide only:
$$$$ = above 300EEK
$$$ = 100–300EEK
$$ = 50–100EEK
$ = below 50EEK per head.
Drinks will double the bill.

vanaema.juures@mail.ee
Open Monday–Saturday
noon–10pm, Sunday noon–6pm
This place offers Estonian home cooking at its best. *Mulgikapsas* and wild boar are dished up in a small cosy cellar restaurant. Service is friendly and attentive. The place is very popular, so reservations are essential. **$$**

INTERNATIONAL

Eeslitall
Dunkri 4/6
Tel: 631 3755
Fax: 631 3210
Open Monday–Thursday
11am–midnight, Friday and
Saturday 10am–1am, Sunday
10am–midnight
In a central location just off the Town Hall Square, the "Donkey's Stable" has been one of Tallinn's most popular restaurants since the early 1990s. The restaurant upstairs is rather upmarket and relatively expensive (for Estonia) but lighter, less expensive meals are available in the cellar. The food is good and the management occasionally bring in foreign cooks to add a little ethnic diversity to the menu. **$$**

Carina
Pirita tee 26e
Tel: 641 9175
Fax: 641 9176
Open daily noon–midnight
The restaurant on the coast road out to Pirita offers pleasant views of the sea. This establishment is a 1-mile (3-km) walk from the town centre. Alternatively you could catch bus 1, 8 or 34. **$$$**

Egoist
Vene 33
Tel: 646 4052
fax: 646 4025
egoist@gourmet.ee
Open Monday–Saturday
noon–midnight
An exquisite meal in Egoist, Tallinn's premier gourmet restaurant, will set you back at least 480EEK excluding drinks. The owner will help you choose from his extensive collection of 1000 wines. Very pricey. **$$$$**

Gloria
Müürivahe 2
Tel: 644 6950
Fax: 646 6180
gloria@gourmet.ee
Open daily noon–midnight
Run by the same man who owns Egoist, Gloria has played host to a quirky range of celebrities, from currency speculator George Soros to Pope John Paul II. **$$$$**

Gnoom
Viru 2
Tel: 644 2488/644 1073
Fax: 644 0947
Open Sunday–Thursday 11am–
11pm, Friday and Saturday
11am–1am
Gnoom is a beautiful 16th-century townhouse offering a choice of four different dining rooms. The Linnakodanike cellar in the basement offers light fare. **$$**

Karl Friedrich
Raekoja plats 5
Tel: 627 2413
Fax: 627 2411
Open daily 10am–1am
Fine dining in Tallinn's Town Hall Square. Karl Friedrich concocts international classics that can be also sampled on the terrace. Try the cellar bar for a casual pint. **$$$**

Roosikrantsi
Roosikrantsi 1/Vabaduse väljak 7
Tel: 640 4499/640 4487
Fax: 644 6536
Open weekdays 8am–midnight and weekends noon–midnight
A Belgian chef dishes up French and international classics including *steak au poivre, coq au vin* and *carpaccio*. The restaurant is particularly popular with foreign businessmen. **$$$**

Indian
Maharaja
Raekoja plats 13
Tel: 644 4367
Fax: 631 3057
Open daily noon–11pm
The Maharaja enjoys a prime location on Town Hall Square and offers very formal service, excellent spicy treats from the subcontinent and stiff prices. **$$$**

Italian
Controvento
Vene 12/Katariina käik
Tel: 644 0470
Fax: 631 3520
Open daily noon–11pm; café open Sunday–Thursday 11am–midnight, Friday–Saturday 11am–1am
One of the best Italian restaurants in Estonia if not in the Baltics, this establishment is run by an Italian and has been a winner ever since it opened. The atmosphere in this 15th-century townhouse situated next to the cloister is unbeatable, as are the Italian pasta and meat dishes. Alternatively, try the more relaxed café on the ground floor. The prices are very high but worth every penny. **$$$$**

Fast Food
There are several McDonalds in and around Tallinn, the most central being on on Viru 24. For something different try the Finnish-run Carrols or Hesburger outlets or the local Chick-King. Kloostri Toidutare on Kloostri 6 in Pirita serves *hot dogi* the Estonian way. For a pizza on the run go for the thin-crust "Peetri Pizza" or the thick American deep-dish variety at Pizza Americana.

Cafés
In summer the Town Hall Square becomes a huge terraced outdoor café. In the colder seasons go for a quick bite at the Café Anglais, the Millennium on Raekoja plats or any of the following:
Maiasmokk
Pikk 16
Tel: 646 4079
Open Monday–Saturday 8am–6pm, Sunday 10am–6pm
Tallinn's oldest coffee-house was in

existence during the First Independence and probably looked no different then than it does now. Maiasmokk also has an affordable restaurant upstairs.

Neitsitorn
Lühike jalg 9a
Tel: 644 0896
Open daily 11am–10pm
The café on four floors in the fortified Neitsitorn tower has been a tourist favourite for years. Care has been taken to keep the interior in character with the building, although this means that there is very little light on the lower floors. During the colder months mulled wine is served in the cellar.

Wiiralt
Vabaduse väljak 8
Open daily 9am–8pm
Popular meeting place with good coffee and great pastries.

Drinking in Estonia

In the past Estonians have tended to do their drinking at home, with a few friends and more than a few bottles of vodka. The proliferation of vodka *(viin)* is a result of Russification. The true national drink of Estonia is beer *(õlu)*. In rural areas beer drinking is still very much a part of daily life and cloudy, thick ales with sediment are often brewed at home. In certain areas, notably the islands, vast consumption of beer has led to the ruin of many farmsteads, many men have literally drunk themselves to early deaths.

Locally produced beers such as *Saku* are served on tap in most bars and cafés throughout the country. The latest concoction is *Saku* ice beer.

Avenüü
Suur-Karja 10
Tel: 631 4602
Open 24 hours
True to its name, Tallinn's all-night bar is decked out like an avenue. This is the only decent place to hang-out when you arrive by bus at 6 o'clock in the morning.

Embassy/Nimeta Baar
Suur-Karja 4/6
Tel: 631 3257
Open Monday–Thursday 11am–2am, Fri, Saturday 11am–4am
"The Pub with No Name" is now called Embassy, probably because of its status as the favourite ex-pat hang-out. The Scottish owner has also opened the Nimega Baar and The Pub with a Name – this last drinking hole is located just a couple of houses down the street from its nameless equivalent, at Suur-Karja 13 and offers dancing until the wee hours of the morning.

George Browne's
Harju 6
Tel: 631 0512
Open daily 11am–2am
Tallinn's first and largest Irish pub, shipped in lock, stock and barrels from Dublin. A quiet lounge with food upstairs.

Tipping

Estonia: Service is included on most bills. However, if you feel especially pleased with the service you have received, leaving a tip will not offend.
Latvia: The Soviet tradition was simply to round up the sum of the bill and this forms the basis of tipping in restaurants. Local porters and taxi drivers also expect tips.
Lithuania: Tipping is becoming increasingly standard practice. In restaurants a tip of one Litas is an ideal amount.

Hell Hunt
Pikk 39
Tel: 631 3723
Open Monday–Thursday 11am–1am, Friday–Saturday 11am–3am
Hell Hunt is a lively local variant on the Irish-pub theme with live folk music. The bar has recently lost some of its cult status.

Kloostri Ait
Vene 14
Tel: 644 6887
Open daily 11am–midnight
The Cloister Garden is a quiet and civilised bar, where you can sip beer or mulled wine around the huge old fireplace.

Vodka

The Baltics use the metric system and Vodka is often ordered in grams – 50g equates to a single measure, 100g is a double etc.

Molly Malone's
Mündi 2
Tel: 631 3016
Open daily 10am–2am
Situated in a prime location overlooking Town Hall Square, Molly Malone's is a favourite with expats and tourists. Football matches are shown on a large screen here.

Tehas N°43
Pikk 43
Tel: 646 4115
Open daily 11am–11pm
The brewery has been revived and serves the locally produced Albert le Coq beer that was brewed on the premises at the beginning of the 20th century. Live bands and billiards on two floors.

Von Krahli Theatre Baar
Rataskaevu 10/12
Tel: 626 9096
Open Sunday–Thursday noon–1am; Friday–Saturday noon–3am
Atmospheric bar with a diverse clientele. Live music most nights.

Eating out in Latvia

Latvian traditional meals are usually mild with a strong emphasis on the use of dairy produce – local cheese, cheese with cumin seeds and curdled milk. Potatoes are usually served as a separate dish and are cooked in a variety of ways. Latvia is famous for its many types of bread, the sweet-and-sour variety being the most popular. If you stay here you should take the time to taste some national Latvian dishes. These include pearl-barley soup with dried mushrooms, fried ham and tomatoes, grey peas with smoked pork and black bread layered with whipped cream. If you have something to celebrate, why not try *pīrãgi* – little croissants with bacon and onions.

RIGA

Riga is a food haven with almost every type of ethnic cuisine from American to Russian and Ukrainian represented. There are excellent (and expensive) upmarket restaurants in the Hotel de Rome, Konventa Sēta, the Metropole Hotel and the Park Hotel Rīdzene.

Latvian
Excellent Latvian home-cooking is served in a number of Lido establishments, notably at Alus Sēta, Dzirnavas, Lido atpūtas centrs, Staburags or Vērmanītis (further details are given below). These places have made country cooking their trademark.
Alus Sēta
Tirgoņu 6
Tel: 722 2431
Open daily 11am–1am
Latvian home-cooking in a self-service cafeteria-style establishement. Help yourself to the grey peas and ribs that are sizzled in front of you. Fine views of Dome square from the seats outside. **$**
Dzirnavas
Dzirnavu 76
Tel: 728 6204
Open 8am–11pm
Treat yourself to a selection of Latvian goodies at the buffet located within the Mill. **$**
Kalanda
Jāņa 8/10
Tel: 722 9775
Open daily 11am–midnight
Latvian restaurant with bags of style. Try the bulls' balls if you are feeling brave. **$$**
Lido atpūtas centrs
Krasta 76
Tel: 781 2187
Open daily 10am–11pm
This vast food court on three levels serves only Latvian fare. The Lido leisure centre, slightly out of town, is packed to the rafters on weekends with Latvian families out for a cheap and hearty meal. Beer is brewed on the premises. Credit cards are not accepted. **$**
Lielais Kamielis
Vecpilsētas 3

Price Guide: Latvia
These ranges are for a starter, main dish and dessert for one person and should be taken as a guide only:
$$$ = over 20 Lats
$$ = 10–20 Lats
$ = less than 10 Lats
Drinks will double the bill.

Tel: 721 2614
Open noon–11pm
Situated in an elegant 17th-century cellar restaurant, the "Big Camel" offers authentic Latvian fare. **$$**
Senā Rīga
Aspazijas bulv. 22
Tel: 721 6869
Open noon–midnight
Set in the cellar of the Riga Hotel this kitschy traditional restaurant is decked out with log cabins, representing the different Latvian regions. A band often performs in the unusual setting of a reconstructed merchant boat. **$**
Staburags
Čaka 55
Tel: 299 787
Open noon–1am
This is the best place for hearty Latvian fodder served in oversized portions. Get a big party together and go for the roast pig. **$$**
Vērmanītis
Elizabetes 65
Tel: 728 6289
Open 8am–11pm
Set next to Vermanes park, this Lido restaurant offers Latvian and international cuisine in a wonderful rustic atmosphere. **$$**

International
Charlestons
Blaumaņa 38/40
Tel: 777 0573/777 0572
Fax: 777 0571
charlestons@zl.lv
www.charlestons.lv
Open noon–midnight
Charlestons is a classy and trendy – albeit expensive – restaurant with a beautiful outside terrace. It's popular, so reservations are essential. **$$**

Melnie mūki
Jāņa sēta 1.
Tel: 721 5006.
Open noon–2am
This establishment, which is situated in the heart of the old town, has quickly become Riga's most popular modestly priced restaurant. **$$**
Samsons
Mārstaļu 4
Tel: 722 9572
Open noon–midnight
The designer furniture makes this restaurant one of the most elegant places to dine in Riga. Classy and pricey international delights. **$$$**
Symposium
Dzirnavu 84/I
Tel: 724 2545
Fax: 724 2546
www.zagars.lv
Open noon–midnight
The first restaurant of Opera director Andrējs Žagars has a warm Mediterranean feel about it and is one of the best dining options in Riga. Also check out the Jaunais Restorāns, Žagars' New Restaurant around the corner. **$$$**
Vincents
Elizabetes 19
Tel: 733 2634/733 2830
ritins@mbox.riga.lv
www.vincents.lv
Open daily 11am–midnight
Renowned chef Martinš Ritinš has cooked up culinary delights for international visitors such as cellist Mstislav Rostropovitch and fashion designer Paco Rabanne. Vincents is pricey but worth it. **$$$**

Fast Food
Riga was the first Baltic capital to see McDonalds open in the very heart of the city. The chain is well established around town and there are a number of cheap copycats. For local fast food try the Latvian pīrāgi at Pīrāgi on Kr. Barona 14 (open daily 9am–10pm). Russian-style meat dumplings can be had at Pelmeņi XL. Kaļķu 7 (open daily 9am–4am). For cheap pancakes of all sorts look no further than Šefpavārs Vilhelms on Šķūņu 6 open daily 9am–10pm. Subs are assembled at Subway, Kaļķu 10,

which is open daily 9.45am–11pm. The best pizza in town is made at Pizza Lulū, Ģertrūdes 27. Tel: 800 5858 800 LU LU, www.lulu.lv. (open 8am–midnight). Run by two Latvian-Canadians, the company have five outlets throughout town and can deliver to your hotel room.

Cafés
During the summer months café tables spill out onto Dome Square (Doma laukums). In winter, however, you can warm up and enjoy the view of the square from **Možums** on Šķūņu 19 (open daily, 9am–1am). Other cafés and fun spots include:

Ai Karamba!
Pulkveža Brieža 2
Tel: 733 4672
aikaramba@aikaramba.lv
www.aikaramba.com
Open 8am–midnight
An authentic American diner in the Jugendstil quarter.

A. Suns
Elizabetes 83/85
Tel: 728 8418
Open 8am–1am, Thursday–Friday 8am–3am, Saturday 11am–3am, Sunday 11am–1am
Funky arty hangout located in a former workshop with a small cinema upstairs.

Osiris
Kr. Barona 31
Tel: 724 3002
Open weekdays 8am–midnight and weekends 10am–midnight
Osiris is the place to go for a calm breakfast or a coffee and a chat in uptown Riga.

Pūt
Jaun 18/22
Tel: 721 2291
Open noon–midnight
Café/bar/restaurant just off Dome square. The upstairs is a fancy restaurant, while you can get cheap burgers, pasta and nachos downstairs or in the courtyard.

Drinking in Latvia
Like its neighbours, Latvia has delicious beers (alus). Local vodka is also good. The most distinctive Latvian drink is Riga Black Balsam, (melnais balzāms), a liqueur made

of herbs and reminiscent of cough medicine. Note: don't drink the tap water in Riga.

Cita Opera
Raiņa bulv. 21
Tel: 722 0770
Open noon–5am.
The "other opera" is a dimly lit cellar bar where the young dance the night away. Admission costs between 3–5Ls

Dickens
Grēcinieku 11
Tel: 721 3087
Open Sunday–Thursday 11am–1am, Friday–Saturday 11am–2am
This plush English pub is popular among Riga's expatriate boozers.

Paddy Whelan's
Grēcinieku 4
Tel: 721 0249
Open Sunday–Thursday 10am–12am, Friday–Saturday 10am–2am
Riga's first Irish pub is still popular with crowds of young Latvians in search of a cheap drink. The upstairs Roisin Dubh (Black Rose) is calmer, more sedate and slightly more expensive.

Pulkvedim Neviens Neraksta
Peldu 26/28
Tel: 721 3886
Open daily noon–3am, Friday–Saturday noon–5am
Riga's hippest restaurant/bar/club in the old town is named after Gabriel Garcia Marquez's novel *Nobody writes to the Colonel* and draws an artsy, intellectual crowd. An admission fee of between 1 and 2 Lats is charged.

Slepenais Eksperiments
Šķūņu 15
(entrance from Amatu iela)
Tel: 722 7917
Open noon–5am
The Secret Experiment, with its high-tech stainless-steel interior, is located in the depth of the old town. By day this place is an affordable restaurant and by night it's a fashionable nightclub.

Eating out in Lithuania
Lithuanian cuisine, which is mainly based on potatoes, is rich and rather fatty. The national dish, cepelinai zeppelins (mashed potato

rolls filled with meat and dripping in a buttery bacon sauce), is quite a mouthful. Most menus are written in Lithuanian, Russian, English, German or French.

VILNIUS

Vilnius' restaurants have vastly improved in recent years. Here, you can find anything from authentic Japanese to Indian and vegetarian restaurants. The top hotels such as the SAS-Radisson Astorija, the Šarūnas, the Shakespeare and the Stikliai all have excellent international restaurants. Interestingly, Vilnius has seen a revival of traditional Lithuanian home-cooking recently and many restaurants offer traditional Lithuanian dishes.

Lithuanian
Amatininkų Užeiga
Didžioji 19/2
Tel: 617 968
Open weekdays 8am–5am, weekends 11am–5am
This place offers simple, hearty Lithuanian fare in a basement situated in the old town. In summer there is outside seating in the town hall square. **$$/$$$**

Lokys
Stiklių 8/10
Tel: 629 046
Open daily noon–midnight
This establishment, set in a gothic cellar, has been around for years and specialises in game, ranging from deer to wild boar. **$$$**

Neringa
Gedimino pr. 23
Tel: 681 958
Open daily 8am–11pm

Price Guide: Lithuania

These ranges are for a starter, main dish and dessert for one person and should be taken as a guide only:
$$$ = over 40 Litas
$$ = 25–40 Litas
$ = under 20 Litas
Drinks will double the bill.

This 1960s' literary cafe still draws in the Lithuanian intellectual crowd, if only for its retro interior. Inexpensive but tasty food. **$$/$$$**

Ritos Smuklė
Žirmūnų 68
Tel: 770 786
smukle@rita.lt
www.rita.lt
Open daily 10am–midnight
Arguably Lithuania's best traditional restaurant. Here you can see how many dishes can be made from pork and potatoes. Wash it all down with Lithuanian *gira*, a fermented drink made from black bread, before dancing to Lithuanian folk music. The place is a drive out of town but worth it. Reserve. **$$/$$$**

Stiklių Aludė
Gaono 7
Tel: 624 501
Open daily noon–midnight
Lithuanian food served in raucous style. The beer bar serves beer and a wide selection of potato dishes. Loud and lively Lithuanian folk music while you dine. **$$$**

Stiklių Bočiai
Šv. Ignoto 4/3
Tel: 621 983
Open daily 11am–11pm
Run by the same team who own the Aludė. The grandiose hall of this former monastery refectory has been transformed into an authentic Lithuanian country tavern. Waiting staff wear traditional dress. **$$$**

Vandens malunas
Verkių 100
Tel: 711 666
Open daily 11.30am–midnight
Traditional Lithuania comes to life in this watermill on the river situated several kilometres out of town. Definitely worth the trip. **$$/$$$**

Zemaičių Smuklė
Vokiečių 24
Tel: 616 573
Open Wednesday–Monday 11am–midnight, Tuesday 1pm–midnight
This cellar tavern is notable for its metre-long sausages. **$$$**

International
Freskos
Didžioji 31
Tel: 618 133

These ranges are for a starter, main dish and dessert for one person and should be taken as a guide only:
$$$ = over 40 Litas
$$ = 25–40 Litas
$ = under 20 Litas
Drinks will double the bill.

www.freskos.lt
Open daily 11am–midnight
Situated under the old town hall, Freskos is a relaxed restaurant with a warm and friendly atmosphere and a good menu. Try any of their delicious salads. **$$$**

Ritos Sleptuvė
Goštauto 8
Tel: 626 117
sleptuve@rita.lt
www.rita.lt
Open Monday–Thursday 7.30am–2am, Friday–Saturday 7.30am–4am
Excellent American/Italian/Mexican fare and a fantastic interior décor. One of the liveliest places in the whole of Lithuania. **$$$**

Cafés
Mano Kavinė
Bokšto 7
Open daily 10am–11pm
"My Café", hidden in the old town, is a small and cosy establishment with excellent coffee. Light dishes are served at lunchtime.

Poniu Laime
Gedimino pr. 31
Tel: 625 687.
Open Monday–Saturday 11am–10pm, Sunday 11am–6pm
Enjoy coffee and cakes and an excellent view of Vilnius' main artery.

Užpio Kavinė
Užpio 2
Open daily 9am–11pm
Bohemian café in the arty Užpis district. In summer, you can dine outside under the trees which overlooking the Vinele River.

Drinking in Lithuania

Lithuania has some excellent beers. Look out for Kalnapilis, Utena and the unfiltered Biržai beer, which is served on tap in some bars.

Bix
Etmonų 6
Tel: 627 791
Open daily 11am–5am
A fun and funky bar on three floors brought to you by the Lithuanian rock band of the same name.

Prie Parlamento
Gedimino pr. 46
Tel: 621 606
crew@prieparlamento.lt
www.prieparlamento.lt
Open Monday–Thursday 8am–2am, Friday 8am–4am, Saturday 10am–4am, Sun 10am–2am
Next to Lithuania's parliament, this is a favourite with expats. There is a calm café on the ground floor and a more sedate café/bar on the second floor. In the basement, things are a little different. There is a lively nightclub in the cellar called *Ministerija*, which heaves until the small hours. For a quiet summer brunch, sit on the small balcony overlooking the street.

The P.U.B.
Dominikonų 9
Tel: 618 393
www.pub.lt
Open daily 11am–2am
Run by the same team who own Prie Parlamento, the Prie Universiteto Baras (The Bar near the University) is the most popular student hangout in town. Inexpensive, good food in an unbeatable atmosphere. Live bands often perform here.

Fast Food
McDonalds has transferred its Baltic headquarters to Lithuania, with outlets in every major town. In Vilnius, the opening of their drive-in went hand in hand with a thorough clean-up of the entire train station area. For inexpensive local fast food try Greitai, Gedimino pr. 10/1 (open weekdays 7am–10pm, weekends 10am–10pm) for Lithuanian fast food on the run, or go to Šavarma, at Aušros Vartų 8 (open daily 10am–midnight). Here you can snack on bread stuffed with humus, shavarma or falafel. For cheap pizza look out for the Čili outlets.

Attractions

TALLINN

Art Galleries

Information on current exhibitions can be found in the magazines *Tallinn In Your Pocket* and *Tallinn This Week*. Most galleries also extensively promote their exhibitions with posters around the town centre.

Draakoni
Pikk 18
Open Tuesday–Friday 11am–6pm, Saturday 11am–4pm. Print and graphic work by contemporary Estonian artists. Exhibitions change each month.

Kristjan Raud Museum
Raua 8
Nõmme
Tel: 670 0023
Fax: 442 094
Open Wednesday–Sunday 11am–6pm. The work of Kristjan Raud plus temporary exhibitions.

Linnagalerii
City Gallery
Harju 13
Tel: 644 2818
Fax: 644 8747. Open Wednesday–Monday noon–6pm.

Sammas
Vabaduse väljak 6
Tel/fax: 631 4553.
Open Wednesday–Sunday noon–6pm. Contemporary art shows.

Tallinna Kunstihoone
(Tallinn Art Hall)
Vabaduse väljak 8
Tel: 644 2818
Open Wednesday–Sunday noon–6pm State exhibition gallery.

Vaal
Väike-Karja 12
Tel: 627 0161
Fax: 627 0160

Open Tuesday–Friday 11am–6pm, Saturday 11am–4pm. Tallinn's most prestigious gallery.

Museums

The admission price to most museums is still pretty inexpensive and, irrespective of the collection, it's often worth paying this fee just to look inside the building. Several of Tallinn's main museums are loacted in beautifully preserved medieval guild houses, complete with oak galleries and stairs.

The Applied Arts Museum is in a renovated warehouse with large, arched halls, and Kiek in de Kök and the Maritime Museum are both housed in restored medieval towers. The view from the upper floors of Kiek in de Kök is impressive, as is the panorama from the roof of the Maritime Museum, which has been transformed into a viewing platform. This is one of the few places from where you can appreciate Tallinn as a coastal town, and if you have a camera it is well worth taking some pictures here. Another fine museum

Tallinn's Top Areas

The Old Town: Tallinn's Old Town *(vanalinn)* is home to one of the best-preserved collections of medieval buildings in Europe. The Old Town is enclosed by a solid 16th-century city wall, with eight gates and 48 towers. Much of the wall remains and many of the towers now house cafés, museums and galleries. Within the Old Town the cobbled streets wind around irregularly shaped buildings, which date mainly from the 15th and 16th centuries. Though individual buildings may be of particular architectural or historical merit, the true beauty is in the area as a whole.

Toompea: This is the upper part of the Old Town, which is reached by the cobbled incline of Pikk jalg or the steps of Lühike jalg. It is the ancient seat of government, the site where fortifications were first built in the 13th century to strengthen the Danes' hold on their newly conquered territory. Toompea still retains an air of detachment – despite their narrowness, its streets are much less intimate than those in the lower town and the buildings are more austere. The garish colours of the Alexander Nevsky cathedral (19th century) also seem to be something of an intrusion.

Pirita: Situated beside the mouth of the Pirita river are the skeletal remains of the Convent of St Bridget. They have stood in this ruinous state since the convent's destruction during the 16th-century Livonian wars. The ruins serve as a venue for occasional open-air concerts and performances. The walk from town to the ruins, along the sea front, is a pleasant one leading past Kadriorg Park, the Song Festival ground and the Maarjamäe Palace museum. Alternatively take a 1, 5, 8 or 34 bus from Narva mnt.

for open-air photography is the Rocca al Mare museum. Scattered through woodland beside the sea are exact replicas of rural buildings from the 18th–19th centuries; quite a few interiors have also been impressively recreated.

Adamson-Erik Museum
Lühike jalg 3
Tel: 644 5838
Fax: 644 2094
Open Wednesday-Sunday 11am–6pm. Paintings and applied art.

Applied Arts Museum
Tarbekunstimuuseum
Lai 17
Tel: 641 1927
Fax: 641 1937
Open Wednesday–Sunday 11am–6pm.

Health Museum
(Tervishoiumuuseum)
Lai 28/30
Tel: 641 1730
Fax: 641 1732
Open Tuesday–Saturday 11am–6pm

Historical Museum
(Ajaloomuuseum)
Pikk 17
Tel: 641 1630
Fax: 443 446

Parks in Tallinn

On a summer's day from the viewing platforms on Toompea, Tallinn appears as a loose collection of buildings scattered throughout a dense and verdant forest. Only the concrete masses of the Soviet suburbs give any real impression of urbanisation. The Old Town is surrounded by a green belt of parks laid out over what were once medieval bastions and moats. These green spaces bear evocative names: Hirvepark (Deer Park), Tornide väljak (Towers Place) and Rannavärava mägi (Coast Gate Hill). Walking through these parks enables visitors to imagine what the original fortress at Toompea was like.

The largest of Tallinn's parks is Kadriorg, which was created in 1718 under the instructions of Peter the Great. The park was designed by an Italian architect, Niccolo Michetti, and its centrepiece is a baroque palace. Pathways meander through the trees, connecting a lake, tennis courts, an ice rink and numerous statues and monuments. The park lies at the terminus of trams 1 and 3.

Beyond Kadriorg, interrupted only by the four lanes of Narva mnt, the parkland continues. Set into the slope of a hill, so as to form a natural amphitheatre, is the enormous concrete shell of the Song Festival Ground. Every five years a large proportion of the populace gather here, together with massed choirs, in a celebration of Estonia.

The Exhibition Grounds are visible further along the coast. Throughout the year, the halls here are filled with trade fairs, art sales, car shows and all manner of other displays and exhibitions. A short ride on buses 1, 5, 8, 34 or 38 leads to the tranquil Woodland cemetery Metsakalmistu, which is the resting place of a great number of famous Estonians.

Open Thursday–Tuesday 11am–6pm. Displays chart the early history of Estonia.

Kiek in de Kök
Komandandi tee 1
Tel: 644 6686
Open Tuesday–Friday 10.30am–5.30pm, weekends 11am–4.30pm
Documents the history of Tallinn's fortifications. Photographic shows.

Maritime Museum
Meremuuseum
Pikk 70
Tel: 641 1412
Fax: 641 1414
Open Wednesday–Sunday 10am–6pm.

Maarjamäe Palace
Maarjamäe Loss
Pirita tee 56
Tel: 237 071
Open Wednesday–Sunday 11am–5.30pm. Neo-gothic, 19th-century summer residence, now a museum of 20th-century Estonian history. Buses 1, 4, 8, 12, 34 or 38.

Natural History Museum,
(Loodusmuuseum)
Lai 29
Tel: 641 1739
Fax: 641 1738
Open Wednesday–Sunday 11am–6pm.

Rocca al Mare Open-air Museum
(Vabaõhumuuseum)
Vabaõhumuuseumi tee 12
Tel: 654 9117
Fax: 654 9127
Open daily 10am–8pm. In winter 10am–4pm. Dancing and folk displays on Sunday mornings. Located around 6 miles (10 km) west from the centre of town. Take bus No 21.

State Art Museum
Kiriku plats 1
Tel: 644 1478
Fax: 644 2094
muuseum@ekm.estnet.ee
Open Wednesday–Sunday, 11am–6pm.

Theatre and Music Museum
(Teatri- ja muusikamuuseum)
Müürivahe 12
Tel/fax: 644 2132
Open Wednesday–Sunday 10am–5.30pm.

TARTU

Tourist Attractions

Stately and faded, the town of Tartu is dominated by classic architecture; notable, exceptions however, include the Town Hall (1789) and the University Building (1809). Much of medieval Tartu was destroyed either in the Great Fire of 1775 or by the Nazis during World War II. Still standing are the 14th-century Jaani Church, which features some unique terracotta figures, and the outer structure of the Cathedral of Tartu Castle, which is now home to the University History Museum. A great number of Tartu's attractions, including the Botanical Gardens (1803) and the Observatory, are now connected in some way to the town's university.

Museums

K.E. von Bauer Museum
Veski 4
Tel: 07 421 514
Open weekdays 9am–4pm.

Estonian National Museum
Kuperjanovi 9
Tel: 07 421 311/422 040
Open Wednesday–Sunday 11am–6pm.

F.R. Kreutzwaldi Literary Museum
Vanemuise 42
Tel: 07 430 053
Open weekdays 9am–5pm.

Oskar Luts Museum
Riia 37
Tel: 07 428 060
Open Wednesday–Saturday 11am–5pm, Sunday 1pm–5pm.

Tartu Town Museum
Oru 2
Tel: 07 422 022
Open Wednesday–Sunday 11am–6pm.

Tartu University Art Museum
Ülikooli 18
Tel: 07 375 677
Open Wednesday–Sunday 11am–5pm.

Tartu University History Museum
Toomemägi
Tel: 07 375 674
www.ut.ee/REAM
Open Wednesday–Sunday 11am–5pm.

Zoology Museum
Vanemuise 26
Tel: 07 375 833
Open Wednesday–Sunday
11am–4pm.

National Parks
Lahemaa National Park
Palmse
Tel: 32 34 196
ekal@estpak.ee
Soomaa National Park
Viljandi, Paala 4
Tel: 43 44 153
soomaa@vil.ee
Karula National Park
Ähijärve, Antsla
Tel: 78 52 456
pille@karula.envir.ee
Western Estonian Biosphere Reserve
Hiiumaa, Vabriku 1
Tel: 46 96 276

Latvia

RIGA

Old Riga is rich in medieval, Renaissance and late 19th-century architecture. It is especially beautiful along Elizabetes Street, between Kr. Valdemāra Street and the riverfront, and along the side streets around L. Antonijas, Alberta and Rūpniecības. In many parts of the city, entire neighbourhoods of old wooden houses built in the late 19th century are still standing. Although many of these dwellings are in a state of disrepair, they exude charm and character. Quirky shops can also be found along many of these streets. Although Riga is safe compared to Western cities, be careful, especially at night.

List of Attractions

Freedom Monument
Brīvības piemineklis
(On the corner of Raiņa bulv. and Brīvības bulv.)
Built between 1931 and 1935, this monument was designed by one of Latvia's greatest sculptors, Kārlis Zāle. To Latvians, it symbolises the country's struggle for freedom under centuries of occupation.

Occupation Museum of Latvia
(Okupacijas muzejs)
Strēlnieku laukums 1
Tel: 721 2715
Fax: 722 9255
omf@latnet.lv
Open daily 11am–5pm. Free admission. Housed in what was once the Soviet Museum of the Latvian Riflemen, the permanent exhibition documents the Soviet and Nazi occupations of Latvia from the signing of the Hitler-Stalin pact in 1939 to the independence struggle in 1991.

House of Blackheads
Ratslaukums 7
Tel: 721 0269
Open Tuesday–Sunday 10am–5pm. Adjacent to the Occupation Museum is this Guild House, originally built in 1344. The House was destroyed during World War II and its ruins were levelled in 1948. It was reconstructed in 1999.

National Opera
(Nacionālā Opera)
Aspazijas bulv. 3
Tel: 722 5803/8496
Fax: 722 8240
mail@opera.lv
www.opera.lv
This stately 19th-century building has been renovated, thanks to a large grant from Western Latvians.

Warehouses
(Ventspils iela, Alksnāja and Vecpilsētas iela)
Built in the 17th century, these buildings are a reminder of Riga's history as a city of trade.

Reuthern's House
Reiterna nams
Mārstaļu 17
Erected in 1685, this building, which is also known as the Journalists' House, is a fine example of baroque architecture. It now houses an exhibition hall.

Dunnerstern's House
(Dunnersterna nams)
Mārstaļu 21
This baroque building dates from 1696 and was constructed by Reuthern's son-in-law. It is currently undergoing renovation work.

St George's Church
Jura baznīca
Skārņu 10/16

Constructed in 1208, St George's Church is the oldest stone building in Riga. The church has been rebuilt several times, and is now home to the **Museum of Decorative and Applied Arts** (Dekoratīvās mākslas muzejs). Tel: 722 9736/722 7833. Open Tuesday–Sunday 11am–5pm.
St Peter's Church (Pēterbaznīca)
Skārņu 19
Open Tuesday–Sunday 10am–5.15pm. Dating from the 13th century, this church features elements of Gothic, Romanesque and baroque architecture. Until the steeple burned down in 1941 during the advance of the Germans and retreat of the Russians, it was considered the highest wooden edifice in the world. Visitors can take the elevator up to the first and second floors for a wonderful bird's eye view of the city. Services are held on Sunday at 1pm.
St John's Church and Court
(Jāņa baznīca and Jāņa sēta)
Skārņu 24
Tel: 722 4028/722 5171
Open every day 11am–6pm. This 13th-century church has suffered from storms and fires and has been rebuilt many times. It is now a working church again.
The Courtyard (Jāņa sēta)
Located next to St John's, this courtyard is flanked on one side by a restored fragment of the old fortification wall that surrounded the city in the 13th century. Street musicians sometimes play here.
The Big and Small Guilds (Lielā un mazā gilde): neighbouring buildings on Amatu 6 and 5.
The Leilā gilde now houses the Philharmonic Concert Hall, and the Mazā gilde can be rented for public and private events.
The Dome Cathedral
(Doma katedrāle)
Doma laukums
Tel: 721 3213
Open Wednesday–Friday 1–6pm, Tuesday 11am–6pm, Saturday 10am–2pm. Constructed in 1211, this building unites elements of Gothic, Romanesque and baroque architecture and has been rebuilt several times over the years. The organ in the cathedral ranks among

the best in the world, and concerts are still held here. The **Museum of the History of Riga and Navigation** adjoins the cathedral, in the quarters of the old monastery.

Riga Castle
(Rīgas pils)
Pils laukums 3
Dating from the 14th century, this castle once housed the German Order of the Brethren of the Sword. The President of Latvia resides in the northern wing. The southern wing houses two museums, the **Museum of the History of Latvia**, (Latvijas Vēstures Muzejs), tel: 722 1357 (open Wednesday–Sunday 11am–5pm) and the **Museum of Foreign Art**, tel: 722 6467 (open Tuesday–Sunday 11am–5pm).

The Three Brothers medieval houses (Trīs brāļi)
Mazā pils 17, 19 and 21
Built at the end of the 15th century, the white house at No.17 is the oldest residential building in Riga.

St Jacob's Church
(Jēkaba baznīca)
Klostera 2
Built in 1225, this church held the first Reformation service in Latvia in the 16th century. It is now a working Roman Catholic church.

Saiema parliament building
On Jēkaba, next to Jēkaba baznīca. The parliament building was erected in the 19th century to house the Knights of Vidzeme.

Swedish Gate
(Zviedru vārti)
Torņa 11
Built during Swedish rule in the 17th century, this is the only surviving gate into the Old City.

City Wall
(Torņa iela)
Dating from the 13th century, the city wall surrounded Riga until the mid-19th century, when it was torn down to make way for further expansion. The fragment on Torņa was restored by Polish workers in the late 1980s.

Powder Tower
(Pulvertornis)
Smilšu 20
This 14th-century building is the only surviving tower of the medieval city wall, which originally featured

28 such look-out posts. The 85-ft (26-metre) structure still bears battle scars: cannon balls can be seen sticking out of the 10-ft (3-metre) thick walls. It is part of the War Museum (Kara muzejs).
Tel/fax: 722 8147. Open Wednesday–Sunday 10am–6pm.

National Theatre
(Nacionālais teātris)
Kronvalda bulv. 2
Tel: 732 2759
This is where Latvia declared its independence on 18 November 1918. The building has a fine, stately, late 19th-century interior.

Academy of Arts
(Mākslas akadēmija)
Kalpaka bulv. 13

Art Museum
(Valsts makslas muzejs)
Kr. Valdemāra 10a
Tel: 732 5021
Open Wednesday–Monday 11am–5pm.

Jewish Museum
Skolas 6
Open weekdays noon–5pm. This small museum traces the history of the Jews in Latvia including the holocaust and the rebirth of the community since independence.

Open-Air Museum of Ethnography
(Brīvdabas muzejs)
Brīvības 440
Tel: 799 4515/4106
Open every day 10am–5pm. The museum is located by the shores of Lake Jugla to the north of Riga. It includes some authentic examples of rural, fully furnished Latvian architecture dating from the 17th to 19th centuries. Various events are held here in the summer, including, on the first weekend of June, an open-air craft market that is attended by thousands of people from all three Baltic States and hundreds of Western tourists.

Around Latvia

Cēsis Castle
Open Tuesday–Sunday 10am–5pm.

Rundāle Castle
Bauska. Open Wednesday–Sunday 11am–6pm.

Turaida Castle
Sigulda. Open daily 10am–5pm.

Art Galleries

Agija Suna
Kalēju 9
Tel: 708 7543
Open Monday–Saturday 11am–6pm.

Art-G
Šķūņu 15
Tel: 722 0039
Open daily 10am–6pm.

Ars Longa
Gleznotaju 5
Tel: 728 5789
Open Tuesday–Sunday 11am–6pm. Modern and classic Latvian art: paintings, graphics, glassware.

Bastejs
Basteja bulv. 12
Tel: 722 5050
Open weekdays noon–6pm, Saturday noon–4pm. Modern Latvian art.

Centrs
Kaļķu 16
Tel: 722 5475
Open Monday–Saturday 11am–8pm. Modern Latvian art.

Ķīpsalas keramika
Balasta dambis 34
Tel: 761 2467
Open daily 10am–5pm. Ceramics.

Kolonna
Šķūņu 16
Tel: 722 6070
Weekdays 10am–6pm, Saturday 10am–5pm. Modern Latvian and Baltic art.

Mākslinieku nams
(Artists' House)
11. Novembra Krastmala 35
Tel: 722 8997
Open Tuesday–Saturday 11am–5pm.

M6
Mārstaļu 6
Tel: 721 2640
Open Tuesday–Saturday noon–7pm.

Cemeteries

The north of the city is testimony to Latvia's long history of warfare and occupation. The Brāļu kapi (Brethren Cemetery) houses some of the state's most notable works of memorial architecture. The Raiņa kapi (Rainis Cemetery) and Meža kapi (Forest Cemetery) are also worth visiting.

Noktirne
Amatu 6
Tel: 721 0073
Open daily 11am–7pm.
Ornamenta Lettonica
Kalēju 21
Open Monday–Saturday
11am–5pm. Latvian art.
Rīgas Galerija
Aspazijas bulv. 20
Tel: 722 5887. Open
Monday–Saturday noon–7pm.
Tifana
Jāņa 16
Tel: 721 6021
Open Tuesday–Saturday 11am–6pm.

Museums & Exhibitions
Occupation Museum of Latvia
(Okupacijas muzejs)
Strelnieku Laukums 1
Tel: 721 2715
Open daily 11am–5pm.
Free entrance.
**Museum of the Riga Dome
Cathedral** (Doma Baznīcas muzejs)
Doma laukums 1
Tel: 721 3213
Open Wednesday–Friday 1–6pm,
Tuesday 11am–6pm Saturday
10am–2pm. Tours of the interior of
the cathedral. You can also visit the
excavations inside the Cathedral
courtyard. Entrance from Palasta 4.
Open daily 10am–5pm.
Museum of St Peter's Church
(Pēterbaznīcas muzejs)
Skārņu 19
Tel: 722 94 26
Open Tuesday–Sunday
10am–5.15pm.
State Art Museum
(Valsts Mākslas muzejs)
Kr. Valdemāra 10a
Tel: 732 5021
Open Wednesday–Monday
11am–5pm. Early and modern
Latvian and Russian painting. The
best art museum in the Baltics.
**Museum of Decorative and
Applied Art** (Dekoratīvi Lietišķās
mākslas muzejs)
Skārņu 10–20
Tel: 722 9736/722 7833
Open Tuesday–Sunday 10am–6pm.
Museum of the History of Latvia
(Latvijas Vestures Muzejs)
Pils laukums 3
Tel: 722 1357

Open Wednesday–Sunday
11am–5pm.
Museum of Foreign Art
Tel: 722 6467
Open Tuesday–Sunday 11am–5pm.
Museum of Foreign Art
(Aizrobezu Mākslas muzejs)
Pils laukums 3
Tel: 722 6467
Open Tuesday–Sunday 11am–5pm.
**Museum of the History of Riga and
Navigation** (Rīgas Vēstures un
kugniecības muzejs)
Palasta 4
Tel: 721 2051/721 1358.
Open Wednesday–Saturday
11am–5pm. The city's most
important historical collection.
Jewish Museum
Skolas 6
Open weekdays noon–5pm.
Latvian Photography Museum
(Fotogrāfu nams)
Mārstaļu 6
Tel: 722 7231/2713
Open Wednesday and Thursday
9am–5pm, Friday, weekends
9am–7pm.
**P. Stradiņa Museum of the
History of Medicine**
(P. Stradiņa Medicīniskās
vēstures muzejs)
Antonijas 1
Tel: 722 26 56
Open Tuesday–Saturday
11am–5pm.
Latvian Museum of War
(Latvijas kara muzejs)
Smilšu 20
Tel/fax: 722 8147
Open Wednesday–Sunday
10am–5pm. Military memorabilia.
Nature Museum of Latvia
(Latvijas Dabas muzejs)
Kr. Barona 4
Tel: 722 6078
Open Wednesday–Sunday
10am–5pm.
Riga Motor Museum
(Rīgas Motormuzejs)
Eizenšteina 6
Tel: 709 7170
Open Tuesday–Sunday 10am–6pm.
Old and new cars, bicycles and
other vehicles.
Riga Circus
(Rīgas cirks)
Merķeļa 4
Closed during the summer.

Zoo
Meža prospekts 1
Tel: 751 86 69
Open daily 10am–6pm.
Open-Air Museum of Ethnography
(Brīvdabas muzejs)
Brīvības 440
Tel: 799 4515/799 4106
Open every day 10am–5pm.
Museum of Latvian rural life
Dauderi, Tvaika 44
Tel: 739 1780
This was the summer residence of
Latvian President Kārlis Ulmanis in
the 1930s. Open Wednesday–
Monday 11am–5pm.
Arsenāls exhibition hall
Torņa 1
Tel: 722 9570
Open every day 11am–5pm.
Modern Latvian art.

National Parks
Gauja National Park
Visitor's Centre
Sigulda, Baznīcas 3
Tel: 2 974 006
Fax: 2 971 344
gnp@gnp.lv
Open daily 9am–6pm.
Slītere State Reserve
Dundaga
Tel: 32 42 542
Fax: 32 42 505
slitere@mail.bkc.lv
Open weekdays 8am–5pm.

Lithuania

The cities of Lithuania have much in
the way of fine architecture and
museums to offer to visitors. Of
special note in Vilnius are some
fine baroque churches; Kaunas
offers many notable old merchants'
buildings and museums. During the
summer months, Lithuania's
seaside towns are lively places with
much to offer visitors.

VILNIUS

Monuments & Sites
Castle Hill and Gediminas Tower,
Arsenalo 5 (behind the Cathedral).
The high point of the Old Town
offers good views over the city. The
Higher Castle Museum on Castle

Hill showcases archaeological finds and the history of the castle, tel: 617 453. Open Sunday–Monday 11am–6pm. You can also tour the excavations of the grand dukes' palace in the Lower Castle Museum just behind the Cathedral on Katedros aikšte 3, tel: 629 988. Open weekdays 10am–5pm.
Three Crosses, on the hill of the same name northeast of Castle Hill. Originally erected for seven Franciscan martyrs, these newly re-erected crosses have become symbolic of the nation.
Cathedral
(Arkikatedra Bazilika)
Arkikatedros aikšte. 1
Tel: 611 127
The original church on this site was built in 1387 to mark the country's conversion to Catholicism.
Gates of Dawn
(Aušros Vartai/Ostra Brama)
Aušros Vartų 12
The city's most famous shrine has Mass daily in Lithuanian and Polish.
St Anne's church
(Šv. Onos)
Maironio 8
Tel: 611 236
This 16th-century brick church is one of the finest examples of gothic architecture in Lithuania.
St Casimir's church
(Šv. Kazimiero)
Didžioji 34
Tel: 221 715
Open Monday–Saturday 4–6.30pm, Sunday 8am–1.30pm. The oldest baroque church in the city, founded in 1604, is dedicated to the patron saint of Lithuania and bears a distinctive crown on its dome.
St John's church
(Šv. Jono)
Šv. Jono 12
Tel: 611 795
A fine late baroque church that once belonged to the university.
St Michael's church
(Šv. Mykolo)
Šv. Mykolo 9
Tel: 616 409
Open Wednesday–Monday 11am–5.30pm
This early 17th-century church contains the mummified remains of the Sapieha family. Also of interest

is a a small museum of architecture contained within the church.
St Nicholas's church
(Šv. Mikalojaus)
Šv. Mikalojaus 4
Tel: 623 069
The oldest standing church in the country, dating from 1320, before the country became Christian.
Saint Peter and Paul church
(Šv. Petro ir Povilo)
Antakalnio 1
Tel: 340 229
Fine stucco work, depicting more than 2,000 figures.

Museums

Museums are relative inexpensive – the entrance fee is usually the equivalent of about US$1; entry is normally free on Wednesday.
Museum of Genocide Victims
Gedimino pr. 40
(entrance from Auku 2a)
Tel: 622 449
Open Tuesday–Sunday 10am–6pm. Vilnius' KGB museum is one of the most interesting sites in the Baltics. Wander through the eerie cells in the basement of the former KGB HQ.
Adam Mickiewicz Memorial Apartment
Bernadinų 11
Tel: 618 836
Open Tuesday–Friday 11am–5pm, weekends 10am–2pm. This is the the house where Lithuania's most celebrated poet lived in 1822.
Artillery Bastion
Bokšto 20/18
Tel: 612 149
Open Wednesday–Sunday 11am–5pm. A 17th-century bastion with medieval armour and cannons.
Lithuanian Art Museum
Didžioji 4
Tel: 628 030
The Art Museum is the umbrella organisation for several museums across the country.
Vilnius Picture Gallery
Didžioji 4
Tel: 224 251
Open Tuesday–Sunday, noon–6pm. Permanent exhibition of Lithuanian painters and sculptors.
Lithuanian State Jewish Museum
Pamenkalnio 12
Tel: 620 730/624 590

Open Monday–Thursday 9am–5pm, Friday 9am–4pm. Also on Pylimo 4. Tel: 613 105. Open weekdays 10am–5pm. A permanent exhibition pays homage to the victims of the holocaust. A visit to Paneriai Forest, southwest of the city, makes for an exceptionally moving experience, as around 100,000 Jews were executed here by the Nazis.
Museum of Applied Art
Arsenalo 3
Tel: 628 080
Open Tuesday–Sunday noon–6pm. The museum is home to recently uncovered cathedral treasure. Over 250 gold, silver and amber crosses, chalices, monstrances and other religious items were hidden under the cathedral in 1655. This treasure was briefly uncovered in 1985 but kept secret from the Soviets. Only in 1998 – well after Lithuania had regained its independence – was the existence of the invaluable 17th-century religious hoard revealed.
Lithuanian National Museum
Arsenalo 1
Tel: 629 426
Open Wednesday–Sunday 11am–6pm. Charts the country's history from the Stone Age through to the 20th century.
Museum of Recent History
Studentų 8
Tel: 755 164
Open Tuesday–Sunday noon–6pm. The exhibition gives an interesting insight into Lithuania through 50 years of Soviet occupation, from the forcible incorporation into the Soviet empire in 1940 to the declaration of independence in the 1990s.
Puškin Memorial Museum
Subačiaus 124
Tel: 690 080
Open Wednesday–Sunday 10am–5pm. The house of Alexander Pushkin's son is located slightly out of town. The 1863 uprising against the tsar was hatched in its tranquil 47-acre (19-hectare) grounds.
Radvilų Palace
Vilniaus 22
Tel: 620 981
Open Tuesday–Saturday 11am–5pm, Sunday 11am–4pm. This is the former home of the

Radziwill aristocracy. The palace's collection now contains family portraits and etchings of Vilnius.

Television Tower
Sausio 13-osios 10.
Tel: 458 877.
Open daily 10am–9pm.
On January 13, 1991 the Soviet army stormed the television tower killing 14 civilians. Small monuments mark the spots where the "defenders of freedom" were crushed by tanks.

Art Galleries

There are dozens of art shops and galleries (dailė) in Vilnius, a selection of which are listed below. Among the most fascinating ones are the two private amber galleries.

Amber Museum
(Gintaro Muziejus)
Šv. Mykolo 8
Tel: 623 092
Open Tuesday–Sunday 10am–7pm.

Amber
Aušros Vartų 9
Tel: 221 988
Open weekdays 9.30am–7pm,
Saturday 9.30am–5pm, Sunday 9.30am–3pm.

Arka
Aušros Vartų 7
Tel: 221 319
Open Tuesday–Friday 11am–7pm,
Sat noon–5pm. Exhibitions by contemporary artists.

Jonas Bugailiškis workshop
Aušros Vartų 17–10

Tel: 617 666
Visit the workshop of the woodcarver.

Juskus Gallery
Barboros Radvilaitės 6
Tel: 226 611
Open Tuesday–Friday 10am–6pm,
Saturday 10am–5pm, Monday 10am–4pm. Landscapes and cityscapes by Lithuanian artists.

Medalių galerija
Šv. Jono 11
Tel: 224 154
Open Tuesday–Friday 10am–6pm,
Sat 10am–4pm. This magnificent hall shows sculpture at its best.

Photographic Gallery
(Fotografijos galerija)
Didžioji 19
Tel: 611 665
Open Tuesday–Sunday noon–7pm.

Russian Art Gallery
Bokšto 4/2
Tel: 223 236
Open Monday–Saturday 11am–6pm. Holds temporary exhibitions of work by contemporary painters.

Vartai
Vilniaus 39
Tel: 222 949
Open Tuesday–Saturday noon–7pm.
Contemporary art exhibitions are held on the second floor.

Vilnius Contemporary Art Centre
Vokiečių 2
Tel: 629 891
cac@cac.vno.osf.lt
Open Tuesday–Sunday 11am–7pm.

Continually changing exhibitions of contemporary art.

KAUNAS

Museums

Museum of Exiles and Political Prisoners
Vytauto pr. 46
Tel: 7 227 526
Open Thursday–Sunday 10am–4pm.
A small exhibition about the struggle of the "Forest Brothers", the Lithuanian anti-Soviet partisans.

Ceramics Museum
Rotušės aikšte 15
Tel: 7 203 572
Open Tuesday–Sunday noon–6pm.
Modern ceramics.

Military Museum of Vytautas the Great
Donelaičio 64
Tel: 7 320 939/320 874
Wednesday–Sunday 10am–6pm.

M.K. Čiurlionis Art Museum
Putvinskio 55
Tel: 7 204 446
Fax: 7 204 612
MKC@takas.lt
Open Tuesday–Sunday noon–6pm. This museum celebrating Lithuania's most important creative genius should not be missed.

Museum of Lithuanian Folk Music and Instruments
Zamenhofo 12
Tel: 7 207 636/206 820
Open Wednesday–Sunday 11am–7pm. Covers an important part of the country's folklore.

Museum of Lithuanian Medicine and Pharmacy
Rotušės aikšte 28
Tel: 7 201 569
Fax: 7 201 575
Open Wednesday–Sunday 11am–5pm. This museum is housed in an original pharmacy in Town Hall Square.

Ninth Fort
IX Fortas
Žemaičių plentas 73
Tel: 7 237 645
Open Wednesday–Monday 10am–4pm. This site, formerly a concentration camp, is now a memorial to Nazi victims.

Parks & Cemeteries in Vilnius

Vilnius is surrounded by a number of pleasant open spaces. At **Kalnų Park** at the foot of the Hill of Crosses is Song Valley, where folk dancing, singing and rock concerts are held. However, the biggest music venue is among the pines in the 395-acre (160-hectare) **Vingis Park** on the west side of the city. A huge stage was built here in 1960 for a major song festival that now takes place every five years. **Pasakų Park** is home to large wooden statues of fairy-tale heroes, which usually prove popular with children. **Burbiškės Park** near the Paneriai forest 5 miles (8 km) southwest of the city is dotted with wood carvings. **Sereikiškės Park** is the oldest in Vilnius. North of the city, along the banks of the River Neris is the 740-acre (300-hectare) **Valakampiai Park**. Also worth a visit, both for their historical interest and as places of quiet reflection, are the city's cemeteries, which are held in great respect by the Lithuanians. **Antakalnis Cemetery** (Karių kapų) is the soldiers' resting place; here, communist leaders are buried alongside the seven border guards killed in July 1991. **Rasų Cemetery**, Rasų 32, is a pantheon of the famous, including Polish Marshal Pilsudski.

Picture Gallery
Donelaičio 16
Tel: 7 200 520
Open Tuesday–Sunday, noon–6pm.
M. Žilinskas Art Museum
Nepriklausomybės aikštė 12
Tel: 7 204 906/201 381
Open Tuesday–Sunday noon–6pm.
Eclectic private collection.
A. Žmuidžinavičius Collection
Devils Museum
Putvinskio 64
Tel: 7 208 472
Open Tuesday–Sunday noon–6pm.
Collection of devil figures.
Zoological Museum
Laisvės al. 106
Tel/fax: 7 229 675/222 543.
Open Tuesday–Sunday 11am–7pm.

Art Galleries
Kauno Langas
Vilniaus 22
Tel/fax: 7 201 227
kaunolangas@kaunas.omnitel.net
www.omnitel.net/kaunolangas
Open weekdays 11am–6.30pm,
Saturday 11am–6pm, Sunday
11am–3pm. Also on Rotušės aikšte
26. Tel/fax: 7 205 538. Weekdays
10am–6.30pm, Saturday
1am–5pm.
Photography Gallery
(Fotografijos galerija)
Rotušės aikštė 1
Tel: 7 321 789
Open Tuesday–Sunday 11am–6pm.
Dizaino Salonas
Valančiaus 25
Tel: 7 228 731
Open weekdays 10am–2pm and
3–6pm, Saturday 10am–4pm.
Zita
Vilniaus 25
Tel: 7 220 301
Open weekdays 10am–6pm,
Saturday 10am–3pm.

KLAIPEDA & THE COAST

Clock Museum
Liepų 12
Tel: 6 213 531
Open Tuesday–Sunday
noon–6pm. Horological
collection covering items from
the beginning of time to the
present day.

Lithuania Minor Museum
Didžioji vandens 6
Tel: 6 210 600/210 860
Open Wednesday–Sunday
11am–7pm.
**Maritime Museum and Aquarium
and Dolphinarium**
At Smiltynė on the Neringa Spit
Tel: 6 391 133/391 170.
Open June, July, August Tuesday–
Sunday 10.30am–6.30pm. Dolphin
shows: noon, 2pm, 4pm. May and
September Wednesday–Sunday
10.30am–6.30pm. Dolphin shows:
noon and 3pm. October to April
weekends 10.30am–5.30pm.
Dolphin shows: noon and 3pm.
This fully fledged sea world, set in an
old fortress, enables you to see
dolphins, penguins and porpoises
etc, all at close proximity.

National Parks

Aukštaitija National Park
Paluse
Tel: 29 47 430
Fax: 29 53 135
anp@is.lt.
Džukija National Park
Marčinkonys Tourist Information
Centre
Miškininkų 61
Tel: 60 44 466
Fax: 60 44 471
Merkinė Tourist Information
Centre
Vilniaus 2
Tel: 60 57 245
dzukijanp@is.lt
Kuršių Nerija National Park
Klaipėda, Smiltynės 11
Tel: 6 391 179
Fax: 6 391 113
Trakai National Park
Trakai, Kęstučio 1
Tel: 38 51 528
Fax: 38 51 546
Žemaitija National Park
Plateliai Tourist Information
Centre
Didžioji 10
Tel: 18 49 231
Fax: 18 49 337
Žemaičių Kalvarijos Tourist
Information Centre
Tel: 18 43 200
znp@plunge.omnitel.net

JUODKRANTÒ

Open-air Museum of Sculpture
Raganų kalnas.
Carvings and folk tales depicted
through sculpture.

NIDA

Fisherman's Museum
Kuverto 2
Open from May to September
Wednesday–Sunday 11am–5pm.
Fishing memorabilia.
Thomas Mann House
Skruzdynės 17
Tel: 59 52 260
Open Tuesday–Saturday
11am–5pm. The esteemed German
writer and Nobel Prize winner spent
his summers here in 1930–31.
Palanga
Amber Museum
Vytauto 17
Tel: 36 53 501
Open Tuesday–Sunday 11am–7pm.
Learn all about "Lithuanian Gold".

DRUSKININKAI

M.K. Čiurlionio Memorial Museum
Čiurlionio 41
The house where the artist/
composer grew up. Concerts are
sometimes performed here.

SIAULIAI

Bicycle Museum
Vilniaus 139
Tel: 1 524 395
Open Tuesday–Friday 11am–7pm,
weekends noon–6pm.
An exhibition of more than 70
bicycles from around the world.

Culture

Theatre

The first professional Estonian theatre group, the Vanemuine Theatre, was formed in Tartu in the early 20th century. The second professional group to be established was the Estonia Theatre in Tallinn. Although the Vanemuine still exists as a drama theatre, housed in an large, ugly building in the centre of Tartu, during the early years of Soviet occupation the Estonia Theatre was transformed into a music theatre.

The Estonian Drama Theatre emerged during the thaw of the 1950s as Tallinn's pre-eminent theatre. It was joined in the 1960s by the Youth Theatre (now the Tallinn City Theatre). Along with the Endla Theatre in Pärnu and the Ugale in Viljandi these remain the major theatres in Estonia. The season is from mid-September until the end of May. Performances usually start at seven and tickets must be booked in advance. Note that all performances, except those at the Russian Drama Theatre, are in Estonian.

Endla Theatre, Pärnu, Keskväljak 1. Tel: 44 42 480.
Estonian Drama Theatre, Eesti Draamateater, Pärnu mnt. 5. Tel: 644 3378; fax: 440 503; draama@teleport.ee.
Puppet Theatre, Eesti Nukuteater, Lai 1. Tel: 641 1617/641 1609; fax: 641 1112.
Linnateater, Lai 23. Tel: 665 0800; fax: 665 0802; lteater@teleport.ee
Old City Studio, Vanalinna Stuudio, Sakala 3. Tel: 660 4500.
Raeteater, Mahtra 22/79. Tel: 634 5286/644 0819 (beautiful décor; fine period plays).

Russian Drama Theatre (Vene Draamateater), Vabaduse väljak 5. Tel: 641 8246.
Salon Theatre (Salong Teater), Kaarli pst. 9. Tel: 645 3875; allan.raim@tallinn.ee.
AH Tammsaare/TEO Theatres, Vene 6. Tel: 646 4080; fax: 631 3596
Theatrum, Vene 14. Tel: 644 6889; fax: 641 1519; marius@colleduc.ee.
Von Krahl Theatre, Rataskaevu 10. Tel: 626 9096; fax: 626 9099; krahl@online.ee.
Vanemuine Theatre, Tartu, Vanemuine 6. Tel: 07 442 272; fax: 07 442 253; teater@vanemuine.ee; www.vanemuine.ee.

Classical Concerts & Opera

Virtually every night of the week, except for the summer break between May and September, a classical performance is held at the **Estonia Concert Hall**, Estonia pst. 4. Tel: 614 7700/614 7760; fax: 614 7769; info@concert.ee, www.concert.ee. More often than not the performance is given by the Estonian State Symphony Orchestra, though performances are also given by the Symphony Orchestra of the Tallinn Conservatoire or the Estonian Philharmonic Chamber Orchestra and Choir. Guest orchestras, choirs and ensembles are also invited from around the world. A garden café adjacent to the concert hall often hosts smaller ensembles and solo artists. These performances usually transfer to other concert halls, notably to Tartu's Vanemuine Theatre and Pärnu's Endla Theatre. Details of performances are posted on notice boards outside the theatre.

In Tallinn there are a number of smaller venues for performances, including **the Town Hall** (Raekoda), Raekoja plats 1, tel: 644 0819; the **Niguliste church**, Niguliste 3, tel: 644 9911; the **House of the Brotherhood of the Blackheads**, Mustpeade Maja Pikk 26, tel/fax: 631 31 99; and the **Matkamaja**, Raekoja plats 18. Check venues for details or consult the calendar of events in *Tallinn In Your Pocket*, www.inyourpocket.com. Also look out for performances by the **Tallinn**

Philharmonic Society, tel: 645 2453; fax: 645 3421; fila@datanet.ee; www.filharmoonia.ee.
A few performances of opera and ballet are held at the **Estonia Theatre**, Estonia pst. 4. Tel: 626 0211/0215; fax: 626 0299; info@opera.ee; www.opera.ee.

Music Festivals

Foremost in the Estonian musical calendar is the **National Song Festival**, which takes place every five years. During the great period of intense Russification towards the end of the 19th century, when the use of the national tongue was almost completely forbidden, the first Estonian Song Festival proved the means by which the steadily growing subterranean nationalist movement was kept alive. The Estonian love of singing was well known and so when a deputation of Estonians laid a petition to hold a festival of song near Tartu in 1869 the authorities saw no harm in allowing the natives of this province of Russia to go ahead with the festival. The first one was ostensibly given in honour of the tsar, but Estonian leaders realised how important such meetings were for boosting moral and a feelign of national pride and they vowed to continue them. At the 1990 Song Festival at the height of the drive for independence, there were 500,000 people in attendance – half the population of ethnic Estonians.

The annual **Rock Summer** festival is also held at the Song Festival grounds. Taking place in early July, Rock Summer offers three days of international acts, featuring rock, blues, world music and classical music.

Since 1984 an **International Organ Music Festival** has taken place every year in Estonia. The festival is held during early August and recitals are given in Tallinn and throughout Estonia. Early October sees the **Jazz and Blues Festival**. The names are possibly not as high profile as those attracted by Rock Summer but the performances are still world class and well worth watching if you have time.

Latvia

Theatre

Latvians have traditionally been seen as a nation of theatre-goers. Under the Soviets, the theatre was the last fortress of Baltic culture but this has changed since independence. Old-style state subsidies are no longer available and theatres are forced to finance themselves. Many theatres are on the verge of bankrupcy, their buildings are run down, actors are finding it hard to make ends meet and tickets are becoming too costly for people to buy on a regular basis. Nevertheless, performances are still shown at the following venues:
National Theatre (Nacionālais teātris), Kronvalda bulv. 2. Tel: 732 2759; info@teatris.lv; www.teatris.lv.
Russian Drama Theatre (Krievu drāmas teātris), Kaļķu 16. Tel: 722 4660.
New Riga Theatre (Jaunais Rīgas teātris), Lāčplēša 25. Tel: 728 3323; fax 728 2945; www.jrt.lv.
Dailes Theatre (Dailes teātris), Brīvības 75. Tel: 270 278.
Kabata Theatre, Peldu 19. Tel: 951 6517/6779.

OUTSIDE RIGA

Daugavpils Musical Drama Theatre (Daugavpils Muzikāli dramatiskais teātris), Gogoļa 23a. Tel: 54 26 700.
State Liepāja Theatre (Valsts Liepājas teātris), Teātra 4. Tel: 342 0145.

Estonian films

Estonian cinema is experiencing something of a rebirth with foreign investment and partnerships stepping in to replace the Moscow hand-outs that previously kept the industry afloat. In Tallinn the House of the Cinema Union (kinomaja), at Uus 3, operates like a club, screening small independent features and documentaries from around the world. Details are posted in the cinema's window.

Valmiera Drama Theatre (Valmieras Drāmas teātris), Lācplēsa 4. Tel: 42 249 43.

Opera & Ballet

Riga was renowned for its ballet in the Soviet Union and many stars of the genre, including Mikhail Baryshnikov, trained here. Like the theatre, however, it has suffered considerably since state funding has dwindled. Riga's opera house, however, has been beautifully restored thanks to private donations from overseas.
National Opera (Nacionālā opera), Aspazijas bulv. 3. Tel: 722 5803; tel/fax: 722 8240; mail@opera.lv; www.opera.lv.

Classical Music

Dome Cathedral, Doma laukums 1. Tel: 721 34 98.
The cathedral's celebrated organ has a wonderful sound and visitors should not miss the chance of hearing a concert here. Tickets for organ concerts can be bought at the Wagner Concert Hall or at the entrance before the performances.
Filharmonija, Amatu 6. Tel: 721 3798. The Concert Hall of the Philharmonic Society is in the Great Guild Hall.
Ave Sol Concert Hall, Citadeles 7. Tel: 327 670.
Wagner Concert Hall, Vāgnera 4. Tel: 721 0814. This charming building in the old town is a good place to hear chamber music.

Cinema

The Baltic states have produced some excellent award-winning films, particularly documentaries, but movie houses mostly show the latest Western releases with the original soundtrack and subtitles.
Daile, Kr. Barona 31. Tel: 728 3854.
Kino 52, Lačplēša 52/54. Tel: 728 8778
Maska, Prusu 2. Tel: 718 7236.
Oskars, Skolas 2. Tel: 733 3643.
Kinogalerija, Jaun 24. Tel: 722 9030.
K. suns, Elizabetes 83/85. Tel: 728 7282.
Palladium, Marijas 21. Tel: 728 1610.

Riga, Elizabetes 61. Tel: 728 1105

Lithuania

Theatre

In spite of funding difficulties the main theatres in Vilnius still show a broad range of plays. The country has a strong acting tradition and many players still enjoy excellent reputations. Look out for performances at the university and by troupes such as the 15-strong Lithuanian National Theatre, as these tend to be particularly good. Performances usually start at 7pm, and resumés are sometimes available in English.
National Drama Theatre (Lietuvos nacionalinis dramos teatras), Gedimino pr. 4. Tel: 629 771; fax: 620 051; info@teatras.lt; www.teatras.lt. The theatre has two stages – a main one and a small platform located round the back of the building.
Vilnius Small Theatre (Vilniaus mažasis teatras), Gedimino pr. 4. Tel/fax: 613 195; mazasis@teatras. lt; www.vmt.lt.
Keistuoliai Theatre (Keistuolių Teātras), Laisvės pr. 60. Tel: 424 585; fax: 424 585; keisti@takas.lt; www.keistuoliai.lt. Children's theatre.
Puppet Theatre (Lėlės Teātras), Arklių 5. Tel: 628 678. Productions of fairy-tales for children.
Raganiukės teatras, Vilniaus 22. Tel: 629 620/769 260; fax: 614 005; raganiukes@teatras.lt. Children's theatre.
Russian Drama Theatre (Rusų dramos teatros), Basanavičiaus 13. Tel: 627 133/620 552. Puts on Russian-language plays.
Youth Theatre (Jaunimo teatras), Arklių 5, Tel: 616 126. Ambitious productions of classical and modern works.

Opera & Ballet

Productions are wide ranging but on the whole tend to be classical and conservative.
Opera and Ballet Theatre (Operos ir baleto teatras), Vienuolio 1. Tel: 620 636; fax: 623 503/620 515 info@opera.lt; www.opera.lt.

Classical Concerts

Tickets for most of the classical concerts can be purchased beforehand at the central ticket office of the **National Philharmonic** Aušros Vartų 5, tel: 627 165/222 290, fax: 622 859, info@ filharmonija.lt, www.filharmonija.lt. Concerts are also performed at: **Artists' Palace** (Menininku Rumai), Didžioji 31. Tel: 618 179. **M. K. Čiurlionis' House**, Savičiaus 11. Tel: 226 414. **Music Academy**, Gedimino pr. 42. Tel: 610 144. **Teacher's House**, Vilniaus 39. Tel: 222 949.

Music Festivals

May: Jazz festival, Birštonas. **June:** Vilnius Festival, Philharmonic. Tel: 627 165/222 290; fax: 622 859; info@filharmonija.lt; www.filharmonija.lt **August:** Visagino Country, International country music and bluegrass festival in Visaginas. Tel: 66 32 411; fax: 66 32 411; v.stakenas@siauliai.omnitel.net; www1.omnitel.net/visagino-country **September:** Griežynė folk music festival, Vilnius and International pop music festival, Vilnius. **Autumn:** Grok Jurgeli, folk music festival, Kaunas **October:** Vilnius Jazz Festival, www.vilniusjazz.lt **November:** Italian opera week, Vilnius; Gaida Baltic Music Festival. **Every five years:** "Dainų Sventė" traditional song festival.

Cinema

The following cinemas in Vilnius show major Western productions in the original language with Lithuanian subtitles: **Helios**, Didžioji 28. Tel: 614 843. **Lietuva**, Pylimo 17. Tel: 623 422. **Skalvija**, Goštauto 2/15. Tel: 611 403. **Vilnius**, Gedimino pr. 5a. Tel: 612 676. **Vingis**, Savanorių 7. Tel: 651 625.

Shopping

Estonia

WHERE TO SHOP

Estonia is a great place to shop. Notable local products include the local Saku beer and the wide selection of handicrafts. Much of the delight of casual shopping here is not the goods but rather the shops themselves, many of which, particularly those in Tallinn's Old Town, possess great character.

WHAT TO BUY

Antiques

The trade in religious icons is still going strong here, although this is the cause of much consternation because it encourages their removal from isolated country churches. More reputable items to buy from antiques shops include medals and distinctive metal-worked items of jewellery.

Fine Art & Graphics

There is no great tradition of painting in Estonia, and Estonian national art only truly came into being in the later part of the 19th century. An Estonian painter of international repute has yet to emerge and the country's most famous artist, Eduard Wiiralt, is recognised more for his skill in drawing and etching than for his painting. Graphics remain the strongest aspect of Estonian art and in some ways the production of graphic works for sale has become something of a cottage industry. The work is of a high standard and reasonably priced although it is probably produced with the tourist in mind.

Ars Boutique, Vabaduse väljak 8. Weekdays 10am–6pm, Saturday 11am–4pm. **Diele Galerii**, Vanaturu kael 3. Monday–Saturday 10am–6pm, Sunday 10am–3pm. **Draakoni**, Pikk 18. Weekdays 10am–6pm, Saturday 11am–4pm. **Galerii 2**, Lühike jalg 1. Monday–Saturday 10am–6pm, Sunday 10am–5pm. **Helina Tilk**, Voorimehe 3. Weekdays 10am–7pm, Saturday 10am–5pm, Sunday 11am–3pm. **Keraamika Ateljee**, Pikk 33. Weekdays 10am–6pm, Saturday noon–5pm. **Ku Te Re**, Pikk 37. Weekdays 11am–6pm, weekends 11am–4pm. **Lühikese Jala Galerii**, Lühike jalg 6. Weekdays 10am–6pm, weekends 10am–5pm. **Molen**, Viru 19. Weekdays 10am–6pm, Saturday 11am–3pm. **Navitrolla Galerii**, Pikk jalg 7. Monday–Saturday 11am–6pm, Sunday 11am–3pm. **Shifara Galerii**, Vana-Posti 7. Weekdays 11am–2pm and 3–6pm, Saturday 11am–4pm.

Books

There are various English-language books available in Estonia including works by local author Jaan Kross. **Antikvaar**, Rataskaevu 20/22. Monday–Saturday 10am–6pm. Antique books. **Bukinist Juhan Hammer**, Voorimehe 9. Tuesday–Friday 11am–5pm, Saturday until 2pm. Second-hand and antiquarian books. **Allecto**, Juhkentali 32-5. Weekdays 9am–6pm. Saturday 11am–4pm. **Euro Publications**, Tartu mnt. 1. Weekdays 10am–6pm, Saturday 11am–5pm. **Kupar**, Harju 1. Weekdays 10am–7pm, Saturday 11am–3pm. Books plus original cartoons and caricatures by local artists. **Rahva Raamat**, Pärnu mnt. 10. Weekdays 9am–7pm, Saturday 10am–4pm. **Viruvärava**, Viru 23. Weekdays 10am–7pm, Saturday 10am–6pm, Sunday 11am–3pm. Imported German books and tourist-orientated literature on Estonia.

Handicrafts

Leatherwork and beautifully patterned, hand-knitted jumpers, socks and mittens are Estonian specialities. Each parish in the country has its own belt and mitten designs and each district of Estonia wears a slight variation on the national costume. Different regions are also famed for particular crafts; Haapsaluu, for example, produces fine cobwebby shawls of woollen lace while the island of Muhu excels in colourful hand-embroidered floral patterns, which are stitched onto slippers, blankets and sweaters.

In addition to wool, linen has is a traditional Estonian fabric. Tablecloths, place mats, linen towels and clothes combine age-old local skills with modern style.

TALLINN

You can find the best handmade sweaters, mittens and caps in Müürivahe street.

Bogapott, Pikk Jalg 9. Daily 10am–8pm.

Hansakaup, Apteegi 2. Daily 9am–8pm. fabrics by the yard.

Joosepi Pood, Vene 16. Weekdays 10am–6pm, weekends 10am–4pm. Sweaters and wooden articles.

Kodukäsitöö, Müürivahe 17. Monday–Saturday 10am–6pm, Sunday 10am–4pm.

Nukupood, Raekoja plats 18. Monday–Saturday 9am–6pm, Sunday 11am–3pm. Wooden dolls and toys.

Puupood, Lai 5. Weekdays 10am–7pm, weekends 10am–4pm. Wooden toys.

Sepa Äri, Vanaturu kael. Weekdays 11am–6pm, Saturday 11am–5pm. Jewellery and Estonian brooches.

Suveniir, Dunkri 2. Daily 10am–8pm.

Latvia

WHERE TO SHOP

Latvians are renowned for their craftsmanship and a wide range of paintings, ceramics, jewellery, glassware, porcelain, textiles, amber, leather, wood crafts and locally made clothes are available to tourists.

WHAT TO BUY

Antiques

Note that you will need an export licence for antiques produced prior to 1945.

Antiqua, Valdemāra 20. Weekdays 10am–7pm, Saturday 10am–4pm. Also on Torņa 4-llc.

Marika, Basteja bulv. 14. Daily 9am–7pm.

Raritets, Čaka 45. Weekdays 10am–7pm, Saturday 10am–6pm.

Vecais gramatnieks, Lāčplēša 9. Weekdays 10am–7pm, Saturday 10am–6pm. Old books.

Volmar, Brīvības 39. Daily 10am–8pm. Another branch on Šķūņu 6.

Folk Art & Souvenirs

Best buys are the locally made woollen mittens and socks in bright patterns. Some lovely shawls are also available. Linen is a speciality – it comes in all shapes and sizes and is usually of especially high quality. Traditional leather shoes with long thong laces make very good slippers.

Amber Free Souvenirs/Nordwear Clothing, Grēcinieku 1. Tel: 750 3546. Also on Kaļķu 2. Tel: 750 3546. Weekdays 10am–7pm, Sunday 11am–7pm. The best hand-knitted sweaters in town and other amber-free souvenirs.

Dzintara galerija, Torņa 4. Open Monday–Saturday 10am–7pm, Sunday 11am–5pm. Amber gifts.

Ezerciems, Kaļķu 7/9. Weekdays 9am–7pm, Saturday 11am–5pm. Glassware, ceramics.

Sakta, Brīvības 32. Weekdays 9am–7pm, Saturday 9am–6pm. Also on Aspazijas bulv. 30. Latvia's traditional souvenir shop has everything from traditional costumes to Rīgas Balzams.

Senā klēts, Barona 28a. Weekdays 11am–6pm. Sells Latvian folk costumes.

Jewellery

There are some well designed, locally made pieces available in Latvian shops. The most interesting modern jewellery incorporates ancient and pagan styles, including the distinctive designs of the interlocking Latvian ring. Amber is relatively cheap here.

A&E, Jaun17. Daily 10am–6pm. Beautiful but pricey amber jewellery

Greznumlietas, Meistaru 21. Open Monday–Saturday 10am–7pm, Sunday 10am–6pm. Amber and silver jewellery.

Līvs, Kalēju 7. Weekdays 10am–6pm, Saturday 10am–4pm. Traditional Latvian jewellery.

Rota, Kalēju 9/11. Daily 10am–7pm. Amber and ceramics.

Books

You can find picture books, guides and maps in the following shops:

Globuss, Vaļņu 26. Weekdays 9am–7pm, Saturday 10am–6pm. English-language literature.

Jāņa Rozes, Elizabetes 85a. Weekdays 10am–7pm, Saturday 10am–5pm. Probably the biggest bookstore in Riga with six other locations in town.

Jāņa Seta, Elizabetes 83/85. Weekdays 10am–7pm, Saturday 11am–5pm. Maps and guides.

Jumava, Vāgnera 12. Weekdays 10am–6.15pm, Saturday 10am–5pm. Antique books.

Planēta, Tērbatas 5. Weekdays 10am–7pm, Saturday 11am–5pm. Old books.

Valters un Rapa, Aspazijas bulv. 24. Weekdays 9am–7pm, Saturday 10am–5pm.

Flowers

The best place to buy flowers is the flower market on Terbatas next to Vērmanes garden. The market is open 24-hours. Note that a small bunch of flowers traditionally makes a very welcome gift if you are visiting a Latvian home.

Markets

Every town has its market, selling a wide selection of food and other trinkets and providing a fascinating view of local life. As in any market,

watch out for pickpockets. In Riga
the main venues are:
Central Market Centrālais tirgus,
Prāgas 1. Open Tuesday–Saturday
8am–5pm, Sunday and Monday
8am–4pm. This vast market in five
old Zeppelin hangars spills down
across a flea market towards the
river. Friday and Saturday are its
busiest days.
Latgales Market, Sadovnikova 9a.
Open Monday–Saturday
8am–4.30pm, Sunday 8am–3pm.
Vidzemes Market Vidzemes
tirgus, Matīsa 2. Open
Monday–Saturday 8am–6pm,
Sunday 8am–3pm.
Āgenskaln Market Āgenskalna
tirgus, Laicēna 64. Open
Tuesday–Saturday 8am–5pm,
Sunday and Monday 8am–3pm.

Lithuania

WHERE TO SHOP

You can buy almost anything in
Vilnius, including amber jewellery.

Antiques

Bear in mind customs regulations
when buying items made pre-1945.
An export licence is needed for
antiques produced before this date.
Antika Kieme, Labdarių 3. Daily
10am–6pm.
Antikvariatas, Dominikonų 3-12.
Weekdays 11am–6pm, Saturday
11am–4pm.
Maldis, Basanavičiaus 4.
Weekdays 9am–6pm, Saturday
10am–3pm.
Senasis Kuparas, Dominikonu
14/16. Weekdays 10am–7pm,
Saturday 10am–5pm.
Versme, Didžioji 27. Open
Tuesday–Friday 10am–6pm,
Saturday 10am–4pm.
Vilniaus Senovė, Pylimo 6.
Weekdays 10am–6pm, Saturday
11am–2pm.

Books

The choice of foreign-language
literature and guides is steadily
improving in Lithuania.
Akademinė Knyga, Universiteto 4.
Weekdays 10am–7pm, Saturday
noon–5pm.

Antikvarinė Knyga, Basanavičiaus 1.
Weekdays 10am–2pm and
2.30–6.30pm. Antique books.
Draugystė, Gedimino pr. 2.
Weekdays 10am–7pm, Saturday
11am–4pm.
Džaneila, Dominikonų 9. Daily
10am–6pm. English-language
magazines.
Humanitas, Vokiečių 2. Open
Monday–Thursday 8.30am–1pm
and 2–5pm, Friday 8.30am–1pm.
Littera, Šv. Jono 12. Open
Monday–Thursday 9am–5pm, Friday
9am–4pm. University bookstore.
Neta, Trakų 5. Weekdays
9am–6pm, Saturday 10am–3pm.
Foreign books.
Vaga, Gedimino pr. 50. Weekdays
10am–7pm, Sat 11am–4pm.

Flowers

Lithuanians offer flowers on many
occasions and for almost any
reason. You can find flowers around
the clock at the Flower Market on
Basanavičiaus 42.

Records

It is worth hunting out records of
Čiurlionis's work, as well as local
jazz and folk music for souvenirs.
The Versme bookshop on Didžioji
27. Weekdays 10am–6pm,
Saturday 10am–4pm has a good
selection of Lithuanian music. Also
check **Audis**, Gedimino pr. 50.
Weekdays 10am–7pm, Saturday
11am–4pm.

Amber

Amber is best bought at the
two private amber galleries
mentioned above or at the
following two shops:
Jūva, Aušros Vartų 21. Weekdays
10am–6pm, Saturday 10am–4pm.
Sagė, Aušros Vartų 15. Weekdays
10am–7pm, Saturday 10am–4pm,
Sunday 10am–3pm.

Souvenirs

There are countless souvenir
shops along Pilies street, the
main tourist road in Vilnius.
Look out for verba, dried-flower
and twig willow, and yew bouquets,
which are especially popular on
Palm Sunday.

Elementai, Stiklių 14/1. Open
Tuesday–Friday 11am–2pm and
3–7pm, Saturday 11am–4pm.
Glass, ceramics and tablecloths.
Kuparas, Šv. Jono 3. Weekdays
10am–6pm. Folk art.
Kuparėlis, Didžioji 38. Weekdays
10am–6pm.
Lietuviški suvenyrai, Aušros Vartų
11. Open Monday–Saturday
10am–7pm, Sunday 10am–5pm.
Mažoji Galerija, Vytauto 6.
Weekdays 11am–7pm, Saturday
11am–5pm. Jewellery.
Sauluva, Pilies 22 also on Pilies
13. Daily 10am–7pm. Wide range of
traditional Lithuanian crafts:
ironwork, ceramics, glass and
leather and dried flowers.
Suvenyrai, Šv. Jono 12. Weekdays
10am–7pm, Saturday 10am–2pm.
Sells linen products.

Markets

Local markets are well worth a
visit for the wide choice of
products on offer. **Gariūnai flea
market** outside Vilnius has
everything you ever dreamed of
finding in the former USSR. The **big
bazaar** is the meeting point of
Lithuanians, Poles, Russians and
Belarusians, who sell items from
cheap watches and toothpaste to
cars and machine-guns. However,
make sure you watch out for
pickpockets. The private farmers'
markets in Vilnius sell meat, milk,
fruits and vegetables:
Halė, Pylimo 58/1. Open
Tuesday–Sunday mornings only.
Kalvarijų, Kalvarijų 61. Open
Tuesday–Sunday mornings only.

Sport

SPECTATOR

Sporting events do not loom large in the Estonian calendar. The areas in which Estonians have excelled in the past have always been individual disciplines rather than team sports. As well as cycling and yachting, during Soviet times Estonians performed well in wrestling and weight-lifting, and the country also produced the world chess-master, Paul Keres.

These days, by far the most popular sport in Estonia is basketball and the home games of the national team always draw a full house. The ice-hockey games at Tallinn's Linnahall are popular and the rink is also the venue for figure-skating and ice-dancing performances.
Kalev Sportshall, Juhkentali 12. Linnahall indoor arena, Mere pst. 20. Tel: 641 2250; fax: 644 9847

PARTICIPANT

Yachting is now a popular sport here and facilities are improving. A new port has been created at Lehtma on the island of Hiiumaa and facilities have been upgraded on Saaremaa and the mainland ports of Haapsaluu, Pärnu and Pirita Tallinn. Yachts can be chartered at Pirita and skippers can be provided.

Ports
Pirita. Tel: 623 7862.
Haapsalu. Tel: 47 455 82.
Lehtma. Tel: 49 214.
Pärnu. Tel: 44 419 48.

Chess
Tallinna Malemaja, Vene 29.

Cycling
Cycling track, Rummu tee 3.

Swimming
Kalev indoor pool, Aia 18. Tel: 644 2286.

Tennis
Tallinn Tennis Centre, Koidula 38. Tel: 601 3280.

Latvia

Tennis
Central Tennis Club, Kronvalda bulv. 2b. Daily 7am–9pm.
Riga Technical University, Kronvalda bulv. 3. Daily 7.30am–10pm.

Swimming Pools
Akvalandija, Aqualand, Mukusalas 45/47. Daily 10am–11pm.
Riga Technical University, Ķipsala 5. Weekdays 8am–9.30pm, weekends 8am–8pm.
VEF swimming pool, Brīvības 197. Weekdays 7am–9pm, weekends 8.30am–9pm.

Golf
Golfs Viesturi, Jaunmarupe, Viesturi 1. Tel: 921 9699; fax: 747 0030. sandra.golfs@parks.lv

Horse Riding
There are a number of stables around the country, including an excellent one at **the castle of Turaida**. Jūrmala, Vaivari, Asaru pr. 61. Tel. 776 6151.

Skydiving
Cēsis Aeroklub, Skydive Sensations, Viesturi. Tel/fax: 41 22 639; jms@skydive.riga.lv; www.skydive.riga.lv

Sailing and Watersports
Central Yachting Club, Stūrmaņu 1a. Tel: 743 3344.

Winter sports
Sigulda bobsleigh and sledging sports centre, Sveices 13, Sigulda. Tel: 2 973 813.

Lithuania

Aeronautics
Vilnius Aeroclub, Kyviškės. Tel: 674 422/86 67 176. Parachute jumps from a small Russian plane.

Tennis
Ministry of Foreign Affairs Tennis Club, Žirmunų 1. Tel. 751 030.
Sereikiškės Tennis Club, Barboros Radvilaites 6. Tel: 612 534;

Horse riding
Zemosios Riešės Žirgiynas, Mažoji Riešė, Žirgų 12. Tel. 504 275/652 901. Traditionally, horse races are organised every year on the second Saturday in January, when riders qualify for the Sartų *lentynés*, the Republican races held on the first Saturday in February. The event is held on Lake Sartų near Utena if the lake is frozen, otherwise it's held in the city.

Fishing
Vilnius Society of Hunters and Fishers, Stiklių 6. Tel: 618 491.

Sailing
Events are held every summer on the Lakes at Trakai. Neringa Yacht Club, Lotmiškių 2.

Rowing club
Irklavimo Sporto Baze, Žirmūnų 1d. Tel: 732 031/750 716.

Swimming pools
Lazdynu Laisvalaikio Centras, Erfurto 13. Tel: 269 041;
Lietuvos Vaiku ir Jaunimo Centras, Ukmergés 25. Tel: 725 657;
Moksleiviu Sveikatos Centras, Žirmunų 37. Tel: 766 729; Žalgiris, Rinktinés 3/1. Tel: 753 375.

Language

Estonian

The Estonian language, the official language of the Republic of Estonia, is closely related to Finnish and Hungarian. Although it uses a Latin alphabet, and each letter represents only one sound, it is a difficult language to master. There are 14 different cases of any noun, verb conjugation is complex and the verb's meaning may also change according to how its root is pronounced. There are, however, no articles or genders in Estonian. If you can manage to pick up a few of the words listed below, this will no doubt be appreciated by the locals.

NUMBERS

1	üks
2	kaks
3	kolm
4	neli
5	viis
6	kuus
7	seitse
8	kahekas
9	ühekas
10	kümme
11	üksteist
12	kaksteist
13	kolmteist
20	kakskümmend
21	kakskümmend-üks
30	kolmkümmend
100	sada
400	neli sada

DAYS OF THE WEEK

Sunday *pühapäev*
Monday *esmaspäev*
Tuesday *teisipäev*

Estonian Sounds

Vowels
a – as in car
e – as in bed
i – as in hit
o – as in on
u – as in up
ä – a as in cat
ö – o as in hurt
õ – as in girl
ü – oo as in shoot.
When a vowel is doubled its sound is lengthened.

Consanants
These have the same sound values as in English, except:
g – always hard, as in gate
j – as the y in yet
s – tch as in match
z – as in pleasure

Wednesday *kolmapäev*
Thursday *neljapäev*
Friday *reede*
Saturday *laupäev*

COMMON EXPRESSIONS

hello *tere*
good morning *tere hommikust*
good evening *tere õhtust*
goodbye *head aega*
see you *nägemist*
thanks *aitäh or tänan*
please *palun*
sorry *vabandust*
excuse me *vabandage palun*
yes/no *jaa/ei*
fine *hästi*
as a greeting or a toast *tervist*
bon appetit *head isu*
The general purpose negative – ei ole – is used to encompass every inconvenience from "we're sold out" to "she's not here".

USEFUL WORDS

airport *lennujaam*
train station *raudteejaam*
(in Tallinn **the station** is known as *Balti jaam*)
harbour *sadam*
shop *kauplus/pood*

town centre *kesklinn*
market *turg*
hairdresser *juuksur*
pharmacy *apteek*
street/road *maantee mnt./ puieste pst.*
every day *igapäev*
holiday *puhkepäev*

Latvian

Latvian is the native language of about 1,690,000 of the 2,686,000 people living in Latvia and one of the world's endangered languages. It is one of two surviving Baltic languages of the Indo-European language group, the other being

Latvian Sounds

Vowels
These have the same sound values as in English, with several additions:
a – as in cat
e – as in bed
i – as in hit
o – as in floor
u – as in good
a line over a vowel lengthens it:
ā – as in car
ē – as in there
ī – as in bee (Riga = Rīga)
ū – oo as in cool

Diphthongs
au – ow as in pout
ie – e as in here
ai – I as in sight
ei – ay as in sway

Consanants
Consonants have the same sound values as in English with the following exceptions:
c – ts as in tsar
č – ch as in chin
g – always hard, as in gate
ģ – as in logical. The accent can also be a "tail" under the letter.
j – as the y in yet
ä – tch as in hatch
ļ – as in failure
ņ – as in onion
r – always rolled as in Spanish
š – sh as in shoe
ž – as in pleasure

Lithuanian. Remotely related to the Slavic languages Russian, Polish, Ukranian, etc., Latvian has 48 phonemes – speech sounds distinguishing one word from another – 12 vowels, 10 diphthongs and 26 consonants. Stress is placed on the first syllable.

NUMBERS

1	*viens*
2	*divi*
3	*trīs*
4	*četri*
5	*pieci*
6	*seši*
7	*septiņi*
8	*astoņi*
9	*deviņi*
10	*desmit*
11	*vienpadsmit*
12	*divpadsmit*
20	*divdesmit*
30	*trīsdesmit*
100	*simts*
1,000	*tūkstotis*

DAYS OF THE WEEK

Sunday *svētdiena*
Monday *pirmdiena*
Tuesday *otrdiena*
Wednesday *trešdiena*
Thursday *ceturtdiena*
Friday *piektdiena*
Saturday *sestdiena*

COMMON EXPRESSIONS

hello, hi *sveiki*
good morning *labrīt*
good afternoon *labdien*
good evening *labvakar*
goodbye *uz redzēsanso/visu laub*
yes *jā*
no *nē*
Please; You're welcome *lūdzu*
Thank you *paldies*
I am sorry! Excuse me *Atvainojiet!*
That's all right *Nekas*
May I ask a question? *Vai drīkstu jautāt?*
May I come in? *Vai drīkstu ienākt?*
Where can... be found? *Kur atrodas...?*

How much is it? *Cik tas maksā?*
Would you please tell me/show me *Vai Jūs lūdzu mannepateiktu/neparādītū?*
Pleased to meet you. *Patīkami ar Jums iepazīties.*
Let me introduce myself. *Atļaujiet stādīties priekšā.*
My name is... *Mani sauc...*
Do you speak English? *Vai Jūs runājat angliski?*
I don't understand/speak Latvian *Es nesaprotu/nerunāju latviski.*
We need an interpreter *Mums ir vajadzīgs tulks.*

USEFUL WORDS

doctor *ārsts*
hospital *slimnīca*
first aid *ātrā palīdzība*
hotel *viesnīca*
restaurant *restorāns*
shop *veikals*
airport *lidosta*
bus station *autoosta*
rallway station *dzelzceļa stacija*
petrol station *degvielas uzpildes stacija*
post office *pasts*
street *iela*
boulevard *bulvāris*
square *laukums*
closed *slēgts*
open *atvērts*

Lithuanian

Lithuanian and Latvian both belong to the Baltic family of the Indo-European languages. Lithuanian is one of the oldest surviving languages related to Sanskrit and it has kept its sound system and many archaic forms and sentence structures. When the language was first formalised in 1918, there were a variety of distinctive dialects across the country and Suvalkiecių. The southern "sub-dialect" of Western High Lithuania was adopted as the official dialect. Today, local dialects have been largely assimilated. There are 32 letters in the alphabet. One of Lithuanian's idiosyncrasies is the tail that appears beneath its vowels.

Lithuanian Sounds

Vowels
a – as in arm
e – as in there
ė – as in make
i – as in sit
o – as in shot
u – as in should
ū – oo as in stool
y – ee as in see
ą, ė, į and ų appear in special cases and are slightly longer than the equivalent letters without a "tail".

Diphthongs
ai – as in i
au – as in now
ei – as in make
ie – as in yellow
uo – as in wonder

Consanants
c – ts as in tickets
č – ch as in chin
j – as in yes
š – sh as in she
z – as in zoo
ž – as in vision

NUMBERS

1	*vienas*
2	*du*
3	*trys*
4	*keturi*
5	*penki*
6	*šeši*
7	*septyni*
8	*aštuoni*
9	*devyni*
10	*dešimt*
11	*vienuolika*
12	*dvylika*
20	*dvidešimt*
30	*trisdešimt*
100	*šimtas*
1,000	*tūkstantis*

COMMON PHRASES

hello *laba diena*
hello Mr... *laba diena, pone...*
hi *sveikas*
please *prasom*
excuse me *atsiprašau*

sorry *apgailestauju*
good morning *labas rytas*
good evening *labas vakaras*
good night *abanakt*
goodbye *Sudiev viso gero*
welcome *sveiki atvykė*
How are you? *Kaip sekasi?*
Pleased to meet you *Malonu su jumis susipažinti*
See you later *Iki pasimatymo*
yes/no *taip/ne*
okay *gerai*
perhaps *galbūt*
when? *kada?*
where? *kur?*
who? *kas?*
why? *kodėl?*
Do you understand me?
Ar mane suprantate?
I don't speak Lithuanian
Aš nekalbu lietuviškai
I understand Lithuanian
Aš suprantu lietuviškai
Do you speak English, German, French, Russian, Polish? *Kalbate angleškai, vokiškai, prancūziskai, rusiškai, lenkiškai?*
I speak English, German...
Aš kalbu angliškai, vokiškai...
May I have...? *Prašyčiau...?*
May I smoke? *Ar galima uzsirūkyti?*
What time is it? *Kelinta dabar valanda?*
At what time? *Kuriuo laiku?*
How much is it? *Kiek kainuoja?*
Where is the nearest shop, hotel, restaurant, café, bar, toilet? *Kur artimiausia parduotuvė, viešbutis, restoranas, kavinė, baras, tualetas?*
thank you (very much) *(labai) aciū*

USEFUL WORDS

left *kaire*
right *dešine*
straight *tiesiai*
bread *duona*
butter *sviestas*
cheese *sūris*
beer *alus*
wine *vynas*
tea *arbata*
coffee *kava*
the bill *saskąitą?*

Further Reading

General

Amongst The Russians, by Colin Thubron. Penguin, 1980. Thubron describes a few days spent in Tallinn before moving on to be less complimentary about Riga.
Baltic Countdown, by Peggie Benton. Centaur Press, 1985. An extraordinary account of the wife of a British diplomat caught up in Riga at the outbreak of World War II.
Rates Of Exchange, Malcolm Bradbury. Vintage, 1990. This sharply observed novel about a hapless visit to a mythical Eastern European state, gives a feel of life under the Soviet system.
The Baltic Revolution, by Anatol Lieven. Yale, 1993. A fine background to the cultural, economic and political life in the region by a member of one of the foremost Baltic families.
The Baltic Nations and Europe, by John Hiden, Patrick Salman. Longman, 1991. A history of the 20th century in the three countries.
The Baltic States: A Reference Book, 1991. Lots of facts.
The Baltic States: Years of Dependence (1940–1980, by Romanuld J. Misiunas, Rein Taagepera. C. Hunt & Co, London; and University of California Press, 1983. This is a follow up to the classic Years of Independence (1917–1940) by Georg von Rauch.
The Czar's Madman, by Jaan Kross. Harper Collins, 1993. Estonia's premier writer brilliantly evokes life in the times of the Russian occupation in the 19th century. Also by Kross: **Professor Marten's Departure**, 1994.
The Good Republic, by William Palmer. Secker & Warburg 1990. An excellent and imaginative novel about an emigre returning to the Baltic city he fled during World War II and encountering some ghosts on his return 40 years later.

The Singing Revolution, by Clare Thompson, Michael Joseph, 1992. Personal account of the rebirth of the Baltics by a British journalist who was there in 1989–90.

Other Insight Guides

Europe is comprehensively covered by over 400 books in Apa Publications' three series of guidebooks, which embrace the world. *Insight Guides* provide a full cultural background and top-quality photography. *Insight Pocket Guides* highlight recommendations from a local host and include a full-size, fold-out map. *Insight Compact Guides* combine portability with encyclopedia-like attention to detail and are ideal for on-the-spot reference. Eastern European destinations covered in these three series include: **Eastern Europe**; **Hungary**; **Budapest**; **Czech Republic**; **Prague**; and **Poland**. In addition, a new range of *Insight Maps* combine durability and elegance of design with accurate and up-to-date information. *Insight Maps* are available to **Budapest** and **Prague.**

ART & PHOTO CREDITS

Photography by
Lyle Lawson except for:

Central Independent Television 230
Anders Gunnartz/Panos Pictures
103
Fred Jussi 84
Gregory Wrona 38/39, 42L, 42R,
68/69, 98, 101, 105, 222/223,
304/305
Gregory Wrona/Panos Pictures 41,
Topham Picturepoint 33L, 34, 113
Roger Williams 74
World Wide Fund for Nature 108,
back cover centre bottom

Map Production Lovell Johns
Visual Consultant V. Barl

INSIGHT GUIDE
BaLTIC STaTes

Cartographic Editor **Zoë Goodwin**
Design Consultants
Carlotta Junger
Picture Research **Hilary Genin**